Transnational Trade Unionism

T0289697

Transnational trade union action has expanded significantly over the last few decades and has taken a variety of shapes and trajectories. This book is concerned with understanding the spatial extension of trade union action and, in particular, the development of new forms of collective mobilisation, network-building and forms of regulation that bridge local and transnational issues.

Through the work of leading international specialists, this collection of essays examines the processes and dynamics of transnational trade union action and provides analytical and conceptual tools to understand these developments. The research presented here emphasises that the direction of transnational solidarity remains contested, subject to experimentation and negotiation and includes studies of often overlooked developments in transition and developing countries with original analyses from the European Union and NAFTA areas. Providing a fresh examination of transnational solidarity, this volume offers neither a romantic or overly optimistic narrative of a borderless unionism, nor does it fall into a fatalistic or pessimistic account of international union solidarity. Through original research conducted at different levels, this book disentangles the processes and dynamics of institution building and challenges the conventional national-based forms of unionism that prevailed in the latter half of the twentieth century.

Peter Fairbrother is a professor of International Employment Relations and Director of the Centre for Sustainable Organisations and Work at RMIT University, Australia. He is also a core researcher at the Interuniversity Research Centre on Globalization and Work (CRIMT). He has published nine books and numerous articles and book chapters.

Christian Lévesque is a professor of Employment Relations at HEC Montréal, Canada, and Co-director of the Interuniversity Research Centre on Globalization and Work (CRIMT). His research focus concerns the impact of globalisation on trade unions, employment practices in multinational corporations and union-management relations. He has co-edited a book and four special journal issues and published several articles and book chapters.

Marc-Antonin Hennebert is an assistant professor in HR and Labour Relations at HEC Montréal, Canada and a core researcher at the Interuniversity Research Centre on Globalization and Work (CRIMT). He holds a PhD from Université de Montréal and recently completed a postdoctoral fellowship in the Department of Management at King's College London. He has recently published a book on international union alliances, as well as various articles.

Routledge Studies in Employment and Work Relations in Context

Edited by Tony Elger and Peter Fairbrother

The aim of the *Employment and Work Relations in Context Series* is to address questions relating to the evolving patterns and politics of work, employment, management and industrial relations. There is a concern to trace out the ways in which wider policy-making, especially by national governments and transnational corporations, impinges upon specific workplaces, occupations, labour markets, localities and regions. This invites attention to developments at an international level, marking out patterns of globalization, state policy and practices in the context of globalization and the impact of these processes on labour. A particular feature of the series is the consideration of forms of worker and citizen organization and mobilization. The studies address major analytical and policy issues through case study and comparative research.

1 **Employment Relations in the Health Service**
The Management of Reforms
Stephen Bach

2 **Globalisation, State and Labour**
Edited by Peter Fairbrother and Al Rainnie

3 **Sexualities, Work and Organizations**
Stories by Gay Men and Women in the Workplace at the Beginning of the 21st Century
James Ward

4 **Vocational Training**
International Perspectives
Edited by Gerhard Bosch and Jean Charest

5 **Industrial Relations in Education**
Transforming the School Workforce
Bob Carter, Howard Stevenson and Rowena Passy

6 **Social Regionalism in the Global Economy**
Adelle Blackett and Christian Lévesque

7 **Unions and Globalization**
Governments, Management, and the State at Work
Peter Fairbrother, John O'Brien, Anne Junor, Michael O'Donnell and Glynne Williams

8 **Privatization of Public Services**
Impacts for Employment, Working Conditions, and Service Quality in Europe
Edited by Christoph Hermann and Jörg Flecker

9 **Rediscovering Collective
Bargaining**
Australia's Fair Work Act in
International Perspective
*Edited by Breen Creighton and
Anthony Forsyth*

10 **Transnational Trade
Unionism**
Building Union Power
*Edited by Peter Fairbrother,
Marc-Antonin Hennebert and
Christian Lévesque*

Previous titles to appear in Routledge Studies in Employment and Work
Relations in Context include:

**Work, Locality and the
Rhythms of Capital**
The Labour Process
Reconsidered
Jamie Gough

Trade Unions in Renewal
A Comparative Study
*Edited by Peter Fairbrother and
Charlotte Yates*

**Reshaping the North American
Automobile Industry**
Restructuring, Corporatism and
Union Democracy in Mexico
John P. Tuman

**Work and Employment in the High
Performance Workplace**
*Edited by Gregor Murray, Jacques
Belanger, Anthony Giles and
Paul-Andre Lapointe*

**Trade Unions and Global
Governance**
The Debate on a Social Clause
Gerda van Roozendaal

**Changing Prospects for
Trade Unionism**
*Edited by Peter Fairbrother and
Gerard Griffin*

**Unionization and Union
Leadership**
The Road Haulage Industry'
Paul Smith

**Restructuring the Service
Industries**
Management Reform and Workplace
Relations in the UK Service Sector
Gavin Poynter

Trade Unions at the Crossroads
Peter Fairbrother

Between Market, State and Kibbutz
The Management and Transformation
of Socialist Industry
Christopher Warhurst

**Globalization and Patterns of
Labour Resistance**
Edited by Jeremy Waddington

The State and "Globalization"
Comparative Studies of Labour and
Capital in National Economies
Edited by Martin Upchurch

**State Regulation and the
Politics of Public Service**
The Case of the Water Industry
Graham Taylor

Global Humanization
Studies in the Manufacture of Labour
Edited by Michael Neary

Women, Work and Trade Unions
Anne Munro

**The Global Economy, National
States and the Regulation of Labour**
*Edited by Paul Edwards and
Tony Elgar*

**History of Work and Labour
Relations in the Royal Dockyards**
*Edited by Ann Day and
Kenneth Lunn*

**Japanese Management Techniques
and British Workers**
Andy Danford

Young People in the Workplace
Job, Union and Mobility Patterns
Christina Cregan

**Globalization, Social Movements
and the New Internationalisms**
Peter Waterman

**Young Adult Women,
Work and Family**
Living a Contradiction
Ian Procter and Maureen Padfield

The Sociology of Industrial Injury
Theo Nichols

**Global Tourism and Informal
Labour Relations**
The Small Scale Syndrome at Work
Godfrey Baldacchino

Transnational Trade Unionism

Building Union Power

**Edited by Peter Fairbrother,
Marc-Antonin Hennebert
and Christian Lévesque**

NEW YORK AND LONDON

First published 2013
by Routledge
711 Third Avenue, New York, NY 10017

Simultaneously published in the UK
by Routledge
2 Park Square, Milton Park, Abingdon, Oxon OX14 4RN

First issued in paperback 2018

*Routledge is an imprint of the Taylor & Francis Group,
an informa business*

Library of Congress Cataloging-in-Publication Data

Transnational trade unionism : building union power / edited by Peter
    Fairbrother, Marc-Antonin Hennebert, and Christian Levesque. — First
    Edition.
        p cm. — (Routledge studies in employment and work relations in context ; 8)
Includes bibliographical references and index.
    1. Labor unions—History.   2. Labor unions and international relations—
History.   I. Fairbrother, Peter.   II. Hennebert,
Marc-Antonin.   III. Lévesque, Christian, 1958–
    HD6451.T73 2013

ISBN 13: 978-1-138-34087-9 (pbk)
ISBN 13: 978-0-415-81880-3 (hbk)

Typeset in Sabon
by Apex CoVantage, LLC

Contents

List of Tables   xi
List of Figures   xiii
List of Abbreviations   xv
Acknowledgements   xix

1   Understanding Transnational Trade Unionism   1
    PETER FAIRBROTHER, CHRISTIAN LÉVESQUE AND MARC-ANTONIN
    HENNEBERT

PART I
Workplace Trade Unions: Bridging the Local to the Global

2   Workers' Power in Global Value Chains: Fighting Sweatshop
    Practices at Russell, Nike and Knights Apparel   23
    MARK ANNER

3   Building North-South Transnational Trade Union
    Alliances: Prospects and Challenges   42
    MÉLANIE DUFOUR-POIRIER AND CHRISTIAN LÉVESQUE

4   Trade Union Strategies in Cross-Border Actions: Articulating
    Institutional Specificity with Local Power Dynamics   57
    CHRISTIAN LÉVESQUE, GREGOR MURRAY, CHRISTIAN DUFOUR
    AND ADELHEID HEGE

5   The Strike at Renault-Dacia: A Challenge for
    East-West Trade Union Cooperation   81
    MICHÈLE DESCOLONGES

PART II
National Trade Unions: Shaping New Forms of Solidarity

6 Building Transnational Unionism: Australian Transport
   Maritime Unions in the World   101
   PETER FAIRBROTHER

7 Creating Spaces for Labour Internationalism: National Industrial
   Unions in the Southern Hemisphere and Their Strategies   121
   ARMEL BRICE ADANHOUNME AND CHRISTIAN LÉVESQUE

8 Local Actors and Transnational Structures: Explaining Trends
   in Multinational Company-Level Negotiations in Europe   141
   VALERIA PULIGNANO, ISABEL DA COSTA, UDO REHFELDT
   AND VOLKER TELLJOHANN

9 European Trade Unions and the Long March through
   the Institutions: From Integration to Contention?   161
   RICHARD HYMAN

PART III
International Trade Unionism: Crafting Institutions
for the 21st Century

10 The International Labour Movement: Structures
    and Dynamics   183
    REBECCA GUMBRELL-McCORMICK

11 Transnational Solidarity around Global Production
    Networks? Reflections on the Strategy of International
    Framework Agreements   203
    MICHAEL FICHTER, MARKUS HELFEN AND KATHARINA SCHIEDERIG

12 Opening the Black Box of Cross-Border Union Alliances:
    A Case Study   223
    MARC-ANTONIN HENNEBERT AND REYNALD BOURQUE

13 Labour Standards in Segmented Markets:
    The Construction Industry in Delhi and Moscow   243
    NIKOLAUS HAMMER

PART IV
Conclusion

14 Futures of Transnational Trade Unionism   265
    CHRISTIAN LÉVESQUE, MARC-ANTONIN HENNEBERT
    AND PETER FAIRBROTHER

    List of Contributors   281
    Index   287

Tables

4.1	Description of the firms	63
4.2	Dimensions and patterns of workplace union involvement in cross-border interaction	66
4.3	Supranational institutional arrangements and local power dynamics	70
7.1	Patterns of labour internationalism in the Ghanaian and Mexican cases	135
11.1	Major Global Union Federations with IFAs	211
12.1	Trade union presence in Quebecor World establishments	226
13.1	Market despotic and coercive labour control regimes	250

Figures

2.1   The Dynamics of Anti-Sweatshop Activism   35
10.1 The historical evolution of international trade
      union organisation   184
11.1 The IFA Process. Transnationalising Labour Relations   206

Abbreviations

AFL	American Federation of Labor
AFL-CIO	American Federation of Labor and Congress of Industrial Organizations
ALGI	A. & L. Group Inc.
ANS	Australian National Stevedores
ATC	Agreement on Textiles and Clothing
ATUF	Australian Transport Union Federation
BNS	National Trade Unions Block
BOT	build-operate-transfer
BWI	the Building and Wood Workers' International Union
CAFTA-DR	Central American-Dominican Republic Free Trade Agreement
Cartel ALFA	National Trade Union Confederation
CBTPA	U.S. Caribbean Basin Trade Partnership Act
CCOO	Federación de Comunicación y Transporte
CEEP	European Centre of Employers and Enterprises providing Public Services
CEP	Communications, Energy and Paperworkers Union of Canada
CES	Confédération Européenne des Syndicats
CFDT	Confédération française démocratique du travail / French Democratic Confederation of Labour
CFTC	Confédération française des travailleurs chrétiens
CGC	Confédération générale des cadres
CGT	Confédération Générale du Travail / General Confederation of Labour
CISC	Confédération internationale des syndicats chrétiens
CLAT	Central Latinoamericana de Trabajadores
CLSs	Core Labour Standards
CONAGRA	Confederación Nacional Gráfica
CSDR	Democratic Trade Union Confederation of Romania
CSI	Confédération Syndicale Internationale
CT	Congreso del Trabajo

CTM	Confederación de los Trabajadores de Mexico
DG EMPL	Directorate-General for Employment and Social Affairs
DPW	DP World Corporation
ECFTU	European Confederation of Free Trade Unions
ECJ	European Court of Justice
ECOWAS	Economic Community of West African States
EEC	European Economic Community
EES	European Employment Strategy
EFAs	European Framework Agreements
EFTA	European Free Trade Association
EIFs	European Industry Federations
EMF	European Metalworkers' Federation
EMU	Economic and Monetary Union of the European Union
ERO	European Regional Organisation
ETUC	European Trade Union Confederation
ETUFs	European Trade Union Federations
ETUI	European Trade Union Institute
EU	European Union
EWC	European Works Council
EWU	Elementary Work Units / UET—unités élémentaires de travail
FDI	Foreign Direct Investment
FEM	Fonds européen d'ajustement à la mondialisation
FES-UGT	Federación sectorial estatal—Unión General de Trabajadores
FGP	Federación Gráfica del Perú
FILPAC	Fédération des travailleurs des industries du livre, du papier et de la communication
FLA	Fair Labor Association
FNV	Federatie Nederlandse Vakbeweging (Federation Dutch Labour Movement)
FO	Force Ouvrière
FOC	Flags of Convenience
GCC/IBT	Graphic Communications Conference of the International Brotherhood of Teamsters
GCIU	Graphic Communications International Union
GDP	Gross Domestic Product
GME	General Motors Europe
GMWU	Ghana Mine Workers Union
GPA-DJP	Gewerkschaft, Druck, Journalismus, Papier
GPNs	Global Production Networks
Grafiska-LO	Grafiska Facföbundet Mediafacket
GUFs	Global Union Federations
GVCs	Global Value Chains
HERE	Hotel Employees and Restaurant Employees Union

HHBV	Dutch investment group Hombergh/De Pundert
ICEM	International Federation of Chemical, Energy, Mines and General Worker' Unions
ICFTU	International Confederation of Free Trade Unions
IFAs	International Framework Agreements
IFBWW	International Federation of Building and Wood Workers (IFBWW)
IFC	International Finance Corporation
IFTU	International Federation of Trade Unions
IG BCE	IG Bergbau, Chemie, Energie
ILO	International Labour Organization
IMF	International Metalworkers Federation
IMO	International Maritime Organisation
IRES	Institut de recherches économiques et sociales
ISNTUC	International Secretariat of National Trade Union Centres
ITF	International Transport Federation
ITGLWF	International Textile, Garment and Leather Workers' Federation
ITSs	International Trade Secretariats
ITUC	International Trade Union Confederation
IUF	International Union of Food, Agricultural, Hotel, Restaurant, Catering, Tobacco and Allied Workers' Associations
IWW	Industrial Workers of the World
MNC	Multinational Company / Multinational Corporation
MUA	Maritime Union of Australia
MUAV	Maritime Union of Australia, Victorian Branch
NAFTA	North American Free Trade Agreement
NBA	National Basketball Association
NBS	National Business Systems
NFCCW	National Federation of Chinese Construction Workers' Union (Taiwan)
NGO	Non-Governmental Organization
NUBCW	National Union of Building and Construction Workers (Philippines)
OECD	Organization for Economic Co-operation and Development
ORIT	Organización Regional Interamericana de Trabajadores
PAN	Conservative Party
PERC	Pan-European Regional Council
PGE	permanent guaranteed wages
PILs	Public Interest Litigations
PPPs	public-private partnerships
PRI	Institutional Revolutionary Party
PUDR	People's Union for Democratic Rights
QFL	Quebec Federation of Labour
QMV	qualified majority voting
RNUR	Régie nationale des usines Renault

RTBU	Rail, Tram and Bus Union
SAD	Dacia Automobile Union
SAK	Viestintäalan Ammattiliitto ry
SAPs	Structural Adjustment Programs
SEC	Siemens Employee Committee
SEIU	Service Employees International Union
SETCA-FGTB	Syndicat des Employés, Techniciens et Cadres
SINDGRAF	Sindicato dos Trabalhadores nas indústrias Graficas do Estado
SITAG	Sindicato Industrial de Trabajadores de Artes Gráficas
SNTMMSRM	Mexican Miners' Union
SUTGMA	Sindicato Unico de Trabajadores de Gráficos Monte Albán
TNC	Transnationally Operating Corporations
TUAC	Trade Union Advisory Committee
TUC	Trade Union Congress
TUN	Transnational Union Networks
TWU	Transport Workers Union
UNI	Global Union Network
UNICE	Union of Industrial and Employers' Confederations of Europe
USAID	United States Agency for International Development
USAS	United Students Against Sweatshops
USWA	United Steelworkers of Americas
VTUWG	Victorian Transport Union Working Group
WCL	World Confederation of Labour
WFTU	World Federation of Trade Unions
WRC	Worker Rights Consortium
WTO	World Trade Organization

Acknowledgements

This book is very much the result of a collaborative process between all contributors. It benefits from the support of colleagues in the Interuniversity Research Centre on Globalization and Work (CRIMT), through the Social Sciences and Humanities Research Council of Canada Major Collaborative Research Initiatives Project, 'Rethinking Institutions for Work and Employment in a Global Era'. In addition, the book project received support for strategic groups from the Fonds québécois de recherche sur la société et la culture.

The collaboration began in 2010. The structure and the focus of the book were crafted at an international workshop that we organised at HEC Montréal in September 2010, entitled 'Transnational Union Action: New Capabilities for Building Labor Institutions'. We gratefully acknowledge the generous support for this seminar and subsequent work towards the publication from the Social Sciences and Humanities Research Council of Canada.

We wish to thank the contributors for their willingness to attend and participate in the workshop. Subsequently, they worked through their chapters with us in a helpful and gracious way, taking comments and advice in a positive way that helped all of us develop the ideas presented in the book.

We especially wish to thank the following for their support and work on the project. Francine Jacques and Nicolas Roby of CRIMT provided superlative support to the workshop, and we acknowledge with thanks their ongoing guidance in the preparation of this publication. Staff at the HEC Montréal were wonderful hosts. We wish to thank the dedicated CRIMT students who provided research assistance and general support in preparing the workshop and the completed volume. Special thanks to Florina Nicoleta for logistical support and attention to detail. We also wish to thank Chau Nguyen from Montreal and Susan Monti from Geneva who provided excellent translation services. Andy Wilson from Manchester revised several of the chapters presented in this book. Finally, we extend special thanks to the editorial staff at Routledge for their strong support throughout the publication process.

1 Understanding Transnational Trade Unionism

Peter Fairbrother, Christian Lévesque and Marc-Antonin Hennebert

Transnational trade unionism is becoming increasingly important for workers around the world. Transnational trade union organisation and action, a form of trade unionism defined by cross-border activity and focus, has become features of contemporary employment and work over the past decades. These types of trade unionism take a range of forms and have followed a number of distinct trajectories. The context for these developments is the changing political economy of work and employment. Multinational corporations have acquired significance in relation to finance, production and trade relations. Concurrently, and as part of corporate development, governments have increasingly embraced a neo-liberal agenda, with decisive implications for union embeddedness within the international political economy (Cramme and Diamond 2009). Of equal note, the global unions, the international confederations such as the International Trade Union Confederation (ITUC) and the global union federations (GUFs) have been transformed from relatively remote bodies to more active and engaged global trade unions (Croucher and Cotton 2009). This book is concerned with understanding these emerging forms of trade unionism, in particular the development of new forms of collective mobilisation, network-building and regulation that bridge local and transnational issues via trade unions.

There has been much debate about trade unions, with unions having been depicted as 'old social movements' (Castells 1996; Touraine 1982). The argument presented in this book is that the distinction between 'old' and 'new' is rather opaque and loses sight of the ways in which trade unions have resources and capacities to renew themselves, often in uneven and contested ways. Thus, we claim that unions retain relevance in the changing international political economy as collective organisations able to articulate the class interests of members. Unions derive their legitimacy from such representation and the expression of their interests (Offe and Wiesenthal 1980; Dufour and Hege 2010). Our argument is that unions can build a counter legitimacy to the apparent legitimacy of corporations and states to secure their bottom line in terms of profit and economic gain. Trade unions, thus, have a transformative capacity that may be unevenly realised, and is certainly contested, both by employers and states as well as within trade unions. Nonetheless, transnational unionism opens up possibilities, and this book explores the conditions for them.

A second debate focuses on unions within a global world, with much analysis raising varied questions about unions' capacities to deal with these changes. One strand of writing focuses on forms of organisation, and union resources and capacities, to address the impacts of globalisation (Bronfenbrenner 2007; Cohen 2006; Lévesque and Murray 2010). One dimension of this debate examines the external and contextual forces that may shape the way unions have begun to organise and operate transnationally, at the workplace and at other levels. Nonetheless, as frequently noted, unions remain bound by views that unions are nation-state based, even when cross-border alliances are in place (Tattersall 2007; Myconos 2005). From the other side of the relationship, there have been many recent changes in the ways that trade unionism has developed internationally. Over the last few decades, international union bodies, such as the International Confederation of Free Trade Unions (ICFTU), the International Trade Secretariats (ITSs) and other organisations have reorganised and relocated themselves to address the changes in process (Gumbrell-McCormick 2000; Windmuller 1980). These developments have also involved re-evaluating relations with either national union confederations or individual unions. These various features of transnational unionism are also taken up in this book.

Trade unions are part of a changing set of international class relations, defined by the way in which capitalist firms operate internationally as part of increasingly complex global value chains, linking production and consumption across territories and regions and linking north and south, often in heterogeneous ways, as part of the profit-maximising strategies of firms (Coe et al. 2007). These relations are often underwritten and shaped by government policy at state levels as well as in relation to international forms of regulation. International agencies, such as the International Monetary Fund, have pushed for the implementation of neo-liberal policies, thereby contributing to a reduction of the relative autonomy of nation states. This process not only affects developing countries, but also developed countries, as underscored by the successive Greek crises. In these circumstances, trade unions both seek to shape and influence these complex relations and, in turn, are moulded by them. In short, trade unions seek to realise their interests in relation to their class location in this emerging world, which in turn requires that workers have the capacity to realise their interests and concerns (Harvey 2000; Wright 2000).

TRANSNATIONAL TRADE UNIONISM

Over the last two decades, there has been growing interest in transnational cooperation, labour internationalism, transnational labour solidarity and several related themes. These themes rest on an assumption that the national form of unionism can be refocused on an international level. This aspect has been well documented in union histories (Gumbrell-McCormick 2003) and has become a key focus in more recent contributions (e.g., Anner 2007).

A more focused definition draws attention to the importance of cooperation across borders. Greer and Hauptmeier (2008) define labour internationalism as:

> spatial extension of trade unionism through the intensification of co-operation between trade unionists across countries using transnational tools and structures. (p. 77)

This focus on cooperation has been taken up by a number of scholars. Gordon and Turner (2000: 257), for example, consider that perception of interdependence is a precondition for transnational union cooperation, while Kay (2005) goes further and argues that labour internationalism is precisely:

> a process of creating a transnational culture based on cooperative complementary identities, defined as a shared recognition of mutual interest coupled with a commitment to joint action. (p. 725)

However, several scholars have pointed to the difficulty of building complementary identities and commitment to joint action (Johns 1998; Gajewska 2009). This emphasis led Lillie and Martinez (2012) to assert that:

> Trans- and—inter-national strategies can only be understood in the context of the interaction between unions' embeddedness in national regulation, and globalizing production, resulting in transnational unionism consisting of a set of relationships between competing national players with competing visions of the 'global' within global production structures. (p. 75)

While 'spatial extension' appears to be a defining feature of transnational trade unionism, it is also a place for cooperation between trade unions as well as a site of potential conflict and competition.

A complementary range of studies has focused on various forms of international activity, solidarity and engagement involving workers and activists from civil society, including trade unionists. This focus is illustrated by two core publications on the subject by Tarrow (2005) and Webster et al. (2008). In the first book, Tarrow (2005) focuses on what he terms 'transnational activism'. The focus is very much on the way that labour activists are increasingly in positions to reshape and focus their activities on a transnational level rather than functioning as domestic actors with restricted views and understandings of the broader context in which they organise and operate. For Tarrow (2005: 25), international alliances are defined as structures of relations among trade unionist and supranational institutions that produce opportunities for actors to engage in collective action at different levels. Alongside this contribution, the text by Webster et al. (2008) emphasises the capacities of labour movements to integrate different struggles at various spatial scales and to counter the oppressive and seemingly inescapable dominance of capital, particularly an increasingly globalised capital.

One implication of these observations is that transnational union activity, be it via individual trade unions or other union organisations, is likely to be uneven, reflecting the way that the pace of change varies throughout the world. These are not unilinear processes; rather, they are varied within countries and from country to country. Not only do particular states play a part in the globalisation process, but broad patterns are at work, with India and China emerging as major players (Pringle and Clark 2010), while countries like the United Kingdom and Japan are repositioning themselves in less dominant ways than in the past. In addition, forms of work and employment are changing, particularly in the advanced capitalist countries. These features raise questions about the forms of transnational trade unionism that may be emerging.

FORMS OF TRANSNATIONAL TRADE UNIONISM

Transnational trade unionism refers to the way that union actors in local, national and international arenas organise and operate so that local and global interests are inter-connected. In the course of these developments, unions are involved in processes, as agents, to articulate a set of inter-linked relations between the local and the global (Barton and Fairbrother 2009).

Several scholars have attempted to capture the evolving forms or models of transnational unions. Hyman (2005) distinguishes various models of organisation and action by international trade unions, ranging from an agitator to a bureaucratic model. Hyman argues that there is an enduring tension between internationalism from below and from above. In a similar type of account, Martinez (2010) attempts to go beyond the opposition between network and bureaucratic models, suggesting that both can be more or less democratic. Drawing on a spatial/social matrix, Munck (2010) makes a distinction between various parameters of the labour movement repertoire of collective action, which vary according to the focus of action (market or society) and its spatial scale (local/global). These contributions suggest that transnational unionism is a contingent and contradictory process involving various forms of action at different spatial scales that can be more or less formalised and centralised.

The most obvious form of action is international organisation and operation linking national unions and global union federation and confederations. In this respect, the way unions signify their involvement and activity in relation to cross-border activity is as members of GUFs and via national union confederations, which in turn are members of the international confederations. There has been increasing activity by the ITUC, formerly the ICFTU, following the collapse of the Soviet Union and the dismantling of the regimes in Eastern Europe. The ICFTU expanded mainly at the expense of the World Federation of Trade Unions (WFTU), which lost most of its European affiliates and a large number of its members in the Soviet Union and Eastern Europe.

Nonetheless, locally or nationally-based unions can develop internationally focused capacities and seek to express transnational objectives and purpose without relying on overarching organisations. In such cases, unions use domestic resources to indicate support for trade unions and union members across borders (e.g., demonstrations of support/campaigns for others elsewhere), unions contact other unions across borders to promote or deal with domestic cases or unions address the implications of decisions taken off-shore that impact on unions locally by seeking support from unions elsewhere (e.g., decisions taken to reorganise plants in one country by corporations based in another).

More complex forms of transnational unionism are those that qualify the starkness of unionism from above or below and emphasise the nested nature of this type of unionism. Two forms stand out. The first form involves trade union organisation across borders in alliances or coalitions, together with international union organisations. Often under the auspices of both GUFs and European federations, clusters of unions have begun working with each other on World Works Councils and European Works Councils (EWCs) (Papadakis 2011; Stevis 2010). In the second form, national unions have sought each other out, establishing cross-border alliances and extending their national practices as inclusive, active and campaigning unions in the international arena (Bergene 2007; Bronfenbrenner 2007). Such practices are evident in unions, such as in the maritime sector (Lillie 2005). Complementing this aspect, such unions also seek to define their immediate concerns as international ones, either by example or in relation to employer practices internationally. This activity is a way of framing national events and activities as international in both reach and implication (Tarrow 2005).

Another form of transnational unionism involves unions that organise and represent members across borders, sometimes as a single union and in other cases as *de facto* unitary organisations or as formal partnerships. One variant involves mergers between national unions across borders (e.g., Nautilus and the financial unions in Scandinavia). In 2009, Nautilus International was created from a merger between Nautilus UK and Nautilus Netherlands, representing professional maritime staff with an integrated executive. There are few examples of this form of transnational unionism, although there are indications that unions are beginning to think of lesser versions than complete mergers. Examples of formal partnerships include the alliance established in 2008 between two major unions, the United Steelworkers (US) and UNITE the union (UK), who signed a framework agreement establishing a new global union entity called Workers Uniting. This union has three million members in the US, Canada, Republic of Ireland and the United Kingdom, and the stated purpose of the partnership is to 'challenge global capital'.

The varieties of transnational unionism are best characterised by experimentation. Trade unions at different spatial scales are creating new mechanisms and new rules and developing new narratives to increase their capacities. In undertaking these possibilities, trade unions are addressing questions related to power.

THE QUESTION OF POWER

The question of power is central to our understanding of trade unionism in general and of transnational trade unionism more specifically (Hyman 1975; 2005). The very existence of trade unions indicates the presence of asymmetrical power relations between labour and capital. Power and its twin sister domination are embedded in employment relations, and trade unions need to exercise power over other actors to realise their purpose (Edwards 1986). Trade unions at the local, national or international levels are primarily concerned with influencing other actors, such as the state and employers, to do something that they might not otherwise do. Power is thus a relational concept.

While there is much debate about the concept of power (Bourdieu 1980; Friedberg 1993; Lukes 2005), there is strong agreement about the fact that power encompasses a variety of logics and arrangements. As argued by Held (1995):

> power expresses at one and the same time the intentions and purposes of agencies and institutions and the relative balance of resources they can deploy with respect to each other. (p. 170)

Focusing on the resources deployed by actors, Wright (2000) distinguishes two general forms of power: structural and associational. First, structural power results from workers' positions and locations within work and employment relations and more generally within the economic system (Wright 2000; Silver 2003; Silver and Arrighi 2001). In many industries, such as the automobile and maritime industries, workers traditionally were in a position to use structural power because the labour process was characterised by large numbers of workers undertaking routine but essential core tasks. This form of the labour process has been in decline in developed countries, although in developing countries it still remains a feature of the plants and workplaces that supply many of the goods to the developed countries. Hence, while the car factories, for example, in developed countries such as the US are no longer sites of large non-specialised workforces, in China, mass production has become increasingly prevalent.

Second, associational power is closely related to the institutional context and results from the formation of a collective organisation of workers, such as trade unions, work councils and political parties (Wright 2000: 962). Several scholars have pushed this line of analysis further by emphasising the dispositional dimension of associational power, referring to the resources and capabilities developed through collective organisation (Frost 2000; Hyman 2005; Kelly 1998; Lévesque and Murray 2010; Pocock 2000). One example of the ways in which unions exercise associational power is by building the organisational capacity of trade unions, colloquially termed the 'organisational model' in many of the Anglo-American unions (Fairbrother and Yates 2003). Here, unions have turned their attention to the features that make for effective organisation: representation and participation, recruitment and campaigning and education and research. The aim is to construct and promote unions as agents, with resources and capabilities to realise their purpose in a changing world.

The focus in this book is on the ways that transnational unionism is shaped by the exercise of structural and associational power. Unions increasingly are operating in a global context that is characterised by deterritorialisation. The production, movement and consumption of goods and services are no longer confined to the nation state, and unions seek to address this feature of the modern world. It may be that, with these changes in the world of work and employment, the relation between the exercise of structural power and associational power is also beginning to change. There is evidence to suggest that as global value chains are established, traditional arrangements for the exercise of structural power will be undermined. The question becomes how can unions and forms of trade unionism develop their resources and capacities to lead to the exercise of new forms of associational power that are more adaptive to these new contexts.

EXERCISING POWER OVER TIME

Transnational unionism has a long history that has been described and analysed by several scholars (Gordon and Turner 2000, Gumbrell-McCormick 2003; Lorwin 1953). Our purpose here is to give a brief account of transnational institutional arrangements over different periods of time. We distinguish three periods: the formative years characterised by fragmented institutional arrangements; the 'les trente glorieuses' period shaped by many divisions and tensions; and the current period, which involves emerging forms of multi-level arrangements.

Formative Years: Fragmented Institutional Arrangements

In the mid-nineteenth century, with the emergence of modern trade unionism, usually as craft-based organisations, the major arrangement for transnational unionism took the form of confederations, drawing individual and often lo-cally based unions together. Such organisations as the International Working Men's Association (IWMA) in the United Kingdom were an early expression of the recognition that cross-border links were important, both to share con-cerns about national and employer-based terms and conditions of employ-ment and to define concerns as cross-border. Such links exposed tensions between so-called industrial and political aims (whether or not to support the Paris Commune) and the specific concerns with nation-state based rights or oppression (Olle and Schoeller 1977). The IWMA was founded in 1864 in Saint Martin's Hall, London and brought together trade unions and a range of left political groups. Its first congress was held in 1866 in Geneva and at its peak the IWMA had 5 to 8 million members. This International was disbanded in 1876 in Philadelphia, after an irreconcilable breakdown in relations between the various political groups that made up the IWMA. Sub-sequent Internationals focused on political groups rather than trade unions.

This first International was followed by the International Secretariat of National Trade Union Centres (ISNTUC) (1901) and the International Sec-retariat of Christian Workers (1914). The ISNTUC was an international consultative body of trade unions. Europe-based and located in Germany, the then renamed International Federation of Trade Unions (IFTU) col-lapsed during the First World War. In 1919, a IFTU was established. The IFTU had close links to the Labour and Socialist International and had a social democratic focus. It was principally a European body that lobbied national governments and the League of Nations. It operated in close alli-ance with the International Labour Organisation (ILO). It was dissolved in 1945 and succeeded by the WFTU. This new federation initially brought together trade union confederations from both social democratic and com-munist backgrounds. One variant in this trajectory was the International Secretariat of Christian Workers, which developed into the International Confederation of Christian Trade Unions in 1920 and then was renamed the World Confederation of Labour (WCL). It arose out of Christian Demo-cratic politics and was an alternative to the secular union confederation, the IFTU (Myconos 2005). In 1945, it became the WCL.

Complementing these developments, unions have long participated in cross-border forums. The first such union organisations were created in the nineteenth century as ITSs: International Typographers' Union (1892); International Miners' Federation (1890); Shoe Workers (1889); Clothing and Metal Workers (1890); and Textile Workers (1894). The goal of these ITSs was to facilitate cross-border links between unions in specific crafts and industries. These organisations grew rapidly in the first part of the twentieth century, from seventeen ITSs in 1900 to twenty-seven in 1914. The more active proponents of this form of union organisation were found in France, Britain, Germany and Austria, and initially this form of interna-tionalism was characterised by numerous associations of skilled workers in Europe.

During this formative period, the architecture of transnational union-ism was put in place. Nonetheless, trade unions primarily drew their power from their positions within local and sub-regional labour markets. They were primarily local and industrial collective organisations.

Les Trente Glorieuses: The Great Divide

In the twentieth century, transnational unionism was characterised by a ten-sion between national-based trade unionism and international trade union bodies. These national-based unions were marked by specific histories and institutional arrangements, often reinforced by law, while the international union bodies, such as ITSs were secondary and often dependent bodies.

In 1949, US unions led a breakaway from the WFTU and founded the ICFTU (Gordon and Turner 2000; Gumbrell-McCormick 2000). This rup-ture took place in the context of the Cold War between the United States and the Soviet Union. Ostensibly, the ITSs were threatened by a proposal by the WFTU to integrate them into the confederation as affiliated federations. In response, the ITSs largely supported the emergence of the ICFTU, join-ing the ICFTU in 1951 (Bendt 2003). In the main, the ICFTU worked with intergovernmental organisations, such as the ILO, the OECD and the UN, on issues relating to the recognition of union rights and the respect of inter-national labour standards. Of note, the ITSs helped develop World Councils during the 1960s–70s. The first permanent and operational instruments de-veloped by trade unions within multinational corporations were put in place during the 1960s–70s and usually took the form of World Works Councils (Bendiner 1974; Litvak and Maule 1972).

A different trajectory developed out of the shift from colonial and im-perial political arrangements to the North-South arrangements, now char-acteristic of the twenty-first century world of work. Many unions in the non-industrial south developed out of the colonial relationships that pre-vailed until the late 1950s and 1960s. They were created and sponsored by unions from home countries, such as the engineering unions in Austra-lia and New Zealand. Often, there were institutional links between these unions, reflected in voting rights and other links. Not infrequently, unions in the south were major players in independence struggles (e.g., Malaysia and Kenya). In a number of cases, these unions also became prominent actors in the revolutionary and anti-colonial struggles of the time. Many promoted left and 'communist' politics as well as challenged the often patronising and exploitative relations between the colonies and their metropolitan 'home' countries. In addition, the promotion of reformist unions in the colonies by the 'home' country unions was often part of an attempt to counter the influ-ence of communist and revolutionary politics, as was the case in Malaysia in the 1950s and in South Korea by US personnel in the 1970s. As part of this mix, the Soviet bloc also underwrote trade union development in former colonies as part of their international outreach.

A further variant of this type of unionism took the form of limited and quasi-colonial cross-border trade unionism. One example is illustrated by the North American Internationals, where unions in the US and Canada operate as single, although uneasy, union bodies. Increasingly, these unions have established distinctive spheres of influence and responsibility in each country. Historically, similar practices, although less developed and comprehensive, characterised some unions in the UK and the Republic of Eire.

During the 1960s and 1970s, with the emergence of multinational corporations, there was a renewed concern about transnational trade unionism. One prominent argument was that there should be a more explicit division of labour between these actors, between national unions on the one hand and parallel forms of international trade unionism on the other. This view is perhaps best articulated in the writings of Levinson, General Secretary of the International Confederation of Chemical and General Workers' Unions (ICEM) in a series of publications (1971, 1972 and 1974).

The institutionalisation of transnational unionism involved many organisational and ideological tensions and struggles between trade unions. The political divisions between the main confederations led to often remote and sclerotic forms of union organisation and activity. The development, and then the existence of the institutions, became a prime concern of the union leaderships of the time, favouring the proliferation of 'international bureaucrats' (Hyman 2005). In this context, the confederations became the focus of union internationalism, and union leaders became rule-takers or simply bureaucrats, applying rules and promoting limited forms of labour internationalism for much of the post-war period, up until the 1980s.

One notable exception to this pattern of international trade unionism is the maritime industry. Under the auspices of the International Transport Workers' Federation's (ITF) 'Flag of Convenience' campaign, maritime unions throughout the world have promoted transnational trade unionism for over fifty years. As Lillie (2005) argues, the ITF, the London-based global union federation for transport unions, provides the institutional arrangements and forums for seafarers and port workers to promote their cross-border interests and concerns. These involve a proactive set of network arrangements between seafaring unions and port worker unions focused on minimum pay agreements for seafarers and challenging union busting by port terminal operators and others. Indeed, the unions have an organisational capacity, via the transnational ship inspector network, which is not the case in other unions in other sectors and industries.

The Current Period: Towards Multi-Level Arrangements

Over the last three decades, unions have faced major challenges. There has been a relative decline in the formal influence and effectiveness of the long-established national unions in advanced capitalist countries, particularly in the Anglo-US bloc of countries. Here, trade unions began to lose their formal place in the polity, as governments embraced neo-liberal ideals and supported employers in their relations with trade unions (e.g., Daniels and McIlroy 2008). In effect, these changes marked the end of the social demo-cratic period that either formally or by default characterised much of the im-mediate post-war period. Increasingly, trade unions found it hard to recruit members or replace members who lost their jobs. During the late 1980s and 1990s, these trade unions faced declining memberships and a diminution of influence. They began to look to their organisational practices and forms and to develop their resources and capacities (Brecher et al. 2006; Breiten-fellner 1997). As unions began to rebuild, they also began to look to forms of transnational trade unionism to address the internationalisation of work and employment that was underway.

One major variant to these developments, centred on trade unions in the European Union (EU), particularly those that were at the founding of the EU (and its forerunners). Unions in these countries, and a number of the Scandinavian countries, committed themselves to social democratic prac-tices, which took the form of 'social dialogue' policies and their associated arrangements. One important feature of this form of trade unionism is that the EU encouraged cooperation between employers and trade unions (par-ticularly national union leaderships). Nonetheless, with the establishment of the EU as a monetary union and trade bloc, unions also faced pressures in relation to the increasing internationalisation of work and employment. One outcome has been a questioning of the long-term saliency of 'social dialogue' practices and arrangements (Turner 1996).

Today, the GUFs' main activities involve disseminating information on the working conditions that prevail in some multinational corporations or industrial sectors, organising international support for affiliated unions. The most important developments have concerned representational structures within multinational corporations. The first permanent and operational instruments developed by trade unions within multinational corporations were put in place during the 1960s and 1970s, usually taking the form of World Works Councils (Litvak and Maule 1972). In North America, these early initiatives aimed at creating transnational union-based dialogue resulted largely from the position of the AFL-CIO and the United Auto Workers (UAW) which were facing increased competition from European subsidiaries. These union bodies feared that jobs would be moved offshore, and in this context, they created plural-national trade union coordination structures within the major automobile companies.

Transnational trade unionism has become a feature of the contemporary trade union movement particularly in relation to multinational corpora-tions (MNCs). Thus, several GUFs have recently become involved in the development of new forms of international solidarity by setting up *global trade union alliances*, which bring together trade unions from different countries representing workers from a single MNC (Croucher and Cotton 2009; Gajewska 2009; Hennebert 2011). Their principal goal is to open up space for dialogue and negotiation at the international level to defend and promote workers' rights wherever the firm's activities are carried out. One of the means employed to this end has been the negotiation of International Framework Agreements (IFAs) that include the eight fundamental ILO conventions and other international labour standards. While these agreements do not replace collective bargaining processes at the national and local levels, they do set out a framework of rights related to trade union recognition and social negotiation at the supranational level (Fairbrother and Hammer 2005).

THE CHAPTERS

This brief account sets the scene for the analysis presented in this book. Workplace unions are facing increased pressures from state policies promoting neo-liberal arrangements within the state, as well as in relation to private capital, nationally and internationally. National unions in many countries, and particularly in the Anglo-US ones, have faced uncertainty, uncooperative if not hostile states and a major decline in union membership, in absolute as well as relative terms. Where unions operated in seemingly sympathetic political arrangements, such as in the EU, through the highpoint of the 'social dialogue' period, unions now face pressures from state policies committed to opening up their economies, as well as pressure internally, within the EU, from Eastern European entrants to the EU, such as Romania (as discussed below), and externally. In this context, the global unions and related confederations have undergone processes of renewal, with the result that the 'international bureaucrats' of the past have now become more active and involved with local and national unions, if not more accountable, than in the past. These are the concerns of the contributors to this book.

The contributions are divided into three major parts, each addressing a core feature of the analysis and explanation of transnational unionism.

Part One

Part One addresses the question of transnational unionism from the starting point of the workplace. The core focus is on the ways in which trade unions manage to bridge the gap between the local and the global.

> **Chapter Two:** In the opening chapter, Mark Anner focuses on the bases and forms of worker power. With reference to Latin American apparel workers, he explores the relationships that are involved in shaping and focusing worker power through an analysis of the effort to unionize Russell apparel factories in Honduras. The importance of this case is that it shows that the apparel workers, despite their

considerable structural weakness, achieved several important successes in 2009 and 2010. The Russell case is then compared and contrasted with the campaign that forced Nike to pay $US 2.2 million to dismissed workers in Honduras, and Knights Apparel's decision to open a 'sweat-free' factory in the Dominican Republic. This study draws on field research in the region as well as interviews with activists in the United States. The success of these campaigns can be attributed to the creative leveraging of four sources of workers' power: structural, associational, normative and political.

Chapter Three: The main purpose of this chapter is to learn how, and under what circumstances, a North-South union alliance can be constructed. Mélanie Dufour-Poirier and Christian Lévesque examine a North-South alliance in the Americas. The alliance was set up without the support of a supranational structure and/or a set of work-based institutions that may have facilitated such an alliance. The authors examine how actors structured their relations between and among each other over time. In this way, they are able to explain the impact of (internal and external) constraints on the ways the workplace unions behave and operate. Drawing on interviews with trade unionists from local, regional, national and international organisations located in Canada, Chile and Peru, a comprehensive analysis is developed that identifies the factors associated with the success and the eventual disintegration of this alliance.

Chapter Four: The focus of this chapter is on the interplay between institutional specificity and local power dynamics in shaping workplace trade union involvement in cross-border interaction. The authors Christian Lévesque, Gregor Murray, Christian Dufour and Adelheid Hege provide an analysis of the prospects and limits of cross-border cooperation in the EU and the NAFTA regions, with particular focus on France and Canada. The purpose of their study is to understand how workplace trade unionists move in and out of transnational spaces to fulfil local needs and objectives. Drawing on longitudinal and multiple case studies, they analyse the logics, trajectories and evolution of workplace union involvement in transnational activity. They show that workplace trade unions, albeit in different ways, make strategic use of international space according to local priorities and supranational opportunities. In particular, they propose that the strategic capabilities of workplace union leaders clearly play pivotal roles in shaping their cross-border actions.

Chapter Five: This chapter provides an understanding of the dynamics of collective action between trade unions from Eastern and Western Europe. Drawing on extensive field work, Michèle Descolonges studies a strike at Dacia (subsidiary of Renault) in Romania in the spring of 2008. This strike was the first 'European strike' in the company, and it involved Romanian and French trade unions. The strike was noteworthy. The dispute was supported by unions in Europe, including French trade unions and in particular the CGT (Confédération générale du travail). The size and the range of activity associated with the strike surprised many. Nonetheless, this strike brought to light many of the difficulties associated with the construction of sustainable trade union cooperation in the context of asymmetric resources and institutional disparities.

Part Two

Part Two has a different focus. Here, the primary emphasis is on national unions, drawing out the relationships between local, national and international unions.

> **Chapter Six:** The first chapter in this part considers the ways that unions, embedded in the workplace but prominent internationally, are able to renew and refocus their purpose. Drawing on extensive field research, Peter Fairbrother develops an analysis of transnational unionism that locates national unions within a matrix of relations that begin at the local level, involve unions as national actors and actively operate within the global union federations. The Maritime Union of Australia (MUA), the major union focus of the study, has a long history of involvement and engagement with international unions. This union was locked out in an infamous challenge to the existence of the union by a major employer that was publicly supported by the government of the day. This event provided an occasion for a renewal of the union's commitment to transnational trade unionism and the promotion of solidaristic forms of organisation and activity with other unions involved in goods transportation and movement through seaports. The conditions for these developments are a reflective and experienced leadership, opportunities for leaders to meet each other and for activists to develop practices of solidarity and information exchange and union cooperation with each other at all levels.
>
> **Chapter Seven:** The theme of building union power is further examined in this chapter. Armel Brice Adanhounme and Christian Lévesque continue to develop this theme, with reference to two sets of unions from the South, Ghana and Mexico. The authors draw on in-depth interviews with key actors to identify different processes in the two countries. They argue that the choice is not between going global or remaining local, but rather navigating between the local and the global by seizing opportunities to strengthen the union's capacity to act at the global level, while enhancing the capabilities of actors at the grassroots level. They propose the idea of rooted labour

internationalism. These variations are explained by the dynamic of the political context in which unions are embedded and the position of these developing countries within the global value chains that link the unions together in each case.

Chapter Eight: This chapter focuses on transnational structures in Europe, in particular on multinational company-level negotiations. The authors, Valeria Pulignano, Isabel da Costa, Udo Rehfeldt and Volker Telljohann, note that both cross-national diversity in systems of employment regulation and weak institutional basis for transnational bargaining at the European level hamper the negotiations of framework agreements in Europe. By drawing on a less deterministic view of institutional structures the authors use their extensive interview-based research data to provide an understanding of how social actors at different levels (European, national and local) shape and reshape regulatory settings. Departing from a multi-actor and multi-level analytical framework, they focus on the strategies of the social actors (management, trade unions and employee representatives) at both European, national and company levels.

Chapter Nine: The last chapter in this part builds on these themes and presents an overview of transnational unionism in Europe. As the author, Richard Hyman, notes at the outset, trade union internationalism has often been primarily European in composition and focus: all formal organisations of global unionism have been located in Europe, headed by Europeans and largely funded by European affiliates. Eurocentrism has contributed to the North-South tensions of recent years, reinforced by the re-orientation of much of the emphasis of the European trade union movement to the regulatory processes of the European Union. This chapter explores some of the contradictions of this process. It concludes by asking how far European unions are moving from integration to contention and whether this process is in turn accompanied by increased sensitivities to global solidarity.

Part Three

Part Three focuses on the international dimension of transnational unionism. The key feature of this section is the examination of the ways in which international forms of trade unionism have developed and promoted new forms of organisation and activity, sometimes successfully and at other times less so.

Chapter Ten: In the opening chapter for this part, the concern is to provide an overview of the international trade union organisations, tracing out their origins and identifying the principal challenges they face in the global world today. The author, Rebecca Gumbrell-McCormick, provides a detailed examination of the structure and dynamics of the international labour movement, focusing on the principal trade union organisations. The creation of the ITUC in 2006 marked the beginning of a new era in relationships between structures, primarily between the ITUC itself and the GUFs. The latter have retained their formal autonomy within a new mechanism for collaboration with each other and the ITUC through the Council of Global Unions. Building on extensive archival research and key interviews, she analyses the strategic direction of the new organisation and examines the relationship between the new formal structures and the living dynamics of local, national and international trade union action.

Chapter Eleven: This chapter develops an account of international union organisation and activity through a focused study of one feature of recent global union federation activity, namely the promotion of IFAs. The authors, Michael Fichter, Markus Helfen and Katharina Schiederig, focus on how global unions can support transnational solidarity across institutional distances by making IFAs a tool for anchoring corporate-specific labour relations throughout global production networks. The authors present a critical examination of these organisational issues, with a study of five GUFs. Their major finding is that IFAs increase the recognition of GUFs as legitimate transnational bargaining agents, both by their affiliates and by management 'across the table'.

Chapter Twelve: Continuing the analysis of global union federations, this chapter studies the conditions for success of international alliances. The authors, Marc-Antonin Hennebert and Reynald Bourque, propose that such cross-border union alliances are one of the main trade union innovations for the social regulation of transnational firms. In an extensive interview-based study of the Canadian multinational firm Quebecor World, the authors examined the ways that union officials sought to coordinate action among unions as represented by the firm's worldwide activities. Under the leadership of Union Network International (UNI), a new form of international alliance was established and a worldwide campaign for union rights initiated. The authors show that although such alliances require the development of common projects and solidarity among members, they are not monoliths. The way these alliances function also involves strategic interplay and a structuring of industrial relations, conferring varying positions and roles on their constituents.

Chapter Thirteen: One object of international union organisation and activity, particularly via IFAs, is to lay the foundation for the regulation of work and employment in ways that benefit and protect workers. Nikolaus Hammer's contribution brings us back to the local level by considering how workers and their local unions cope with the challenges of work and employment despite IFAs applying to the industry. Drawing on material from research projects on construction MNCs in India, Russia and South Africa, this contribution explores the extent to which regulations of work and employment can be extended across labour control regimes in different institutional contexts and labour market segments. The author argues that large infrastructure developments in global growth poles have led to the emergence of an international segment of construction labour in particular forms of labour control regimes. The latter are characterised by the extension of subcontracting and the state-sponsored attraction of a migrant workforce as well as an increase in informal labour.

Final Chapter

Chapter 14: In this chapter, the editors, Christian Lévesque, Marc-Antonin Hennebert and Peter Fairbrother, aim to provide an overview of the main themes addressed by the contributors to this book. They present an understanding of the key features of transnational trade unionism, explore the question of power in relation to these developments and identify the conditions to build and sustain union solidarity. This final chapter lays out the foundation for the development of a framework to understand transnational trade unionism.

REFERENCES

Anner, M. (2007), 'The Paradox of Labour Transnationalism: Trade Union Campaigns for Labour Standards in International Institutions', in Craig Phelan (ed.), *The Future of Organised Labour: Global Perspectives*, Oxford: Peter Lang.

Barton, R., and Fairbrother, P. (2009), 'The Local is Now the Global: Building a Union Coalition in the International Transport and Logistics Sector', *Relations industrielles / Industrial Relations*, 64(4), 685–703.

Bendiner, B. (1974), 'Unions Expanding International Coordination', *Harvard Business Review*, 52(2), 12–23.

Bendt, H. (2003), *Worldwide Solidarity. The Activities of the Global Unions in the Era of Globalisation*, Bonn: Friedrich-Ebert-Stiftung, Division for International Cooperation, Global Trade Union Program.

Bergene, A.C. (2007), 'Trade Unions Walking the Tightrope in Defending Workers' Interests: Wielding a Weapon Too Strong?', *Labor Studies Journal*, 32(2), 142–166.

Bourdieu, P. (1980), *The Logic of Practice*, Stanford: Stanford University Press.

Brecher, J., Cossello, T., and Smith, B. (2006), 'International Labor Solidarity: The New Frontier', *New Labor Forum*, 15(1), 9–18.

Breitenfellner, A. (1997), 'Global Unionism: A Potential Player', *International Labour Review*, 136(4), 531–555.

Bronfenbrenner, K. (2007), *Global Union: Challenging Transnational Capital through Cross-Border Campaigns*, Ithaca, NY: Cornell University Press.

Castells, M. (1996), *The Rise of the Network Society. The Information Age: Economy, Society and Culture*, Malden, MA: Oxford, UK: Blackwell.

Cohen, S. (2006), *Ramparts of Resistance: Why Workers Lost Their Power and How to Get It Back*, London: Pluto Press.

Coe, N., Kelly, P., and Yeung, H., (2007), *Economic Geography. A Contemporary Introduction*, Malden, MA: Blackwell Publishing.

Cramme, O., and Diamond, P. (2009), *Social Justice in the Global Age*, Cambridge: Polity.

Croucher, R., and Cotton, E. (2009), *Global Unions Global Business. Global Union Federations and International Business*, London: Middlesex University Press.

Daniels, G., and McIlroy, J. (eds) (2008), *Trade Unions in a Neoliberal World: British Trade Unions under New Labour*, London: Routledge.

Dufour, C., and Hege, A. (2010), 'Légitimité des acteurs collectifs et renouveau syndical', *La Revue de l'IRES*, n° 65, 2010/2, 67–85.

Edwards, P. K. (1986), *Conflict at Work: A Materialist Analysis of Workplace Relations*, Oxford: Basil Blackwell.

Fairbrother, P., and Yates, C. (eds) (2003). *Trade Unions in Renewal: A Comparative Study*, London: Routledge.

Fairbrother, P., and Hammer, N. (2005), 'Global Unions: Past Efforts and Future Prospects', *Relations industrielles / Industrial Relations*, 60(3), 405–431.

Friedberg, E. (1993), *Le pouvoir et la règle. Dynamiques de l'action organisée*, Paris: Le Seuil.

Frost, A. C. (2000), 'Explaining Variation in Workplace Restructuring: The Role of Local Union Capabilities', *Industrial and Labor Relations Review*, 53(4), 559–578.

Gajewska, K. (2009), *Transnational Labour Solidarity. Mechanisms of Commitment to Cooperation within the European Trade Union Movement*, New York, Routledge.

Gordon, M., and Turner, L. (2000), *Transnational Cooperation among Labor Unions*, Ithaca, NY: ILR Press.

Greer, I., and Hauptmeier, M. (2008), 'Political Entrepreneurs and Co-Managers: Labour Transnationalism at Four Multinational Auto Companies', *British Journal of Industrial Relations*, 46(1), 76–97.

Gumbrell-McCormick, R. (2003), 'The ICFTU and the World Economy: A Historical Perspective' in Ronald Munck (ed.) *Labour and Globalisation: Results and Prospects*, Liverpool: Liverpool University Press.

Gumbrell-McCormick, R. (2000), 'Globalisation and the Dilemmas of International Trade Unionism', *Transfer: European Review of Labour and Research*, 6(1): 29–42.

Harvey, D. (2000), *Spaces of Hope*, Berkeley: University of California Press.

Held, D. (1995), *Democracy and the Global Order: From the Modern State to Cosmopolitan Governance*, Cambridge: Polity Press.

Hennebert, M-A. (2011), 'Cross-Border Union Alliances and Transnational Collective Bargaining: A Case Study in a Canadian MNC', *Just Labour, A Canadian Journal of Work and Society*, 17 & 18, 1–17.

Hyman, R. (2005), 'Shifting Dynamics in International Trade Unionism: Agitation, Organisation, Bureaucracy, Diplomacy', *Labor History*, 46(2), 137–154.

Hyman, R. (1975), *Industrial Relations: A Marxist Introduction*, London: Macmillan Press.

Johns, R. (1998), 'Bridging the Gap between Class and Space: U.S. Worker Solidarity with Guatemala', *Economic Geography*, 74(3), 252–271.

Kay, T. (2005) 'Labor Transnationalism and Global Governance: The Impact of NAFTA on Transnational Labor', *American Journal of Sociology* 111(3): 715–756.

Kelly, J. (1998), *Rethinking Industrial Relations: Mobilization, Collectivism and Long Waves*, London: Routledge.

Lévesque, C., and Murray, G. (2010), 'Trade-Union Cross-Border Alliances within MNCs: Disentangling Union Dynamics at the Local, National and International Levels', *Industrial Relations Journal*, 41(4), 312–332.

Lillie, N. (2005), 'Union Networks and Global Unionism in Maritime Shipping', *Relations industrielles / Industrial Relations*, 60(1), 88–111.

Lillie, N., and Martinez Lucio, M. (2012), 'Rollerball and the Spirit of Capitalism. Competitive Dynamics within the Global Context, the Challenge to Labour Transnationalism, and the Emergence of Ironic Outcomes', *Critical Perspectives on International Business*, 8(1), 74–92.

Litvak, I. A., and Maule, C. J. (1972) 'The Union Response to International Corporations', *Industrial Relations*, 11(1), 62–71.

Lorwin, L. L. (1953), *The International Labor Movement: History, Policies, Outlook*, New York: Harper.

Lucio Martinez, M. (2010), 'Dimensions of Internationalism and the Politics of the Labour Movement. Understanding the Political and Organisational Aspects of Labour Networking and Co-ordination', *Employee Relations*, 32(6), 538–556.

Lukes, S. (2005), *Power: A Radical View*, Basingstoke: Palgrave Macmillan.

Munck, R. (2010), 'Globalization and the Labour Movement: Challenges and Responses', *Global Labor Journal*, 1(2), 218–232.

Myconos, G. (2005), *The Globalization of Organized Labour: 1945–2005*, Basingstoke: Palgrave Macmillan.

Offe, C., and Wiesenthal, H. (1980), 'Two Logics of Collective Action: Theoretical Notes on Social Class and Organizational Form', *Political Power and Social Theory*, 1, 67–115.

Olle, W., and Schoeller, W. (1977), 'World Market Competition and Restrictions on International Trade Union Policies', *Capital and Class*, 1(2), 56–75.

Papadakis, K. (2011), *Shaping Global Industrial Relations. The Impact of International Framework Agreements*, Geneva: International Labour Organizations, International Institute for Labour Studies.

Pocock, B. (2000), *Union Renewal: A Theoretical and Empirical Analysis of Union Power*, Adelaide: University of Adelaide, Centre for Labour Research.

Pringle, T., and Clark, S. (2010), *The Challenge of Transition: Trade Unions in Russia, China and Vietnam*, Basingstoke: Palgrave Macmillan.

Silver, B. (2003), *Forces of Labour: Workers Movements and Globalization since 1870*, Cambridge: Cambridge University Press.

Silver, B., and Arrighi, G. (2001), 'Workers, North and South', in L. Panitch and C. Leys (eds.), *Socialist Register 2001: Working Classes, Global Realities*, London: Merlin Press.

Stevis, D. (2010), *International Framework Agreements and Global Social Dialogue: Parameters and Prospects*, International Labour Organization, Employment Sector, Employment Working Paper No. 47, Geneva: International Labour Organization.

Tarrow, S. (2005), *The New Transnational Activism*, Cambridge: Cambridge University Press.

Tattersall, A. (2007), 'Labor-Community Coalitions, Global Union Alliances, and the Potential of SEIU's Global Partnerships', in K. Bronfenbrenner (ed.), *Global Unions: Challenging Transnational Capital through Cross-Border Campaigns*, Ithaca, NY: ILR Press.

Touraine, A. (1982), 'Triumph or Downfall of Civil Society', in D. Reiss (ed.), *Humanities in Review*, Vol. 1, Cambridge: Cambridge University Press.

Turner, L. (1996), 'The Europeanization of Labour: Structure before Action', *European Journal of Industrial Relations*, 2(3), 325–344.

Webster, E., Lambert, R., and Bezuidenhout, A. (2008), *Grounding Globalization: Labour in Age of Insecurity*, Oxford: Blackwell Publishing.

Windmuller, J.P. (1980), *The International Trade Union Movement*, Boston: Klumer.

Wright, E. (2000), 'Working-Class Power, Capitalist-Class Interests, and Class Compromise', *American Journal of Sociology*, 105(4), 957–1002.

Part I

Workplace Trade Unions: Bridging the Local to the Global

2 Workers' Power in Global Value Chains

Fighting Sweatshop Practices at Russell, Nike and Knights Apparel

Mark Anner

On November 17, 2009, one of the United States' largest sportswear and collegiate apparel companies, Russell,[1] announced it would re-employ 1,200 Honduran garment workers who were subject to anti-union discrimination. The workers' union would be respected and allowed to bargain collectively. The announcement came after two years of local and international activism targeting the company. It was heralded by the movement and by independent observers as one of the largest contemporary success stories of the international labour movement (Greenhouse 2009). It was also a bit of a surprise. The global apparel industry has long been considered an industry where labour has the weakest structural and associational power (Silver 2003). Over the past two decades, even some of the largest and most creative international anti-sweatshop campaigns eventually resulted in plant closings and the destruction of labour unions (Armbruster 2005). Thus, the Russell campaign is a call to reflect on what, in this most precarious and hyper-mobile of global value chains, allowed for this favorable outcome.

An exploration of sources of workers' power in global value chains and an analysis of the dynamics of the Russell case indicate that several overlapping factors contributed to labour's success. It is argued here that recent shifts in trade rules, new forms of associational power, an empowering normative frame and political opportunities in the form of non-state governance institutions all influenced the movement's ability to leverage the corporation and achieve the movement's goal. This chapter first explores these four sources of worker power. Next, the chapter illustrates these powers by examining the case of Russell in Honduras and then compares and contrasts this case to the successes at Nike in Honduras and Knights Apparel in the Dominican Republic.

WORKERS' POWER

Power generally refers to the ability of one group to get another group to do something it would not otherwise do. For apparel workers, this most often means the ability to get apparel manufacturers to recognise a union and engage in collective bargaining in order to improve wages and working conditions. The legal establishment of a union often also requires leveraging the state. Drawing on the research of scholars of political economy, international relations, social movements and industrial relations, at least four forms of power can be identified: (1) structural power, (2) associational power, (3) normative power and (4) political power. Each of these traditional sources of workers' power has been transformed by the dynamics of global value chains and evolving labour strategies. Understanding these sources of power and their transformations provides insights into the recent successes of apparel workers and lessons for workers in other sectors of the economy.

Most discussions of workers' power begin with economic structures. For Marx and Engels ([1848] 1992), the industrial revolution entailed the centralisation of production, which included the bringing together of large masses of workers under a single factory roof. Capital in these more advanced industrial sectors had, in a sense, 'organised' labour. This suggests that the greater the centralisation of production, the greater the potential strength of labour. This helps explain why large industries like the automotive industry historically have had stronger trade unions than the smaller and more dispersed apparel factories. Capital-intensive industries that have high value-added per worker also provide labour with more strength since there is a larger pie for employers to share with labour (Marshall 1920). For apparel production workers, the pie is notoriously small, which is another reason why their structural power is so limited.

John Commons was more concerned with the structure of the market over the structure of production. It was the market and its 'competitive menace' that most adversely affected labour and market expansion from a local to a national level added to labour's challenges (Commons 1909). For apparel workers, the dramatic globalisation of the industry has presented perhaps its greatest obstacle to sustained organisational success.

Economic sociologists note that the structure of the market and the structure of production are part of the same capitalist process, one that has increasingly segmented and dispersed the production and distribution of goods and services through global value chains (Gereffi, Humphrey and Sturgeon 2005; Gereffi, Korzeniewicz and Korzeniewicz 1994). If labour's initial strength came from the centralisation of production, it follows that decentralisation through global value chains would weaken labour's power. But this observation must be qualified. If labour can disrupt a strategic segment of the global value chain, then decentralisation may not be such a conundrum. This is what Perrone (1983) refers to as positional power, and why Silver (2003) argues that outsourcing may in fact increase workers' power (or the 'forces of labour'). Yet, the global apparel industry has relied predominantely on *horizontal* outsourcing, where corporations farm out *duplicate* production functions to countless factories. In this structure, the ability of workers to disrupt the supply chain had been greatly curtailed (Anner 2011).

Nonetheless, as we will see ahead, recent changes in trade rules may in fact be contributing to the greater centralisation of production and more direct ownership of suppliers, which decreases firm mobility and makes companies more vulnerable to activist campaigns. And, as Naomi Klein eloquently observed, apparel corporations that have invested so heavily in their brand image have made themselves vulnerable to consumer campaigns and economic boycotts, something the anti-sweatshop movement was quick to capitalise on (Klein 2000).

Workers located in structurally unfavorable sectors have the potential to achieve some of their goals through strong organisations, or associational power. This is what social movement scholars refer to as 'resource mobilisation'. They argue that the more resources that movements have (funds, personnel, infrastructure, etc.), the better positioned they will be to achieve their goals (McCarthy and Zald 1977). For labour, most accounts of associational power begin with trade unions, since these have the organisational structure, economic resources, staff, and infrastructure that facilitate collective action (Wright 2000: 962).

Yet, too many resources over a long period of time may be a liability. Robert Michels, in the *Iron Law of Oligarchy*, famously declared that large organisations (including trade unions) are eventually overcome by bureaucratic tendencies (Michels 1911 [1962]). More recent critiques of traditional and international trade union organisations highlight their rigidity and vertical structures, noting that they are particularly unsuitable for the task of international labour solidarity (Jakobsen 2001; Waterman 2001). For Waterman, the preferred forms of international solidarity are social movement networks (Waterman 2008). Of course, networks are not without their limitations, including problems with accountability and global north-south power imbalances (Anner 2006). Their more limited resources also restrict the number of campaigns they can pursue at a given moment. At the same time, many trade unions have found ways to revitalise and remain relevant in the global economy (Turner, Katz and Hurd 2001; Voss and Sherman 2000).

Many of the most effective campaigns have involved the joining together of revitalised trade unions and activists networks (Turnbull 2006). This is also true of contemporary anti-sweatshop activism, which has been built on alliances among workers, unions, labour rights groups, women's groups and student organisations. The prominent role of non-union groups adds greater legitimacy to transnational efforts in that—when students or women's group denounce sweatshop practices in Honduras or Bangladesh—they cannot be criticised for acting out of a hidden agenda to protect the jobs of their members. Finally, the incorporation of young activists affects organisational tactics, because these activists often employ disruptive and creative actions, from anti-sweatshop sit-ins to 'Twitter bombs'.

Adding to organisational strength is the manner in which movements frame their goals. Sociologist and international relations scholars argue that norms—by which they mean socially accepted standards of appropriate behaviour—have the ability to change opponents' behaviour, even that of power dictatorial states (Katzenstein 1996; Risse and Sikkink 1999; Tannenwald 1999). Thus, while traditional political analysis focuses on the 'logic of consequences' (use of military or economic power to change conduct), the normative approach suggests that opponents can be shamed into changing their conduct through a 'logic of appropriateness' (March & Olsen 1998). For labour activists, what this suggests is that multinational corporations may avoid certain actions—for example, the use of thirteen-year-old girls to make their products—not only because they fear economic sanctions, but also because they desire legitimacy, which is obtained by adhering to socially-accepted conduct.

The power of norms lies in the ability of activist networks to expose their violations and shame the violator into appropriate behavior (Finnemore and Sikkink 2005; Keck and Sikkink 1998; Risse and Sikkink 1999). Norms have been evoked by labour movements ever since worker organisations first demanded an end to *inhumane* conditions of work. Webster, Lambert and Bezuidenhout refer to 'symbolic' power used in contemporary campaigns of janitors, undocumented immigrants and workers with HIV/AIDs. They define symbolic power as 'the struggle of right against wrong' that takes place in the public domain (Webster, Lambert and Bezuidenhout 2008: 12–13). Normative power has long been an important aspect of the global anti-sweatshop movement. References to 'starvation wages', 'intolerable working hours' and 'abusive child labour' are common normative frames effectively used by activists to generate moral outrage among consumers and shame among corporations.

The final source of workers' power is political power. Governments establish rules for the economy, determine levels of social benefits and decide who can and who cannot form a union, bargain collectively and strike. And they establish how many resources should be dedicated to enforcing rules governing the workplace. Not surprisingly, labour has had a strong interest in obtaining political power in order to influence these decisions (or, perhaps, to transform the entire system). Workers have sought political power through alliances with or participation in political parties or movements. In some countries, tripartite mechanisms of consultation give labour influence in key policy decisions. In countries where labour is denied institutionalised political access, workers may be more likely to organise protest events that target state institutions.

Social movement scholars of the political process tradition add that labour's political power is related to its ability to exploit political opportunities and respond to political threats (Tarrow 1989; Tilly 1978). Divisions in governing elites might, for example, provide labour with an opportunity, whereas a coup d'état and subsequent anti-union repression is a political threat that might spark labour mobilisation, as was the case of the 2009 coup in Honduras. Scholars of transnational advocacy add that movements facing political threats at home may seek out political opportunities abroad via foreign governments that are more receptive to their concerns (Keck and Sikkink 1998).

For the anti-sweatshop movement, transnational governance structures include the emerging world of private labour rights monitoring, investigation and remediation. Two prominent American non-state governance institutions are the Fair Labour Association (FLA) and the Worker Rights Consortium (WRC). The FLA was founded with the support of the United States government and includes corporate members on its board. The WRC is a student and labour initiative, and does not have corporate members. WRC investigations often provide the anti-sweatshop movement with the needed documentation and thus legitimacy to their claims of abuses. At the same time, its findings and the strategic dissemination of its research reports may push multi-national corporations (MNCs) to change their conduct in what some scholars refer to as the dynamics of 'information politics' (Keck and Sikkink 1998).

To summarise, even workers traditionally considered among the most vulnerable and powerless can sustain organisational success in global value chains by synergistically leveraging structural, associational, normative and political power. For global apparel workers, this might entail targeting vulnerabilities in production and consumption segments of supply chains, forming transnational activist networks, shaming brand-sensitive corporations that violate fundamental workers' rights and exploiting transnational political opportunities through information politics and politically-oriented activism.

ANTI-SWEATSHOP ACTIVISM IN APPAREL GLOBAL VALUE CHAINS

To understand current anti-sweatshop activism, it is first necessary to understand how and why sweatshop practices proliferated. In Central America in the 1990s, in order to re-activate economies after prolonged civil war and social strife, local governments worked with international aid agencies like USAID and the World Bank to develop a model of export-oriented growth via low-end outsourcing in manufacturing. U.S. trade laws liberalised quotas for apparel assembled in Central America and the Caribbean but required the use of US made fabric in order to receive full exempt status. Since apparel production requires much lower capital investments than textile production, and since industries with much lower investment costs are more mobile, the US rules relegated to Central America a hyper-mobile form of production and resulted in labour's weak structural power, which weakened workers' ability to organise and improve conditions.

In the mid-1990s, Central America workers sought to compensate for their structural and associational weaknesses by joining an international anti-sweatshop movement. American activists had already been active in the region opposing US intervention during the wars of the 1980s. They had developed deep social trust networks, understood the context and many had developed language skills that facilitated communication. The end of the civil wars in the region led these activists to shift their focus from issues related to physical integrity and other basic human rights to new issue areas based on social justice at the workplace related to the boom in export processing zones (Krupat 1997). Thus, an activist network had already been established prior to the start of the anti-sweatshop movement. What changed were the issue areas and the targets. Instead of protesting the assassination or arrest of a union leader, the activists protested the 'starvation wages' and 'oppressive factory conditions' of the workers. And instead of directing most of their energy at the state, they combined state-centric protest with protests that targeted the MNCs that made sizeable profits off the structures of international outsourcing.

The movement employed normative power in one of the first major anti-sweatshop campaigns by focusing on child labour. Producers such as Kathie Lee Gifford were effectively shamed and backed into a 'normative corner' by movement allegations and media documentation that under-aged workers were making their clothing. Apparel MNCs were then forced to ensure more effective monitoring of the age requirement in their suppliers. The problem for workers in Central America was that the 'child labour' normative frame did not result in greater empowerment via stronger unions.

By the late 1990s, as American and international trade unions became more active in the anti-sweatshop campaigns, they brought with them an organising perspective. While abusive conditions were highlighted in all their public denouncements, associational power was more fully developed. Workers went on strike at the same time activists picketed the stores and targeted the headquarters of the MNCs. Political power was also employed, often in the form of pressure on the US government's trade representative through General System of Preference petitions that alleged unfair trade practices due to labour rights violations.

The combination of activist and union associational power with political leverage contributed to the formation of several important unions and several collective bargaining agreements in the Dominican Republic, El Salvador, Guatemala, Nicaragua, Honduras and Mexico. But the weak structural power of apparel workers eventually undermined these successes. With time, each unionised factory with a collective bargaining agreement closed and moved elsewhere. The hyper-mobility of capital in the apparel global value chain trumped the normative, associational, and political power of labour.

Then the apparel global value chains underwent a series of important changes in the early 2000s. The U.S. Caribbean Basin Trade Partnership Act (CBTPA) in 2000 allowed for duty-free access for products made in the region using certain regional knit fabrics. The Central American-Dominican Republic Free Trade Agreement (CAFTA-DR) in 2005 deepened this trend and made the trade benefits permanent. The World Trade Organization through the Agreement on Textiles and Clothing (ATC) provided for the global dismantling of controlled trade in textiles by January 1, 2005.

There were two results of these regulatory changes. First, the elimination of the quota system allowed manufacturers to geographically concentrate production to their liking. One the other hand, production flowed to China and increased in very low-wage countries such as Vietnam and Bangladesh. Yet, at the same time, producers that stayed in Central America began to expand their operations to include textile production. This meant greater investment costs, which lowered capital mobility. Several large firms that stayed in the region also directly owned the factories making their products. The end result was that apparel workers' structural power in these facilities increased, if ever so slightly. The stage was set for a new round of anti-sweatshop activism in the region.

WORKERS' POWER AND RUSSELL IN HONDURAS

In perhaps the single most significant success of the contemporary anti-sweatshop movement, on November 19, 2009, the athletic apparel giant, Russell, was pressured to accept the re-hiring of 1,200 Honduran workers and unionists by opening a new factory. It was also forced to recognise the union, begin collective bargaining and adopt a union neutrality clause at all its facilities in the country. This success can be understood as a result of the sources of workers' power developed above and recent structural changes due to changing trade regulations that allowed Russell to concentrate production in Honduras. Political power was employed by leveraging transnational non-state governance structures. Associational power built on the historic alliance between Honduran workers and transnational anti-sweatshop activists, particularly student activists. And normative power developed in the form of an empowering anti-sweatshop frame.

Russell has been characterised for much of its over 100 year history by its aim to achieve vertical integration. By the 1930s, Russell was making not only fabric and garments but also its own yarn and dyes. In 1960, Russell was the largest manufacturer of athletic clothing in the US, and by 1994, its sales topped USD 1 billion.[2] Yet soon afterwards, rising costs in the US and escalating competition pushed Russell into a process of deep restructuring. In the late 1990s, it closed approximately one-third of its US facilities and began shifting production abroad. Offshore production shot from 17 per cent to 70 per cent of production over the course of the 1990s.[3]

What is notable about the Russell restructuring process is that it did not entail outsourcing. Rather, new foreign-based facilities were directly owned by the corporation. Indeed, Russell continues to do its own spinning, knitting, cloth finishing, cutting, sewing and packaging. This is important because ownership made Russell directly accountable for violations committed at these facilities, which also meant that the most common strategy of apparel MNCs—terminating an independent supplier's contract and moving elsewhere in the face of a labour organising drive—was not an option. The suppliers were part and parcel of Russell.

In 2006, Russell was purchased by Berkshire Hathaway (headed by billionaire Warren Buffett) for USD 600 million and became a part of Berkshire Hathaway's Fruit of the Loom unit. In the process, Central America and the Caribbean became a major site of Russell's offshore activities. Honduras emerged as a regional hub where, following the changes in trade regulations that allowed for duty-free exports of textiles, Russell built a new textile manufacturing plant in Choloma. Russell established a total of eight garment production facilities and became the largest private sector employer in the country.

In many ways, the choice of Honduras is not surprising. Since the 1980s and early 1990s, the country was the preferred site of US apparel corporations for either offshoring or, far more often, outsourcing. By the mid-1990s, Honduras was the fourth largest exporter of apparel to the US market. Unlike its more tumultuous neighbors—Guatemala, Nicaragua and El Salvador—Honduras had avoided a full-scale civil war. Honduras also offered good roads and the region's best deep-water port, the infrastructural legacy of a two-century endeavor to provide European and American markets with quick access to silver, zinc and bananas.

The absence of civil war should not suggest the absence of authoritarian rule and civil unrests. The 1950s through the early 1980s were characterised by military governments and a relatively strong and active labour movement (Meza 1991). Yet, many Honduran military rulers had a reformist bent and were equally skilled at repression and cooptation. As James Mahoney notes when contrasting Honduras to El Salvador and Guatemala, 'the body count was in the hundreds, not the thousands' (Mahoney 2001: 254). Political access was always greater for labour in Honduras relative to its closest neighbors. In the contemporary era, access escalated after the progressive Manuel Zelaya became president in January 2006, but then declined dramatically following the coup d'état of June 2009. Access historically has also been undermined by the systematic under-funding of the Ministry of Labour and its department of workplace inspection.

In this context, at two Russell-owned factories—Jerzees Choloma and Jerzees de Honduras—aggrieved workers sought out the support of union organisers at their Choloma office for assistance. The organisers held workshops and meetings with the Russell workers, recruited new members and then presented the Ministry of Labour with documentation to legalise a labour union with the purpose of collective bargaining. These unionists were part of the moderate CGT labour confederation, and they explained to management that they did not want conflict, but rather sought to work together to resolve common issues and concerns.[4]

Russell, however, made it apparent that it did not shift production out of the US and into Honduras to develop a high-end model of employer-union partnership. According to one account, organisers received death threats, and by September 2007, management had dismissed 145 workers at the plants due to their union activity (WRC 2008). Then, in April 2008, Russell closed the Jerzees Choloma plant, but agreed to relocate all of its workers to Jerzees de Honduras. At Jerzees de Honduras, in response to what workers saw as arbitrary and abusive treatment by management, they formed a union to represent the 1,800 workers. Three months later, the union and management entered into a collective bargaining process as required by law. During that time, workers claimed they were subjected to continued harassment and threats of plant closure (WRC 2008). By October 2008, bargaining had reached an impasse and Russell announced it would close the plant for 'economic reasons'.[5]

The local labour union was now at a crossroads. With limited domestic political power and weak associational power, it was unable to take on the country's largest private sector employer. But what could it do? As Sidney Tarrow has suggested, actors unable to resolve their grievances domestically could seek to exploit transnational political 'opportunity structures' (Tarrow 2005). Labour rights clauses in trade agreements with the US had provided such a mechanism in the past. In this case, the movement found the emerging non-state labour rights governance institutions to be a more immediate option. In the case of Russell, unionists contacted the WRC and asked them to inspect the situation in the factory.[6]

Through repeated trips to the country, the WRC conducted detailed and systematic analysis of what transpired in the factories and posted its reports on its website. The WRC concluded that the closing of Jerzees was motivated in part by the desire to rid the company of the union (WRC 2008, 2009). WRC reporting, a form of 'information politics', put pressure on Russell to look more closely at conditions in its factory. The WRC report also vindicated the Honduran workers in their assertion that their rights had been violated and motivated American student activists organised in United Students Against Sweatshops (USAS) to take on the Russell campaign as its next major endeavor.

USAS proved to be an effective ally for the Honduran union. It has characterised itself for creative, direct-action tactics that have included not only picketing retail stores, but also sweatshop fashion shows in which, as students model a brand-named apparel, a commentator explained how these products were made in an impoverished country for 'starvation wages'. 'Naked' marches[7] were also used to indicate that, unless sweatshop conditions were addressed, consumers with a strong moral consciousness would be forced to stop purchasing clothing altogether. These actions were an effort to leverage normative power by catching consumer's attention and appealing to their deeper sense of what is right and wrong.

At the time of the Russell campaign, USAS already had approximately ten years of transnational organising experience.[8] Over the course of numerous anti-sweatshop campaigns involving Honduran-based producers, student and Honduran activists had developed what Sidney Tarrow refers to as a 'trust network' (Tarrow 2005). The worker-student alliance made sense for an additional reason: Russell was one of the largest producers of American collegiate apparel. This gave the students a source of economic leverage that they could exploit by demanding universities cut their contracts with Russell until such time that Russell respected internationally recognised workers' rights.

American trade unionists also became involved in the campaign. Notably, the American Federation of Labour and Congress of Industrial Organisations (AFL-CIO)'s American Center for International Labour Solidarity provided support to the Honduran union and offered training activities. Long-time American union activist Jeff Hermanson was particularly instrumental in providing strategic advice and lending his considerable negotiating skills at crucial junctures. Yet, the American textile workers' union, UNITE, was not strongly involved partly as a result of its process of separation from the Hotel Employees and Restaurant Employees union (HERE) and partly because it had dramatically cut back its solidarity work in the region as it chose to focus more on organising domestic industrial laundry and apparel distribution centers. The Textile, Garment and Leather Workers' Federation (ITGLWF)—the sector's Global Union Federation—was also not strongly involved in this campaign, partly as a result of the untimely passing of its long-time general secretary, Neil Kearney.

Russell was a member of the Fair Labour Association, and the FLA code of conduct requires its members to respect internationally recognised labour rights, including the right to form a labour union. Russell insisted that the factory closing was strictly due to changing demand for its fleece products. Yet, as attention on the case mounted with activists insisting labour rights were indeed violated, the FLA was compelled to inspect the factory. To do so, the FLA turned to A. & L. Group Inc. (ALGI), one of its accredited external monitors. ALGI monitors travelled to Honduras and reported that they did not detect evidence of anti-union behavior (FLA 2009: 12).

International labour activists and Honduran union representatives were enraged with the ALGI report. According to the FLA, it received ten procedural challenges from labour rights organisations and the CGT labour center in Honduras regarding the impartiality of the ALGI (FLA 2009). Their pressure led the FLA to contact an International Labour Organization (ILO) consultant, Adrian Goldin, to examine the case. Goldin visited Honduras, interviewed workers, unionists and managers, and, in direct contrast to the ALGI, found that the closure was related to the presence of the union (Goldin 2009). After reviewing the ALGI and Goldin reports, the FLA maintained that the decision to close the factory was motivated by changes in market demand, not anti-unionism (FLA 2009: 15).

The USAS protests escalated. The students had organised three speaking tours of fired Russell unionists, which covered influential universities from the east to west coast of the US. In December 2008, the University of Miami had become the first school to cut its contract with Russell. Later, other universities cut their ties, some soon after the workers visited their campuses. Eventually, major American universities—including Columbia, Cornell, Harvard, Michigan, Penn State, Rutgers, Wisconsin, New York University and the entire University of California system—terminated their licensing agreement with Russell based on evidence of anti-union activities in Honduras. The Canadian Federation of Students and the British student network People & Planet also became involved, resulting in two Canadian schools and approximately ten British schools terminating their Russell contracts.

USAS also began to shift its strategy by targeting not only Russell's collegiate consumers, but also non-collegiate business relations. For example, when USAS learned that Russell's subsidiary, Spalding, which had a long-standing relationship with the National Basketball Association (NBA), had signed a USD 125 million deal with the National Basketball Association, it went to the playoffs and hung a four-story-high banner that denounced Russell's sweatshop practices and demanded the NBA terminate the deal. Student activists began also aggressively targeting several of Russell's main retail partners. Activists went into Dick's Sporting Goods and Sports Authority and slipped protest material inside apparel products. When customers held up an item to look at it or went into the dressing room to try it on, anti-Russell fliers fell on the floor. To the tremendous annoyance of these retailers, fliers would continue to appear days after the protest action.

Activists also went to Russell's headquarters in Kentucky and travelled to Warren Buffett's home to express their discontent with the billionaire's apparel producer. And, as a result of student activism, on May 13, 2009, sixty-five members of Congress wrote to Russell CEO John Holland expressing their concern over the labour violations at Russell's facilities in Honduras. Adding to the corporation's discomfort were USAS 'Twitter bombs' and Facebook 'wall attacks' that would bombard these services with messages such as 'Did you know that Russell just closed a factory and illegally destroyed 1,800 jobs?' Russell responded by shutting down its Facebook wall.

USAS's strategy was to combine economic power in the form of a boycott and disruption of business as usual with normative power. In contrast with anti-sweatshop protests of the 1990s, USAS chose freedom of association as its core normative frame. Instead of depicting very young women in the campaign fliers, they used two older elected leaders of the factory union, one male and one female. And instead of depicting them as vulnerable victims, the image of the unionists was one of strength and determination. The solution suggested by the message and the image was one of worker organisation through respect for internationally recognised freedom of association rights, not paternalism. This was a deliberate decision on the part of the Honduran unionists and their USAS allies. Indeed, the activists took the picture for the flier several times in order to capture the right expression of strength and determination on the workers' faces.[9]

This normative frame was a strategic choice that had consequences on the movement's outcomes. Earlier anti-sweatshop activists learned that the child labour normative frame engendered the strongest and most positive consumer response. Yet, the result of pursuing a victimisation frame is that, even when the movement successfully pressures a corporation to change its conduct, the outcome is more likely to be top-down standards on working ages, hours of work for minors and external enforcement mechanisms. Pursuing an empowering frame is less likely to receive the same level of consumer concern, but, when successful, the result is more likely to involve bottom-up worker organisation.

The students and workers' message that Russell had violated fundamental workers' rights helped to convince university administrators to cut contracts with Russell. And the termination of contracts put economic pressure on Russell. Notably, unlike previous campaigns, there was not a single student sit-in during the Russell campaign. That is, the 'logic of appropriateness' was used when targeting the universities. Collegiate administrators changed their conduct because they were influenced by the message that a fundamental right had been violated, not because students took over the president's office or because students stopped buying Russell t-shirts in the campus store. Yet, the consequence of the schools' actions, the termination of contracts with Russell, put direct and significant economic pressure on Russell. Thus, the 'logic of consequences' was employed when universities and retailers cut their contract with Russell. In the end, approximately 110 colleges and universities ended their contracts with Russell, as did Sports Authority.

In early 2009, Russell was still publicly insisting that it respected workers' right to unionise. In fact, it noted that it had promoted 'collective pacts' with workers as a display of its respect for freedom of association. On June 19, 2009, the WRC issued a scathing report on the practice, emphasising that such 'employer-dominated representation schemes' are recognised by the International Labour Organization and the US Department of State as undermining the genuine exercise of freedom of association (WRC 2009: 3). The report was distributed to universities and the FLA in an effective use of information politics.

Less than one week later, the FLA announced that it was putting Russell under a 90-day review, the only time it had imposed a review process on a collegiate corporate member since its founding in 1999.[10] Coincidentally, three days later, Honduran president Manuel Zelaya was removed from office by the military and forced into exile. The new regime, which was strongly backed by large business owners, was quick to repress anti-coup union protesters. For Russell, accusations of violating labour rights were now compounded by the reputational risks of violating rights in a post-coup, militarised country.

On November 17, 2009, after years of union organising efforts and an intense one-year transnational campaign, Russell announced it would re-open the factory and re-hire 1,200 workers. Russell also agreed to recognise the union, begin collective bargaining and adhere to a neutrality clause for all of its other seven factories in Honduras (Hobbs 2009; Russell Athletic 2009). It was, as Steven Greenhouse of the *New York Times* proclaimed, the most important victory for the anti-sweatshop movement to date (Green-house 2009).

By 2010, the new factory, Jerzees Nuevo Día, was operating and its union negotiated a collective bargaining agreement, increased wages by 25 per-cent and achieved free lunches and transportation for workers. Leveraging the neutrality clause, a second union was formed at another Russell plant, which, in 2012, began collective bargaining, and third unionization drive began at yet another Russell factory.[11] Notably, the post-coup government of Porfirio Lobo had selected the CGT labour confederation's long-time general secretary, Felicito Avila, to be its Minister of Labour. Avila quickly granted legal recognition to the new union.

The dynamics of the campaign are depicted in Figure 2.1. Activism began with domestic (Honduran) workers and their union. They employed asso-ciational power in an attempt to organise the Russell apparel supplier, and

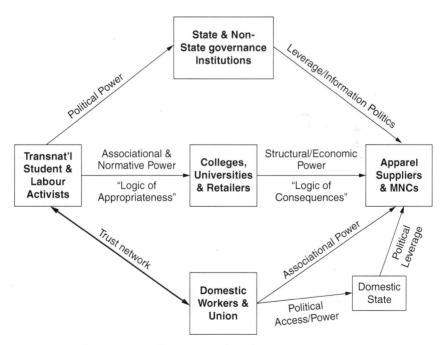

Figure 2.1   The Dynamics of Anti-Sweatshop Activism

they attempted to use political leverage via the state. When this proved insufficient, they developed a trust network with transnational student and labour activists. The activists framed the problem in terms of a violation of fundamental workers' rights in order to pressure colleges and universities via the logic of appropriateness to cut their contracts with Russell. These actions resulted in direct economic pressure on Russell via the logic of consequences. During this entire period, activists took advantage of political opportunity structures via non-state governance institutions (notably the WRC) to employ information politics in order to further leverage Russell. The end result of this synergistic use of workers' four powers is one of the biggest successes of the anti-sweatshop movement, the re-hiring of hundreds of union activists, the opening of a unionised plant with collective bargaining and the commitment of the largest private sector employer in Honduras to a union neutrality clause throughout the country.

DIFFUSING THE SUCCESS AT RUSSELL, NIKE AND KNIGHTS APPAREL

The success at Russell in Honduras was immediately followed by a large transnational activist campaign led by USAS that forced Nike to pay USD 2.2 million to laid-off workers at two of its sub-contractors in Honduras who had been denied their benefits (Greenhouse 2010b; Palmquist 2010). Then, Knights Apparel in the Dominican Republic negotiated with the WRC the establishment of a 'sweat-free' facility that would triple the average wage paid in the apparel sector, improve benefits and embrace the union. The factory's products would then be sold at special stands located inside the bookstores of prominent American universities.

The Nike 'Just Pay It' campaign success was unprecedented. Nike had long insisted that, since its suppliers were independently owned firms, it was not responsible for the wages, benefits and severance pay of those workers. USAS activists saw things differently, arguing that since Nike had the market power to set the terms and conditions of its supplier contracts, it was largely responsible for the economic conditions of its suppliers, and thus the ability of its suppliers to pay worker termination costs. The Nike campaign built on the same trust network of the Russell campaign that involved a local CGT union in Honduras, USAS, and American labour activists. USAS activists repeated many of the campaign tactics: universities were pressured to cut Nike contracts, Nike retail outlets were picketed and Nike's Facebook wall was quickly covered with anti-sweatshop messages. WRC research reports also once again provided leverage through information politics.

Yet, there were two important differences between the Nike campaign and the Russell campaign. It took far fewer universities cutting Nike contracts to get the corporate giant to rescind and agree to provide money to the laid off workers. Wisconsin University and Brown cut their contracts and

Cornell University announced it would let its exclusive Nike contract with its athletics program expire unless Nike paid the workers what they were owed. The University of Washington (a Nike athletic school) also threatened to terminate its contract, with its president, provost and licensing committee putting considerable pressure on the company.[12] These few universities contrast with the 110 universities that it took to terminate their relationship with Russell before Russell acted. This seems to be an indication of the reputation USAS had developed during the Russell campaign. Nike could see that USAS had the capacity to cut more contracts. That is, USAS was able to issue a credible threat against Nike. Rather than waiting for USAS to repeat its 110 university boycott organised against Russell, Nike decided to resolve the issue sooner in order to limit the potential economic and public relations damages that a prolonged campaign might cause.

The campaign results differed, too. While in both cases, workers received payment for lost benefits due to factory closures, in the case of Russell, a new factory was opened in which a union and collective contract were allowed, and workers in the seven other Russell plants in Honduras were given the promise of management neutrality in the face of any further unionisation drives. No such offers were made in the case of Nike, because, since Nike does not own factories, it was not in a position to open one for the fired workers. Nike did agree to run a re-training program for these workers and request that its other suppliers in Honduras give them priority re-hiring. But by late 2012—much to the dismay of the workers and the union—Nike had not implemented this agreement.

Knights Apparel is the result of a history of activism in the Dominican Republic and an agreement between the WRC and Joseph Bozich, the C.E.O. of Knights Apparel. The factory is located at the site of an old factory, BJ&B, which was once the target of a temporarily successful labour and student campaign in the early 2000s. The USAS and the WRC had long been attempting to turn the logic of apparel global value chains on their heads by pushing universities to agree to source from suppliers that pay a living wage and respect workers' basic rights. The initiative, known as the Designated Suppliers Program, had run into anti-trust concerns and many universities were left waiting for U.S. Justice Department approval before embracing the idea.

Knights Apparel provided an opportunity to move forward with this model in one factory after Knights' CEO, Joseph Bozich, faced serious health concerns and decided that he wanted to do more with his life than increase his firm's market share (Greenhouse 2010a). Bozich entered into negotiations with the WRC to pursue the idea of a 'sweat-free' factory. USAS made its 'non-opposition' contingent on the location of this effort in the old BJ&B factory.[13] Bozich accepted the proposal. The 125 workers at the new factory, Alta Gracia, are paid USD 2.83 an hour, 3.4 times the minimum wage. The products are sold at bookstores located on college campuses, including those owned by Barnes & Noble (Greenhouse 2010a).

On first blush, it appears that the Russell case was the most successful because it resulted in the most jobs and the largest union. However, the Nike and Knights Apparel cases were significant for other reasons. The Knights Apparel case shows that it is possible to triple wages and remain financially viable. This is because production wages make up such a small segment of the sales price of garments. This example thus raises the question of why other retailers with products in the same store do not also pay a living wage and respect workers' right to unionise. The Nike victory, while not resulting in the defense of a union, holds considerable symbolic importance for the movement. It showed the movement's ability to force one of the largest and most publicly recognised corporations in the world to change its policy and cover the termination costs of an independent supplier. This example has emboldened the student anti-sweatshop movement perhaps more than any other success to date.

CONCLUSIONS

Garment workers in global value chains are assumed to be extremely weak and largely unlikely to achieve organising success. The industry is considered too hyper-mobile and the low-skilled workforce too easily replaceable to allow for sustainable unionisation. Yet, union successes at firms like Russell in Honduras impel a re-evaluation of these assumptions and a re-examination of the sources of workers' power in global value chains.

This chapter has argued that workers have four sources of power. Structural power refers not only to plant size, profit margins and skill levels, but also to degrees of plant mobility and corporate vulnerability to boycotts. Associational power includes not only traditional trade union structures, but also transnational activist networks and the tactics they employ. Political power refers to the ability to leverage not only traditional centers of political power, but also emerging voluntary governance structures in the global economy, such as labour rights institutions like the WRC. Activists also used normative power. Every flier, speech and document of the movement displayed a choice of words designed to maximise public outrage, shame corporate targets and empower workers.

The final chapter in the anti-sweatshop movement is far from written. The industry remains highly dynamic as a result of shifting trade rules, global economic changes and evolving corporate strategies. Indeed, it seems each time the movement develops a successful strategy to improve conditions in global value chains, corporations and their suppliers find new ways to work around these successes. This forces activists once again to re-think their strategies. Yet, what remains relevant is the role that the four sources of workers' power will continue to have in shaping movement outcomes.

NOTES

1. Over the course of its history, Russell has had many names, including Russell Manufacturing Co., Russell Mills Inc., Russell Athletic, and Russell Corporation. In 2009, Russell renamed itself Russell Brands, LLC. For simplicity, I will refer to Russell.
2. Hoovers.com, accessed January 20, 2011.
3. Hoovers.com, accessed January 20, 2011.
4. Author's interview with union organisers, San Pedro Sula, May 2010.
5. The plant ceased operations on January 30, 2009.
6. Author's interviews with CGT organisers, San Pedro Sula, Honduras, May 2010.
7. Activists did not march entirely in the buff, most often opting to wear undergarments.
8. Although, it is important to note that national USAS representatives were limited to two-year terms with the goal of reducing bureaucratising tendencies, so there was a certain degree of re-learning.
9. Author's interviews with US activists, June 2010.
10. In addition to the external pressure, there was some internal debate and pressure on the FLA leadership, particularly by Maquila Solidarity Network, one of the NGO participants in the FLA.
11. Author's interviews with Russell unionists, San Pedro Sula and Choloma, Honduras, June 2010 and with USAS representatives in the United States, January 2011 and correspondence from Jeffrey Hermanson, November 2012.
12. Author's phone interview with Rod Palmquist, USAS national representative 2008–2010, January 31, 2011 and correspondence with Margaret Levi, October 2012.
13. Author's phone interview with Rod Palmquist, USAS national representative, January 31, 2011.

REFERENCES

Anner, M. (2006), 'The Paradox of Labour Transnationalism: Trade Union Campaigns for Labour Standards in International Institutions', in C. Phelan (ed.), *The Future of Organised Labour: Global Perspectives*, Bern: Peter Lang Publishing, 63–90.

Anner, M. (2011), 'The Impact of International Outsourcing on Unionization and Wages: Evidence from the Apparel Export Sector in Central America', *Industrial & Labor Relations Review*, 64(2), 305–322.

Armbruster, R. (2005), *Globalization and Cross-Border Labor Solidarity in the Americas: The Anti-Sweatshop Movement and the Struggle for Social Justice*, New York, London: Routledge.

Commons, J. (1909), 'American Shoemakers, 1648–1895: A Sketch of Industrial Evolution', *Quarterly Journal of Economics*, 24(1), 39–84.

Finnemore, M., and Sikkink, K. (2005) 'International Norm Dynamics and Political Change', *International Organization*, 52(4), 887–917.

FLA (2009), *FLA Report on the Closure of Jerzees de Honduras*, Washington D.C.: Fair Labor Association.

Gereffi, G., Humphrey, J., and Sturgeon, T. (2005), 'The Governance of Global Value Chains', *Review of International Political Economy*, 12(1), 78–104.

Gereffi, G., Korzeniewicz, M., and Korzeniewicz, R. (1994), 'Introduction: Global Commodity Chains', in G. Gereffi and M. Korzeniewicz (eds.), *Commodity Chains and Global Capitalism*, Westport: Praeger, 1–14.

Goldin, A. (2009), 'Mission Report: The Closure Process of Jerzees de Honduras, Previous Investigations, and the Right of Freedom of Association', San Pedro Sula, Buenos Aires: FLA.

Greenhouse, S. (2009), 'Labor Fight Ends in Win for Students', *The New York Times*, November 18.

Greenhouse, S. (2010a), 'Factory Defies Sweatshop Label, but Can It Thrive?', *The New York Times*, July 18.

Greenhouse, S. (2010b), 'Nike Agrees to Help Laid-Off Workers in Honduras', *The New York Times*, July 27.

Hobbs, S.R. (2009), 'Russell Factory in Honduras to Reopen In Response to U.S. Student Pressure', *BNA Daily Labor Report, November 23*.

Jakobsen, K. (2001), 'Rethinking the International Confederation of Free Trade Unions and its Inter-American Regional Organization', *Antipode*, 33(3), 363–383.

Katzenstein, P.J. (1996), 'Introduction: Alternative Perspectives on National Security', in P.J. Katzenstein (ed.), *The Culture of National Security: Norms and Identity in World Politics*, New York: Columbia University Press.

Keck, M.E., and Sikkink, K. (1998) *Activists Beyond Borders: Advocacy Networks in International Politics*, Ithaca: Cornell University Press.

Klein, N. (2000), *No Logo, No Space, No Choice, No Jobs: Taking Aim at the Brand Bullies,* 1st ed. Toronto: A.A. Knopf Canada.

Krupat, K. (1997), 'From War Zone to Free Trade Zone', in A. Ross (ed.) *No Sweat: Fashion, Free Trade, and the Rights of Garment Workers,* New York: Verso, 51–77.

Mahoney, J. (2001), *The Legacies of Liberalism: Path Dependence and Political Regimes in Central America*, Baltimore: Johns Hopkins University Press.

March, J.G., and Olsen, J.P. (1998), 'The Institutional Dynamics of International Political Orders', *International Organization*, 52(4), 943–969.

Marshall, A. (1920), *Principles of Economics: An Introductory Volume*, 8th ed., New York: MacMillan.

Marx, K., and Engels, F. ([1848] 1992), *The Communist Manifesto*, New York: Oxford University Press.

McCarthy, J.D., and Zald, M.N. (1977), 'Resource Mobilization and Social Movements: A Partial Theory', *American Journal of Sociology*, 82(6), 1212–1241.

Meza, V. (1991), *Historia del Movimiento Obrero Hondureño*, Tegucigalpa: Centro de Documentación de Honduras.

Michels, R. (1911 [1962]), *Political Parties: A Sociological Study of the Oligarchical Tendencies of Modern Democracy*, New York: Free Press.

Palmquist, R. (2010), 'Student Campaign Takes on Nike Like Never Before', *The Huffington Post,* July 12, http://www.huffingtonpost.com/rod-palmquist/student-campaign-takes-on_b_643375.html.

Perrone, L. (1983), 'Positional Power and Propensity to Strike', *Politics & Society*, 12(2), 231–261.

Risse, T., and Sikkink, K. (1999), 'The Socialization of International Human Rights Norms into Domestic Practices: Introduction', in T. Risse, S.C. Ropp, and K. Sikkink (eds.), *The Power of Human Rights: International Norms and Domestic Change*, New York: Cambridge University Press.

Russell Athletic (2009), 'Russell Athletic and Union Announce Landmark Agreement', http://digitalcommons.ilr.cornell.edu/cgi/viewcontent.cgi?article=1711&context=globaldoc.

Silver, B.J. (2003), *Forces of Labor: Workers' Movements and Globalization since 1870*, New York: Cambridge University Press.

Tannenwald, N. (1999), 'The Nuclear Taboo: The United States and the Normative Basis of Nuclear Non-Use', *International Organization*, 53(2), 433–468.

Tarrow, S. (1989), *Democracy and Disorder: Protest and Politics in Italy, 1965–1975*, Oxford: Oxford University Press.

Tarrow, S. (2005), *The New Transnational Activism*, New York: Cambridge University Press.

Tilly, C. (1978), *From Mobilization to Revolution*, Reading: Addison-Wesley.

Turnbull, P. (2006), 'The War on Europe's Waterfront: Repertoires of Power in the Port Transport Industry', *British Journal of Industrial Relations*, 44(2), 305–326.

Turner, L., Katz, H. C., and Hurd, R. W. (eds.) (2001), *Rekindling the Movement: Labor's Quest for Relevance in the Twenty-first Century*, Ithaca: Cornell University Press.

Voss, K., and Sherman, R. (2000), 'Breaking the Iron Law of Oligarchy: Union Revitalization in the American Labor Movement', *The American Journal of Sociology*, 106(2), 303–349.

Waterman, P. (2001), 'Trade Union Internationalism in the Age of Seattle', *Antipode: A Radical Journal of Geography*, 33(3), 312–336.

Waterman, P. (2008), 'A Trade Union Internationalism for the 21st Century: Meeting the Challenges from Above, Below and Beyond', in A. Bieler, I. Lindberg, and D. Pillay (eds.), *Labour and the Challenge of Globalization: What Prospectus for Transnational Solidarity?*, London: Pluto Press, 248–263.

Webster, E., Lambert, R., and Bezuidenhout, A. (2008), *Grounding Globalization: Labour in the Age of Insecurity*, Malden: Blackwell Publishing.

WRC (2008), *Worker Rights Consortium Assessment: Jerzees de Honduras (Russell Corporation) Findings and Recommendations*, Washington, D.C.: Worker Rights Consortium.

WRC (2009), *Worker Rights Consortium Assessment of regarding Rights of Association of Russell Athletic and Fruit of the Loom Employees in Honduras: Analysis of 'Collective Pacts,* Washington, DC: Worker Rights Consortium.

Wright, E. O. (2000), 'Working-Class Power, Capitalist-Class Interests, and Class Compromise', *American Journal of Sociology*, 105(4), 957–1002.

3   Building North-South Transnational Trade Union Alliances

Prospects and Challenges

Mélanie Dufour-Poirier and Christian Lévesque

This chapter seeks to understand the dynamics of cross-border alliances between workplace trade unions from Canada and South America. Its main objectives are twofold: first, to document the process through which unions build and develop alliances in the absence of transnational structures or mechanisms; second, to identify the conditions that foster and sustain relationships between workplace trade unions from different countries. The case studies under investigation here appear particularly interesting because the alliance was launched, developed and sustained on the initiative of workplace trade unions. This type of alliance constitutes a form of transnational trade unionism from below involving local actors. By local actors we mean workplace trade union representatives and staff from industrial unions who support and coordinate action at the plant level.

There is a growing body of research on transnational trade unionism from below, particularly following the adoption of the directives on European work councils (EWCs). Research shows that the presence of EWCs has triggered greater involvement by workplace trade unions in cross-border actions. These consultative bodies provide resources and communications channels and ensure some form of monitoring (Lillie et al. 2004). Despite the presence of this consultative mechanism, the future of workplace trade union cooperation appears to be uncertain. This is particularly true in a context in which actors have little experience at the transnational level or where there are great disparities between employee representatives in terms of resources or opportunities (Wils 2000; Whittall 2000).

In recent decades, global union federations (GUFs) have also played a pivotal role in the involvement of workplace trade unions in cross-border actions. *Flags of Convenience* (Lillie 2005) and the *Rio Tinto* mining (Goodman 2004) campaigns symbolise the importance of developing original strategies to enhance the activity of workplace trade unions at the transnational level. They also highlight the difficulty of convincing actors with unequal resources to pursue a common strategy and the necessity of maintaining tight interdependence between trade union actors. This appears particularly important since the temptation to rely on a traditional repertoire of action is often very strong (Anner et al. 2006). Raising awareness and framing transnational trade unionism appears to be an ongoing challenge.

Our study focuses on a particular form of transnational unionism from below: transnational union organisations, such as GUFs, were not actively involved in the process and the workplace trade unions could not rely on any formal institutional mechanisms, such as EWCs. In the absence of a coordinating structure (GUFs or consultative mechanisms, such as EWCs), we believe that actors need to be creative when they are crafting this form of transnational unionism. They must develop new capabilities, particularly when the alliance involves actors with heterogeneous and unequal resources.

Our approach places considerable emphasis on the dynamics of cross-border alliances and, in particular, on the interactions between actors, on the sources of cooperation and tension that shape the process of coalition-building and on the way actors frame transnational solidarity. From previous research (Kay 2005; Lévesque and Poirier-Dufour 2005; Turnbull 2006), we expect that this dynamic of cross-border alliances will be shaped by the resources (financial, informational, logistical, technical, etc.) that actors can mobilise and the context within which the alliance develops.

The first part of this chapter describes the research method and case studies. It is followed by a chronological account of the action undertaken by trade unions to build the alliance. The third part highlights the issues and challenges related to the process of building a North/South trade union alliance, while the conclusion identifies the conditions that foster and sustain transnational unionism from below.

DESCRIPTION OF THE CASE STUDIES

This research examines cross-border actions involving workplace and national trade unions from Chile, Peru and Canada within a sole multinational firm of European origin (Euromin). As of 2007, this firm had 37,698 direct employees (and some 22,323 indirect), working in 18 countries worldwide, over five continents. Euromin operations involve both ore extraction and refinement and processing. In Canada, the company has seven mining sites and six refineries; in Chile, the company reports on three properties and various projects at the exploratory phase; in Peru, Euromin has multifunctional sites and a few projects at the exploratory phase. In mid-2006, Euromin acquired these operations from a Canadian company (Canmin2) that had previously been bought by another Canadian company (Canmin1) in 2005. As will become obvious, these changes of ownership over a very short period shape significantly the nature and the intensity of cross-border action between the trade unions under scrutiny.

The data were gathered through semi-structured interviews between 2004 and 2009 in the three countries. In total, 70 interviews were conducted with 44 trade unionists from Canada, Chile and Peru operating at the workplace, national and international levels. In Canada, in addition to interviewing staff and officers from the national industrial union, we met on several occasions with workplace trade union representatives from two refineries and a mine. In Chile, we interviewed the national union leaders and workplace representatives from a copper refinery. In Peru, we met with national industrial trade union leaders and workplace trade union representatives of the two largest mines in the country. The interview data were supplemented with an analysis of various types of documentation (labour, corporate, public and other) and on-site visits in the three countries. Ethical constraints forbid us from revealing the identity of the company and the representatives consulted (Dufour-Poirier 2011).

PHASE ONE: GROWTH AND INCLUSION (1990–2004)

Prior to the 1990s, workplace trade unions at Canmin1 in Canada had gradually developed strong ties and a tradition of cooperation. Union representatives gathered at least once a year and met regularly with the employer. The Canadian industrial trade union had been able to establish a form of pattern bargaining whereby each workplace trade union was entitled to receive any improvements in terms and conditions granted to its neighbour. The negotiations took place every three years. Although everyone knew the terms negotiated by others beforehand, nothing could be taken for granted. This form of pattern bargaining combined with biannual meetings involving the employer and trade union representatives strengthened the bargaining power of workplace trade unions. They were well informed of current problems, modernisation plans and projects, and they knew what to expect from upcoming negotiations.

The wave of closures of plants and mining sites in Canada in the late 1980s, coupled with the company's expansion into foreign countries, prompted workplace trade unions to reassess their bargaining power. This reassessment led them to initiate discussions on developing links with trade unions from other countries, in particular South America, where Canmin1 had facilities. These early discussions led to the appointment of a regional staff member of the industrial trade union to work with an internal committee on coordinating the transnational activities of workplace trade unions from Canmin1 in Canada.

At the start of the 1990s, several meetings were organised between industrial and workplace trade unions from Canada, Chile and Peru where the company had operations at that time. These meetings helped nurture a relationship of trust among trade unionists, both in the North and the South, and allowed them to gauge the differences between countries in terms of workplace health and safety, environmental issues and union security and protection. These initial contacts persuaded workplace trade unionists to develop their relationships further and to monitor them thoroughly. However, it was not an easy task, as this Canadian workplace trade union representative made clear:

> *I'll show you the letters I had to send to the Industrial Trade Unions to create events (related to the coalition)! I was the one who had to push! It takes structures to allow these meetings! Yes, we heard, but it is complicated to structure these things, there are costs, we must look at it. (. . .) It's expensive, we don't have time. I had to work from the grassroots and write to all the local unions! (. . .) Despite the pressure of all concerned, I won my point!*

The 2001 Summit of the Americas in Quebec City served as a springboard for cross-border actions and propelled the alliance into a phase of *expansion and inclusion*. Participants included leaders of the Canadian industrial union, workplace trade unions from Canmin1 sites in Canada, as well as workplace and national leaders from Chile and Peru. In this historic setting, this colourful mix of organisations attended the meetings that would lead later to the organisation of a consultative transnational round table. Following this meeting, a temporary committee was established '*to investigate the behaviour of four Canadian multinationals in the South*', including Canmin1. Several workplace trade unionists from Canada demanded that certain clauses in the Canadian collective agreement should be included in agreements covering the Chilean and Peruvian operations. The following quotation from a Canadian workplace representative shows that this claim reflected a desire not only to upgrade working conditions in the South but also to protect jobs in the North.

> *They say, look out for your 'jobs'; you will lose them because investments are being made in the South now. (. . .) Increasing wages there means keeping 'jobs' in Canada, [sic]. (. . .) When trade unions from the North go to South, people say "it is certain that if you want to increase your wages, it can also help us keep our 'jobs!'" There must be benefits on both sides! Otherwise, it will just be charity, nothing more!*

This period of intense activity was followed by a period of much reduced activity. From 2001 to mid-2004, there were occasional email exchanges or conference calls between union representatives (local and national) from Canada and Chile but no permanent exchanges. Difficulties in maintaining regular and sustainable ties between workplace trade unions created much disappointment among workplace trade unions in both Chile and Canada. Discontent was exacerbated by the fact that the Canadian trade union representatives could not fulfill the pledge they had given in 2001 to organise a tour of Canmin1's sites in Chile. Trade unionists in Chile wanted to use the close links the Canadian industrial union had established with Canmin1's headquarters to put pressure on managers in Chile.

Finally, three years later, in May 2004, a delegation of Canadian trade unionists went to Chile to restore the links established a few years earlier. To organise this project, workplace trade unions relied on human, technical and financial resources dedicated to international activities by the Canadian national industrial union. Without these resources, such an endeavour would not have been possible. The meetings held with Chilean trade unions in the mining and metal-processing industry fostered the establishment of closer links in the areas of working conditions, collective bargaining and management strategies and objectives. These discussions raised awareness among trade unionists of the disparity in working conditions between the North and the South. The Canadian delegation also contacted other trade unions in the country for the first time. These new contacts were used to exchange collective agreements and spawned the idea that '*all workers are in the same boat*'. Chilean managers did not welcome the arrival of the Canadian delegation, viewing the development of such cross-border relations as a threat: access to key mining sites in Chile was blocked, despite the promise made by corporate headquarters. The Chilean employers became increasingly hostile to the nascent North-South alliance, but this hostility merely made the participants even more determined to pursue their collaboration.

This initial phase suffered several setbacks but was nevertheless characterised by the creation of a network of committed actors. In the North, this progression by trial and error led to a position of *openness and inclusion*. In Canada, the wave of plant closures pushed trade unionists to develop further their collaboration with trade unions from the South. In the South, the desire to raise workers' living standards, coupled with the fear of having to suffer job losses, convinced union leaders to participate actively in cross-border actions. In both the North and South, the relevance of the alliance was easily justified and activists were able to identify common interests and converging zones of action. The resources made available by the Canadian industrial union, as well as its coordination efforts, created areas of understanding and compromise among activists, which in turn alleviated the North/South divide. These successes were consolidated during the second phase.

PHASE TWO: EXPANSION AND CONSOLIDATION (2005–2006)

In 2005, Canmin1 was under threat of takeover by multinational companies of dubious reputation in terms of union practices, among which was a Canadian company with supposedly more ethical practices than its competitors. This threat of takeover spurred the Canadian national industrial union to accelerate and expand the dialogue between trade unions. There was an urgent need to prevent potential job losses in the North and to force the emerging company to assume its social responsibilities in the South. The whole structure of the Canadian industrial trade union was mobilised with the twin aims of maintaining the company's Canadian origins and building a larger union community. For several months, official press releases, electronic documents and press conferences reiterated the strategic nature of this acquisition for the economic development of the mining industry in Canada and the safeguarding of jobs. At the same time, the issue of trade union rights received extensive coverage.

The campaign was successful, since Canmin1 was bought by another Canadian company (Canmin2). Following this acquisition in June 2005, a transnational meeting was held in Canada. Most of the trade unions in the new entity attended this meeting; they included workplace trade unions from Canada as well as workplace and national trade union organisations from Germany, Chile, Peru and the Dominican Republic. A guest from a GUF also attended. The objective of this meeting was to expand and consolidate the alliance. During the meeting, summary tables showing the benefits, wage gains and due dates for collective agreements in Canada were distributed to encourage a form of pattern bargaining with the employer. Visits to operating sites were also organised in order to enable trade unionists from the South to observe working conditions, operating techniques and health and safety measures that were prevalent in North America. The 2005 meeting ended with a recommendation to broaden the coalition through the inclusion of trade union organisations operating in various multinational firms in the mining industry.

A second meeting was organised in Chile in November of the same year. Thanks to logistical and linguistic support from the Canadian industrial trade union and its staff responsible for international activities, a broader delegation participated in this meeting. Most of the participants at the 2004 meeting also travelled to the meeting in Chile, together with some additional trade unionists from Canada. Union leaders from a large mining site in Peru and trade unions from other companies (operating in the ten largest mining firms worldwide) were also involved. Seminars and training workshops were organised in order to facilitate the transfer of expertise and experience. The exchanges focused on several challenges facing workplace trade unions, such as workplace harassment, overtime, working hours, compensation and health and safety. Common irritants were pointed out, such as subcontracting, precarious jobs, the collective bargaining process, occupational diseases associated with working at high altitudes, environment issues and workplace trade union security. An information newsletter describing the objectives and activities of the coalition was published, and the participants discussed for the first time the prospect of creating a global trade union council. Pamphlets were distributed among participants at the conclusion of the meeting that emphasised '*the need to establish and strengthen these inter-union relations*'. With upcoming negotiations at several Canadian sites, it was agreed to organise preparatory exchanges to restrain company attempts to downgrade working conditions. Participants agreed to meet again in May 2006.

Following the announcement of a possible takeover of Canmin2 by a Chinese conglomerate, another transnational trade union meeting took place in Canada in December 2005. The Canadian industrial trade union leaders feared the worst in terms of union representation and job protection. They took advantage of the presence of several trade unionists from other countries to generate maximum media coverage in order to influence the government and public opinion. It sought to prevent at any cost the damaging impact of a buy-out by a foreign group. A coordinated trade union strategy under the auspices of a global council was adopted on this occasion.

As planned, a third Canadian delegation travelled to Chile in May 2006. Trade unionists from Canada, Chile and Peru then discussed numerous issues facing trade unions at the workplace level. The meeting also enabled participants to identify common problems and to draw up effective strategies to deal with them. Outsourcing and occupational diseases rapidly stood out as major problems that should be dealt with through a comprehensive global strategy. The need to upgrade collective bargaining practices and capabilities was also reaffirmed. The Canadian industrial trade union acted as the 'official coordinator' and took on the responsibility of centralising the information and disseminating it through the alliance. In order to deal with the language problem, representatives from each country agreed to help with compiling an information newsletter published in French, Spanish and English.

The successful collective bargaining rounds in Chile and Peru in the summer of 2006, as well as the publication in December of the third information newsletter, indicated the alliance's strong potential for development. The sense of urgency created by the corporate situation led several Canadian trade unionists to work harder to consolidate the emerging network and to strengthen contacts with the trade unions from the South. However, some Canadian workplace trade unionists were more skeptical about the progress likely to be made by a larger and increasingly complex alliance built around a corporate actor likely to experience both constant and unpredictable change. In the South, the urgent need to operate on a global scale was not called into question. Trade unionists shared the view that transnational unionism was necessary to prevent any attempts by the company to downgrade working conditions: expectations were particularly high in Chile and Peru. At this stage, nobody could have predicted the rapid collapse of the alliance.

PHASE THREE: BREAKUP AND WITHDRAWAL (2007–2008)

The event that the unions had most feared took place in June 2006, when Canmin2 was suddenly taken over by Euromin. This change of ownership considerably disrupted the trade union strategy. The takeover, coupled with the retirement of a leading figure in the alliance's development, led to a major slowdown in transnational activities and a noticeable drop in contacts among participants. This situation created frustration at the workplace level, notably in Chile:

> *After these meetings, it is as if everything was lost and we started again from scratch! What we need is just that we do not lose the fluidity of contacts! (. . .) There is no feedback on the issues. (. . .) We send a fax to Canada and there is no answer; I do not know what is happening! We also note that the contacts remain in place with the federations; the information never gets to the workplace unions!*

In March 2007, a transnational meeting was organised in Canada involving Euromin unions for the first time. The entire structure of the Canadian industrial trade union as well as workplace affiliates from various Canadian provinces participated in this one-day event. Several international guests attended, including delegations from Germany, the Dominican Republic and Chile. The agenda and its headlines highlighted the difficulties in coming to grips with a sprawling employer in constant flux. The monumental scale of the figures characterising Euromin appeared intimidating indeed. No mention was made of the global trade union council discussed at the previous meetings. No meeting schedule was determined and no guideline was issued. The same sense of drift was evident in the writing of the information newsletter. In the end, many uncertainties and unresolved issues remained.

In November 2007, trade unions from Canada met in an attempt to revive the alliance. Developing new contacts abroad turned out to be more difficult than expected since many former union leaders from Chile and Peru had been replaced after losing elections. This meant that the bonds of trust that had been built up between workplace trade union leaders had to be completely re-established. The exchange of personal impressions and general comments about the failure and apparent abandonment of the project provided a better measure of the scale of the disavowal and reflected the anger felt by some participants. Nevertheless, many trade unionists shared a desire to resume discussions on the establishment of a global council as soon as possible. Hope was restored to some degree, though difficulties remained.

In October 2008, an impressive group of trade unionists attended a meeting; it included trade union leaders from Australia, Germany, Chile, New Caledonia, Peru and the Dominican Republic. Canadian trade union leaders were also present, as well as an official researcher from a GUF. Several issues were highlighted, including the rapid growth of the Euromin workforce and productivity worldwide. Many participants doubted the promise made by the company to lower the risk of workplace accidents, adopt fair employment policies, promote sustainable development measures and invest in cooperative relationships with surrounding communities, in short to respect stakeholders' interests in the production process. However, they were eager to change the course of events by adopting global trade union strategies. Successful union experiences in this regard were mentioned by a representative from a GUF as examples of how these aspirations can be put into practice at the transnational level.

Delegates also discussed the possibility of setting up a communication network within Euromin. The major concrete achievement of these exchanges was the establishment of an international monitoring and action committee made up of four members. It was agreed that the committee should meet at least three times a year and present a progress report to the Canadian industrial trade union and its related affiliates in order to ensure network coordination and the proper dissemination of information.

These proposals led to the adoption of a statement on the participants' commitment to follow up rapidly on the suggestions made over the two days of the meeting. The delegates agreed to meet again soon afterwards in order to consolidate the guidelines of the resurgent alliance. They revived the idea of building a *global network,* but several participants, particularly from the South, were doubtful about the wisdom of restarting a process that had encountered so many drawbacks and difficulties over the years. For this Peruvian leader:

> *Canadians have a different vision from us. For us all to arrive at a single viewpoint, a lot of water needs to go under the bridge! Canadians are at the top! They will have to lower (their standard of living) and come down to the level we're at and we need to go up! A long time is needed to go up.*

To date, the future of the alliance remains uncertain. In the North, changes in ownership and access to the decision-making centre have prompted workplace trade unions to question the relevance of the alliance, particularly when benefits at the workplace level have not really materialised yet. The slowdown in exchanges and coordination problems have also revealed tensions and frustrations amongst trade unionists. In the South, skepticism and disapproval shape the relations with the North, putting in jeopardy the alliance. Moreover, attending an international meeting has been detrimental to some of the Southern participants who have lost their jobs, thus further complicating the dynamic of North-South relations. The problems encountered by the Canadian industrial trade union in terms of coordination and the progressive reduction and centralisation of resources allocated to the coalition have also created serious obstacles to maintaining inter-union contacts.

ISSUES AND CHALLENGES

The evolution of this alliance highlights several issues related to the process of building North/South trade union alliances. In this section, we focus on three of them: autonomy and control, renewal of the way transnational trade unionism is framed and the management of diversity.

The alliance under investigation here was initiated by workplace trade unions that in the early stages enjoyed a considerable degree of autonomy. This autonomy was attributable to several factors: direct access to the Canadian corporate HQ of Canmin1, the tradition of coordinated bargaining between the Canadian facilities, the strategic positions of the Canadian sites within the corporation and the involvement of trade union staff with considerable experience at the transnational level in coordinating the activities of workplace trade union representatives. However, the locus of control in terms of decision-making and resources gradually shifted to higher levels within the industrial trade union organisation. Again, a number of factors seem to have contributed to this process of centralisation: the takeover of Canmin1 by Canmin2 and then Euromin, which substantially reduced trade union access to the decision-making center of the company; the early retirement of the staff coordinator, who was the leading figure at the beginning of the project; and a decision to centralise transnational activities at a higher level of the trade union organisation. This process of centralisation affected the ability of local actors to monitor the contacts made within the alliance, thus creating much frustration and disappointment. This situation was felt in the South as well as in the North, where some trade unions were unable to maintain contacts with their counterparts. Local trade unions lost ownership of the project and started to reduce their involvement and engagement.

These findings highlight the importance of simultaneously promoting bottom-up and top-down processes in order to ensure the survival of an alliance based on multiple centres of influence and action (Gallin 2000; Ion et al. 2005). They also underline the need for national industrial unions to create space for debates and for workplace trade unionists to develop their own repertoire of action and understanding of transnational unionism. Concurrently, national industrial unions must assume leadership and devote resources to transnational activities, since workplace trade unions do not have the resources, not least the financial resources, to sustain long-term involvement in transnational alliances. In short, there needs to be a delicate balance between bottom-up and top-down processes.

The findings also underscore the limited capacity of a single national industrial union to coordinate international alliances. The role of the Canadian industrial trade union was pivotal in creating the conditions to build the alliance. It devoted human, technical and financial resources to the project and, by various means, actively supported the involvement of trade unions from South America. However, it reinforced the North/South divide and placed trade unions from South America in a position of dependency, not only in terms of access to financial resources but also in the planning of activities. When international activities were centralised at a higher level, the relative strategic importance of this alliance lessened, and the financial and technical resources devoted to it diminished. The allocation of these resources was crucial to sustaining the involvement of trade unions from the South. This turn of events underlines the difficulty a single trade union may encounter in supporting transnational actions and the importance of sharing the burden of those actions among several national trade unions in order, in particular, to reduce the dependency of trade unions from the South, which often do not have the resources to engage in transnational action. It also emphasises the importance of relying on transnational mechanisms or structures, such as GUFs, to coordinate cross-border actions (Lillie 2005; Lillie et al. 2004; Pulignano 2011; Turnbull 2006).

The second issue is related to the importance of developing and renewing a clear vision of transnational trade unionism and disseminating it through the alliance. Updating the way transnational unionism is framed in response to changes in context and employer strategies emerges as a crucial prerequisite for sustaining local actor's involvement in the alliance. Transnational unionism, without such a frame, may often appear irrelevant and inaccessible for workplace trade union leaders, who may have a hard time justifying their actions at the transnational level to their rank-and-file members. They need external legitimacy to convince workers of the necessity to build international alliances. This statement from a Canadian trade union official in 2008 highlights the importance of developing and renewing a frame of reference for transnational trade unionism:

> If there were a strategy, if we said this is what we intended to develop in the coming months, you have to join our rank-and-file movement, informing them there is a world council, what is it used for, this is what we want you to say to general meetings as a local leader. What does the world council do? What will it do for us? We cannot say anything to members we do not know! (. . .) We created undue expectations.

Transnational unionism also needs to be located in time and space. Workplace trade unions are often locked into local issues that need to be dealt with over very short periods. This is especially true when the survival of a site or union is at stake. A delay in the activities undertaken by the alliance can threaten not only its stability but also any form of commitment on the part of trade unionists. In this regard, this workplace trade unionist from Peru admits:

> Unfortunately we are seeking tangible results almost immediately. We too often fall into the trap of short term. If you do not achieve immediate results, members feel nothing has been done . . . A long-term strategy, four or five years, when you are elected for two years, it's political suicide, nothing less!

The third issue concerns the problem of managing diversity. This is illustrated by the necessity of bridging global demands with local issues, which inevitably vary according to the specific problems in each workplace. This challenge is exacerbated in a North/South alliance in view of the disparities in working and life conditions. Even though the trade unionists were able to identify common issues, such as health and safety, they were not able to translate them into a common platform for collective bargaining. Perhaps most importantly, and over and above a certain commonality of interests, trade unionists from both the North and South were seeking to safeguard jobs in their own countries and workplaces. Managing this tension appeared particularly challenging in the context of an asymmetrical relation between workplace trade unions from the North and the South.

The various experiences and practices of workplace representatives further complicated relations between trade unionists from the North and South. In Canada, at least until Canmin2 was bought by Euromin, collective bargaining was generally conducted in a rather routine way with the support of experienced staff from the national industrial trade union. In the event of a breach of contract, the agreement could be enforced through legal channels. Unions competed to represent workers by standing for election under the monopoly model of union representation, which limits division at the workplace level. In Chile and Peru, in contrast, union representation is fragmented at the workplace level, and there is fierce competition between trade unions divided along political lines. Collective bargaining is always far from being a routine process, and it is often difficult for workplace representatives to force employers to implement the agreement. Trade unionists from Canada had some difficulties understanding the role of trade unions in the South and assessing the pressure they had to deal with on a daily basis.

Finally, following the acquisition of Canmin2 by Euromin, the alliance became larger and the trade unions much more diverse in terms of country of origin, which further exacerbated differences in practices, customs and traditions. This complex amalgam further highlighted the limited capacity of a single national industrial trade union to coordinate a transnational alliance of this scale. It also reduced the likelihood of establishing high-trust relations between participants, which in turn weakened their commitment to and support for the action undertaken at the transnational level (Beck 2003; Caire 2000).

CONCLUSION

This chapter has sought to analyse the process of building an alliance between workplace trade unions from the South and the North. Our results are limited by the scope of the comparisons, the type of transnational unionism from below under study and the fact that the alliance examined here is not necessarily representative of other existing or potential cross-border alliances. With these methodological reservations in mind, it would appear that three conditions have to be met if sustainable, transnational trade unionism from below is to be established.

The first condition concerns organisation. One particularity of the alliance examined in this chapter is that it developed in the shadow of existing transnational organisations, such as GUFs. The coordination of actions by workplace trade unions was undertaken by a Canadian industrial trade union, which played a pivotal role in the development of the alliance. It provided resources and at the same time created space so that local actors could put forward their own vision of transnational unionism. However, as the alliance grew and became more complex as the nature of the employer changed, the national union's limited capacity for coordination became obvious. Evans (2010) has convincingly argued that national industrial unions need to play an active role in a transnational campaign. Our study supports this argument, but it also highlights their limited capacity to act and the importance of linking their actions with transnational organisations such as GUFs. As well as reducing the workload of individual national unions, these organisations can help to ease relationships between trade unions with asymmetrical resources and increase the legitimacy of transnational alliances.

The second condition concerns the need to articulate the different levels of action, activism and leadership. Linking the global and the local is relevant to the three issues discussed in the previous section. The issue of autonomy and control is related to the decision-making process and the allocation of resources. Renewing the frame of reference for transnational trade unionism helps to provide a direction and a road map for workplace trade union action. Finally, the management of diversity involves establishing links between local issues and global initiatives. The articulation between space and action highlights the need to build a multi-level transnational trade unionism that breaks with the binary oppositions of the past (*local/global, top/down*), and their intersection and alternation (Sassen 2007). In our case study, dealing with these issues was quite challenging, and trade unionist did not necessarily have the resources and capabilities to address them thoroughly. Developing the capabilities to frame issues, mediate conflicting interests and connect repertoires of action across time and space seems crucial to sustaining transnational unionism.

Finally, the third condition is related to the recognition that transnational unionism involves competitive as well as collaborative relationships (Dufour-Poirier 2011; Erne 2008; Johns 1998). It is often assumed that workers across borders have more in common than conflicting interests. Conflict is generally associated with selfish attitudes, opportunistic behaviours or a narrow conception of solidarity. Our data suggest that transnational unionism entails both competitive and collaborative relations around conflicting and common interests. Workplace trade unions define transnational trade unionism according to local issues. Their perception of transnational trade unionism is grounded in and shaped by local issues and problems that may be at odds with global imperatives. Trade unionists need to recognise the existence of these conflicting interests and to develop the mechanisms and capabilities required to manage these conflicts. Recognising the existence of these conflicts and dealing with them is probably the first step towards building sustainable transnational unionism.

REFERENCES

Anner, M., Greer, I., Hauptmeier, M., Lillie, N., and Winchester, NJ. (2006), 'The Industrial Determinants of Transnational Solidarity: Global Interunion Politics in Three Sectors', *European Journal of Industrial Relations*, 12(1), 7–27.

Beck, U. (2003) *Pouvoir et contre-pouvoir à l'ère de la mondialisation*, Paris: Alto Aubien.

Caire, G. (2000), 'Syndicalisme ouvrier et mondialisation', in A. de Fouquet, U. Rehfeldt, and S. Le Roux (eds.), *Le syndicalisme dans la mondialisation*, Paris: Les Éditions de l'Atelier, 21–30.

Dufour-Poirier, M. (2011), 'Construction d'une coalition syndicale internationale: analyse d'une perspective Nord-Sud', Ph. D. dissertation, Montréal: HEC Montréal.

Erne, R. (2008), *European Unions: Labor's Quest for a Transnational Democracy*, Ithaca: Cornell University Press.

Evans, P. (2010), 'Is it Labor's Turn to Globalize? Twenty-first Century Opportunities and Strategic Responses', *Global Labor Journal*, 1(3), 352–379.

Gallin, D. (2000), *À l'heure de la mondialisation, quel mouvement syndical?*, Geneva: Global Labour Institute, http://www.globallabour.info/fr/2008/05/a_lheure_de_la_mondialisation.html.

Goodman, J. (2004), 'Australia and Beyond: Targeting Rio Tinto', in R. Munck (ed.), *Labour and Globalisation: Results and Prospects*, Liverpool: Liverpool University Press, 105–127.

Ion, J., Franguiadakis, S., and Pascal, V. (2005), *Militer aujourd'hui,* Paris: Collection Cevipof / Autrement.

Johns, R.A. (1998), 'Bridging the Gap between Class and Space: U.S. Worker Solidarity with Guatemala', *Economic Geography*, 74(3), pp. 252–271.

Kay, T. (2005), 'Labor Transnationalism and Global Governance: The Impact of NAFTA on Transnational Labor', *American Journal of Sociology*, 111(3), 715–756.

Lévesque, C., and Dufour-Poirier, M. (2005), 'International Union Alliances: Evidence from Mexico', *Transfer*, 11(4), 531–548.

Lillie, N. (2005), 'Union Networks and Global Unionism in Maritime Shipping', *Relations industrielles*, 60(1), 88–111.

Lillie, N., and Martínez Lucio, M. (2004), 'International Trade Union Revitalization: The Role of National Union Approaches', in C. Frege and J. Kelly (eds.), *Varieties of Unionism: Strategies for Union Revitalization in a Globalizing Economy*, Oxford: Oxford University Press, 159–179.

Pulignano, V. (2011), 'European Works Councils and Trade Union Networking. A New Space for Regulation and Workers' Solidarity in Europe?', in A. Blackett and C. Lévesque (eds.), *Social Regionalism in the Global Economy*, Oxford: Routledge, 111–139.

Sassen, S. (2007), 'L'émergence d'une multiplication d'assemblages de territoires, d'autorités et de droits', in M. Wieviorka, A. de Debarle, J. Ohana (eds.), *Les sciences sociales en mutation*, Auxerre, France: Éditions Sciences humaines, 205–221.

Turnbull, P. J. (2006), 'The War on Europe's Waterfront—Repertoires of Power in the Port Transport Industry', *British Journal of Industrial Relations*, 44(2), 305–326.

Whittall, M. (2000), 'The BMW European Works Council: A Cause for European Industrial Relations Optimism?', *European Journal of Industrial Relations*, 6(1), 61–83.

Wils, J. (2000), 'Great Expectations: Three Years in the Life of a European Works Council', *European Journal of Industrial Relations*, 6(1), 85–107.

4 Trade Union Strategies in Cross-Border Actions
Articulating Institutional Specificity with Local Power Dynamics

Christian Lévesque, Gregor Murray,
Christian Dufour and Adelheid Hege

When thinking about transnational trade unionism, we often have the image of union representatives in Brussels or Geneva working for either global union federations (GUFs) or some other type of supranational trade union organisation dealing with global issues and actors. We rarely consider workplace union representatives, who typically handle grievances and solve workers' daily problems, as transnational activists. Yet these workplace reps are often involved in transnational action and can play a pivotal role in shaping international campaigns and cross-border actions. They are located in the intersection between the local and the global and can act as brokers who bridge these different levels and who can frame local issues in a wider perspective and transpose international issues on to the local agenda (Tarrow 2005). The purpose of this chapter is to understand how workplace trade unionists move in and out of transnational space to fulfill local needs and objectives.

In the European Union (EU), the adoption of the European Works Council (EWC) Directive has sparked much interest in the involvement of workers' representatives in cross-border actions. Although their involvement in transnational activities often surpasses what is engendered by their participation in these consultative bodies, the existence of EWCs has triggered a greater awareness of the importance of international issues and pulled workplace trade unionists into transnational space (Marginson et al. 2004; Pulignano 2006). Even though the North American Free Trade Agreement (NAFTA) does not provide any such mechanisms for cross-border consultation on employment issues, it has intensified cross-border trade union cooperation in some industries (Babson and Juarez 2007; Kay 2005). Indeed, some workplace unions in Canada and the US already have a long tradition of cross-border interaction because several 'international unions' in the private sector have brought together Canadian and US workplace trade unions within the same industrial union since the 1930s as, for example, the United Steel Workers of America or the International Association of Machinist and Aerospace Workers.

There is considerable evidence that national and supranational institutions shape trade union approaches towards transnational unionism. For Greven and Russo (2006), in contrast with German trade unions, US unions are less likely to engage in social dialogue with employers and more likely to engage in transnational corporate campaigns. Similarly, according to Burgoon and Jacoby (2004), US unions are more likely to focus on organising, while EU unions will emphasise collective bargaining. Workplace power dynamics also appear to shape the logic and patterns of trade union involvement in cross-border action. Greer and Hauptmeier (2008) show how inter-site competition shapes workplace trade union strategies, while Ryland and Sadler (2008) suggest that the bargaining power of workplace trade unions influences their definition of solidarity.

This study focuses on the interplay between institutional specificity and local power dynamics in shaping workplace trade union involvement in cross-border interaction. Drawing on multiple longitudinal case studies conducted in Canada and France, our aim is to identify the factors that push and pull workplace trade unions in and out of transnational space. In so doing, this chapter addresses three questions: first, what are the patterns of union involvement in cross-border action; second, what are the factors that push and pull them into transnational space; and, finally, to what extent are these patterns of workplace union involvement integrated into their strategic repertoires of action.

We first present the research problem and our theoretical propositions before giving an overview of the study and the detailed research results from our observations of workplace trade unions in both France and Canada. In the final part of the chapter, we argue that the integration of international space into workplace trade union repertoires of action is shaped by the interplay between institutional opportunities provided at the supranational level and local power dynamics.

BUILDING TRANSNATIONAL UNIONISM IN THE GLOBAL ECONOMY

Munck (2004), among others, has convincingly argued that trade unions must extend their practices into transnational space in order to match global capital. The growth of multinational corporations (MNCs) has increased the asymmetrical distribution of power between employers, who are increasingly international in scale and scope, and trade unions, which remain largely embedded in local or national contexts. The development of production networks and the ability of MNCs to transfer production between countries reinforce management bargaining power vis-à-vis workplace unions. MNCs use coercive comparisons and threats of relocation to obtain wage concessions and more flexible work and employment arrangements. The extension of global value chains (GVCs) in Eastern Europe, South America and Asia accelerates this process and puts unions operating in quite different economic and institutional contexts in competition with one another.

The shift in the scale and scope of production creates formidable barriers to the construction of cross-border actions. For example, the fragmentation of GVCs is weakening local union bargaining power, in particular the power resources associated with a strategic location within these networks (Coe et al. 2008). However, by increasing the interdependence between different locations within the GVC, this fragmentation creates space for cross-border actions (Herod 2002). Babson's study (2003) of two sister Ford plants located in Mexico and the US shows that a work stoppage in one site can, in a very short time, have an impact throughout the supply chain, making a local dispute immediately international in scope and creating space for greater cross-border cooperation between unions.

This process has also prompted the extension of supranational institutions and mechanisms to follow the movement and flow of production within GVCs. The negotiation and implementation of International Framework Agreements (IFAs), and to a lesser degree of codes of conduct, is often considered as a mean to regulate employment relations issues within the MNC and their supplier networks (Blackett 2004; Bourque 2005; Hammer 2005). European and Global Works Councils are also seen to be new forums to regulate employment issues and even to reshape the balance of power between workers and employers (Pulignano 2005). According to Marginson and Sisson (2004), each of these mechanisms may offer an opportunity structure for cross-border actions and create a new dynamic within local and national unions. They can act as a springboard for cross-border cooperation, bringing representatives to work closely together (Marginson et al. 2004).

While these new mechanisms drive some unions towards transnational activity, there is much evidence showing the difficulties of building a community of interest across borders and of sustaining cooperation. Trade union involvement in cross-border action, particularly in a context of competitive relations between sites, drives unions towards a 'localist' conception of their interests and leads them to weigh up their involvement in cross-border action through an instrumental lens (Hege and Dufour 2007; Greer and Hauptmeier 2008; Lévesque and Murray 2010a). Their initial enthusiasm often disappears, to be replaced by skepticism and/or disengagement (Babson and Juarez 2007; Dufour-Poirier 2011; Ryland and Sadler 2008).

The spatial extension of trade union practices into transnational space thus appears to be a contradictory process that both favours and undercuts co-operation between trade unionists across borders. It can drive workplace trade unions into transnational space while accentuating localist pressures. Our objective is to understand this contradictory process through an analysis of the dynamic interplay between global and local imperatives. Our working hypothesis is that patterns of workplace trade union involvement in cross-border actions are shaped by both supranational institutions and local power dynamics.

Drawing on Campbell's expansive definition of institutions, including 'formal and informal rules, monitoring and enforcement mechanisms, and systems of meaning that define the context within which individuals, corporations, labour-unions, nation states, and other organisations operate and interact with each other' (Campbell 2004: 1), institutions may be both constraining and facilitating. They can limit prospects for change by engaging actors in path dependence, thus locking these actors into particular repertoires of action and constraining the range of future options. But institutions are also created and developed through actor contention and negotiation and may offer resources that facilitate actor agency and that can be mobilised to reshape patterns of relations. EWCs, global company councils, GUFs, IFAs, codes of conduct or any other transnational mechanisms define the scope and nature of the supranational institutions available to a workplace union. These supranational institutional arrangements in which workplace trade unions are embedded can thus narrow or open up opportunities for workplace trade union involvement in cross-border interactions. We might expect that patterns of involvement in cross-border action will vary according to the thickness (scope and nature) of these supranational institutions. Thicker institutional opportunities should pull workplace trade unions into international space.

However, the way workplace trade unions seize these institutional opportunities and transform them into institutional resources is related to the local power dynamic in which they are embedded. Several studies suggest that a reduction in the bargaining power at the local or national level pushes trade unions to invest in cross-border organising or collective bargaining (Burgoon and Jacoby 2004; Greer and Hauptmeier 2008). Other studies show that active union involvement in cross-border interaction requires the mobilisation of trade union power resources and capabilities (Lévesque and Murray 2010a; Pulignano 2007; Turnbull 2006). In particular, the capability to provide overarching narratives as a frame of reference for workplace union action seems to be an essential ingredient to enlarging repertoires of action at the transnational level (Turnbull 2006; Tarrow 2005). This is clearly a complex issue since the capability to frame issues is related to other trade union power resources and capabilities and also to the context in which they are located (Murray et al. 2010).

These mixed results points to the need to better understand how the different dimensions of local power dynamics play out. Drawing on the work of Wright (2000) and many others (see Anner's chapter in this book), we distinguish between two forms of power: structural and associational.

Structural power refers to the position of workers and their representatives within production networks and related product and labour markets. According to their position, workers may be more vulnerable to competitive pressure or have more leverage over the bargaining of work conditions. It can be anticipated that a position of vulnerability in a production network will push a workplace trade union into transnational space to increase its capacity to act. The position of a workplace trade union within a production network and related product and labour markets is shaped in large part by firm strategies and location within the GVC (Gereffi, Humphrey and Sturgeon 2005). However, workers and their representatives are not passive agents in this process. As demonstrated by Coe, Dicken and Hess (2008), the strategies of production networks and firms are inherently dynamic and contested. Indeed, Herod, Rainnie and McGrath-Champ (2007) strongly argue that worker agency can improve relative position and bargaining power.

Associational power concerns precisely agency that stems from the collective organisation of workers. Drawing on previous analyses of variations in union capacity (for a synthesis, see Dufour et al. 2009), we extend the initial conceptualisation of associational power of Wright (2000) and focus on the power resources and strategic capabilities of workplace unions (Lévesque and Murray 2010b). Power resources are captured through three components: *internal resources*, which refer to the mechanisms that ensure internal solidarity and deliberative vitality (for example, the relative density of internal steward networks, the extent of membership participation or the existence of different workplace representative structures); *external resources*, which result from the integration of workplace unions in horizontal or vertical networks through affiliations with union structures, ties with other unions or community groups, political parties, educational institutions or government agencies; and *narrative resources*, which consist of the range of values, shared understandings, stories and ideologies that aggregate identities and interests and translate and inform motives. Even though resources are essential to improve the relative position and bargaining power of workplace trade unions, they may not be sufficient. Workers' representatives also need to interpret, express and act upon current situations. This is what we refer to as strategic capabilities. We focus here on two aspects of strategic capabilities: framing, which refers to the capacity of unions to develop and put forward their own projects and to relate them to a larger whole; and articulating between actions, space and time (Lévesque and Murray 2010b).

We expect that union involvement in cross-border action requires the mobilisation of power resources and capabilities. We need however to understand how each of these dimensions of associational power play out and how they are related to structural power and supranational institutional arrangements. It is our contention that the dynamic interplay between supranational institutions, on the one hand, and structural and associational power, on the other, provides an explanation of how workplace trade unionists move in and out of transnational space to fulfill local needs and objectives.

RESEARCH METHODS AND CASE DESCRIPTION

This research is part of a larger project on union renewal. It is built around multiple longitudinal case studies undertaken in different institutional contexts. Research for this study involved cross-national, comparative ethnographies.

The data were gathered between 2003 and 2010 through numerous site visits and observation of the production process by the four authors of this bi-national team.

In this chapter, we focus on six of these case studies. Individual and group interviews were conducted with roughly seventy workplace union leaders and activists, union officials beyond the worksites and other local actors, in particular managers. These open-ended, semi-structured interviews focused on a wide range of issues: the role of the worksite and its links with the larger firm; the characteristics of the workforce; the local union's history, structure and internal dynamics; conceptions of solidarity and worker interest; the relations between the workplace union and various external groups, including the union to which it is affiliated; the nature and intensity of networks in which the workplace union is involved; and the strategic capabilities of the local leadership.

A key condition for open access to these unions and their worksites was the promise to protect their identity when reporting results; therefore, we use acronyms in describing the cases. In this chapter, we present the experience of six workplace unions in three industries in Canada and France: vehicle assembly, auto parts and aerospace. Each local union leadership represents workers in a subsidiary of an MNC. In each case, the parent MNC either has a EWC or has been targeted for the development of a global company council. Table 4.1 describes the main characteristics of the six cases.

The first pair of subsidiaries, one in France (Transfra) and one in Canada (Transcan), are part of the same division of a North American manufacturer of transport equipment. This division has expanded rapidly over the last two decades, primarily through the acquisition of domestic firms in a variety of national settings. As of 2010, it had over 35,000 employees worldwide. The new facilities are in both higher-cost and lower-cost locations, ranging from Western Europe to Eastern Europe, Mexico and China. Employment at the Canadian site (Transcan) was stable for a longer period, but has declined sharply from 1,200 production workers in 2002–2003 to just 350 in 2009–2010, with the prospect of further lay-offs. At the French site (Transfra), employment has remained stable with around 1,000 employees since the 1990s. With several plants in the European Union, the division has established a EWC with employee representatives from its various plants. The division has not signed an international framework agreement but, as a result of recent discussions with trade union representatives in North America, has agreed to apply a code of conduct.

The second pair of subsidiaries belongs to two different MNCs with operations in the same highly competitive and concentrated segment of the auto parts industry. The French site (Autofra) and the Canadian site (Autocan) are subsidiaries of a European and a Japanese MNC, each with, respectively, 87,000 and 100,000 employees worldwide. Although the 1,000 employees at each of the sites are increasingly subject to the pressures of benchmarking, as they have to bid for product mandates in order to defend

Table 4.1 Description of the firms

	Transfra	Transcan	Autofra	Autocan	Aerofra	Aerocan
Profile of the firm						
– Industry	Transport equipment	Transport equipment	Auto parts	Auto parts	Aerospace	Aerospace
– Region of origin	North America	North America	Europe	Asia	Europe	North America
– Number of employees in the division	35,000	35,000	87,000	100,000	15,000	30,000
– Number of employees at site	1,000	350	1,250	1,175	4,000	7,000

jobs, levels of employment have remained relatively stable in recent years. The Autofra workers face particular competitive pressures from sister sites in Eastern Europe, the Autocan workers from sites within their MNC in the United States and Mexico. The Japanese MNC has been targeted by a GUF to establish a global network but does not have an IFA or a code of conduct. The European MNC has a EWC but has not yet signed an IFA.

The third pair of subsidiaries are located in two different MNCs in the aerospace industry. The French site (Aerofra) is part of a division of 15,000 employees within a European MNC. Employment at Aerofra has been stable over the last decade at roughly 4,000 employees. The Canadian site (Aerocan) is in the aerospace division of a North American MNC, with 30,000 employees worldwide in that segment of its operations. Employment at the Canadian site had declined from 10,000 in the early 1990s to 7,000 in 2010. Both the French and Canadian sites are in the high-end segment of their company's GVC, and each plays a leading role within the worldwide firm. The European MNC has a EWC but has not signed an IFA. The aerospace division of this North American MNC has established a global company council that brings together worker representatives from most of its sites worldwide.

While this particular research design clearly cannot aspire to be representative of an overall population of MNC subsidiaries in the two countries, and the variations in the composition of the six cases certainly limit our capacity to generalise from these particular cases, our methodological approach does offer important advantages in the light of our research objectives. The focus on matched pairs of subsidiary unions in two different institutional contexts allows us to consider the impact of industry and national institutional variations while providing insight into different regional (EU vs. NAFTA) contexts. Longitudinal comparative workplace ethnographies of comparable local unions within the international production networks of MNCs allow us to link levels of analysis over time, yielding a larger set of arguments about how local union leaderships deal with the impact of globalisation. Moreover, the design gives us a better understanding of the articulations between the local and international levels and, ultimately, helps us to disentangle the relations between these different levels and patterns of workplace trade union involvement in cross-border action.

THE DYNAMICS OF CROSS-BORDER INTERACTION

Transnational unionism encompasses a variety of forms. It can mean the spatial extension of trade union practices in the international context (Lillie and Martinez Lucio 2004) or the intensification of co-operation between trade unionists across countries (Greer and Hauptmeier 2008). We will assess two dimensions of workplace trade union involvement in cross-border actions: the spatial and the modes of interaction.

The spatial dimension concerns the articulation between the local and global. It captures how actors extend local practices to the international level by mobilising domestic resources to move in and out of supranational space and how local issues are externalised and how international issues are internalised at the national level and adapted to local strategic projects that then become part of an international agenda (Tarrow 2005). This spatial dimension will be measured by three indicators: the scales where contentions are voiced (local, national, regional, international), their domains of concern (education, working conditions, labour rights, environment, etc.) and the scope for rank and file involvement.

The modes of interaction concern three aspects: the strength of the ties established with other actors at different levels; the extent of cooperation and conflict between these actors; and the repertoire of actions local unions are mobilising through these interactions, in particular whether their actions are oriented towards information-sharing, organising, transnational collective bargaining, strike-support or networking. Table 4.2 exhibits the distribution of our six cases according to those two dimensions.

There are important variations in local union involvement in cross-border action between our cases. In terms of the spatial dimension, all workplace union leaderships voice their contention at the local level. However, while some remain almost exclusively at this level (Transfra and Autocan), others try to articulate local contentions at the regional (Autofra and Aerofra) and even transnational levels (Transcan and Aerocan). The domain of contention always covers issues of cost and working conditions, but it can also embrace larger issues, such as labour rights (Aerofra and Aerocan). At Aerofra, issues of contention include training and social meetings between workers from different European countries. With the exception of Aerofra, rank-and-file involvement appears relatively limited, although local union positions can be subject to customary deliberative processes (Autofra and Aerocan).

Modes of interaction are also quite unevenly distributed across the cases. The workplace unions in two cases (Transfra and Autocan) are mainly concerned with information gathering, entailing weak ties and competitive relations with other unions. In complete contrast, two other workplace unions (Aerofra and Aerocan) share information and engage in collective bargaining. These latter local leaderships develop stronger ties with other trade unions that involve both collaborative and competitive relationships. The other two workplace unions (Autofra and Transcan) are situated in between, not going beyond the sharing of information and the cultivation of competitive relations through weak ties.

When the spatial dimension and the modes of interaction are combined, we can identify three distinct patterns of workplace trade union involvement in cross-border actions: a localist pattern that characterise workplace unions that choose to stay in their box (Autocan and Transfra); a risk reduction pattern that typifies workplace representatives that are moving in

Table 4.2 Dimensions and patterns of workplace union involvement in cross-border interaction

	Transfra	Transcan	Autofra	Autocan	Aerofra	Aerocan
Spatial						
– Scale	Local	Transnational	Regional	Local	Regional	Regional and transnational
– Domain	Protection of national market	Cost and working conditions	Cost and working conditions	Cost and working conditions	Working conditions and labour rights, social encounter	Working conditions and labour rights
– Scope for rank-and-file involvement	Weak & defensive	Weak	Through deliberative process	None	Strong	Through deliberative process
Modes of interaction						
– Repertoire of actions	Information gathering and mobilisation	Information gathering	Information sharing	Information gathering	Information sharing, collective bargaining	Information sharing, collective bargaining
– Strength of relationships	Very weak	Weak ties	Weak ties	Very weak	Strong ties	Strong ties
– Nature of relationships	Competitive	Competitive/ collaborative	Competitive	Competitive	Collaborative	Collaborative/ competitive
Pattern of union involvement in cross-border interaction	Localist	Risk reduction	Risk reduction	Localist	Proactive	Proactive

and out of their box (Autofra and Transcan); and a proactive pattern that exemplifies unions that are trying to enlarge the box (Aerofra and Aerocan).

The Autocan and Transfra workplace unions share many similarities. Both operate almost exclusively at the local level, and their movement into supranational space is invariably instrumental, either to protect their national market (Transfra) or to secure information about cost and working conditions at other sites in order to improve the position of their site (Autocan). There is not much scope for rank and file involvement at the supranational level, and when it occurs, it is geared towards the protection of site interests. For example, when a decision was taken to outsource a segment of the Transfra assembly process to Eastern Europe, Transfra workers blocked the exit at their site so that the equipment could not be transferred. This demonstrated that the safeguarding of jobs is paramount. Both workplace unions have very limited interaction with other trade unions. The Autocan workplace trade union has had only sporadic contacts with sister unions in the United States and does not have any systematic contact with unions beyond its region, despite the existence of a global company network within one of the GUFs. Indeed, Autocan local union leaders demonstrate little knowledge of sister unions in other countries with whom their relationship is more competitive than collaborative. The Transfra workplace union leaders are well aware of the situation of sister plants in Europe and seek to obtain information about them but do not develop strong ties with the unions at those sites. Transfra workplace union leaders rarely participate in the annual meeting of their company's EWC. When they do participate, it is primarily to gather information relevant to the fortunes of their site. Accordingly, the workplace unions at both Autocan and Transfra can be described as isolated since they clearly prefer not to venture beyond local space.

The workplace unions at Autofra and Transcan share many features that distinguish them from the more localist pattern observed in the two previous cases. Both Autofra and Transcan local union leaders try to articulate the local to the supranational albeit in a rather limited way. They move in and out of international space to voice their local concerns, which are mainly about cost and production issues. Confronted with local managers constantly comparing the productivity and cost structure of their sites with other sites in their MNC, these leaders seek to gather information that is immediately relevant to their local needs. Even though Autofra worker representatives are critical of the functioning of their company's EWC, they use it for information gathering. They complain that their EWC is dominated by trade unionists from the home country of their MNC and that these unionists are subjugated to the employer's competitive agenda. The Canadian union leaders in Transcan cannot rely on such a consultative body. They have had to initiate their own contacts with unions from other countries and have visited several sites in Europe to obtain relevant information about cost structure, production process and labour relations issues. In collaboration with the workplace unions of other sites of this MNC in Canada and industry unions affiliated to rival union federations, Transcan union leaders participated in meetings to establish a global coordinating structure within the company. However, Transcan workplace union leaders withdrew from this initiative to protest against significant layoffs implemented by the corporation. At Transcan, there is practically no space for rank-and-file involvement in cross-border action, and such union involvement is a contentious issue among the membership, who question the necessity of building cross-border alliances when the survival of their plant is at stake. At Autofra, the involvement of local leaders in cross-border actions is a subject of frequent discussion among leaders and with their members. These deliberative processes enhance the scope for rank-and-file involvement. The similarities between these two workplace unions far outweigh this dissimilarity, especially as regards their modes of interaction. Both unions have developed only weak, or even very weak, ties with their sister plants based on competitive rather than collaborative relationships. The competitive nature of those relationships is exacerbated in the case of Autofra by the proximity of sister plants competing in the same market segment. Overall, it appears that these two workplace unions have both sought to venture into transnational space in order to reduce the risk of job losses and secure the future of their site.

The workplace unions at Aerofra and Aerocan both display a more proactive pattern of involvement in cross-border actions than is evident in the other four cases in this study. Both Aerofra and Aerocan actively seek to shape their transnational space. Aerofra is a key player within their EWC and has initiated an annual meeting that brings together 10 per cent of workers from each of four European sites in the company. Organised around training, cultural and sporting activities, these meetings aim to create a sense of belonging and community between workers from sites located in different countries and thus facilitate active rank-and-file involvement. The Aerofra leaders have also sought to extend local practices to the regional (EU) level. For example, the French practice of profit-sharing has been extended to the European level through the EWC and now applies in national sites where no such legal obligation exists. The objects of cross-border actions are therefore more wide-ranging than comparisons of working conditions and the sharing of information. The modes of interaction developed by the Aerofra union entail strong ties and collaborative relations with other workplace unions as regards a range of issues relevant to the collective regulation of employment. Despite certain differences, the experience of the Aerocan union exhibits many similarities. The Aerocan leaders play a central role in bringing workplace trade unionists from different sites together and are able to frame local issues in a broader context. Drawing on the experience of several global works councils, the Aerocan union has been instrumental in the creation of a mechanism that seeks to bring together all local and industrial unions in that division of their MNC on a bi-annual basis. This global council not only focuses on the sharing of information about working conditions and management approaches; it has also initiated the negotiation of a corporate code of conduct that specifies the company's social responsibility, notably as regards worker rights. The Aerocan workplace union has developed strong ties with a variety of unions in Europe and in North America, and these are based on a collaborative approach, despite the obvious competition between sites to obtain new product mandates.

Our study of workplace trade union teams in Canada and France reveals quite different patterns of union involvement in cross-border action. At one extreme, there are two workplace unions (Transfra and Autocan) with almost no enduring links at the supranational level: their approach is confined to local space. At the other extreme, two workplace teams (Aerofra and Aerocan) exhibit a proactive stance and play a leading role in the construction of cross-border actions. In between these two extremes, two other workplace unions (Autofra and Transcan) are characterised by a more uneven trajectory, where bursts of strong cross-border involvement at some times are punctuated by periods of weak and even non-existent involvement at other times.

UNDERSTANDING PATTERNS OF WORKPLACE UNION INVOLVEMENT

We now turn to supranational institutional arrangements and local power dynamics in which workplace unions are embedded to understand how they navigate between the local and the global. Table 4.3 displays the characteristics of the supranational institutional arrangements and the local power dynamics for each case.

What is the impact of supranational institutional arrangements on patterns of union involvement in cross-border actions? At first glance, the substantial variations in supranational institutional arrangements among our cases suggest a very limited impact. In France, there are three different patterns even though the workplace unions all have access to a EWC, a GUF and European union federations. However, as we will argue below, under certain conditions (cf. Autofra), the existence of a EWC appears to pull workplace unions into supranational space, which raises the question of whether these local leaders would move into this space in the absence of an EWC. While there is a similar variation in patterns of union involvement in cross-border actions, the only workplace union that displays a proactive pattern (Aerocan) is able to tap into richer and thicker supranational arrangements than in the other two cases. The Aerocan workplace union is part of an international (Canada-US) union, which certainly facilitates relations with sister plants in the US. Aerocan local leaders can also rely on a global company council that they have helped to put in place.

Local power dynamics, in terms of sources of structural and associational power (see Table 4.3), are also clearly associated with variations in patterns of union involvement in cross-border interaction.

Table 4.3 Supranational institutional arrangements and local power dynamics

Pattern of local union involvement	Localist		Risk reduction		Proactive	
Case	Transfra	Autocan	Autofra	Transcan	Aerofra	Aerocan
Supranational institutional arrangements						
– Firm-specific	EWC	None	Code of conduct & EWC	Code of conduct & Global company council	EWC	Code of conduct & Global company council
– Union-specific	GUF and European Federation	Global company network	GUF and European Federation	None	GUF and European Federation	GUF and international union
Local power dynamics						
Structural power						
– Position in the GVC	Strong	Modest	Modest	Strong	Strong	Strong
– Inter-site competition	Weak	Strong	Strong	Medium	Weak	Medium
– Market cycle	High	High	Medium	Low	High	Medium/low
Associational power						
– Internal resources	Low	High	High	Low	High	High
– External resources	High	Low	Low	High	High	High
– Narrative resources	High	Intermediate	Intermediate	Low	High	High
Strategic capabilities						
– Framing	High	Low	Intermediate	Low	High	High
– Articulating	Low	Low	Intermediate	Low	High	High

An explanation focused on exogenous factors might readily point to the impact of structural power on patterns of union involvement. However, the direction and strength of this relationship are too variable to draw any firm conclusions regarding the importance of sources of structural power on patterns of union involvement in cross-border interaction (see Table 4.3). The Aerofra and Transfra sites both produce a high value-added product with a stable and even increasing demand, apparently sheltered from competition, which suggests a very strong position within their respective production networks and product markets. However, their patterns of cross-border involvement are quite different. The Autofra and Autocan workplace unions also share comparable market conditions, but this structural power yields different patterns of cross-border interaction. Their parent companies cultivate intense product mandate and product market competition between sites in an industry characterised by a high degree of spatial mobility. Both Autofra and Autocan produce relatively low value-added products, for which the demand remains strong, but the production at each site could conceivably be moved to lower-cost locations. Transcan and Aerocan produce high value-added products, but they have encountered a sharp decline in the demand for their products and increasing competition for segments of their production process from sites located in lower-cost regions, notably Mexico. The Transcan and Aerocan unions also adopt different approaches towards cross-border interaction. In other words, similar conditions as regards the structural power of these workplace unions are associated with different patterns of local union involvement.

Associational power is clearly important for patterns of union involvement. Workplace union leaders who can draw on associational power resources and capabilities are more likely to exhibit a proactive pattern of involvement in cross-border interactions (see Table 4.3). This situation characterises workplace unions at Aerofra and Aerocan. Their internal resources include a vibrant deliberative process and a network of shop floor delegates that can act as a bi-directional transmission belt between workers and their leaders at the site. In terms of external resources, they are embedded in their industry union, have strong access to their regional labour federation and participate actively in both. Their narrative resources are characterised by a long history of cooperation and partnership with management that informs their strategies. In contrast to the other cases in our study, the mobilisation of these associational resources comes together with a workplace union leadership that demonstrates a strong strategic capacity in terms of capabilities both to frame issues and to articulate them at different levels. For example, in a context of fierce inter-site competition for a new product mandate, the Aerocan leadership was able to frame a project that articulated the promotion of local employment with MNC requirements to attain cost savings through the outsourcing of segments of production to lower-cost locations in its GVC. These union leaders were able to situate their project over a long time horizon and to mediate between contending interests within and outside the site. At Aerofra, where the composition of union representatives is dominated by one trade union (Force Ouvrière), the union leaders were able to propose a unifying project that brought together different stakeholders. Union leaders at both sites are therefore able to frame issues at different levels and then transpose them on other scales, be they from global to local or local to global.

The workplace unions that have more limited associational power resources and capabilities display either localist or risk-reduction patterns of cross-border interaction. While the Autofra and Autocan workplace unions both have strong internal resources, their pattern of cross-border involvement is either risk reduction (Autofra) or localist (Autocan). The Autocan union is quite isolated in terms of its links within the community and external union structures, but it does have an effective deliberative process and a strong network of shop-floor delegates. Autocan leaders are therefore well connected to the rank and file, and worker participation in the life of the union is quite extensive. Indeed, the Autocan union has a long history of struggle, including a six-month strike in the mid-1990s, but in the current context, this history of struggle is not used to frame a mobilising script for the membership. Autocan leaders increasingly embrace local management's micro-corporatist strategy, which seeks to secure their site's survival in the face of a hostile external environment. In such a context, union leaders have not been able to develop an autonomous agenda and are framing worker interests in terms of site performance.

The internal resources of the Autofra unions are also its main asset. The level of unionisation at the site is 70 per cent of workers, which is quite exceptional by French standards, where union membership tends to be confined to a small group of activists. At the two other French sites in this study, the level of unionisation is between 10 and 15 per cent. Another quite unusual aspect of the Autofra unions' internal resources is that the five major trade unions (CFDT, CGT, CFTC, FO and CGC) present in the plant are represented almost equally in works committee elections. This situation pushes a normally heterogeneous group of union representatives to work together and to develop a wide range of inter-union activities on an ongoing basis. This mode of operation requires a continuous dialogue about the division of tasks between the different union representatives and a need to prioritise the spaces in which the Autofra unions are involved. For example, the Autofra union leadership decided on a strategic basis that they could get more out of their participation in local and national structures of representation, respectively the 'comité d'entreprise' (works council) and the 'comité de groupe' (national company council), than from the EWC supranational structure.

In contrast to Autofra and Autocan with their strong internal resources but relatively weak external resources, the Transcan and Transfra workplace unions are characterised by strong external resources and quite weak internal resources in which a small group of workplace union officers cultivate external links. Deliberative processes and the network of shop floor delegates at Transcan are weak. Local union culture is dominated by an instrumentalist servicing mentality. The framing capabilities of the local leaders are not particularly well developed. Historically, the Transcan workplace union has not been isolated, with active participation in the activities of both its industry union and national union federation and drawing extensively on their staff for servicing expertise. Its industry union is not affiliated to a GUF and, therefore, has few ways to connect with existing international structures. This industry union has, however, supported the international initiatives undertaken by the Transcan workplace union. These international initiatives were not sustained, as local leaders had neither sufficient internal resources to support them nor the strategic capabilities (framing and articulating) to integrate them effectively into their repertoire of action.

The Transfra union has been completely dominated by the CGT representatives since the early 1990s. These leaders use the rich history of their union to legitimise their frame of reference, which rests on a traditional discourse of social class conflict associated with the CGT beyond the site. However, these leaders clearly give priority to local needs over wider forms of solidarity. Despite an active leadership team, the rank-and-file involvement in the deliberative process at Transfra is relatively weak, and the level of unionisation barely reaches 10 per cent. Transfra union leaders are able to tap into their extensive political networks to defend local interests through the promotion of new product mandates for their site. These leaders are also skilled in their capacity to frame issues and convince both workers and site managers that their strategic orientations are the right ones. The strength of the Transfra union leadership is the result of its strategic capabilities and of its ability to mobilise extensive external networks cultivated over many years.

Overall, our results show that patterns of union involvement vary across industries and the relative thickness of supranational institutional arrangements. While exogenous influences related to the location of sites in the GVC of their parent company, the extent of inter-site competition and the type of product cycle offer a tempting line of explanation, our analysis of the relationship between sources of structural power and patterns of union involvement does not support such a contention. In contrast, the extent of associational resources, as gauged by trade union power resources and capabilities, provides some understanding of patterns of union involvement. The two cases of proactive workplace union involvement in cross-border actions were both characterised by a consistently high degree of union power resources and capabilities. However, the four cases in the localist and risk-aversion patterns both displayed mixed indicators on the different dimensions of associational power (higher in some respects and weaker in others). In other words, there is not a simple mechanical explanation of the dynamics of union involvement in cross-border actions.

PULLING INSTITUTIONAL AND POWER ANALYSIS TOGETHER

In order to capture the logic of underlying patterns of union involvement in cross-border actions, we now examine the dynamic interplay between these patterns and supranational institutional arrangements and structural and associational power.

The localist pattern of involvement appears to be driven by the interaction between structural and associational power resources. The position of both sites (Autocan and Transfra) seems to bring the workplace leaders towards the local level to pursue their objectives. They mobilise their resources and capabilities to attain these objectives, which are primarily oriented towards securing the site. Production at Transfra is largely sheltered from inter-site competition, but the site has to compete with other firms to obtain new contracts. The links with the community and political allies that the workplace union has cultivated over time are a strategic resource in obtaining new contracts and securing new investment. Union leaders are able to frame issues in a way that makes the workplace union an indispensable actor in the eyes of both workers and local management. They are bridging actors, able to connect different spaces in order to fulfill local needs. In a context where their site is relatively sheltered from inter-site competition and workplace union leaders already act as brokers, engagement at the supranational level does not seem relevant and might even jeopardise their localist strategy.

The same kind of logic underlines the localist pattern of the Autocan workplace union. Its actions are targeted towards securing the future of the site, and this goal is preeminent. In the short term at least, the union's strategic partnership with local management seems to protect workers from the strong inter-site competition encouraged by the parent MNC. This strategy also makes the Autocan workplace union an indispensable partner for local management. The real strength of this union lies in its close proximity to its members, a proximity that it has developed over time. Strategic partnership is, in this case, a two-way street since local management could not easily pursue unilateral changes without compromising the cooperative relations that are a central tenet of its strategy for the survival of the site. Local union leaders are therefore using their main asset, their internal resources centred on deliberative vitality, to cope with a context where threats to the survival of the site are omnipresent. Union representatives have so fully integrated the predominant management discourse on the requirements of competitiveness in a global era that it is sometimes difficult to distinguish their position on this issue from that of management. The close proximity of the local union leaders to both the workers and management reinforces their centrality but also undermines their capacity to develop an autonomous agenda. The main asset of the workplace union—its internal resources—is therefore also the main barrier to the emergence of a more autonomous union project, and this is all the more evident in a context where the workplace union is already quite isolated in terms of its ability to mobilise external resources.

Both workplace unions exhibiting a pattern of risk reduction (Autofra and Transcan) focus on local objectives in a context where the role of their sites and their own bargaining power are at risk. However, they mobilise different sets of power resources. Autofra is characterised by robust internal resources but relative isolation. The presence of a EWC clearly pulls Autofra leaders into transnational space, but their main objective is to protect local interests. Supranational institutions clearly matter, but this does not mean that they become a strategic priority. Unlike the localist position exhibited by the Transfra leaders, the Autofra leaders cannot readily disregard the activities of the EWC because of their weak structural power. Nor is the Autofra union able to change the terms of the debate because it does not have the associational power to overcome the cozy relationship between management and unions in the parent company. In order to maintain prevailing cooperative relations between what could be competing unions at the level of the site, the Autofra union leaders keep their distance from industry and national trade unions outside the site and maintain wary and competitive relations with trade union representatives from the parent company. Such a dynamic basically confines the Autofra union leaders to a risk-reduction strategy.

The vulnerability of the Transcan site creates the conditions for its union to engage in cross-border action. Faced with sharp declines in employment and demand for their products, local leaders, with the strong encouragement of staff in their industry union, decided to move into the supranational space to gather information. However, they do not have sufficient resources and capabilities to sustain such an engagement or, more importantly, to go beyond a merely instrumental outlook. Indeed, despite taking an early initiative in this new transnational engagement, the Transcan union was not able to build on this experience to renew its narrative stock. It continues to favour the same interpretative frame premised on 'bread and butter' issues in order to mobilise its membership. There are clear limits to such a discourse that provokes much criticism in the union and in the surrounding community. Transcan leaders find it difficult to counter these criticisms, and this in turn undermines their involvement in cross-border actions and, ultimately, their own legitimacy.

The workplace unions, characterised by a proactive pattern (Aerocan and Aerofra), share three key features. First, their industry is highly integrated and consolidated and, located at the apex of their respective value chains, the two sites produce high value-added products in complex organisational settings. Despite significant layoffs at Aerocan, neither workplace union is in a particularly vulnerable position as regards their product markets and their location in the parent company's GVC. Second, not only can both workplace unions draw on extensive power resources and capabilities, but they are able to articulate them over time and through space. Third, both of them are actively engaged in the development of supranational institutions. They are, of course, already participating in cross-border actions, but they are also seeking to shape the emerging supranational institutions. Their involvement in cross-border actions is therefore completely integrated into their strategic repertoires of action.

The interaction of supranational institutional arrangements and local power dynamics appears to shape patterns of union involvement in different ways. The localist pattern emerges in a context where jobs are relatively sheltered from intense competition, albeit in different ways, and the workplace unions have sufficient resources and capabilities to be an indispensable interlocutor for both workers and local managers. Active union involvement in cross-border action could undermine this fragile compromise. Risk reduction is characteristic of workplace unions where their site is vulnerable because of threats to product market or location in the parent company's GVC. This weakened structural power appears to push workplace union leaders into transnational space in order to gather the information so vital to the pursuit of their local objectives. Neither leadership has sufficient resources and capabilities to create a new dynamic at the supranational level (Autofra) or to ensure the support of members to engage in ambitious cross-border initiatives (Transcan). Finally, the proactive pattern emerges from a context where the structural sources of power do not undermine the capacity of the workplace union leadership and where these leaders are able to mobilise both extensive resources and particular capabilities in order to engage in the construction of the new supranational institutional arrangements, which they have fully integrated into their strategic repertoires of action.

CONCLUSION

The purpose of this chapter is to understand how workplace trade unions move in and out of supranational space to attain their objectives and meet local needs.

A first conclusion concerns how the variability in the way that workplace unions exploit the institutional opportunities available at the supranational level depends on their reading of local imperatives. The workplace unions displaying a localist pattern do not get involved because they consider that such involvement could endanger their strategies to safeguard employment at their sites. For the workplace unions engaged in risk aversion, the international is not fully integrated into their strategic repertoires; they make forays into supranational space in order to gather information for the protection of local interests. The workplace unions exhibiting a proactive pattern have completely integrated this supranational space into their repertoires of action, seeking both to promote the role of their sites within larger GVC strategies and to shape the rules of the game in the emerging supranational institutions.

A second conclusion concerns the factors that pull and push workplace trade unions into supranational space and enhance sustained involvement in cross-border action. Consistent with previous research (Marginson and Sisson 2004), our cases support the proposition that supranational institutional arrangements can act as a springboard and pull trade unions into international space. The presence of thick institutional arrangements appears to favour an initial cross-border involvement of workplace trade unions. Our results also reinforce previous findings as regards the influence of structural power on trade union involvement in cross-border action (Burgoon and Jacoby 2004; Greer and Hauptmeier 2008). Weakened structural power as a result of declining product markets or inter-site competition can push workplace unions into international space, as this vulnerability can make cross-border action a more attractive strategy to increase their capacity to act. Similarly, workplace unions located at the apex of their GVC can be pushed into supranational space in order to defend and promote their interests. However, while institutional arrangements can pull and structural power push workplace unions into supranational space, neither of these factors—alone or combined—is sufficient to create the conditions for sustained trade union involvement in cross-border actions. Such proactive involvement also requires the mobilisation of multiple power resources and strategic capabilities (see also Lévesque and Murray 2010b). Our study suggests that proactive workplace unions must be able to draw on both internal and external resources and a range of strategic capabilities. In particular, our study highlights how these workplace union leaders must be able to frame local issues in relation to the global, but also to bring them back to the level of the local. They must articulate their strategies in multiple spaces and do so over time and in a way that is ultimately integrated into their strategic repertoires. In contrast, the local leaders engaged in localist and risk-reduction patterns mobilise either internal or external resources and are critically limited in their ability to frame the issues (from both local to global and global to local) and to articulate them across different spaces and over time.

A third conclusion concerns the muted impact of institutional differences between Canada and France on the patterns of involvement in cross-border actions. All are contending with pressures on their structural power. Each has to measure the extent of its internal and external resources in relation to the particular institutional arrangements in which their site and union are embedded. The point is not to discount the potential effects of particular institutional arrangements, be they industry, national or supranational, on workplace trade unions but to highlight the ways that union actors mobilise these arrangements and other internal and external resources to increase their capacity to act in an increasingly transnationalised space.

A final conclusion is that workplace unions, albeit in different ways, make strategic use of international space according to local priorities and supranational opportunities. All of these union leaderships are located at a complex intersection between the local and the global: each integrates the global into local issues and each is compelled to infuse local interests into the dynamics of its cross-border actions. Even workplace unions that display a localist pattern of involvement are bridging the local and the global and seeking to frame local issues, such as the safeguarding of jobs and the survival of their site, into a wider strategy of how to contend with global competition. Whether such workplace union leaders can be considered as, using Tarrow's label, rooted cosmopolitan activists might be a step too far, but it is clear that they are acutely aware of the international nature of the challenges faced by their sites and try to address these challenges in ways that are consistent with the resources and capabilities available to them. The strategic capabilities of these workplace union leaders clearly play a pivotal role in shaping their cross-border actions.

ACKNOWLEDGEMENTS

This research is part of a larger project funded by the Social Sciences and Humanities Research Council of Canada (SSHRC) and the *Fonds de recherche sur la société et la culture du Québec* (FQRSC). The authors acknowledge the generous participation of the many trade unionists and managers who shared their time and their insights in the context of this study. The four authors contributed equally to this chapter.

REFERENCES

Babson, S. (2003), 'Dual Sourcing at Ford in the United States and Mexico: Implications for Labour Relations and Union Strategies' in W. N. Cooke (ed.), *Multinational Companies and Global Human Resource Strategies*, Westport, CT: Quorum Books.

Babson, S., and Juarez, H. (2007), 'Emergent Design: The International Research Network on Autowork in the Americas', *Labor Studies Journal*, 32(1), 23–40.

Blackett, A. (2004), 'Codes of Corporate Conduct and the Labour Regulatory State in Developing Countries', in J.J. Kirton and M.J. Trebilcock (eds.), *Hard Choices, Soft Law*, Toronto: Ashgate.

Bourque, R. (2005), *Les Accords-Cadres Internationaux (ACI) et la Négociation Collective Internationale à l'Ère de la Mondialisation*, Genève: Institut International d'Études Sociales.

Burgoon, B., and Jacoby, W. (2004), 'Patch-Work Solidarity: Describing and Explaining US and European Labour Internationalism', *Review of International Political Economy*, 11(5), 849–879.

Campbell, J. (2004), *Institutional Change and Globalization*, Princeton: Princeton University Press.

Coe, N.M., Dicken, P., and Hess M. (2008), 'Global Production Networks: Realizing the Potential', *Journal of Economic Geography*, 8(3), 271–295.

Dufour, C., Hege, A., Lévesque, C., and Murray, G. (2009), 'Les syndicalismes référentiels dans la mondialisation: une étude comparée des dynamiques locales au Canada et en France', *Revue de l'IRES*, 61(2), 3–37.

Dufour-Poirier, M. (2011), 'Construction d'une coalition syndicale internationale: analyse d'une perspective Nord-Sud', Ph.D. Dissertation, Montreal: HEC Montréal.

Gereffi, G., Humphrey, J., and Sturgeon, T. (2005), 'The Governance of Global Value Chains', *Review of International Political Economy*, 12(1):78–104.

Greven, T., and Russo, J. (2006), 'Strategic Campaigns against Multinational Enterprises: the German Experience', paper presented at Global Companies, Global Unions, Global Research, Global Campaigns: An International Conference, New York, February 10.

Greer, I., and Hauptmeier, M. (2008), 'Political Entrepreneurs and Co-Managers: Labour Transnationalism at Four Multinational Auto Companies', *British Journal of Industrial Relations*, 46(1), 76–97.

Hammer, N. (2005), 'International Framework Agreements: Global Industrial Relations between Rights and Bargaining', *Transfer: European Review of Labour and Research*, 11(4), 511–530.

Hege, A., and Dufour, C. (2007), 'Allemagne/Belgique. Restructurations chez Volkswagen Wolfsburg d'abord!', *Chronique Internationale*, 104, 11–21.

Herod, A. (2002), 'Organizing Globally, Organizing Locally: Union Spatial Strategy in a Global Economy', in J. Harrod and R. O'Brien (eds.), *Global Unions? Theory and Strategies of Organized Labour in the Global Political Economy*, London: Routledge.

Herod, A., Rainnie, A., and McGrath-Champ, S. (2007), 'Working Space: Why Incorporating the Geographical Is Central to Theorizing Work and Employment Practices', *Work, Employment and Society*, 2(2), 247–264.

Kay, T. (2005), 'Labor Transnationalism and Global Governance: The Impact of NAFTA on Transnational Labor', *American Journal of Sociology*, 111(3), 715–756.

Lévesque, C., and Murray, G. (2010a), 'Trade Union Cross-Border Alliances within MNCs: Disentangling Union Dynamics at the Local, National and International Levels', *Industrial Relations Journal*, 41(4), 312–332.

Lévesque, C., and Murray, G. (2010b), 'Understanding Union Power: Resources and Capabilities for Renewing Union Capacity', *Transfer*, 16(3): 333–350.

Lillie, N. and Martinez Lucio, M. (2004), 'International Trade Union Revitalization: The Role of National Union Approaches', in C.M. Frege and J.E. Kelly (eds.), *Varieties of Unionism: Strategies for Union Revitalization in a Globalizing Economy*, London: Oxford Scholarship Online.

Marginson, P., Hall, M., Hoffman, A., and Müller, T. (2004), 'The Impacts of European Works Councils on Management Decision-Making in the UK and US-Based Multinationals: A Case Study Comparison', *British Journal of Industrial Relations*, 42(2), 209–233.

Marginson, P., and Sisson, K. (2004), *European Integration and Industrial Relations*, London: Palgrave-MacMillan.

Munck, R. (2004), 'Globalization, Labor and the Polanyi Problem', *Labor History*, 45(3), 251–269.

Murray, G., Dufour, C., Hege, A., and Lévesque, C. (2010), 'Les syndicalismes référentiels dans la mondialisation : une étude comparée des dynamiques locales au Canada et en France', *Revue de l'IRES*, 61(2), 3–37.

Pulignano, V. (2005), 'EWCs and Cross-National Employee Representative Coordination. A Case of Trade Union Cooperation?', *Economic and Industrial Democracy*, 26(3), 383–412.

Pulignano, V. (2006), 'Still "Regime Competition"? Trade Unions and Multinational Restructuring in Europe', *Relations industrielles / Industrial Relations*, 61(4), 615–638.

Pulignano, V. (2007), 'Going National or European? Local Trade Union Politics within Transnational Business Context in Europe', in K. Bronfenbrenner (ed.), *Global Unions: Challenging Transnational Capital through Cross-Border Campaigns*, Ithaca: Cornell University Press.

Ryland, R., and Sadler, D. (2008), 'Revitalizing the Trade Union Movement through Internationalism: the Grassroots Perspective', *Journal of Organizational Change Management*, 21(4), 417.

Tarrow, S. (2005), *The New Transnational Activism*, Cambridge: Cambridge University Press.

Turnbull, P. (2006), 'The War on Europe's Waterfront—Repertoires of Power in the Port Transport Industry', *British Journal of Industrial Relations*, 44(2), 305–326.

Wright, E. O. (2000), 'Working-Class Power, Capitalist-Class Interests, and Class Compromise', *The American Journal of Sociology*, 105(4), 957–1002.

5 The Strike at Renault-Dacia

A Challenge for East-West Trade Union Cooperation

Michèle Descolonges

The changes trade unions underwent following the establishment of foreign multinational companies in the Eastern European countries have been much explored in the literature. However, transnational solidarity between trade unions in Eastern and Western Europe has attracted less attention, or at best has been examined solely from the perspective of trade unions in Eastern Europe. Based on the 2008 strike at Renault-Dacia in Romania, this chapter highlights how trade unions, whether in the East or the West, are shaped by their histories, which explain the economic crisis as well as the form their transnational solidarity takes. The strike elicited a favourable response in Europe and was backed by the French trade unions. It stood out in the European social landscape. The inter-union cooperation it fostered lay at the heart of several issues rekindled by the economic crisis that surfaced in late 2008.

Romania became a 'people's democracy' after the Second World War and experienced an 'uprising for democracy' in 1989. By then, however, it had become one of Europe's poorest nations. After 1989, Romania, like the other Eastern European countries, went through a period of transition during which it sought to align itself with the Western industrial model. The recession of the 1990s led the pro-free-market government elected in 1996 to reform the mining sector, with the loss of 80,000 jobs, and launch a series of privatisations. The first organisations to be privatised were the telephone and cement companies, which were bought by Lafarge.

Trade between France and Romania is governed by a form of protectionism, despite Romania's entry into the European Union (EU) on 1 January 2007 and its corollary, the free circulation of labour and capital. French companies have been prompted to move to Romania by the country's changed political situation, state of development and low labour costs, but few Romanian companies have moved to France. EU membership has encouraged migration. A part of Romania's skilled workforce has left for other European countries, at the same time as workers from Asia are trying to enter Europe through Romania's borders. Aggravated by the economic crisis, inequality between workers from the two countries, particularly in terms of employment, poses a challenge to cooperation between Romanian and French trade unions.

Romanian unions first joined European trade union organisations, including the European Trade Union Confederation (ETUC), in the 1990s. It was not until March 2005, however, that they became involved in European trade unionism, when they took part in the Euro-Demonstration organised in Brussels to protest against the so-called draft Bolkenstein Directive (Pilat 2007). Their massive participation in a European demonstration was underplayed. When Dacia workers laid down their tools in early 2008, conditions in Europe were ripe for the strike to spread and, in response to the ETUC's call for the mobilisation of European trade union organisations, 54 trade unions from 29 countries demonstrated on 5 April of that year in Ljubljana (Slovenia). They voiced demands on subjects such as wages, purchasing power and equality, themes that echoed the Dacia strike.

The European demonstration of September 2010, in which 100,000 people took part, had a common purpose: to denounce the national austerity plans endorsed by the European institutions. It echoed the demonstrations organised in several European countries, including Romania and France.

Thus, while it is true that Romania's trade unions have taken part in various forms of European trade union action, the question is whether, like those of other countries of eastern and central Europe, they are turning towards the European 'model'. The literature tends to underplay the difficulties most Eastern European trade unions have encountered integrating into Europe, chiefly because of their past, which they find hard to shake off. They are having trouble coping with market realities in the context of a global economy. It might be relevant for them to adopt a strategic model along American pro-market lines (Crowley 2004).

However, from what angle should we consider the integration of Romanian trade unions into Europe? Will they continue to be part of the increasingly conflictual situation observed in every crisis-stricken country except the United States, even though the strong trade union mobilisation in early 2010 did not stop the Romanian state's reform process (Lochard and Pernot 2010)? In this context, what is the capacity of Romanian trade unions, and their counterparts in the 15-member EU, to take transnational action over the long term? What can the trade unions of the EU do beyond providing training?

By looking at one case more closely, that of the Renault-Dacia strike in the spring of 2008, this chapter aims to determine the nature of the inter-union cooperation that emerged at the time and to highlight the heterogeneity of trade union dynamics. It is based on empirical studies of how trade union standards, rules and values have been tested by globalisation. The studies were conducted under the umbrella of the *Institut de recherches économiques et sociales* (IRES), at the request of France's General Confederation of Labour (CGT) between 2005 and 2009 and resulted in a compilation of over 100 in-depth interviews with French trade unionists, mainly from the CGT and the French Democratic Confederation of Labour (CFDT). The interviewees were members of labour federations, in particular craft federations, and unions at 12 multinationals whose headquarters are situated on French territory. Several meetings were held with international craft union leaders. In-depth interviews were also held with senior managers from the same multinationals. In Romania, about 30 interviews were conducted in 2008 with trade unionists from Dacia and equipment manufacturers, a sub-contractor's employees, regional political officials and associative stakeholders. Some of the interviews took place during the strike, and we also attended a public demonstration.

On the basis of these field surveys,[1] we will examine the establishment by the multinational Renault of a plant on a brownfield site in Romania, where a powerful trade union was present. We will describe how the strike was conducted and the trade unionists' demands, as well the support and forms of solidarity from which they benefited. Lastly, we will consider the outlook for the future of cooperation between trade union organisations.

FROM NATIONALISED COMPANY TO MULTINATIONAL

The *Régie nationale des usines Renault* (RNUR) became a state-owned corporation at the end of the Second World War. In France, it played the role of social precursor, prefiguring measures that would subsequently be extended to all wage-earners (in 1955, a third week of paid holiday leave, paid public holidays, supplementary pension; in 1962, a fourth week of paid holiday leave). However, even when they were nationalised, French corporations bore little resemblance to the forms of collective ownership introduced in the East under communist control: the single trade union organisations in the communist countries of Eastern Europe did not have the same concepts of economic development or provide the same services (housing, food, access to schools for children, etc.) as the works councils established in France post-World War II.

Renault is representative of globalised manufacturing organisations. The first project engineering agreements were concluded with Romanian government for the manufacture of the Renault 8 Dacia in 1966. A factory was built in Mioveni, next to the town of Pitesti. The first Dacia cars rolled off the assembly lines two years later.

Cooperation between the RNUR and Dacia took the form of technology transfers, i.e., transfers of licences. The socialist state was the majority shareholder and Dacia retained all its prerogatives with regard to labour management and work organisation.

After Renault's change of status in France, the French state became a minority shareholder with a 15 per cent stake in the group. Renault took advantage of the 'Asian Financial Crisis' to go global (Freyssinet 2007). It consolidated its global status in 1999, when it entered into an alliance with the Japanese group Nissan, acquired the Romanian manufacturer Dacia and set up the South Korean company Renault Samsung Motors. In 2008, Renault was present in 118 countries and had 130,000 employees. It is a multibrand group.

In 1999, Renault first acquired 51 per cent of Dacia capital from the Romanian state property fund. It opted for a brownfield site, was awarded tax and customs exemptions and pledged to carry out an industrial and business programme involving investment, modernisation and cost reduction. The programme provided for the transformation of the industrial plant, the network of suppliers, the distribution system and the products. Since then, Renault has upped its stake to 99 per cent. Renault-Dacia, which is setting up a major research centre in Romania, is Romania's second largest exporter.

As a result of this investment, production was gradually rationalised and quality assurance procedures introduced for the performance of technical audits. Production was re-organised into *unités élémentaires de travail/UET* (elementary work units/EWU), and a team of French engineers and technicians was tasked with passing on its know-how about concurrent project management (Angelescou 2008).

New assembly lines were installed. The multinational's management opted for a diversified workforce (including some hired-out workers) and limited automation in order to save jobs. In 1999, Dacia had 29,000 employees. In 2001, a planned redundancy scheme was put in place by the multinational's management. Under the scheme, some of the staff were to be retrained over five years. Laid-off workers were in part absorbed into the local industrial fabric (equipment manufacturers, farmers, pensioners). Two thousand people were trained using European funds. In 2010, the number of wage-earners at Dacia had fallen to below 12,000. The workforce was younger (average age 36), skilled, well educated and 35 per cent female.

The 'Dacia platform' is located on land ceded by the town of Mioveni at an attractive price. Its main product is a low-priced car, the Logan, which was launched in 2004. By the end of 2005, Logans were being sold in 35 countries, but mainly in Eastern Europe, i.e., the local market. Sales rose quickly. In 2007, Dacia's annual sales increased by 17.4 per cent. In February 2008, 1,300 cars rolled off the lines daily. New models were introduced and started to be sold in Western Europe, entering into direct competition with cars produced in other European countries.

The car and equipment manufacturers share the same space, a simultaneous throughput and the same industrial project. Each company continues to be managed independently and the workers have different statuses and wages. The number of first-tier suppliers was reduced from 200 to 143. Romanian suppliers were encouraged to engage in quality assurance so as to bring themselves into line with Western standards. However, the supply contracts for one model required suppliers to be present in both France and Romania. International suppliers were encouraged to set up shop in Mioveni—a source of growing discrimination with regard to local companies (Layan 2003).

THE TRANSFORMATION OF LABOUR INSTITUTIONS

In 2004, in order to prepare Romania for EU membership, the European employers' organisation UNICE (Union of Industrial and Employers' Confederations of Europe, later BusinessEurope) and the International Labour Organisation (ILO) issued a series of conditions to employers. They stressed the need for employer professionalism, in particular with regard to collective bargaining. Employer associations benefited from training provided by German employer organisations. In addition, the Romanian government established a framework for industrial relations: it adopted the Constitution in 2003 and a new Labour Code in 2005 and transposed European directives relating to labour law. Encouraged by the ILO and the EU, tripartism was seen as a means of integrating trade union organisations into decision-making processes. At sector level, Romania adopted a law in 2005 on the establishment of European Works Councils that was implemented in 2007.

Created in 1990, the trade union confederation Cartel ALFA covers the mining, education, banking, tourism, agriculture, transportation and public administration sectors (Pilat 2007). It espouses a set of aspirations that are close to the Christian Democrat ideology. The confederation has 600,000 members. It is willing to deal with all European trade unions, irrespective of their ideological affiliation. For example, its chair, Bogdan Hossu, accepted an invitation to the French CGT Congress in December 2009. The confederation is affiliated with the International Trade Union Confederation (ITUC) and European Trade Union Confederation (ETUC).

Umut Korkut (2006) has described the difficulties encountered by Romania's trade union organisations during the first 10 years of post-communism: the inconsistent application of tripartism, the absence of mutual respect between the social partners, the growing gap between trade union leaders and members and the use of trade unions for political ends. A large number of strikes, in particular in the mining sector, underscored the institutional vacuum and absence of negotiations. For example, the 'social pact' signed in 2000 between the Romanian government and the trade unions was immediately broken by Cartel ALFA. In the view of the European Commission, the negotiating structures had no authority. A new, more successful agreement was signed in 2002.

The trade unions gradually took on board the measures set out by the EU with a view to Romania's integration into the community. Their integration into Europe started in the 1990s, when four confederations obtained observer status with the ETUC, later becoming full members. Well before Romania joined the EU, they had developed relations with the European Economic and Social Committee. As one author has noted, the education of Romanian trade union organisations was one of the priorities of the partnership between Romania and the EU. The unions were urged to reform their internal structures, to participate in national decision-making processes relating to labour affairs and to incorporate the many obligations stemming from EU membership (Pilat 2007).

These forms of institutional participation did not spark immediate interest in Europe. Pilat (2007) shows that unionists were relatively indifferent to the 2002 EU directive on the information and consultation of staff with regard to restructuring plans, which emerged in Europe after Renault's 1997 announcement that it would be closing its factory in Vilvoorde, Belgium. Romania's trade union organisations started to translate the European view and discourse into action, i.e., participating in a demonstration against the 'services' directive organised by the ETUC in March 2005. The so-called 'Bolkenstein Directive' sparked vigorous opposition, chiefly in Belgium and France. Objections centred on the concept of the service provider's 'country of origin', which would determine the rights of the service provider's workers, no matter where the service was provided. The social actors continued to be concerned about the risks of social dumping. This directive has been operational in France since December 2009.

Between 1988 and 2006, ten multinationals with headquarters in France and facilities in Romania signed international framework agreements (Danone, Accor, Carrefour, Club Méditerranée, Renault, EDF, Rhodia, Lafarge, PSA and France Télécom). In 2010, GDF-Suez also signed an international framework agreement. The outcomes were uneven, however, and the Romanian unions became cautious about signing them. Wage-earners at subsidiaries of European firms with a presence in Romania were represented on European works councils. A law on the establishment, organisation and functioning of such councils was adopted in 2005. It entered into force on 1 January 2007.

At the same time, Western countries were helping Romania make the transition to a market economy, promoting the development of a civil society supposedly in favour of the establishment of democratic processes. Numerous associations were created and benefited from Europe's generosity, which has withered since Romania joined the EU. As European subsidies for associations have dried up, civil society is finding it difficult to act. It is also felt in some quarters that democracy was somehow granted to the Romanians, but without them acquiring 'people's sovereignty' (Heemeryck 2006). Whatever the case, the associations and trade union organisations pursue different goals, each following their own path, and the associations appear exceptionally involved in life at work.

At the national level, with the end of the communist societies in Eastern Europe, many trade union organisations were restructured. After the Romanian trade union confederation was dissolved in 1990, a slew of new trade unions were created. Representativeness requirements led to the consolidation of five confederations. They are all affiliated with the ETUC and the International Trade Union Confederation (ITUC). On joining the ETUC in the 1990s, they benefited from training that allowed them to adopt the approaches of Western European trade union organisations long before

Romania joined the EU, and from European subsidies (Pilat 2007). A number also joined European craft federations.

In terms of political orientation, Romania's trade union organisations tend to be either social democratic [Fratia, National Trade Unions Block (BNS)] or Christian democratic [Democratic Trade Union Confederation of Romania (CSDR), National Trade Union Confederation (Cartel ALFA)]. Meridian is said to be influenced by the cooperative sector. It is not unheard of for trade union leaders to invoke these alignments for political purposes. This has made them an object of much criticism and affected social dialogue in particular, for they have more dealings with the state than with tripartite structures.

Since union membership was no longer obligatory, the unions haemorrhaged members in the early 1990s. Romania is, nevertheless, one of the European countries in which the rate of unionisation remained high (roughly 35 per cent), especially in manufacturing (Fulton 2009). Other sources note a rate of unionisation of 50–60 per cent in manufacturing and over 75 per cent in the public sector.[2] The number of union sections is steadily rising, but union membership is practically non-existent in newly established companies.

Dacia has a different trade union structure; there is only one union, the SAD (Dacia automobile union), which was founded in 1990 and is a member of the Metal Workers' Federation within the BNS. The SAD has more members than any other trade union in Romania. Violaine, Delteil and Patrick Dieuaide (2008) suggest that the union structure organised by activity reinforces the management structure introduced by senior management. The SAD's power is bolstered by the fact that its ranks include Dacia employees and those of first-tier suppliers. Its main role is to negotiate the collective work agreements with Dacia and the suppliers. It has 10,000 members at Dacia and 4,000 among the suppliers. After the spring 2008 strike, membership is reported to have risen to 16,000, including 6,500 women (trade union source).

At Renault's French sites, the trade union balance has shifted. The CGT became the predominant trade union in the 1990s but saw its influence erode as the working-class population shrank. The *Confédération générale des cadres* (CGC), the CFDT and *Force ouvrière* (FO) have taken over joint responsibility for workforce representation. At the same time, all trade union organisations have seen their local union structures falter and lose members (Freyssinet et al. 1995). In 2008, the CFDT took the chair of the world committee, succeeding FO. In 2009, having campaigned actively at the grassroots level, the CGT again started to win local craft elections.

As far as Renault is concerned, the substance of the dialogue between Romanian and French trade union organisations changed in the 1990s. All the unions have had to deal with the multinational's strategy of establishing itself in countries where labour costs are low. They have a long-term common interest in allowing the poorest countries to 'catch up' socially, so as to limit social dumping, but in the short term, especially since the onset of the economic crisis, wage-earners are in competition with each other.

The signing of the Renault international framework agreement—along with other French, Belgian and Spanish trade union organisations—in 2004 was seen as symbolising a step forward in industrial relations. For all French trade union organisations, the unionisation of wage-earners whose employment status is poorly protected (employees, subcontractors, subsidiaries, temporary staff, etc.) remains one of the main unresolved issues.

Modernisation of the production facilities involved acceptance by the Romanian trade union leaders of a socio-political compromise. They consented to the lay-offs of the 1990s, which affected mainly less-skilled workers (Ost 2009); in other East European countries, the lay-offs reportedly 'suited' the trade unionists (Ost 2009). At the grassroots level, they developed a form of traditional authority based on the largesse they dispensed and regular wage increases. They emerged from the trade union organisations that were recreated in the early 1990s and are seen as part of the legacy of the past. As one Dacia engineer put it, '*Trade unions here aren't real unions like in France. We grew up with communism and things don't change just like that. Here the rule was: you work and you obey. You don't say anything because of the Securitate'*.

THE ROLE OF THE RENAULT GROUP COMMITTEE

The relationships between the Romanian and French trade unions basically take place at the levels of the confederation and occupational federations. The CES has offered training programs to Romanian trade unionists. Since the beginning of the economic crisis, through conference sessions and working groups, the FEM (to which seven French federations and three Romanian federations are affiliated) and the International Metalworkers' Federation (IMF) have worked to bring trade unionists together and inform them about social movements, bargaining in a market economy and a common strategy for fighting social dumping

At both the CFDT and the CGT, metalworker's federations have developed links with their Romanian colleagues in the form of information exchanges, work meetings, etc. These federations were engaged in the Renault-Dacia strike. They were physically present in Romania; they collected money from the French workers from all occupational and regional sections (for example, the CGT metalworkers' federation gave 27,000 euros to SAD) and disseminated news about the strike through the French media.

Relations between trade union organisations are institutionalised in the Renault Group Committee, which is a representative body of Renault workers worldwide established in 2000 in the wake of the European group committee. It receives information on the group's business activity, financial situation, future plans and employment projections. It is well informed about the group's economic prospects for the years ahead. Members from the Renault Group Committee represent their national trade unions. The committee has 34 titular members and 5 observers. Ten are members of a restricted committee, including, since 2007, the Romanian representative, according to whom the committee's value lies in the information provided on the group's strategy. Indeed, the committee appears to be one of the means used by management to persuade the trade unionists to act 'strategically': the information made available to it provides little indication of the processes that have been initiated. The trade unionists were mere spectators as the multinational expanded in ways that seemed inexorable. Even when the issues were jobs and social dumping, the group committee managed to maintain inter-union contact. According to the CGT representatives, an additional concern was to make trade unionists with no tradition of democratic trade unionism aware of points of view other than those of the multinational's management.

The Renault Group Committee is an important instrument of trade union socialisation at the international level. The established relationships are, in fact, based on historical links—for example, CGT metalworkers with other trade unions, particularly with Renault workers in Brazil. These relationships are also made possible by the strategic position the officials of the group committee hold. It is the group committee office that is in charge of welcoming new affiliates and collecting information on working conditions and wages in different countries. Members have access to the financial resources they need to make site visits. Thus in March 2007, when Romania entered the EU and a dispute about the collective agreement began, representatives from the CFDT, FO and CGT went to Pitesti in order to express their 'trade union solidarity'. Following their visit, they reported to the group committee on the problems they had observed, notably those concerning health and safety. The CFDT was concerned about the Romanian issues, on which their leaders followed up. By the end of 2008, FEM and IFM gave training sessions, which the Renault group committee organised for its membership.

A further issue arose with respect to Romania, where direct clashes between wage-earners and employers were unknown, namely the need to reshape industrial relations. The state, headed by the Communist Party, had been the regulator, and the employers one emanation thereof. And, as Thomas Lowit (1979) highlighted, the trade union organisation restricted any collective action it felt might escape its control.

THE STRIKE: BORROWED FEATURES
AND AN INDELIBLE LEGACY

Industrial action in Romania climaxed in 1999, affecting over one million workers. The number of strikes and participants then reduced to 60,300 people in 2007, as other forms of conflict took their place. Wages topped the list of demands, followed by restructuring and collective agreements and working conditions and hours (Descolonges 2011; Ciutacu 2009).

In Romania, strikes are governed by the 2003 Constitution. A strike can be called only if all other means of conciliation have failed. The employer must be given a 48-hour notice. The strike can have no aim other than defence of workers' economic interests and may not be used for political ends. Breaches of procedure render the strike unlawful, and this obviously has a bearing on strike recognition. The data therefore reflect only strikes recognised as legal, or 4 per cent of the total (Boboc and Calavrezo 2010).

After Renault bought Dacia, the disputes of the early 2000s reflected resistance to lay-offs and the reorganisation of work. The spring 2008 strike unexpectedly mushroomed. It went beyond the ritualised annual strikes called during wage negotiations. Called by the SAD—whose strategic approach we have underscored—we believe it is evidence more of a 'hybrid identity' than trade union 'revitalisation' (Meardi 2007). Indeed, it borrowed issues and expanded the repertory of action, while at the same time extending the possible duration of collective action.

Europe expressed solidarity. The talk was of a 'European strike', and it was even said that the strike was taking place before the gaze of Europe. The strike had a particular resonance in France. In a message affirming its '*support for the wage demands of Dacia workers in Romania*', the bureau of the Renault Group Committee (on which four French trade union organisations were represented alongside Spanish, Belgian and Korean unions) took the view that the volume of output and the '*efforts made*' should give rise to '*wage changes*'.

In a social context riven by tensions, warning strikes took place in the public sector and at three railroad companies. At Dacia, a daily two-hour strike started on 14 March 2008, timed to coincide with the annual wage bargaining round. After this warning strike, management raised its initial proposal of a 10 per cent pay increase to 12 per cent, or 32 euros per month. The trade union organisation considered that offer an '*insult*'. The workers felt that the economic situation worked in their favour—Dacia was said to have made profits of over 300 million euros in the previous two years—and asked for a '*more equitable distribution*' of the benefits. According to management, that demand was unrealistic, as the profits were insufficient to cover the losses of previous financial years or the major investment made by Renault to put Dacia back on its feet.

The wage negotiations having failed, Dacia's factory workers launched an 18-day strike that got them what they wanted on many fronts. Their main demands related to wages. The increase they were demanding—an initial 60 per cent, followed by 40 per cent—has to be viewed in the light of the Romanian socio-economic context. A list of 14 demands was drawn up, the most important being the payment of a general wage increase of 150 euros.

Adopting a time-honoured approach—as we saw earlier—Dacia management contested the strike's lawfulness, citing respect for collective bargaining procedures and the number of strikers and turned to the Argès commercial court to have it stopped. Under Article 40 of the Constitution, a strike can be organised only once all other avenues for settling the dispute have been exhausted. Article 40 further stipulates that the decision to strike has to be approved by half of the employees, and, according to management, the number of strikers was less than half of wage-earners. In response, the trade union collected the signatures of 7,664 Dacia workers who said they supported the strike.

The question of the strike's lawfulness was followed especially closely by Romanian public opinion. The court decision would reflect on the Romanian legal system, whose corrupt nature is widely admitted and whose decisions are frequently contested. On the sixteenth day of the strike, having deferred a decision twice, the Argès court ruled that the strike was lawful. The day after the court handed down its decision, the trade unionists proclaimed: '*The judges have upheld the Law. This shows that the people are qualified and that they represent the future of Romania*'.

The strike having thus been declared legitimate and, following a public meeting of several thousand people in the square at Pitesti, Dacia's management made another offer. It announced an increase of about 100 euros gross, in two instalments, and an annual bonus of about 25 euros. In addition, the workers undertook to make up for some of the lost output, estimated at 17,000 Logans. Seventy per cent of the employees consulted agreed.

The staging of the public meeting in Pitesti testified to the indelible legacy of collective action and to numerous borrowed features. The meeting played out against the backdrop of two kinds of symbols: political and national. Before the first speeches, the *Internationale* rang out for ten minutes in the background. It was followed by the national anthem, and the crowd listened in deferent silence. When the meeting broke up, the national anthem was replaced by a patriotic song asserting, '*We are Romanians*' that was picked up *mezzo voce* by the departing participants (Note: Dacia is the name of the actual partial territory of Romania. This territory was conquered by the Roman Empire in the 2nd century AD; Romanised Dacians are said to be the ancestors of today's Romanians). The *Internationale* could be understood as both an echo of the past and a reference to the future, expressed during the speeches.

The strikers' occupation of a public space was a legitimate act since the gathering had been authorised by the mayor of Pitesti. Should it be seen as a rejection of the violence that had marked the revolt at the Brasov tractor factory, on 15 November 1988—which resulted in the sacking of the town hall and worker repression—or the miners' demonstrations of the 1990s? The crowd remained on its feet, surrounded by watchful, calm policemen, in a square undergoing construction, with paving stones an arm's length away. The speakers held forth from the balcony of the cultural centre.

The crowd hung on every word, it was joyful. People shouted their own slogans and raised their fists in the air. There were many young people and women. Flags and banners were waved, bearing the names of the trade unions present. The media had been invited—trade unionists from different countries spoke to each other before the cameras. A poem written by the strikers was read by a car body repairman. He was loudly applauded. Differences in status were invoked more than once. The presence of trade unionists from equipment suppliers was mentioned ('*They're Dacia's suppliers, they support us. (. . .) This is our family. Our motto: ALL FOR ONE, ONE FOR ALL*' [sic]), but they did not speak. Noisemakers were rattled, small horns tooted. No leaflets were handed out.

It was said that the strike should be expanded into a general social movement. However, the strike could not go on. In 2008, Orthodox Easter was celebrated on May 1. In Romania, where almost 90 per cent of the population are practising Orthodox Christians, Easter is widely celebrated. It is accompanied by numerous rituals, in particular agricultural ones, that require money.

Certain demands were *de facto* excluded. It is true that the strike was sparked by the failure of the annual wage negotiations and, in the European economic situation, wage demands certainly resonated. However, nothing was said of the precarious nature of many jobs; some allusions were made to working conditions ('*The workers say they do not agree to working in four teams*', public meeting), but not to the pace of the work, in other words, its organisation. Lastly, when it came to the role of the multinationals, responsibility was placed on politicians.

The Pitesti demonstration also served as a platform for other disputes and the issues they raised. For example, a strike at the Mangalia shipyard reflected sensitivity to collective action against bureaucratic practices: '*We went on strike and the mentality at Mangalia (shipyard) changed. Everyone was asking: what's the union doing? Not just the leaders, but the whole union. Because the leaders can't act on their own. We can only act, defeat the employer, if we're united. UNITE!*'

Expressed not just as a slogan—*unite* was shouted out twenty times—but also in the fabric of the statements ('*The workers assembled here are the future of Romania's unions*'), united action was a predominant theme. It was underscored in particular by the presence throughout the strike of the BNS and Cartel ALFA confederations, each of which was close to a different political grouping.

The strikers received many forms of support, nationally and internationally. That support was impressive in its scope and diversity. It was not limited to one corporation or country. Public craft unions, post office workers' unions, teachers' unions—where the rate of unionisation is high—voiced support on numerous occasions. Delegations from trade unions at private companies, subsidiaries of the multinationals, were present on more than one occasion, especially those from the new Ford subsidiary, which had been bought two weeks earlier. Mittal employees were present at the public meetings organised by the strikers. Certain messages of sympathy broadened the themes of the strike. For example, the teachers from Argès County, who had themselves been on strike for 20 weeks, said they had not only wage-related demands but also demands relating to the '*conditions of the child*', thereby extending a hand to the many associations in that field.

Hostility was expressed in the same breath as the demand for genuine '*European citizenship*'. It is true that European trade union solidarity was strongly expressed and communicated to the strikers, who were able to position their action against a European backdrop of wage-related demands. The European demonstration in Ljubljana, which took place during the strike, and the speech by ETUC Secretary-General John Monks referring to the strike were announced to the strikers gathered during the public meeting in Pitesti.

> '*One very important thing, for the first time we have experienced the solidarity of European and international unions. We thank them. There has been a huge demonstration in Ljubljana. A National Block representative was there. We prepared a message in your name. It was read by John Monks. For the first time, the name of the Dacia autoworkers' union was mentioned in Ljubljana. All European workers now know that Dacia exists. UNITE.*' (trade unionist, public meeting).

The Renault group French trade union organisations expressed solidarity in messages and declarations. The CGT attended the public meetings in Mioveni and Pitesti, the CFDT was present in Pitesti. Their representatives were visibly moved. Both organisations held collections at Renault sites in France for the Dacia strikers. The French media gave extensive coverage to the strike. Part of the background to this interest was that, in 2005, the majority of the French voted *against* the ratification of the treaty establishing a constitution for Europe. Nonetheless, the treaty was ratified by the parliaments of 13 of the 17 countries concerned and entered into force in 2006.

UNDERSTANDING THE STRIKE

The conduct of the strike highlighted the way in which the trade union organisation and its members remained scarred by the past, while at the same time adopting certain strategies borrowed from European trade unions. Both aspects can be seen in the subjects raised and the construction of a system of opposition. They highlight the importance of worker representation in mobilisation. Four are discussed below. They associate the territorial dimension (Europe) with doubts about global industrial organisation.

Industrial Know-How vs. Relocation

From the start of the strike, Dacia management raised the spectre of relocation, hinting that factories could be opened in Russia and India, where the Renault group already had a presence. Many of those involved saw this as a form of blackmail, and it helped make the strike a prime example of the effects of the multinationals' opportunistic policies of relocating production facilities in countries with low labour costs. It goaded the region's stakeholders, who were fully aware of the region's dependency on industrial installations, into speaking out:

> '*I don't think Renault will leave for another country. They're blackmailing us. But if it did, the workers would leave, too. The repercussions would be serious. And Renault would also lose its skilled workforce.*' (Elected municipal official).

In addition to demanding recognition of their work through a wage increase, the strikers wanted recognition of their skills and acknowledgement of the training they had received and of their capacity to adapt to organisational change. The previous, sequentially organised production system had been replaced by a project-based mode of organisation that brought together French and Romanian technicians and engineers. In a production setting, this project-based system gave precedence to the rate of output rather than to how well the new method had been learned or recognition of Romanian know-how (Angelescou 2008).

The fact that engineers and technicians took part in the strike and were present at the Pitesti meeting was emphasised. Supervisors, for their part, had been asked by the company's management to stay on the sidelines, and they remained in their offices.

Social Justice vs. Europe

The strike was ignited by the Romanians' general demand for a higher standard of living. Since Romania's entry into the EU, its citizens have been better able to gauge their plight against that of other Europeans and to find cause for revolt. A comparison of autoworkers' wages sent out shockwaves (400 euros per month for a highly skilled worker in Romania, 2800 euros for his counterpart in France).

From strikers to institutional officials, all the social players made references to the values of justice and dignity:

> '*For Dacia's unionists, two factors contributed to the situation. The first was pay. The second was a lack of respect.*' '*If we are not united, we won't manage to win rights and respect at Renault.*' (public meeting).

The French trade unionists, who were standing beside the speakers on the balcony of the cultural centre, focused on the theme of social justice: '*We don't want a two-speed social Europe*' (CFDT). '*We know what your working conditions are. All Europe's workers should have equal pay for equal work*' (CGT).

Trust vs. Mistrust

The strikers attributed the difficulties as much to Romania's political and industrial leaders as to the multinational's management. The question took on a national dimension, for Romania had been chosen by many multinationals precisely because of its low labour costs, but also because of its potential for a rapid rise in skills and, by Renault, because of past investments and the inducements offered by the Romanian Government. The strike was followed especially closely by the Romanian media, which more than once relayed concerns about industrial relocation.

The role of the various state bodies was queried, for they seemed to carry little weight in the face of a multinational's decisions. There was no doubt, however, about municipal support for the strikers. The mayors of Mioveni and Pitesti explicitly expressed their support, and each in turn manifested it tangibly by authorising a meeting in a public place. The pre-election context in which the strike took place was not insignificant, and it attracted attention from across the political spectrum. Opposition to and reservations about the strike were expressed by political officials close to the government.

National Identity vs. International Action

In some respects, the *national* character of the Dacia strike is important. Indeed, because there is no European strike law, national particularities, as we have seen, take centre stage.

Another *national* dimension of the strike was the expression of xenophobic sentiments. Foreign multinationals, the French employers and the Romanian employers and governments were repeatedly castigated as thieves. The threats of relocation fomented fear and exacerbated the feeling of injustice. Paradoxically, the call for unity was permanent and rubbed shoulders with the perceived injustices and racist words.

The image of thieves robbing the country of its industrial heritage and the mobilisation of xenophobic sentiments echoed the campaigns conducted during the Ceausescu era and revived in the early 1990s. Certain slogans expressed during the public meeting were almost post-colonial in nature, describing industrial leaders as 'white slaves': '*The French-Romanians, the Korean-Romanians are dangerous.*'

CONCLUSION: HOW HAVE RELATIONS BETWEEN ROMANIAN AND FRENCH TRADE UNIONISTS CHANGED?

The spring 2008 strike, which took place one year after Romania's entry into the EU and after Renault-Dacia had enjoyed two profit-making years, introduced cracks in an apparently stable socio-political compromise. It brought to light two major points: the legacy of the past was very much alive and collective action had possibilities.

In terms of their demands, the outcome of the strike was relatively satisfactory for the Dacia workers. At the political level, the government authorities were at the forefront and ruled on the lawfulness of the strike. As far as the multinational was concerned, the strike did not so much call the production relationship into question as bring to light a mode of work organisation that took no account of local know-how.

There was, nevertheless, something exceptional about this strike: it symbolised both the injustices of the European construct and what happens when a multinational moves to a country with low labour costs. In France and in Europe in general, it was seen as symptomatic of the inequalities between EU member states, and it lay open to question the disparities within the European 'social model'. By aiming to play social catch-up, the dispute became part of the European system of regulation, while maintaining an ideological background of social transformation.

The conduct of the strike was characterised by a number of paradoxical features: the legacy of the past, 'post-colonial' speeches rejecting foreign predators and slogans intended to unite. The negotiating process remained opaque, but the public meetings, the inter-occupational activities, the presence of the suppliers' employees, the range of occupational groups mobilised and the presence of French trade unionists from the CFDT and the CGT were evidence of the possibilities.

Considered at the European level, the strike can be said to have helped change the practices of collective unity. At a time when the nature of disputes is being reconfigured in an increasingly differentiated world, the Renault-Dacia strike, on the contrary, showed the possibilities for mobilisation founded on shared, if constantly conflicting, interests. What came of this? In 2009, the French trade union organisations asked the group's management to allow a second Romanian representative to sit on the group committee. However, other questions were raised that go beyond that institutional measure.

The communist past and the post-communist legacy are often invoked in academic work. It is our view that the East-West inter-union cooperation relationship must be considered from another angle. It is somewhat naïve to think that only the trade union organisations of eastern Europe are bound by their past. The opposite is also true, but there the ties claim to be normative. On the one hand, the compromise reached between the SAD leaders and the company management held and, accepting the variables put forward by S. Crowley, we can speak of an 'alliance' that produced a number of benefits, in particular in terms of pay.

However, the trade union fragmentation that is characteristic of the French situation was replicated, in this case, at the international level. The historical proximity of the CGT to the communist party played against it, in that the SAD's leaders did not wish to establish ties likely to affect their image on the question. This is illustrated by the failed attempt of the CGT leader to visit the Dacia trade unionists in May 2010. Conversely, it worked in favour of ties with other unions. But what could result other than occasional convergence when, as we saw earlier, the SAD ignored the least skilled workers, whereas the French trade union organisations felt they had to include everyone, no matter what their job status? Moreover, if we spoke earlier of a hybrid identity, it was also to emphasise that there are possibilities for greater openness within the SAD.

Their assiduous association with trade union structures at the occupational (FEM) and territorial levels (ETUC) helped the Romanian trade unionists adapt to European thought processes. In periods of social tension over jobs, the European trade unions have a major role to play in uniting and informing. However, the Dacia case would tend to show that interunion cooperation is established on an industrial basis in an ad hoc manner, whereas, over time, territorial or federal trade union structures offer greater possibilities. Thus a trade union organisation, such as Cartel ALFA, kept the requisite distance from the government and political parties. It developed a critical discourse and a new capacity to mobilise, choosing its words with particular care on industrial investment (Apostoiu 2009) and developing relations with the trade union organisations of the EU concerned by the migration of Romanian workers.

NOTES

1. These surveys could not have been conducted without the assistance of Maria Constantinescu and Cornel Constantinescu, professors of sociology at Pitesti University.
2. Eurofound.europa.eu/eira/country/romania.pdf

REFERENCES

Apostoiu, L. (2009), 'The role of trade unions in fighting the effects of crisis', *South-East Europe Review*, 4, 513–516.

Angelescou, G. (2008), 'Solenza, la pré-Logan ou comment l'entreprise roumaine Dacia a appris à développer les projets en mode concourant?', 16th GERPISA International Colloquium, Turin, Italy, June 18–20.

Boboc, C., and Calavrezo, O. (2010), 'Roumanie. Une crise profonde et un dialogue social difficile', *Chronique internationale de l'IRES*, 127(November), 184–198.

Ciutacu, C. (2009), *Romania: Industrial Relations Profile*, Bucharest: Institute of National Economy, Romanian Academy.

Crowley, S. (2004), 'Explaining Labor Weakness in Post-Communist Europe: Historical Legacies and Comparative Perspective', *East European Politics and Societies*, 18(3), 394–429.

Delteil, V., and Dieuaide, P. (2008), 'Le conflit Renault-Dacia en Roumanie. Quand le local et l'européen ont partie liée', *Revue de la régulation*, 3–4, 2nd semester.

Descolonges, M. (2011), *Des travailleurs à protéger. L'action collective au sein de la sous-traitance*, Paris: Hermann-Adapt.

Freyssinet, M. (2007), 'Renault 1992–2007, Mondialisation et quelques doutes', paper presented at 15th GERPISA International Colloquium, Paris, June 20–22.

Freyssinet, M., Fridenson, P., and Pointet J.-M. (1995), 'Les données économiques et sociales de Renault. Les années 70 et 80', paper presented at 13th GERPISA International Colloquium, Paris, June 16–17.

Fulton, L. (2009), *La représentation des travailleurs en Europe*. Brussels: Labour Research Department, ETUI (online).

Heemeryck, A. (2006), 'Gouvernance démocratique, État et ONG en Roumanie: quelques éléments de clarification autour de l'introduction d'une loi de transparence', *L'homme et la société*, 159, 175–190.

Korkut, U. (2006), 'Entrenched Elitism in Trade Unions in Poland and Romania: An Explanation for the Lack of Union Strength and Success?', *Economic and Industrial Democracy*, 27(1), 67–104.

Layan, J.-B. (2003), 'L'intérêt stratégique des périphéries du système automobile européen', paper presented at the 11th GERPISA International Colloquium, Paris, June 11–13.

Lochard, Y., and Pernot. J.-M. (2010), '2010, année terrible. Les relations sociales à l'épreuve de l'austérité', *Chronique internationale de l'IRES*, 127, 40–55.

Lowit, Th. (1979), 'Y a-t-il des États en Europe de l'Est?', *Revue française de sociologie*, April–June, 431–466.

Meardi, G. (2007), 'Multinationals in the New EU Member States and the Revitalisation of Trade Unions', *Debatte*, 15(1), 177–193.

Ost, D. (2009), 'The End of Postcommunism. Trade Unions in Eastern Europe's Future', *East European Politics and Societies*, 23(1), 13–33.

Pilat, N.-M. (2007), 'Towards the Europeanization of Trade Unions in Post-Communist Romania', *South-East Europe Review*, 2, 95–107.

Part II
National Trade Unions: Shaping New Forms of Solidarity

6   Building Transnational Unionism

Australian Transport Maritime Unions in the World

Peter Fairbrother

The global context in which unions now operate is complex, multi-faceted and increasingly involves cross-border activity. For unions, this changing terrain has prompted debate about the ways they should organise, the role and place of global unions in these processes and whether cross-border alliances and unions are feasible (Fairbrother and Hammer 2005; Tattersall 2007: 170). Complicating these considerations, government policy and practice remains a central reference for the way that many unions organise and operate.

The question is, under what circumstances can unions develop forms of transnational unionism? A range of literature examines the external and contextual forces that shape the way that unions organise and operate transnationally, at workplace and other levels (Cohen 2006; Bronfenbrenner 2007). Here, the emphasis is on the organisational arrangements and capacities of unions. Nonetheless, it is also frequently noted that unions remain bound by conceptions of unionism as nation-state based, even when cross-border alliances are established (Myconos 2005; Tattersall 2007). There, however, are a few examples of unions attempting to transform the way they organise and operate, specifically in relation to the linkage between the local and the global, and as part of a process of forging forms of transnational unionism.

The argument here is that transnational unionism rests on a series of relationships that involve union organisation, capacity and purpose; unions are both in and of a set of multi-level relationships in a transnational world. These relationships are power relationships, and it is in this context that unions, as transnational actors, organise and operate. Two faces of power are evident. First, unions organise and operate as participative or hierarchical organisations, with representative or delegated structures and arrangements. Second, unions as collective organisations are potentially in a position to exercise power in ways that are distinct from the exercise of power as individuals (Lukes 2005). These features of transnational unionism are the focus of this chapter. To explore these relations, a study is presented of three transport unions that cover workers in the Port of Melbourne, and particularly the Maritime Union of Australia, Victoria Branch (MUAV), all of which are part of the International Transport Federation (ITF). The purpose is to trace out the complex relations linking the local and the international and to develop an explanation for it. In this respect, the ways in which transnational unionism can become a feature of individual union activity are explored and analysed.

The paper comprises five sections. In the first, a brief review of debates about transnational unionism is presented. This is followed by an outline of the approach taken in studying one set of union relationships. Third, a picture of the complex relations linking the local and the international are presented. In the fourth section an assessment explains this history. Finally, a brief conclusion is presented.

THEORETICAL CONSIDERATIONS

Many workers now find themselves in positions where their livelihoods and, indeed, the quality of their lives are affected directly or indirectly by international developments relating to work and employment relations as well as the security of employment. In such circumstances, it is not surprising that they look to their unions for respite. Occasionally, workers and their unions are tempted to respond in defensive rather than pro-active ways, in other cases, unions and their members take a more offensive stance.

The writing on trade unions in a global world has four strands to it. One strand of analysis focuses on local action by unions in the face of decisions or policies that originate from elsewhere. This may involve a closure, a set of policies that negatively impact on the workforce or changes to the terms and conditions of employment to the detriment of current employees (Gunawardana 2007; Juravich and Bronfenbrenner 1999). In these circumstances, many unions take steps to address such challenges, sometimes successfully, sometimes not. A second strand of analysis considers the way in which unions may respond to developments and events internationally, often in solidaristic ways and elaborating policies and campaigns for change (Clawson 2003; Beasley 1996; Kirkby 2008). Third, another strand of analysis focuses on the way in which unions may reach out to like unions and organisations to develop responses to corporate or government decisions and policy (Turnbull 2007; Stevis and Boswell 2007). Finally, there is a small literature on the ways that unions may begin to forge concrete alliances with each other and, in some cases merge, to create cross-border unions (Tattersall 2007; Gekara 2009).

The argument here rests on an assumption about the nature and character of trade unionism. Unions are a voluntary form of organisation that is rooted in the labour-capital relation. Such relations include the direct control of labour within labour processes, constituted over time through managerial regulation and diverse forms of governance and as a commodity within labour markets. These relations are not confined to the state, nor are they exclusively regulated by the state. Rather, they are part of a complex array of national and international relations.

These relations are complex, involving the exercise of power within and by trade unions. Increasingly, trade unions face an asymmetrical distribution of power between employers and unions at an international level. This recomposition draws attention to the processes of restructuring and reorganisation that are taking place. As part of such processes, it is necessary to consider the way labour-capital relations are being recomposed at the point of production and service. Such processes of change have implications for wage systems, changing forms of work and employment, the articulation of ideologies of management and the changing role of the state. Unions often find themselves in situations where their bargaining power is compromised by the remoteness of decision-making, the competing interests between workplaces and the segmentation of representation within the workplace (Coe *et al.* 2008). Nonetheless, while such experiences at a workplace level may be relatively common, it is also the case that unions operate at a number of different levels and thus can meet the challenge of globalisation by drawing on resources and exercising capacities in a multi-level way.

Such possibilities draw attention to the ways in which unions organise and operate. In general, unions face pressures towards representative forms of governance and towards ensuring the basis of participation and membership involvement. This tension is the conundrum of union democracy (Fairbrother 1984; Lipset et al. 1956). It draws attention to the question of leadership at local, national and international levels and has been addressed in different ways by many writers (Hyman 1979 and 2007; Lipset *et al.* 1956; Martin 1968). On the one hand, actors as leaders at different levels of the union may find themselves constrained by history, experience and position, focusing on limiting repertoires of action (Michels 1962; Hyman 1979). On the other hand, leaders at different levels may be able to break through these self-limiting constraints and open up possibilities for the union and for themselves as leaders.

One way of gaining an understanding of these dynamics is to consider how the exercise of power is worked out in relation to the union as a collective organisation. Much of the recent writing on power and unions has focused on structural and associational power, developing an analysis about the exercise of power in relation to the collective form of organisation embodied by trade unions (Wright 2000; Silver 2003; Anner 2013; and Lévesque *et al.* 2013). Structural power refers to the position and location of workers within employment and work relations. Depending on their position, these workers may either be susceptible to employer pressures and demands or seek to assert a counter position or indeed acquiesce. In many ways, such a response depends on whether and under what circumstances unions can exercise agency and thus represent their members via campaigns, bargaining and so on (Rainnie *et al.* 2007). This reference to agency draws attention to associational power, the other face of these relations. Such power refers to collective organisation and action as a way of harnessing and focusing on the capacity of workers to resist and to assert themselves as members of a collective organisation, a union. As Lévesque and Murray argue (2010: 333, 335–336), the investigation of associational power involves a consideration of 'power resources and strategic capabilities'. However, while they investigate the dimensions of such resources and capacities at a workplace level, the analysis here extends the argument to show how these capacities often involve a set of mutually reciprocal relations across levels within a union.

Thus, while the focus of much study is at the workplace and local level, exploring the way that trade unions have organised, mobilised and operated in conditions of economic decline and insecurity of employment, it is also necessary to consider the broader context within which unions organise and operate. Thus, the focus is on developing an analysis of trade unions with reference to the local, regional and international dimensions of transnational unionism. In this respect, the framework is relational rather than institutional; the purpose is to provide an account of transnational unionism that takes into account the diverse forms of organisation and activity that make for transnational unionism.

THE STUDY

The primary focus is on the relation between one global union, the global union federation (GUF) that is the International Transport Federation (ITF) and a local union, the Maritime Union of Australia, Victorian Branch (MUAV). It examines how this union and two associated unions, the Transport Workers Union (TWU) and the Rail, Tram and Bus Union (RTBU) took steps to initiate forms of transnational trade unionism. It involves the collection of data in Melbourne, Victoria as well as elsewhere in Australia and in London at the head office of the ITF.

The data for the paper come from a variety of sources. First, the core database comprises a series of key informant interviews from 2004 to 2010 with 35 different respondents, involving 46 interviews altogether. Informants were selected according to position within the port or the union. Interviews were cross-checked with other interviewees, documentary sources and observation of union activity. A number of these informants have been interviewed several times, as the relationships within the union were explored, as well as relations with other unions with whom members worked on transnational questions. An additional eight interviews were conducted with ITF head office staff in London, including one interview involving five different staff members. While this material constitutes the core of the research data, it is complemented by documentary materials, including union publications. To a limited extent, we also conducted observational data collection at union offices, on the port side, in public houses and on the street. This material has been written up in the form of field-notes. In addition, we conducted internet searches of company and union material.

FROM LOCAL TO GLOBAL AND BACK AGAIN

The Maritime Union of Australia (MUA) is a recent union, founded in 1993 from a merger between the Seamen's Union of Australia and the Waterside Workers' Federation. Both these unions date back to the nineteenth century in one form or another, with the Seamen's Union of Australia founded in 1872, and the Sydney Wharf Labourer's Union in the same year. The two unions in their modern form date from the early twentieth century, the Waterside Workers Federation (1902) and the Seamen's Union of Australia (1906). These unions have a long history of struggle, representation on ships and wharves and international engagement. They each have contested political histories and a history of violence and struggle typical of this form of work. With the establishment of the MUA, the membership coverage included port workers (services and stevedoring), offshore workers, deep-sea divers and shipping workers. This diverse membership in part arose out of amalgamations with smaller unions, such as the Firemen and Deckhands and the Federated Shipping Clerks' Union, as well as the major merger in 1993.

Currently, the MUA is a small but prominent union. It represents around 11,000 members. It is organised into nine branches covering Australia and has its national headquarters in Sydney, Australia. Many notable leaders have developed out of the union and its forebears, including one prime minister. The union has a strong international commitment, expressed in solidarity actions and active involvement in the ITF (Lockwood 1987; Beasely 1996; Kirkby 2008).

A Local Branch

The Port of Melbourne moves around 36 per cent of Australia's container trade, 6500 containers on average each day. It is used by 42 different shipping lines as well as a number of other general cargo carriers. The port is an important trading gateway handling an estimated $A58 billion in international trade and contributing around $A2.2 billion to the Victorian economy in 2008. The Port of Melbourne achieved 17 consecutive years of trade growth until 2008 and was back on track in 2010–2011, when it handled over 2.39 million container throughput, or 79.7 million revenue tonnes (Port of Melbourne Corporation 2011).

Two main stevedoring operators manage the container movement in the port, DP World (DPW) and Patricks Corporation. DPW has around 260 permanent employers and 100 permanent part-timers. Patricks has around 50 permanent employees, 50 permanent part-timers and 100 supplementary workers. The workforce is organised on the basis of casuals, allowing for adjustments to demand. The pool of permanent casuals is also known as permanent guaranteed wages (PGE) staff. They are retained on a set rate per week to make sure that they are available. Management usually recruits their permanent staff from this pool of labour. This procedure also allows for more flexibility because they are multi-skilled and can multi-task across the yard. At Patricks in 2009, the permanent part-timers earned a minimum of $A48,000 per annum, while there were two categories at DPW: one earning $A46,000 per annum and the second earning about $A28,000 per annum. On top of these basic rates, work teams have the opportunity to earn bonuses and related payment based on performance indicators. Other smaller stevedoring companies have 30 permanents and around 80 permanent part-timers with 60–80 supplementary workers. A smaller operator, Australian National Stevedores (ANS), which usually handles bulk goods has 12 permanents and about 10 permanent part-timers and 40 casual supplementary workers. In addition, there are other workers on the non-wharf side of the port.

Most of these workers are members of the MUA Victoria Branch, along with a range of workers from other smaller ports in Victoria. The Victoria Branch has 2,500 members, nearly 1,000 at the Melbourne Port itself. Casual employment is now a large part of the workforce and the union membership. The union meets with new staff at their induction and to date has been successful in recruiting most new starters. The union branch is organised around delegates, based on the work groups and shifts. These delegates constitute a committee, which deals with problems and takes up issues in the first instance. If matters cannot be resolved at the port level, the branch becomes involved. During the major negotiations on enterprise bargaining agreements, the branch leadership meets with the committee to formulate the claim and then subsequently to develop it. The committees are not limited to one port and are usually company based. The Patricks committee, for example, comprises 76 delegates from the whole country. Agreements are tiered, with Part A covering the whole country and Part C covering particularly ports. A variation takes place with the offshore oil and gas industry, mainly based in Victoria and West Australia and, hence, involving the West Australian branch and the Victoria branch.

A Local ITF Working Group

With two other unions connected with port work, the TWU and the RTBU, the MUA Victorian Branch established an ITF Working Group (for a full history, see Barton and Fairbrother 2009). In the latter part of 2004, each union proposed and agreed to the following motion:

> That this meeting congratulates the MUA, RTBU (Rail Division) and TWU initiative of forming the ITF Victorian Transport Union Working Group (VTUWG).
> The Integration of Logistics Transport through the establishment of multi modal transport companies is happening and the VTUWG is a logical step for our three unions to take. Noting that this is not an

amalgamation in any way shape or form, but a way for our unions to cooperate for the benefit of our members.

We fully support the principle of this working group ". . . to establish a cooperative working relationship for the benefit of maritime, rail, and road and air transport union members." Further, it seeks to uphold the charter of the ITF and identify and support the ideals, principles and campaigns of the ITF. (Maritime Union of Australia 2004)

This motion was agreed upon unanimously at an MUA members' meeting on 26 October 2004.

The coverage of these unions was broadly complementary. The TWU covers aviation, oil, waste management, gas, road transport, passenger vehicles and freight logistics. In 2008, it had 80,000 members across Australia with 21,955 in Victoria. The RTBU is an amalgamated union with 35,000 members organised into three divisions: rail, locomotive and tram and bus. Only the rail division, which covers staff such as signalers, station staff, customer service staff, workshops, shunters and administrative staff, became involved in the ITF Working Group in Victoria.

The ITF Working Group has its origins in the 1997/98 waterfront dispute centred on the MUA. Patricks Corporation in 1998, with government assistance, locked out and dismissed its 1,700 strong unionised (MUA) workforce and attempted to replace them with a non-unionised workforce. After extensive legal action, assisted by 'peaceful community assemblies' outside the wharf gates and an international boycott by the ITF of ships loaded by scab labour, the MUA workforce returned to their jobs. In this process, over half were made redundant or downgraded to casual status (Svensen 1998; Wiseman 1998). A central part of the strategy pursued by the Victorian Branch was to build an inter-union profile via the ITF.

The 1998 dispute provided the initial opportunity for union leaders to build an inter-union coalition, link up with each other and begin to define a pro-active approach to the types of corporate (and government) policies that led to the dispute (Hyman 2007: 198–99). The first steps were taken by the MUA and the ITF. Working closely with and under the auspices of the ITF, the MUA sought to internationalise the campaign, highlighting the way a seemingly narrowly focused dispute about the de-unionisation of cargo handling operations on the Australian coast (promoted by the National Farmer's Federation and supported by the conservative federal government) was in fact a dispute with international ramifications. In the ensuing events, there was supportive action from the International Longshore and Warehouse Union on the West Coast of the United States, protests by Japanese dockers and demonstrations in support of the MUA outside Australian embassies in Japan, Korea, India, the Philippines and Russia (Svensen 1998). These actions were organised by the ITF and their affiliates, often involving links and exchanges between local leaderships elsewhere and the MUA.

The Working Group was also a product of the connections that the RTBU had with the ITF and the way that legitimated the movement by all three unions to set up the Working Group. Briefly, the RTBU, as a predominantly public transport union, historically had very little connection with the GUFs; insofar as it did have an international sentiment, it was with the Public Services International, the GUF that covered public sector workers internationally. However, with privatisation of public transport, the acquisition of tram routes and related public transport by international consortia, including Connex (the French-based multinational transport company), and the increased development of Melbourne Port, the union learnt of the ITF. In 2003, in the middle of a dispute with Connex and at the instigation of the national secretary of the RTBU, the secretary of Inland Transport for the ITF contacted the Victorian RTBU leadership to offer support. Subsequently, he and the education officer for the ITF visited Melbourne and worked with the transport unions on transport-related matters. This connection provided the opportunity for the RTBU leadership to also reach out to the MUA, in relation to local matters.

Hence, in a variety of ways, both the MUA and other members of the Working Group, focused their activity within an international framework, as defined by the ITF. As stated by one of the union leaders:

> The integration of logistics, transport through the establishment of a multi-model transport company is happening and the [Working Group] is a logical step now for three unions to take. Noting that this is not an amalgamation in any way, shape or form but a way for our unions to co-operate for the benefit of our memberships. We fully support the principle of the working group to establish a co-operative working relationship for the benefit of Maritime Union, the Rail, Tram and Bus Union and the Transport Workers Union members and further it seeks to uphold the chart of the ITF and identify and support the ideals, principles and campaigns of the ITF. Members of the MUA fully support this initiative. (MUA Leader, June 2007)

The significance of the ITF in this respect is that by framing the remit of the Working Group in relation to the ITF, it conferred a legitimacy to this form of solidarity that overrode the previous polemical and partisan differences that had traditionally divided the unions.

The critical dimension in this process of coalition building was the question of organisation. A small number of leaders took the initiative to open up a new form of unionism, a 'logical development'. However, while it may be 'logical', it required effort, planning and commitment to a different way of doing things, thereby challenging prevailing power relations and laying the foundations for resistance (Carter et al. 2003). These union members (mainly branch officers and local delegates with a few members) focused recruitment drives on the precinct, delegates worked together and exchanged experiences across unions and with each other. These recruitment drives involved MUA and RTBU members recruiting road transport drivers into the TWU. They attended rallies and participated in other forms of support in relation to other Australian trade unionists and international ones. The leaders met with each other formally and informally, expressed support for each other and planned ways of approaching and dealing with sections of their unions who did not favour these developments.

The activist cadre worked together and exchanged views and experiences with each other; they learnt from each other. As stated by one MUA leader:

[Q]   Do local delegates get involved very much in the ITF type of activities?

[Interviewee]   Yeah. Well, that's probably where these meetings that we have, you know, in the precinct are more important, because it's the sort of sinking it down. It's no use just having us three meeting [the leaders of the unions] and not having it sinking down any further [to the activists and members in the port]. (June 2009)

The main period of activity was between 2004 and 2010, when the union leaderships sought to develop distinct ways of organising and operating as trade unionists. They took what seemed to be a logical development of both the solidaristic moment, symbolised by the 1998 maritime dispute, and the fragmented and parochial form of union organisation that had long characterised the logistics industry; they saw beyond the immediate and the mundane, through the prevailing forms of domination (Lukes 2005: 144–151). In turn, the ITF provided a legitimating rubric for the intersection between these two aspects of unionism. While historically there may be examples of like organisations, where unions come together and in *ad hoc* but ongoing ways attempt to create solidaristic ways of organising, this particular initiative was new for these trade union members. By 2010, however, the initial enthusiasm for the Working Group had begun to taper off, as the three unions began to focus more on their own specific concerns.

Nonetheless, the unions built a collective presence at the port. They developed a structured mutual interest coalition where the membership participated in activities together, irrespective of the particular union to which they belonged. Thus, this was not just the activity of particular individuals in one place at a moment in time; it was a process of building a form of trade union collectivity that went beyond the prevailing sovereign patterns of representation.

MOVING OUTWARDS

The MUA has a long history of engaging in solidaristic activity, with unions in Australia and also international unions. Within Australia, the parameters of engagement were set by the political divisions and relationships that have long characterised the Australian labour movement. This meant the cooperation and engagement were often on political rather than industrial lines. The three unions that comprised the Working Group have historically been at odds with each other, although there has long been political sympathy between sections of the RTBU and the MUA. The qualification in relation to these two unions is that, until relatively recently, the RTBU organised and operated within the state sector, organising public transport workers, whereas the MUA was dealing with the difficulties created by shipping companies and, more recently, the stevedoring companies.

During the 1990s, as globalisation became a defining attribute of the transport and logistics industry, the union nationally began to explore the possibility of alliances with other transport unions in Australia (the same unions that composed the Working Group) as well as like unions based in New Zealand. These developments set the scene for a more formal alliance at a national level in the late 2000s, titled the Australian Transport Union Federation (ATUF). Of note, the Victorian experiment provided the impetus for this development, although in practice the establishment of ATUF was independent of the Victorian Working Party.

The ATUF comprises the three main unions, the MUA, the RTBU and the TWU and was endorsed on 18 November 2009. It built on ongoing work between the three main unions. As stated by one national leader:

> . . . what we did was we moved from a hierarchical, bureaucratic response to organising an industry, [one] that had been confined behind very clear parameters. (National MUA, 2008)

This leader was making reference to the beginning of a change in the collective mindset that had characterised the union in the past. He claimed that the union had begun to move beyond this mindset and to promote alliances with other unions, thereby developing forms of external solidarity, increasingly irrespective of traditional political alignments. No doubt, the collapse of the Soviet Union and the consequential changes in the international political economy were part of this reframing of political relationships and alliances.

An important stimulus was the draconian and invasive deregulation that took place with the Conservative coalition government in the mid-2000s. Under the ubiquitous title of 'Work Choices', attempts were made to demobilise the union movement. But more than that, in the case of the MUA, the union could also draw on the memory of the government-backed attempt by the stevedoring company Patricks to break the union in 1997/98. This was defined thus:

> . . . one of the interesting things about Howard [Prime Minister, coalition government 1996–2007] as he was prepared to totally deregulate the whole of the Australian labour movement but not remove any of the

constitutional constraints from unions like ours. If we were operating like a union in the US or New Zealand then we would have been able to massively expand our organisational base because we have a very good brand name and people understood the type of union we were. So, and against all those constraints that we were put in, it was left to me and the National Council of the Maritime Union to say that we needed to really go out and establish our bonafides and build trust based on . . . our understanding of what was needed and a willingness to engage with any other labour organisation in a co-operative and mutually inclusive way. (National MUA, 2008)

The union nationally began to look to the Working Group and to other unions to build the basis to resist the attack on unions that was taking place. Initially the focus was on shipping and the traditional areas of organisation and activity, but within a framework that recognised that past practices needed to be changed. One example was the Working Group:

> . . . you are seeing in Victoria I guess a local manifestation of the same approach [alliance building on substantive matters] because we are really part of the transformation as in bottom-up unions. It is about practical engagement of the membership and the communities they live in. (National MUA, 2008)

In particular, the union learnt from the 1997/98 lock-out.

> . . . that was something that we learned out of Patricks. So you can't rely on any intrinsic legislative or internal values; you need to go back to the community and sell the values that will have the political presence to be able to challenge . . . and ring in the changes . . .So and to do that you had to have a not a top down but you need to have a bottom up type union and bring in a proper . . .dialogue with all your membership in terms of where they saw their needs. (National MUA, 2008)

One outcome was the establishment of the ATUF.

THE GLOBAL

Central to these two sets of developments is the ITF, the international trade union federation for transport workers' unions. Based in London, it has an affiliation of 751 unions representing over 4,600,000 transport workers in 154 countries. It is one of several GUFs allied with the International Trade Union Confederation (ITUC). While the headquarters is located in London, the ITF has offices in Nairobi, Ouagadougou, Tokyo, New Delhi, Rio de Janeiro, Amman, Moscow and Brussels.

The ITF represents the interests of transport workers' unions in bodies that take decisions affecting jobs, employment conditions or safety in the transport industry, such as the International Labour Organisation (ILO), the International Maritime Organisation (IMO) and the International Civil Aviation Organisation (ICAO).

The ITF engages in solidarity and support activity. It provides a research function to affiliate unions and has a specialist education department (for details see Croucher and Cotton 2009). One ITF strategy is the promotion of national coordinating committees, although their remit was quite limited. These committees bring transport unions together in each country, for the purposes of education and support. The problem, or limitation, is that until recently they were not seen as organising bodies.

There was a clear recognition among the ITF staff, covering inland transport, dockers, research and education, that unions have to rethink their purpose and enhance their capacities. At a meeting with a number of the relevant staff at the ITF in 2007, the comment was made that:

> Yes most unions have no real strategies developed in terms of how they tackle the logistics industry the way that it is organised today. (ITF Staff, 2007)

In a global world for transport, the ITF is about supply chains and the movement of goods, as well as the transportation of people. In relation to the ITF the task became:

> So the ITF's position really is to try and make sure that there is a union structure that is capable of moving forward. And I . . . to my mind it will mean that we will have to pick winners and losers in the end in terms of support, resource allocation. (ITF Staff, 2007)

The question is what is an appropriate structure and focus for both national unions, their constituents and the national committee?

> So the thing is the world is changing faster than even our most progressive unions can think to catch up with it. So the ITF's policy is to look at global organising, to build union solidarity, to build union power, so the theory is there, the commitment to it is there in voice but not in practicalities.
>
> . . .
>
> In my view, unions are going to have to make do, say well we are going to have to go and organise those bloody casuals or those part-timers or those Sheilas in the office or whatever excuse that they have got for not doing it now because by the time that they do finally take the hat off the last peg there will be nothing to replace it. (ITF Staff, 2007)

One way of developing and encouraging these developments is via national coordinating committees. The problem here is that, traditionally, these committees have a limited remit. As stated:

[Interviewee 1]   . . . the national co-ordinating committees have been there for a very long time, every country has a national co-ordinating committee, it is a way of bringing together our affiliates in a particular country.
[Q]   Not for organising?
[Interviewee 1]   Not necessarily, they come together on education issues, they come together on a whole variety of issues.
[Interviewee 2]   They could be good instruments for organising. . . That is the new challenge, as we need to see because everybody is losing. So one way of doing it is together . . . It has not been the traditional role. . . Yes to get them to play a more strategic role . . .
[Interviewee 3]   And, it isn't necessarily enough, it may be that the transport unions getting together under the ITF banner just isn't enough. (ITF Staff, 2007)

The Federation in effect became the national coordinating committee of the ITF. This development dovetailed with the ITF policy on national coordinating committees. There was a recognition that unions had to move beyond a view that they were sovereign bodies. As stated:

It needs a basic change in the thinking of the unions you know, unions are still thinking in terms of . . . their kingdoms . . . So if I am railway as long as the rail track runs you know that is my [kingdom] and then there is the boat, ok there is a boat boundary. So national co-ordinating committees also . . . need to think you know that those boundaries are blurring now . . . And so the train doesn't stop on the track it goes into the port and . . . a loaded empty port goes into the railway you know and from there it goes to the warehouse and then there is a truck carrying it you know. So they have a very national role, they have a very organising role in this, although the perspective may be the supply chains or whatever but a lot of those things are very, very national, very, very basic you know. (ITF Staff, 2007)

Although unacknowledged, the ATUF in 2009 is the national extension of the Working Group established in 2004. With the establishment of the Working Group, the three national unions were faced with a novel development, given the historic political differences between the three national unions, mirrored in the equally tentative and novel approach initially taken by the three Victorian unions. In this way, not only did the three Victorian unions build their capacity in relation to locally based and focused activity, but they also set a precedent for the unions nationally. By setting up the national federation, the national unions also reshaped their purpose in tangible ways, embracing solidaristic activity, albeit in the form of policy initiatives and support in relation to national agreements and representation.

The Federation saw the Working Group as an important step. It brought the unions together locally. The next task was to bring unions together nationally and regionally (at a global level), rather than at a State level or indeed port by port.

> In terms of the Federation, the organisation in Victoria that is different, that is a great initiative and it doesn't take into fact, into account the objectives of those State-based unions. So I suppose that is the ground level and we want them to start organising . . . something called TUF which is a Transport Union Federation [ATUF], which takes into account those things at that level but also ties in [with] New Zealand and . . . so we squared out the base. (National MUA, 2008)

In a comment on the Working Group, the ITF leadership also saw it as an important development but one that was very much within the ITF framework of development.

> The Victorian model that they are pronouncing is in actual fact just picking up on ITF policy. ITF policy is that there be co-ordinating committees in each of the countries so that transport unions do get together and rationalise what is going on with the restructuring of transport and what they can do together. And . . . it has actually been a very very good tool where unions aren't in conflict with each other because they can take their local hat off as they go into the meeting and put an ITF hat on and make some real progress, chewing and spitting and . . . about the politics that are going on. (ITF staff, 2007)

Nonetheless, the best of the knowledge of ITF staff, then and subsequently, is that the development of a Working Group based on a port is unique in the sense of drawing three different unions together to represent and mobilise members beyond representation in relation to agreements and specific grievances. It became a model for development of a transnational form of unionism.

MEDIATIONS

The broader remit and campaigns by the ITF provide part of the melding of the local and global as a form of transnational unionism that links the MUAV, the Working Group, ATUF and the ITF together. As noted, the ITF has long campaigned against the low wages paid on ships sailing under flags of convenience (FOC). It supports a range of ITF Inspectors whose job is to investigate ship conditions, defend seafarers and link local groups to the ITF as part of its FOC campaign. The inspectors are central to the FOC campaign. While the ITF has over 150 inspectors worldwide, six are based in Australia. The MUA is an active promoter of the campaign, with the national coordinator based in the National Office of the union. The objective is to develop the campaign in a bottom-up way, from the ships and a top-down way from the ITF, with the process mediated by the MUA nationally:

> So you can start to see for the first time where it comes from both directions. Because most highly successful campaign in the world, the FOC campaign, with trade union organisation easily linking in with one of the smallest unions' objectives—the seafarers in Australia have got about 4,000 seafarers. . . (National MUA, 2008)

While the Working Group brought together the three main unions in the Port of Melbourne, and is a precursor to the national federation, the ITF inspectors link the MUA (and by implication the other two unions) into the international campaigns and ways of organising internationally. These inspectors are *de facto* lead delegates for the union, with an international remit.

The ITF inspectors come out of the union and provide a link between the branches and the wider ITF movement. As stated by the Melbourne-based inspector:

> I started on the Melbourne waterfront in 1989 as a wharfie with Strang Stevedores then later worked with Strang/Patricks, Australian Stevedores and eventually the evil ones—Patricks. I was a multi skilled wharfie, which involved working as a clerk as well. In 1994 I became a member of the Patrick's shop committee, and in early 1995 I stood for Melbourne Branch Assistant Secretary and was elected as an official of the branch. In early 1996 I was asked to work as part time inspector for the ITF and thus my association commenced with the ITF. For the next three years I was half/ half, that is ITF inspector and branch official. I was offered a full time position in 1999 as ITF inspector in the Port of Melbourne and I accepted that position. As ITF inspector I'm responsible for the ports of Melbourne, Geelong, Portland and Westernport in Victoria, and various ports in Tasmania and South Australia. Earlier this year I was appointed as Assistant Co-ordinator for Australia. In Melbourne we have been able to develop a strong volunteer and supporter base for the ITF which has been of great assistance to our unique cause we all have in the work of the ITF. (Maritime Union of New Zealand 2004)

These inspectors are an important conduit for the local union and the global federations and the national coordinating committees or equivalent, providing a practical and ongoing link between the different levels of the union, including the national coordinating committee. They provide, as an internationally focused and connected union, a capacity for the union engaged in representation and campaigning on an international, rather than a national front. Their role and place in the union means that the union can tangibly shape its purpose as an international rather than a local and parochial body (see any selection of MUA publications, at the Port level, Branch level and nationally).

As argued by Lillie (2005) about the ITF, the inspectorate constitutes an organisational lynchpin for transnational unionism:

> The ITF, a London-based association of transport unions, connects the struggles of seafarers and port workers through a global strategy of union networking and coordinated industrial action. Seafaring unions draw on the industrial leverage of port workers to negotiate minimum standard pay agreements, while dock unions leverage the growing influence of the ITF in fighting union busting in ports. A global transnational ship inspector network provides the power basis for imposing collective agreements on shipowners. Although conceived as a resource for organizing seafarers, the inspectorate also provides port unions with leverage. (p. 88)

Thus, the organisational arrangements, resources and capabilities for transnational unionism are in place. The question is how were these diverse ingredients brought together? The answer lies with the three Victorian branch union leaders. These three leaders have known each other since the MUA lockout in 1997/8. While from different political wings of the trade union movement, they came to know each other and respect each other during campaigns related to the lockout (Barton and Fairbrother 2009). They, in effect, brokered the shift from three independent and sometimes competing union groups to a solidaristic union organisation committed to campaigning and mutual support. This initial step enabled them to utilise their resources strategically, assisting each other, and to focus their actions in relation to transnational issues. From these seemingly small steps, the frequent and often fleeting meetings between these leaders, as brokers, laid the foundations for an effective and notable form of transnational unionism.

ASSESSMENT

This brief history draws together two often overlooked dimensions of power. On the one hand, unions are themselves collective organisations, both structured and operating in relation to complex arrangements about leadership and membership. This feature draws attention to the importance of union democracy, a defining aspect of trade unionism insofar as it refers to power relations within unions. On the other hand, unions are collective organisations where members may be in a position to exercise agency, thereby realising the promise of the potential associated with the exercise of both structural and associational power. In the process of establishing the port-based union form of organisation, the maritime union and its two associated unions in Victoria, Australia took the decisive steps to establish the bases of transnational unionism, building on their resources and thereby forging emergent capabilities.

While the focus of the analysis is on the organisational resources and capacities of the three unions, and particularly the maritime union, with its ability based on a long history to frame international issues as local union concerns, it also points to the way solidarity between unions can be achieved. Thus, there was a two-sided process of developing resources and exercising capacities. First the maritime union built on its own democratic forms, via an accountable local (port-based and provincial leadership) and national leadership and the resources provided by the inspectors that enabled the union to provide an ongoing definition of transnational concerns. This process has long been reinforced by the ongoing engagement with the ITF, and particularly its global campaigns around maritime matters. Second, by building on the base of the MUAV, as an activist and campaigning union, and reaching out to the other transport unions at the port, the three unions created the ITF Working Group at the Port of Melbourne. This solidaristic form of unionism was not built around a single and integrated organisational structure. Rather it comprises a set of interlinked relationships that comprise this emergent form of transnational unionism. The claim is that these developments constitute an example of successful transnational unionism between unions within and around the port and, in relation to individual and collective vertical relationships, from the local to the global. The study thereby enables us to revisit theories about unions, showing how transnational unionism is built out of relationships that address organisation, capacity and purpose.

The first point to note is that these three unions, the maritime and the other two, were organised around local representational structures, with accountable and responsive leaderships who focused on port work and the emerging relationships between the unions at this level. While there may have been differences in the degree of accountability and responsibility within each union, they nonetheless organised in democratic ways. It was this aspect that gave the leaders the authority and capacity to promote the working group and to build a union organisation that was able to look beyond the immediate and local towards the global. As noted, the unions came from very different backgrounds and traditions. Nonetheless, they were each able to exploit the different strengths that their structural location within the port gave them.

The second point of note is that these organisational steps allowed the union leaderships to frame seemingly specific issues, such as recruitment by other union members of road transport workers into the TWU. Beginning with an organisational step to establish a Working Group under the remit of the ITF, the MUAV and the other two unions provided the means for focusing their otherwise disparate international activity. Building on their different locations within the port, they based their joint work on their different locations within the work and employment networks that comprised the port. In this way, they were able to frame the cross-recruiting, campaigning and lobbying activity as solidarity actions, thereby promoting associational power in relation to the port. They used the Working Group as a way of developing solidarity between the three unions and as a way of developing their international profile (see also, Urata 2011). Of course, each union continued to work through their national unions, as well as to deal directly with ITF on occasion. The MUA thus experimented with policies promoting collective practice and networks of activity, policy and power (Lévesque and Murray 2002). They drew on their 'power resources' as collective organisations with leaders and representatives prepared to take up local grievances, agreements and policies. They also drew on their experience of the past, as a union that had a mobile and internationally located membership, and a union that had long been politically engaged. In this way, they consolidated their internal solidarity, exemplified by forms of union democracy and promoted external solidarity with other local unions and with their national and international counterparts (Lévesque and Murray 2002: 45–46).

One strategy, and the third point, is for unions to reshape their purpose in an international direction. Clearly, where unions have long histories of international engagement and political awareness, such moves may be easier. Nonetheless, it does require unions to qualify their sovereign focus and look beyond the immediate and the parochial. Both the local union and the ITF had a clear appreciation of the dilemmas facing unions and the choices they confront. The task is to develop organisational forms that meet the transnational challenges that are emerging, realise capacities and shape their purpose to address these objectives. By looking internationally as a local union and locally as a global union federation, the initial steps to forge a renewed sense of purpose were taken.

CONCLUSION

Unions are bound up in complex relations bringing together labour, capital and the state. Equally, unions face challenges that are international in scope and origin. Nowhere is this clearer than in the transport industry and, particularly, the maritime section of that industry. While one strategy is to form and promote institutional links and relationships in the form of cross-border unions or alliances, the strategy followed by the maritime unions has been to build on past practices and mould their relationships within the unions and between the union group and others. This emphasis on relationships means that the union group is able to build on current strengths while enhancing their capacities and shaping their purpose.

The conditions for such a form of unionism are a reflective and experienced leadership, opportunities for leaders to meet each other and for activists to develop practices of solidarity, information exchange and union cooperation with each other. Nonetheless, at the base is a membership responsive and willing to become engaged, at least on occasion, via campaigns, demonstrations, rallies, attending meetings and talking. In doing this, these unions are constructing distinctive forms of transnational unionism with the capacity and purpose to challenge international capital, such as employers and global forms of governance. This was an expression of democratic trade unionism, based on the exercise of associational power.

REFERENCES

Anner, M. (2013), 'Workers' Power in Global Value Chains: Fighting Sweatshop Practices at Russell, Nike and Knights Apparel', in P. Fairbrother, M-A Hennebert and C. Lévesque (eds.), *Transnational Trade Unionism: Building Union Power*, London: Routledge.

Barton, R., and Fairbrother, P. (2009), 'The Local is Now Global: Building a Union Coalition in the International Transport and Logistics Sector', *Relations Industrielles/Industrial Relations*, 64(4), 685–703.

Beasley, M. (1996), *Wharfies: A History of the Waterside Workers Federation*, Sydney: Halstead Press in association with the Australian National Maritime Museum.

Carter, C., Clegg, S., Hogan, J., and Kornberger, M. (2003), 'The Polyphonic Spree: The Case of the Liverpool Dockers', *Industrial Relations Journal*, 34(4), 290–304.

Clawson, D. (2003), *The Next Upsurge: Labor and the New Social Movements*, Ithica: ILR Press.

Coe, N., Dicken, P., and Hess M. (2008) 'Global Production Networks: Realizing the Potential', *Journal of Economic Geography*, 8(3), 271–295.

Cohen, S. (2006), *Ramparts of Resistance: Why Workers Lost Their Power and How To Get It Back*, London: Pluto Press.

Croucher, R., and Cotton, E. (2009), *Global Unions, Global Business. Global Union Federations and International Business*, London: Middlesex University Press.

Fairbrother, P. (1984), *All Those In Favour: The Politics of Union Democracy*, London: Pluto Press.

Fairbrother, P., and Hammer, P. (2005), 'Global Unions: Past Efforts and Future Prospects', *Relations Industrielles / Industrial Relations*, 60(3), 405–431.

Gekara, V. (2009), 'Two Maritime Sector Unions' Fight against Decline through a Cross-Border Merger—the Nautilus International Project'. Paper presented at the 27th International Labour Process Conference, Edinburgh, April 6–8.

Gunawardana, S. (2007), 'Struggle, Perseverance and Organisation in Sri Lanka's Export Processing Zones', in K. Bronfenbrenner (ed.), *Global Unions: Challenging Transnational Capital Through Cross-Border Campaigns*, Ithaca: ILR Press.

Hyman, R. (1979), 'The Politics of Workplace Trade Unionism: Recent Tendencies and Some Problems for Theory', *Capital and Class*, 3(2), 54–67.

Hyman, R. (2007), 'How Can Trade Unions Act Strategically?', *Transfer*, 13(2), 193–210.

Juravich, T., and Bronfenbrenner, K. (1999) *Ravenswood: The Steelworkers' Victory and the Revival of American Labor*, Ithaca: ILR Press.

Kirkby, D. (2008), *Voices from the Ships: Australia's Seafarers and Their Union*, Sydney: University of New South Wales Press.

Lévesque, C., and Murray, G. (2002), 'Local versus Global: Activating Local Union Power in the Global Economy', *Labor Studies Journal*, 27(3), 39–65.

Lévesque, C., and Murray, G. (2010), 'Understanding Union Power: Resources and Capabilities for Renewing Union Capacity', *Transfer*, 16(3), 333–350.

Lévesque, C., Murray, G., Dufour, C., and Hege, A. (2013), 'Trade Union Strategies in Cross-Border Actions: Articulating Institutional Specificity with Local Power Dynamics', in P. Fairbrother, M.-A. Hennebert, and Lévesque, C. (eds.), *Transnational Trade Unionism: Building Union Power*, London: Routledge.

Lillie, N. (2005), 'Union Networks and Global Unionism in Maritime Shipping', *Relations Industrielles / Industrial Relations*, 60(1), 88–111.

Lipset, S., Trow, M., and Coleman, J. (1956), *Union Democracy: The Inside Politics of the International Typographical Union*, New York: The Free Press.

Lukes, S. (2005), *Power: A Radical View*, 2nd ed., Basingstoke: Palgrave Macmillan.

Lockwood, R. (1987), *War on the Waterfront: Menzies, Japan, and the Pig-Iron Dispute*, Sydney: Hale & Iremonger.

Maritime Union of Australia (2004), Victorian Branch, 26 October 2004, mimeo.

Maritime Union of New Zealand (2004), The Maritimes, 8(December), 10–11.

Martin, R. (1968), 'Union Democracy: An Explanatory Framework', *Sociology*, 2(2), 82–124.

Michels, R. (1962), *Political Parties: A Sociological Study of the Oligarchical Tendencies of Modern Democracy*, New York: Free Press.

Myconos, G., (2005), *The Globalization of Organized Labour: 1945–2005*, Basingstoke: Palgrave Macmillan.

Port of Melbourne Corporation (2011), *Annual Report 2010–11*, Melbourne: Port of Melbourne Corporation, www.portofmelbourne.com.

Rainnie, A., Herod, A., and McGrath-Champ, S. (2007), 'Spatialising Industrial Relations', *Industrial Relations Journal*, 38(2), 2–118.

Silver, B. (2003), *Forces of Labour: Workers Movements and Globalization since 1870*, Cambridge: Cambridge University Press.

Stevis, D., and Boswell, T. (2007), 'International Framework Agreements: Opportunities and Challenges for Global Unionism', in K. Bronfenbrenner (ed.), *Global Unions: Challenging Transnational Capital through Cross-Border Campaigns*, Ithaca: ILR Press.

Svensen, S. (1998), 'The Australian Wharf Lockout', *Capital & Class*, 22(3), 1–11.

Tattersall, A. (2007), 'Labor-Community Coalitions, Global Union Alliances, and the Potential of SEIU's Global Partnerships', in K. Bronfenbrenner (ed.), *Global Unions: Challenging Transnational Capital through Cross-Border Campaigns*, Ithaca: ILR Press, 155–173.

Turnbull, P. (2007) 'Dockers versus the Directives: Battling Port Policy on the European Front', in K. Bronfenbrenner (ed.), *Global Unions: Challenging Transnational Capital through Cross-Border Campaigns*, Ithaca: ILR Press, 117–136.

Urata, M. (2011), 'Building Rank and File Activism: A Study of the Global Action Day Campaign in the History of the International Transport Federation', in A. Bieler and I. Lindberg (eds.), *Global Restructuring, Labour and the Challenge of Transnational Solidarity*, London: Routledge.

Wiseman, J. (1998) 'Here to Stay? The 1997–1998 Australian Waterfront Dispute and Its Implications', *Labour & Industry*, 9(1), 1–16.

Wright, E. (2000), 'Working–Class Power, Capitalist-Class Interests, and Class Compromise', *The American Journal of Sociology*, 105(4), 957–1002.

7 Creating Spaces for Labour Internationalism

National Industrial Unions in the Southern Hemisphere and Their Strategies

Armel Brice Adanhounme
and Christian Lévesque

This chapter seeks to understand how national industrial trade unions in the Southern Hemisphere occupy international space and navigate between the global and the local. This question has prompted a debate on the appropriate articulation between the global and the local. Several scholars argue that trade unions are compelled to go global in order to counter multinational companies (MNCs) (Lambert 2002; Munck 2002; Webster et al. 2008). New forms of labour internationalism are emerging in the Southern Hemisphere that go beyond business unionism, relying on union networking across borders and, 'with civil society associations, setting a new agenda, thus creating a belief that change is possible' (Lambert 2002: 187). Other scholars are sceptical about the need for labour to match these MNCs at the global level (Burawoy 2010; Ghigliani 2005). They insist on local embeddedness, arguing that priority must be given to local endeavours. This 'localist' perspective is best captured by Burawoy (2010), who emphasises the need to develop local networks instead of relying on labour internationalism. He notes the complexity of the emerging new labour internationalism which, as Ghigliani (2005) also mentioned, it appears to be a matter more of form than of substance. Burawoy (2009; 2010) basically challenges the possibility of finding an alternative to globalisation in the global countermovement and suggests that priority should be given to the creation of broader solidarities at the national level instead of building transnational action.

While both groups of scholars insist on grounding globalisation, they diverge on the appropriate strategy. The former insists on linking the global to the local (Webster et al. 2008), while the latter compresses the global into the local (Burawoy 2009; 2010). This chapter seeks to disentangle the articulation between the local and the global by analysing the protagonists' self-understanding of the strategies of globalising the local and localising the global. We argue that neither the local nor the global are enclosed totalities. They are interconnected and interdependent, and their constructed meanings are interwoven and not deterministic. In order to achieve our objective, we propose using the heuristic tool of rooted labour internationalism to understand how Southern Hemisphere trade unions are engaging in cross-border action.

This question is investigated from the perspective of two national industrial trade unions in the mining sector in Ghana and Mexico. Trade unions in both countries are in a position of vulnerability due to their countries' dependence on foreign direct investments (FDIs) and the structural constraints imposed on their national economies by liberal reforms, notably the structural adjustment programs (SAPs). To cope with the pressures generated by globalisation, these unions are engaged in renewal processes that have prompted the development of new repertoires of action and the extension of their practices and relations across spaces.

The first section of this chapter draws on Tarrow's (2005) concept of rooted cosmopolitanism as a means of understanding labour internationalism. The second section describes the research method of the two case studies, while the third presents the results of our investigations in Ghana and Mexico. The fourth section examines the similarities and contrasts between our two case studies, and the conclusion highlights how a perspective on power resources can help to understand the way trade unions bridge the local and the global.

THE CASE FOR A ROOTED LABOUR INTERNATIONALISM

National trade unions play a pivotal role in bridging the local and the global and creating spaces for local unions to build solidarity across borders (Evans 2005; Greer and Hauptmeier 2008; Lévesque and Murray 2010). The way they navigate between the local and the global appears to be shaped by the resources and opportunities that unions can mobilise at the domestic and supranational levels. At both levels, a distinction can be drawn between the power resources resulting from workers' and trade unions' positions within the domestic and international economic system (structural power) and those derived from the norms, rules and practices that strengthen workers' collective organisation (associational power) (Wright 2000). Structural power is linked to the location of workers in the labour market and their position in the global value chain. Associational power is related to national and international institutional settings, such as collective bargaining and consultative legislation, or to the internal resources developed by trade unions to strengthen their collective organisation (Lévesque and Murray 2010). It is our contention that the dynamic interplay between these two types of power resource at the domestic and supranational level pushes and pulls trade unions into cross-border action. A number of studies support this claim.

Some studies show that a reduction in trade unions' bargaining power at the local or national level pushes them to engage in cross-border organising or collective bargaining (Greer and Hauptmeier 2008; Lillie and Martinez Lucio 2002). Ghigliani (2005) also argues that the capacity to shift between levels is related to the institutional and economic domestic conditions in which trade unions operate. The absence of some forms of associational power, such as trade union rights, appears to push trade unions towards cross-border co-operation. Others, like Burgoon and Jacoby (2004), show that it is not only domestic conditions but also international spaces that help to shape labour internationalism. In particular, they note that opportunity structures and resources at the supranational level, such as the presence of transnational consultative mechanisms or trade union rights, can act as a springboard for cross-border action, pulling trade unions into international space. A growing body of research shows how opportunity structures and resources at the supranational level shape the role national industrial trade unions play in connecting the local unions they represent with actors across the global landscape (Kay 2005; Lévesque and Murray 2010; Pulignano 2005).

These findings highlight the way labour internationalism is articulated in the complex intersection between the local and the global. Drawing on Cohen (1992), who first used the concept of rooted cosmopolitanism, Tarrow (2005) argues that cosmopolitan activists are rooted to the extent that they rely on domestic and international resources and opportunities to launch transnational activities. He emphasises the relational aspect of cosmopolitanism, the social relations that connect the local and the global. Among the broad stratum of rooted cosmopolitans that he describes, he mentions the case of labour activists from the South who forge ties with foreign unionists and non-governmental organisations (NGOs) and differentiates these transnational activists from their domestic counterparts, who cannot shift between levels.

As an heuristic tool for analysis, the concept of rooted labour internationalism, by which we mean the embeddedness of transnational solidarity, highlights the structural and associational power through which domestic trade unionists become transnational ones. We seek, firstly, to discover how national industrial trade unions use coordinated strategies to occupy international spaces in accordance with the local priorities they have set and, secondly, to show that the differences between them can be explained by the dynamic interplay between structural and associational resources derived from the national political economy context and the supranational opportunity structures available to them. The choice is not between going global or remaining local; rather, by seizing opportunities to articulate the various levels, unions can strengthen their capacity to act at the supranational level while simultaneously enhancing the capabilities of actors at the grassroots level. Neither exclusively global nor completely local, the diversified and complex strategies of labour internationalism are shaped by the contextual realities each national trade union faces. Based on this perspective, we focus on three dimensions to capture the role national industrial trade unions play in connecting the local and the global: the space of labour internationalism, the modes of interaction and the meaning ascribed to labour internationalism.

The first dimension, the space of labour internationalism, establishes the nature of the articulation between the local and the global. It shapes the ways in which actors seek to extend local practices by mobilising domestic resources to move in and out of international alliances and also the way in which international issues are internalised at the national level and adapted to local strategic projects as they become part of the international agenda (Tarrow 2005). The role of the geography of labour (Herod 2002; Marston 2000) in creating spaces for internationalism will help us to assess this articulation under three headings: the scales where contentions are voiced (local, national, regional, international), the domains they are concerned about (education, working conditions, labour rights, environment, etc.) and the space created for the involvement of rank-and-file and local leaders. The point here is to establish the relevance of the geography of labour in creating spaces for internationalism (Castree et al. 2004), in accordance with the argument that the space and its production are constitutive of social praxis (Herod et al. 2007).

The second dimension expands upon the first by focusing on the modes of interaction between trade unions and between trade unions and NGOs. As several scholars have noted, transnational union interactions are not necessarily cooperative (Greer and Hauptmeier 2008; Lillie and Martinez Lucio 2002). In essence, they may be more competitive than solidaristic, particularly between trade unions from developed and developing countries (Silver and Arrighi 2001). Three aspects are under scrutiny here: the strength of the ties established with other actors at different levels; the extent of cooperation and conflict between these actors; and the repertoires of action trade unions mobilise through their interactions, that is, whether these actions are structured around information-sharing, cross-national organising, transnational collective bargaining, strike support or diplomacy for networking.

The third dimension refers to the meaning attributed to labour internationalism. As shown by social movement scholars (Benford and Snow 2000; Tarrow 2005), material conditions do not necessarily trigger action or, more precisely, a mobilisation process. Trade unions need to assign meaning to material conditions and to locate their actions within a framework that provides a range of values and shared understandings. The way trade unionists define their interests as opposed to those of others is a critical component of labour internationalism (Herod 2002; Johns 1998; Ryland and Sadler 2008). Their local or global framings depend on the representation they have of their community of interests. This can be opposed to those of others, as is often the case for actors in the Southern Hemisphere, where the issue of otherness plays a dominant role in defining the totality, as implied by the very notion of internationalism. Another issue concerns the logic underlying trade union involvement in labour internationalism. Lévesque and Dufour-Poirier (2005) have highlighted three logics: a resource-driven logic, which is mainly geared towards an instrumental approach; a capacity-building logic, the main thrust of which is to enhance skills and capabilities; and a transformative logic, the principal aim of which is to build coalitions in order to increase trade union influence over MNCs. These logics define how trade unions frame the space of labour internationalism.

Our perspective stresses that labour internationalism is a multi-dimensional process involving the spaces, the modes of interaction and the meaning. These dimensions are rooted in the political economy of each country and articulated at the transnational level, both of which shape the power resources of trade unions, be it in terms of associational or structural power. The challenge is to explore how national industrial trade unions bridge the local and the global and to discover the factors that push and pull them into the transnational space.

RESEARCH METHOD

We investigate the case for a rooted labour internationalism through a study of two national industrial unions in the mining sector in Ghana and Mexico. In Ghana, the data were gathered in 2007 and included a total of 22 interviews with various actors: national executives and regional officers from the Ghana Mine Workers Union (GMWU) ($n = 5$), local leaders from three different mines ($n = 10$), social activists ($n = 7$) such as NGOs and the Chamber of Mines and representatives from a local mining community. In Mexico, the data were collected between 2001 and 2004 from 17 key informants at different levels and periods: staff from global union federations ($n = 3$), elected officers from the national industrial unions ($n = 7$), notably from the Mexican Miners Union ($n = 3$) and local union representatives ($n = 4$). We also attended, as observers, three different meetings in Canada and Mexico involving national industrial trade unions from the mining and metal working sectors from different countries.

In both countries, open, semi-structured interviews were used to collect the data. In a narrative format, we covered a wide range of issues: union history; structure and internal dynamics; institutional arrangements; recent trends in the political economy; national perspective on transnational unionism; the place of transnational solidarity in their strategic programs; conception of solidarity and worker interests; and the nature and intensity of networks developed. Documents from local, national and international unions were also gathered in order to obtain a better understanding of labour internationalism in both countries. This combination of methods increases our confidence in the results and our ability to understand the dynamics of union involvement in international alliances.

LABOUR INTERNATIONALISM IN CONTEXT

The development of transnational trade unionism in Ghana and Mexico highlights the relationship between economic structures and institutional arrangements and the way that national industrial trade unions can increase their capacity to act. In Ghana, transnational unionism is framed in terms of capacity building, while in Mexico, domestic and international conditions have favoured a coalition-building approach.

Economic Structure and Institutional Arrangements in the Ghanaian Case

Ghana belongs to the Economic Community of West African States (ECO WAS) where, according to the Bretton Woods standards, the country is regarded as a model of economic growth. Following a period of political and economic instability that started in the mid-1970s, Ghana embarked on a neo-liberal SAP in 1983 (Hutchful 2002; Panford 2001). While official reports indicate an employment rate of 11 per cent (2000 estimates), the informal economy accounts for 80 per cent of national output and explains the high percentage of people living under the poverty line. Artisanal and small-scale miners known as 'galamsey', estimated to number between 100,000 and 200,000 people, most of them unskilled rural workers (Hilson 2002), constitute a vibrant subsector of the mining industry, accounting for about 10 per cent of the total annual gold output and over 60 per cent of total annual diamond output. This informal mining sector is paradoxically acknowledged to contribute to poverty alleviation, particularly in rural areas where employment opportunities are rare (Akabzaa 2009).The conflictive relationship between the indigenous artisanal miners and foreign mining companies on issues of access to land for mining purposes is illustrative of the opposition between the structural formal economy with its concern for macroeconomic stability and the substantive informal economy in which the majority of Ghanaians subsist.

Institutional labour arrangements in Ghana are premised on the favourable political climate and pro-business reforms introduced since the SAP, which the trade unions, namely the Ghana Trade Union Congress (TUC), supported at the beginning before subsequently opposing them. The country returned to a multi-party system in 1991, and in the autumn of 1992, the TUC constitution was amended to prohibit the organisation from entering into an alliance with any political party for the purpose of winning elections. The introduction of this political neutrality clause was motivated by the bitter lessons learnt by the TUC in prior arrangements with political regimes, which had made them dependent and vulnerable (Konings 2006: 375). While the implementation of the SAP resulted in a consistent GDP growth of 6 per cent over the 1990s, socioeconomic and spatial disparities widened, particularly in terms of the distribution of and access to health, education, basic services, etc. (Konadu-Agyemang 2000). In the aftermath of the reforms, a mining code in line with the World Bank's strategy on mining was enacted in 1986 and revised in 2006 (Akabzaa 2009). The reforms were thought necessary to accelerate national development and reduce poverty.

After more than a quarter of a century, however, they have had a negative impact on rural mining communities, where poverty is pervasive and endemic (Aryeetey et al. 2004; Hilson 2004). Ghanaians are right to wonder if the mining sector has been an effective vehicle for poverty alleviation and sustainable national development (Akabzaa 2009).

According to our own field observations, the labour relations regime in the mining sector is shaped by the variable and complex nature of the relationships the workers have with the community, the mining companies and the state. In one particular mine, the workers, who are basically foreigners, are separated from the community and live in their compound, while in many others, they live side by side with the local people and feel part of the same community. The social demands on the mining companies are high in a situation where the state fails to provide the mining communities with basic infrastructural resources, such as health care and education. Because of the high illiteracy rate, education programs are highly valued, as successful, educated children will later provide their parents' pension fund. The informal economy is a space where workers and the local community meet as well: the majority of the miners' wives are informal traders in the local community, where they sell goods. Their husbands, in addition to the mining jobs, usually have a garden where they grow food products to supplement their wages.

The 69-year-old GMWU, one of the seventeen autonomous national unions affiliated to the TUC, has 31 branches including mining plants and mining services. Union membership, which totals 14,877 in all, is open to all employees who fall within the jurisdiction of the union, including the informal mining sector, as well as to managerial and professional personnel. Following the death of the General Secretary, who had been in office for more than 25 years, a new generation of activists took over the leadership of the union. Since then, the GMWU has undergone a process of modernisation that includes the following four elements: (a) training for both manual and managerial personnel; (b) organising the white-collar workers, supervisors and manual workers in the informal sector; (c) a strengthening of social dialogue; and (d) networking. The GMWU's approach to labour internationalism must be located within this modernisation process.

PATTERNS OF LABOUR INTERNATIONALISM IN THE GHANAIAN CASE

The GMWU has been affiliated to the International Federation of Chemical, Energy, Mines and General Worker Union (ICEM) since 1995. This international affiliation provides a new space for the construction of cross-border cooperation. Union officials regularly attend the ICEM international congress, and one of their representatives is a member of the executive committee. The union is also involved in the ICEM at the regional level: one member sits on the executive committee and another is in charge of the African women's committee. As well as facilitating information exchange and networking, these forums give GMWU greater recognition within and across borders. They also create opportunities for change. A union officer claims they belong to 'a new generation of committed activists who campaign for changes rather than being bureaucrats interested in diplomacy'.

The spaces of labour internationalism are, however, segmented, and the tensions between the local and the global in the construction of international links surface at the regional scale. The construction of alliances at the regional level within the ICEM and with African trade unions overshadows relations with NGOs and western trade unions. It is mainly at this scale that workers' needs and grievances are voiced. The domains are determined by the national union. They include youth and gender issues and improving the life of mining communities, particularly through humanitarian assistance.

However, building new capabilities through education and training is the most important need the trade union tries to satisfy. International resources allocated to the unions are used for training in collective bargaining, advocacy, research and planning, organising and recruitment. Training themes include community needs, ILO conventions, HIV, health and safety, etc. National officials select and recommend branch leaders and workers for training or education abroad. Many important leaders at the national level have themselves benefited from the international education programs. Through these education programs, international issues, such as decent work or HIV campaigns, are internalised and adapted to the local context, thereby linking the global to the local.

The space created for rank and file and local leaders to become involved is also geared towards education. The resources made available to the national union are used to empower the membership through capacity building. Transnational solidarity is needed to support educational and training projects for the rank and file in order to facilitate what one national official described as 'the empowerment of human capital'. The GMWU also creates space for the involvement of local leaders in international meetings, notably ICEM regional and international congresses. Although the space created for local leaders is rather limited, it nevertheless increases their awareness of international issues and creates a greater sense of belonging to the labour movement.

The national union's modes of interaction within these spaces are mostly characterised by weak ties. At the international level, the GMWU has participated in support campaigns aimed at forcing companies to respect international and national labour standards. Cooperation with Western countries is limited to general information exchange; one official complained that 'they have not developed any solidarity action so far, especially with the North American unions, whose level of commitment is not very strong'. The relationship is even less cordial with the Wassa Association of Communities Affected by Mining, a local NGO that publicly exposes the damage caused by mining operations. Moreover, Western NGOs that are unsympathetic to the mining operations are excluded from any sort of collaboration. Exchange and information-sharing are deeper at the regional level, mostly with English-speaking countries such as Nigeria and South Africa. The main aim here is the sharing of information on working conditions, health and safety issues and the strategies of MNCs. However, developing contacts among trade unions from the same company on an African regional level is not an easy task. Foreign mining corporations are eager to discourage any local initiative aimed at connecting local unions with each other. One local union leader said that an invitation from South African colleagues to visit a mine had been thwarted by management, who were fearful of such joint activity. Another obstacle to transnational solidarity at the regional level stems from the linguistic barriers that divide the Ghanaian English-speaking workers from the French speakers from neighbouring countries that surround them. The language problem prevents them from discussing at the West African regional level common issues that would help to develop bilateral cooperation.

The spaces of labour internationalism and these modes of interaction are closely linked to the meaning ascribed by trade unionists to labour internationalism. Solidarity rests on a clan-based grouping that determines a mutuality of interests between Ghanaian miners. The strong craft identity is spatially fixed and does not transcend borders. The GMWU does not have common interests or, indeed, conflicts with workers from other countries. Labour internationalism is driven by an instrumental approach geared to capacity-building, a process in which the national industrial union identifies the resources and sets priorities at the local level and carries them through at the international level. Labour internationalism is even instrumental in the development of partnerships with management. Indeed, the national trade union officials are pushing for 'a genuinely good partnership with management'. The employers, however, appear more reluctant. Crucial to the construction of this partnership is the professionalisation of local trade union officers through training programs. At present, local leaderships often lack even the basic skills required to deal with the sophisticated strategies deployed by MNCs. These training programs are geared towards increasing the capabilities not only of local leaders but also of the newly organised white collar workers in the Professional and Managerial Staffs Association Union.

This pattern of labour internationalism, which rests on capacity-building, is consistent with the priorities the trade union has set, though it is limited in scope, especially the articulation and intermediation between the local and the global. Both the logic of professionalism, whereby the trade union frames the discursive capacity of the rank and file, and the emphasis on training and education in order to strengthen their bargaining power meet local needs and reflect the expectations of both workers and the wider community. In so far as it is attuned to the basic educational and material needs of the workers, this pattern is in fact embedded in the local context.

Economic Structure and Institutional Arrangements in the Mexican Case

Globalisation in Mexico, as in many newly industrialising countries, was seen as a way of securing new FDI in order to boost employment and economic opportunities. The North American Free Trade Agreement (NAFTA), signed in 1994, combined with the free trade agreements the country has with over 50 countries, has strengthened a development policy based on low wages as the country's main competitive advantage, which dates back to the earlier period of industrialisation in the mining and manufacturing industries (Caufield 2004). NAFTA has had a strong impact on investment, but China's entry into the global production network has revealed the limits of such a development model. According to a 2008 official report using a food-based definition of poverty, 18.2 per cent of the population is below the poverty line, while asset-based poverty is higher than 47 per cent. The latter figure is consistent with the reality of the informal economy, which accounts for 50 per cent of Mexico's economic activity (Bayon 2009).

The country is an important mineral producer, ranking among the top producers in a variety of minerals (silver, copper, manganese ore, zinc, gold, etc.). Total employment in the mineral sector in 2004 was $ 257,349, a 3.8 per cent increase compared with 2003, and a 9.9 per cent decrease compared with the year 2000. The Mining Law, promulgated in 1992 and amended in 1996 and 2005, covers the exploration, production and beneficiation of minerals. The regulations allow increases in private sector participation in mining companies in Mexico and permit up to 100 per cent private equity ownership in the exploration, development and production, even of commodities previously reserved for the Government (Torres 2004).

The institutional arrangements have been labelled 'authoritarian corporatism' by several analysts of the Mexican industrial relations scene (Bizberg 1999; Middlebrook 1995). Over many decades, the official unions, notably the CTM (*Confederación de los Trabajadores de Mexico*), have built close links with the state. The Institutional Revolutionary Party (PRI), which held power at the federal level from the early 1930s to the year 2000, has always maintained very close ties with the official unions, which acted like a transmission belt for the PRI's policies. The official unions greatly contributed to the PRI's electoral hegemony. In particular, the unions exercised tight control over worker demands (De La Garza 2003). In this classic example of corporatist political exchange, union representatives had access to greater financial resources and played an important role within the state administration in return for their cooperation in industrial and political matters. This was particularly the case with regard to labour courts, which have significant decision-making power in areas such as the determination of union representativeness, union registration and the legality of strikes. These same powers contribute to the continued importance of the official unions within the overall administration of the Mexican industrial relations regime, but they also highlight the vulnerability of trade union bargaining demands to broader political considerations.

The changing geometry of party political power in Mexico and the emergence of independent trade union confederations complicate this interpretation of the institutional arrangements (Bensusán and Cook 2003). The rivalry between the independent unions outside the framework of the *Congreso del Trabajo* (CT) and with the CTM brought about a crisis in the Mexican labour regime following the election of Vicente Fox of the conservative party (PAN) in 2000. While the labour law remains interventionist and protective of workers because of the resistance of the CTM to the various reforms and its affiliation to the ruling party, the weakening of the corporatist framework (Bensusán 2011) has further fragmented the trade union movement.

The mining sector remains outside of CTM control and is dominated by a national industrial union, the Mexican Miners' Union (SNTMMSRM), which represents 160,000 workers in the mining and manufacturing industries. From the early 1950s to 2002, the SNTMMSRM generally called the Mineros, participated and was active in the consolidation of the authoritarian corporatist regime. Their leaders were described as true 'charros' who worked closely with the PRI to control labour struggles. After the death of the General Secretary, who had held power for nearly four decades and was replaced by his son, the Mineros have followed a different path.

Patterns of Labour Internationalism in the Mexican Case

Given its position within the political arena in Mexico, the CTM has historically been able to exercise tight control over access to international space. In fact, for many years it virtually controlled trade union access to international networks, and most international activities were controlled by a small group of CTM bureaucrats who monopolised representation and resources.

In the 1990s, several events weakened the CTM, notably the death of its leader Fidel Velázquez, who was in office from 1941 to 1997, and the discussions over free-trade treaties. In addition, independent unions became both increasingly active internationally and recognised as such by international bodies. The CTM's supportive approach to free-trade agreements prompted several trade unions, such as the AFL-CIO and the Canadian Labour Congress, to seek new allies in order to oppose the imminent signing of NAFTA. In 2001, the International Metalworkers' Federation (IMF) opened a regional office in Mexico with a view to extending its representation, including independent unions, in large and influential sectors such as auto and mining. This regional office prompted the development of a dense network among its affiliates, which provided a source of leverage in annual collective bargaining rounds and opened up a space for collective and coordinated action.

The Mineros joined the IMF during this period and were immediately quite active. They participated regularly in international activities organised by the IMF, such as training programs and colloquiums. The General

Secretary of the union quickly got involved within the IMF and was elected to the international executive committee. The union also established regular contacts with unions from the North and South and took the initiative in organising events that brought together unions from different countries dealing with the same employer. The spaces for labour internationalism were thus enlarged to incorporate different levels (local, national and regional) and to include wider domains. Exchanges focused on concrete issues, such as working conditions, health and safety, workers' rights and quality of life. Local leaders were directly involved in this information exchange process with local leaders from other countries and relayed the information to the rank and file. This top-down communication process was crucial, since the rank and file was directly involved in solidarity actions and campaigns in support of strikes.

The Mineros acted as a powerful relay in building close relationships with unions from North and South America. In particular, the leadership of the Mineros sought to strengthen its links with the United Steelworkers of Americas (USWA). These strong ties became very helpful during difficult periods. In addition to building tight networks at the regional level, the Mineros were also engaged in collective mobilisation at the national level. Indeed, the union became entangled in several bitter struggles with an industry heavyweight that was well known worldwide for its anti-union activities (*Grupo Mexico*). In June 2005, the union, together with Peruvian and American miners, organised a day of protest against *Grupo Mexico* in which over 10,000 workers took part. As the clashes with the employer became more numerous, they attracted the media spotlight and were often punctuated by serious violence. In September 2005, after a 46-day strike, the local union in two *Grupo Mexico* steel mills in Michoacán won major improvements in working conditions. The following year, in April 2006, one of the mills was the scene of a tragic incident. The army decided to intervene in order to stop the disturbances and disorders caused by the strikers. Several workers were wounded, and two of them later died. Violent strikes also broke out in northern Mexico following tragic labour incidents. In particular, in Pasta de Conchos in February 2006, 65 miners died when a mine collapsed. The Mineros Secretary General accused the leaders of *Grupo Mexico* of industrial murder. In the face of the growing strength of industrial conflicts with *Grupo Mexico* and the sympathy the union was winning both within and outside Mexico, the government removed the national executive from office in February 2006 and accused the union of fraud, which it denied from the outset. The USWA—with which the miners had earlier sealed a strategic alliance—launched activities in support of the Mineros during this highly turbulent period. In the following months, several campaigns of international solidarity—directed jointly by the IMF and the USWA—were planned to exert pressure and break the deadlock. In spite of this, and even though the federal judicial authorities ruled in favour of the main Mineros leaders, the latter remains as of June 2011 in exile in Canada.

Thus the modes of interaction depended on two interrelated processes. The first was based on active local mobilisation, which gave a global perspective to what were domestic claims and externalised them into international forums by bringing them to the attention of international actors such as the IMF. This constituted an upward shift in the issues pursued by the union. The second was based on fostering a high level of long-term involvement with other national unions. They were engaged in collaborative means-oriented arrangements with these unions and in building coalitions over a long period. These two processes—mobilisation and coalition building—were the nucleus of the Mineros approach to labour internationalism and an indispensable ingredient in its struggle with the employers, the state and the official unions in Mexico.

Thus transnational solidarity was seen as an opportunity offered to the Mineros to frame a new normative perspective on labour internationalism that went beyond the bureaucratic approach that had characterised the old guard of trade unionists. The leaders see themselves as part of a movement that transcends national boundaries. They believe that the goal of international alliances is not just to build networks but, more profoundly, to transform globalisation and the orientations of the labour movement. Even though they acknowledge that workers' interests are not always the same, they insist on the need to go beyond these divergent interests in order to confront MNCs. Over time, there was clearly an identity shift. The 'we' became far more inclusive, encompassing a broader vision of workers' interests. The numerous struggles the union was engaged in also modified its narrative. The union's success in increasing workers' earnings and benefits was used as an agenda-framing resource to mobilise workers and shape their claims. The upward shift of level in the location of the union's claims entailed a change in the types of actions taken by the union, involving new actors at new levels of interaction. It also involved experimentation with new forms of action, such as international mobilising campaigns and community networking. Further, and perhaps most importantly, union leaders reframed not only their repertoires of action they engaged in but also their agenda. Coalition-building became an integral part of the Mineros strategy. With the USWA, the Mineros are currently engaged in the creation of a cross-border transnational trade union representing 1,000,000 industrial workers in Mexico, Canada, the US and the Caribbean.

UNDERSTANDING PATTERNS OF LABOUR INTERNATIONALISM IN GHANA AND MEXICO

Following important changes in their leadership over the last decade and a half, the GMWU and the Mineros have undergone a process of union renewal that has led them away from their past model of trade unionism. These leaders have been able to rearticulate the space of labour internationalism, to reshape forms of action and relations and to reframe the meaning of solidarity and international action. Agency has been crucial in the extension of their practices and relations across spaces. However, they have followed different paths to labour internationalism: a capacity-building pattern in Ghana and a coalition-building pattern in Mexico. These paths reflect trade unionists' self-understanding of the strategies of globalising the local and localising the global.

As shown in Table 7.1, these patterns differ in each of the dimensions selected to capture labour internationalism: the spaces, the mode of interaction and the meaning of labour internationalism. First, GMWU operates mainly at the regional level and focuses on access to education for the community and on training geared towards increasing local and national leadership skills. The Mineros operate at the regional and the transnational levels and are more concerned with improving labour and working conditions by involving rank-and-file and local leaders in information-sharing and solidarity campaigns. Second, while GMWU maintains weak ties with trade unions based on information sharing, the Mineros have developed strong ties with North American trade unions and the IMF and are engaged in a wider range of action, including campaigns in support of strikes and active mobilisation. Third, GMWU bases its interests on a strong craft identity and sees labour internationalism as a mean to increase its resources to build new capabilities. The Mineros leadership, for its part, frames its interests around class identity and sees labour internationalism as a struggle to build broader coalitions.

The Mineros and the GMWU articulate the local and the global in different ways, and our analysis of this articulation must take account of the dynamic interplay between the structural and associational power resources the unions mobilise at both the domestic and supranational level. The idea here is to identify how these patterns are rooted in each country's political economy and articulated at the transnational level.

In terms of economic location, both countries are far from being at the higher end of the food chain, even though Ghana is by international standards in a far worse position. The GDP per capita is 10 times higher in Mexico ($14,000 compared with $1,300) and the informal economy is more widespread (80 per cent versus 50 per cent of economic activity). Further, the adult illiteracy rate is 25 per cent in Ghana in contrast to 5 per cent in Mexico, and the probability of dying before the age of 40 is much higher in Ghana (25 per cent versus 5 per cent) (World Bank, 2009). The GMWU embeds its approach to labour internationalism in this context of economic vulnerability. In the rural Ghanaian mining communities characterised by a strong informal economy, high illiteracy rates and an absence of educational infrastructures, the GMWU's labour internationalism is expected to alleviate poverty and foster sustainable socio-economic development through an engagement in education and training. Ghana's membership of ECOWAS did not lead to an upgrading in the global value chain, which could in turn have accelerated the development of the infrastructures needed to raise workers'

Creating Spaces for Labour Internationalism 135

Table 7.1 Patterns of labour internationalism in the Ghanaian and Mexican cases

Dimensions of labour internationalism	GMWU: Capacity building	Mineros: Coalition building
Spaces of labour internationalism		
– Scales	Regional	Regional and transnational
– Domains	Training, youth and gender issues, life improvement for communities	Labour conditions and labour rights, health and safety
– Space for rank-and-file involvement and local leaders	Educational programs for rank and file; local leaders' participation in ICEM meetings	Rank-and-file involvement in solidarity campaigns; information sharing between local leaders from different countries
Modes of interaction with unions		
– Repertoire of action	Exchanges and information sharing - more intense at regional level, weaker overseas	Information sharing; campaigns in support of strikes; active mobilisation
– Strength of relationships	Mainly weak ties with trade unions and NGOs	Strong ties with North American unions & IMF; moderate ties with unions from South; weak ties with NGOs
– Nature of relationships	Cooperation with trade unions; arms length with NGO	Strong collaboration with trade unions
Meaning of labour internationalism		
– Solidarity	Strong craft identity spatially fixed; clan-based groupings, mutuality of interest with employers	Class identity; mutuality of interest with other workers and against employers and the state
– International action	Resource-driven; instrumental approach to building new capabilities and new unionism	Mobilisation and struggle to build broad coalitions and renew union agenda and repertoires of action

educational levels. In Mexico, where the economic situation is better, even though the low wage policy designed to draw in FDI is detrimental to workers and their communities, Mineros are not in need of infrastructural resources and do not expect transnational bodies to help launch educational and developmental programs as the Ghanaians do. Although it has its downsides, membership in NAFTA puts Mexico in a better position in the global value chain to attract FDI in the mining and manufacturing industries.

There is also a difference between the two trade unions with respect to the configuration of associational power resources at the domestic and transnational levels. At the domestic level, labour internationalism in Ghana is supported by the cohesive and stable institutional setting in which the leaders work. The policy of political neutrality protects the union from enduring conflict with the state, and its strategic partnership with foreign MNCs under the guiding principle of professionalism preserves the domestic norms and rules that support workers' collective organisation. At the transnational level, the difficulties in establishing bilateral relationships with trade unions from English-speaking countries and the linguistic barriers with the surrounding French-speaking countries have reduced the scope of the GMWU network. Isolated from Western trade unions and, according to their leaders, suffering from the indifference of global bodies, the GMWU cannot expect to draw on many resources from the transnational level to increase its associational power resources. In Mexico, the absence of local allies, the contentious relations with the state and the MNCs and its rivalry with official trade unions weaken the power resources available to the Mineros and call into question the trade union's very existence. Locally isolated, their pattern of coalition-building is aimed at responding to their local needs by strengthening their members' collective organisation. Mineros have literarily been pulled into the transnational arena, as their allies enjoy greater resources. Sharing the same economic space with American and Canadian workers forces them into defining a set of common interests and to engage in cross-borders actions within the NAFTA setting. The IMF regional office in Mexico has also helped them to develop global links and connect worldwide. They went global by networking and campaigning with regional and supranational unions with which they have strong ties and shared interests, thereby transcending national concerns about collective action. The weakening of the resources underlying their collective organisation at the domestic level has compelled the Mineros to invest in the development of associational power resources at the supranational level.

Thus it appears that the dynamic interplay between structural and associational power resources pushing and pulling trade unions in the international space plays out differently in Ghana and Mexico. The GMWU operates within a domestic institutional setting that does not challenge the foundation of its collective organisation. However, workers' economic vulnerability and Ghana's location in the global value chain weaken their structural power resources. The need for infrastructural resources not available at the domestic level pushes the union into the transnational space, basically at the regional level within ECOWAS, to obtain these resources. Thus the GMWU's capacity-building pattern of labour internationalism is shaped by the relative stability of the union's associational power resources and the weakness of the workers' structural power resources at both the domestic and transnational level. By contrast, the Mineros are located in an economic environment that is less detrimental to workers and the community, even though the economic situation in Mexico has worsened over the last decade. Labour internationalism is not shaped by a weakening of workers' structural power resources. The Mineros are pushed out of the domestic arena and pulled into the transnational arena in order to re-establish their weakened collective organisation at the domestic level. In short, the Mineros coalition-building pattern of labour internationalism is geared towards increasing their associational power resources.

These patterns of labour internationalism, developed within a North-South relationship in Mexico and a South-South relationship in Ghana, are consistent with the contrasting regional spaces formed by NAFTA and ECOWAS. The difference between the two cases lies in the nature of the bilateralism and not in the asymmetric relations both have with Western organisations. Thus the spaces, the modes of interaction and the meaning attributed to the renewal of labour internationalism in each national context show that, besides bridging the North-South divide at the heart of the opposing views on transnational solidarity, other fundamental challenges exist. These challenges are located beyond the structural dichotomy, which might appear as a mere surface characteristic that serves only to embellish the existing forms of labour internationalism. The protagonists are much more concerned with the substance than with the form of the new labour internationalism. At both the domestic and transnational levels, the patterns of capacity-building and coalition-building are consistent with the expectations generated by the national political economy in which each national industrial trade union is embedded. As such, they make a strong case for a rooted labour internationalism.

CONCLUSION

Using the notion of rooted labour internationalism as a heuristic tool, the polarised debate on the optimal solidaristic response from labour to transnational MNCs presented in this chapter has focused on how two industrial trade unions in the Southern Hemisphere occupy international spaces and navigate between the global and the local. Transnational solidarity is subordinated to the unions' understanding of the needs and interests of their membership, and their patterns of labour internationalism are shaped by the configuration of the structural and associational power resources available to them. The respective national political economies matter since the patterns of capacity-building and coalition-building are rooted in each country's economic structures and labour institutions. Instead of locating

their patterns on one side or the other of the localist/globalist divide, neither the GMWU nor the Mineros understands labour internationalism as
a choice between matching transnational MNCs or developing local networks. Rather, their strategies are rooted in the constraints and freedoms
inherent in their respective national political economies, which determine
the economic and institutional conditions under which the unions operate
and which impel them into internationalism.

There is an ambivalent movement, from the local to the global and from
the global to the local, led by the ambitious renovators in Ghana and the ex-
iled yet proactive Mineros leaders in Mexico, which illustrates the rootedness
of the domestic process and its articulation with transnational challenges.
The direction of this movement depends on the available structural and associational power resources. Thus when the movement is from the local to
the global, the spaces for transnational unionism are constructed by using
and enhancing the capabilities that push the actors at the grassroots level.
International issues are internalised and adapted to local strategic projects,
thereby becoming part of the international agenda. Burawoy (2010) is right
to emphasise the importance of embedding labour initiatives in local contexts, where the protagonists own their stories. Both the Ghanaian and Mexican trade unions are rooted in the local realities that are the starting point for
their attempts to frame and circumscribe the space for transnational unionism, and both base their strategies on a coherent articulation of the various
levels. Thus, the alternative they propose to economic globalisation is socially
constructed, locally rooted and shaped by the transnational opportunities.

However, the articulation between the local and the global is beyond the
scope of local actors, who have to rely on transnational power resources, as
do the cosmopolitan activists praised by Tarrow (2005) and Webster et al.
(2008). There is also a movement from the global to the local, in which the
spaces for transnational unionism are shaped by the transnational power
resources and pull the trade unions into internationalism. They seize these
opportunities to strengthen their capacity to act at the global level and to extend local practices to the supranational level, where they use their domestic
resources to move in and out of international alliances. As Burawoy himself
recognises in his study of the reproduction of the racial order in the copper
mines in Zambia between 1968 and 1972, external and global forces shape
social processes (Burawoy 2009: 250–1). The global cannot be compressed
at the local level and international space has its own autonomy that creates a
different set of opportunities. The case for a rooted labour internationalism
depends on this double movement, by which the false local/global dichotomy is avoided to make way for a holistic yet contextual approach to labour
internationalism that does not promote 'one best way' of combating transnational, regardless of the national political economy. There is no universal
recipe for creating spaces for labour internationalism. The variable geometry that these Southern Hemisphere cases reveal suggests that future studies
should pay greater attention to the various ways in which national trade
unions bridge the local and the global by mobilising their power resources.

REFERENCES

Akabzaa, T. (2009), 'Mining in Ghana: Implications for National Economic Development and Poverty Reduction', in B. Campbell (ed.), *Mining in Africa: Regulation and Development*, London and New York: Pluto Pres/IRDC.

Aryeetey, E., Osei, B., and Twerefou, D. (2004), 'Globalization, Employment and Livelihoods in the Mining Sector of Ghana', paper presented at Accra ESSER, 2004.

Bayon, M. C. (2009), 'Persistence of an Exclusionary Model: Inequality and Segmentation in Mexican Society', *International Labour Review*, 148(3), 301–16.

Benford, R. D., and Snow, D.A. (2000), 'Framing Processes and Social Movements: An Overview and Assessment', *Annual Review of Sociology*, 26, 611–639.

Bensusán, G., and Cook M. L. (2003), 'Political Transition and Labour Revitalization in Mexico', *Research in the Sociology of Work*, 1, 229–267.

Bensusán, G. (2011), 'Labour Reform from a Regional Perspectives: Experiences in the Americas', in A. Blackett and C. Lévesque (eds.), *Social Regionalism in the Global Economy*, New York and London: Routledge, 207–224.

Bizberg, I. (1999), 'Le syndicalisme mexicain face à la mondialisation et à la décomposition du régime politique', *La revue de l'IRES*, 29, 132–164.

Burawoy, M. (2009), *The Extended Case Method: Four Countries, Four Decades, Four Great Transformations, and One Theoretical Tradition*, Berkeley and Los Angeles: University of California Press.

Burawoy, M. (2010), 'From Polanyi to Pollyanna: The False Optimism of Global Labor Studies', *Global Labour Journal*, 1(2), 301–313.

Burgoon, B., and Jacoby, W. (2004) 'Patch-Work Solidarity: Describing and Explaining US and European Labour Internationalism', *Review of International Political Economy*, 11(5), 849–879.

Castree, N., Coe, N., Ward, K. G., and M. Samers (2004), *Spaces of Work: Global Capitalism and Geographies of Labour*, London: Sage.

Caufield, N. (2004), 'Labor Relations in Mexico. Historical Legacies and Some Recent Trends', *Labor History*, 45(4), 445–467.

Cohen, M. (1992), 'Rooted Cosmopolitanism', *Dissent*, Fall, 478–483.

De La Garza, E. (2003) 'Mexican Trade Unionism in the Face of Political Transition', *Research in the Sociology of Work*, 11, 202–228.

Evans, P. (2010), 'Is it Labor's Turn to Globalize? Twenty-first Century Opportunities and Strategic Responses', *Global Labour Journal*, 1(3), 352–379.

Ghigliani, P. (2005), 'International Trade Unionism in a Globalizing World: A Case Study of New Labour Internationalism', *Economic and Industrial Democracy*, 26(3), 359–382.

Greer, I., and Hauptmeier, M. (2008), 'Political Entrepreneurs and Co-Managers: Labour Transnationalism at Four Multinational Auto Companies', *British Journal of Industrial Relations*, 46(1), 76–97.

Herod, A. (2002), 'Organizing Globally, Organizing Locally: Union Spatial Strategy in a Global Economy', in J. Harrod and R. O'Brien (eds.), *Global Unions? Theory and Strategies of Organized Labour in the Global Political Economy*, London and New York: Routledge.

Herod, A., Rainnie, A., and McGrath-Champ, S. (2007), 'Working Space: Why Incorporating the Geographical is Central to Theorizing Work and Employment Practices', *Work, Employment and Society*, 2(2), 247–264.

Hilson, G. M. (2002), 'The Future of Small-Scale Mining: Environmental and Socioeconomic Perspectives', *Futures*, 34, 863–872.

Hilson, G. M. (2004), 'Structural Adjustment in Ghana: Assessing the Impacts of Mining-Sector Reform', *Africa Today*, 51(2), 53–77.

Hutchful, E. (2002), *Ghana's Adjustment Experience: The Paradox of Reform*, Geneva: UNRISD.

Johns, R. (1998), 'Bridging the Gap between Class and Space: U.S. Worker Solidarity with Guatemala', *Economic Geography*, 74(3), 252–271.

Kay, T. (2005), 'Labor Transnationalism and Global Governance: The Impact of NAFTA on Transnational Labor', *American Journal of Sociology*, 111(3), 715–756.

Konadu-Agyemang, K. (2000), 'The Best of Times and the Worst of Times: Structural Adjustment Programs and Uneven Development in Africa: The Case of Ghana', *Professional Geographer*, 52(3), 469–483.

Konings, P. (2006), 'African Trade Unions and the Challenge of Globalisation: A Comparative Study of Ghana and Cameroon', in C. Phelan (ed.), *The Future of Organised Labour. Global Perspectives*, Bern: Peter Lang, 361–395.

Lambert, R. (2002), 'Labour Movement Renewal in the Era of Globalization: Union Responses in the South', in J. Harrod and R. O'Brien (eds.), *Global Unions? Theory and Strategies of Organized Labour in the Global Political Economy*, London and New York: Routledge, 185–203.

Lévesque, C., and Dufour-Poirier, M. (2005), 'International Union Alliances: Evidence from Mexico', *Transfer*, 11(4), 531–548.

Lévesque, C., and Murray, G. (2010), 'Trade Union Cross-Border Alliances within MNCs: Disentangling Union Dynamics at the Local, National and International Levels', *Industrial Relations Journal*, 41(4), 312–332.

Lillie, N. and Martinez Lucio, M. (2002), 'International Trade Union Revitalization: The Role of National Unions Approaches', in C. Frege and J. Kelly (eds.), *Varieties of Unionism: Strategies for Union Revitalization in a Globalizing Economy*, Oxford: Oxford University Press.

Marston, S. (2000), 'The Social Construction of Scale', *Progress in Human Geography*, 24(2), 219–242.

Middlebrook, K. J. (1995), *The Paradox of Revolution: Labour, the State and Authoritarianism in Mexico*, Baltimore: Johns Hopkins University Press.

Munck, R. (2002), *Globalization and Labour: The New Great Transformation*, New York: Zed Books.

Panford, K. (2001), *IMF-World Bank and Labor's Burdens in Africa: Ghana's Experience*, Westport: Praeger.

Pulignano, V. (2005), 'EWCs and Cross-National Employee Representative Coordination. A Case of Trade Union Cooperation?', *Economic and Industrial Democracy*, 26(3), 383–412.

Ryland, R., and D. Sadler (2008), 'Revitalizing the Trade Union Movement through Internationalism: The Grassroots Perspective', *Journal of Organizational Change Management*, 21(4), 417.

Silver, B. J., and Arrighi, G. (2001), 'Workers North and South', in L. Panitch and C. Leys (eds.), *Working Classes, Global Realities, Socialist Register*, London: Merlin Press.

Tarrow, S. (2005), *The New Transnational Activism*, Cambridge: Cambridge University Press.

Torres, I. (2004), 'The Mineral Industry of Mexico', in *U.S. Geological Survey Minerals Yearbooks-2004*, Reston, VA: United States Geological Survey.

Webster, E., Lambert, R., and Bezuidenhout, A. (2008), *Grounding Globalization: Labour in the Age of Insecurity*, Oxford: Blackwell.

World Bank (2009), *World Development Report 2010: Development and Climate Change*, Washington DC: World Bank.

Wright, E. O. (2000), 'Working-Class Power, Capitalist-Class Interests, and Class Compromise', *The American Journal of Sociology*, 105(4), 957–1002.

8 Local Actors and Transnational Structures

Explaining Trends in Multinational Company-Level Negotiations in Europe

Valeria Pulignano, Isabel da Costa,
Udo Rehfeldt and Volker Telljohann

Various studies concerning labour relations have sought to focus attention on supranational bargaining and labour internationalism as key responses to globalisation and international capital mobility (Levinson 1972). However, with regard to the attempt at launching an international framework for collective bargaining, Rehfeldt (1993) clearly points out the absence of an adequate legal framework as being a crucial precondition for explaining the weaknesses and, in most of the cases, the failure of these initiatives. The main sticking point is a minimal concrete follow up to the initiative taken in 2004 by the European Commission that was aimed at supporting the adoption of a legal framework through a directive on the establishment of a European system of transnational collective bargaining that complements existing national systems. In this context, institutionally weak trade unions' responses to international businesses and bargaining coordination have to date depended greatly, on the one hand, on the financial and organisational resources available internally and, on the other hand, the capacity to build up transnational coordination of action and solidarity in situations of threat at the transnational level. Although there are still some serious obstacles in this regard, some optimistic perspectives have emerged as crucial in promoting European-wide, rather than national, responses (Erne 2008; Fetzer 2008; Greer and Hauptmeier 2010). However, bargaining at the European level still suffers from a number of shortcomings. Some studies report that, in the majority of cases to date, the outcome of the negotiations is a 'joint text' (Telljohann et al. 2009: 24–27). Moreover, in only a few cases have framework agreements been concluded to manage European-wide restructuring or to address particular aspects of the employment policy of multinationals. Among the factors hampering the negotiation of framework agreements at the European level, structural differences between national unions and the cross-national diversity of the systems of interest representations are highlighted (da Costa and Rehfeldt 2008).

By drawing from a less deterministic view of institutional structures, we argue that a systematic analysis of the social processes that have accompanied the evolution of bargaining activity at the European multinational level needs to be developed. This implies examining how policy actors at different levels use existing regulatory settings, not only as constraints, but also as resources for particular courses of action. As Streeck (2011: 142) emphasizes, *'what an institution "really means" must and therefore can be continuously re-invented by actors in the light of both specific situations and changing general circumstances'*. Thus, this paper departs from a multi-actor and multi-level analytical framework by focusing on the strategies employed by the social actors (management, trade unions, and employee representatives) at both the European and local levels in order to explore their interest in engaging (or not) in negotiation within Europe. The paper examines the social processes that have, or have not, contributed to the conclusion of agreements. It explores the conditions under which employee representatives, company management and trade unions have promoted European, rather than local, responses while engaging in European company-level negotiation. The research findings clearly illustrate the difficulty of generalising based on different experiences or company cases. However, they point out that the ways in which different local strategies are developed and evolve, as well as the forms these strategies take, greatly affect the extent to which negotiation at the European company level develops. More specifically, the paper identifies four different conditions influencing bargaining at the EU level: strong cross-border coordination of workers supported and facilitated by a solid articulation between the European Union (EU) level and the national union level; a European Works Council (EWC, structure and practice not predominated by headquarters and with a strong 'home-country' structure for worker representation); local union power; and a centralised human resources (HR) corporate culture with a high degree of centralised autonomy and control of local management over labour relations. These factors contribute to the generation of different strategies developed by local actors to achieve their objectives while complying with their interests. Moreover, cross-company diversity with regard to the subject of the negotiations also plays a key role in explaining the dynamics of the bargaining process at the European level, and therefore contributes to explaining the interest social actors have in being engaged (or not) in negotiation.

Six multinational companies were selected for investigation. We assess the extent to which the strategies of local actors have been bound up with European-level developments and how they have evolved. We do this by exploring the conditions under which trade unions and local management have engaged (or not) in negotiations for framework agreements at the transnational company level. The cases were selected on the basis of the conclusion (or not) of agreements, the diversity of subjects and the social parties signing agreements. The following cases were selected: General Motors Europe and Ford (concluded framework agreements for the management of restructuring); Schneider and Areva (concluded agreements on equal opportunities, the anticipation of change and collective redundancies); and Siemens and

Electrolux (did not conclude agreements). In Areva and Schneider, agreements were signed by the European Metalworkers' Federation (EMF), whereas in GM Europe, the EWC was involved, together with the EMF, in the signing of agreements. By contrast, in Ford Europe, all the company-level negotiations were concluded by the EWC alone.

Data collection was carried out during the period from 2008 to 2010. It consisted of 35 semi-structured interviews with representatives of the European Industry Federation (EIF) in the metal sector and European coordinators within the EWCs, as well as national and local trade union officers, employee representatives and local managers. Observing local works council and EWC meetings, as well as the use of company and union documents (i.e., collective agreements), also provided useful secondary data.

The chapter is structured as follows. The first part discusses the relevance of establishing cross-border, company-level negotiations in Europe for the Europeanisation of industrial relations. It also offers definitions and specificities of European framework agreements (EFAs) in the metal sector in Europe. The second part presents the research findings. It comparatively examines the range of circumstances and the local actors' strategies for the conclusion (or not) of agreements.

EUROPEANISATION AND EMPLOYMENT REGULATION: THE PERSPECTIVE OF EUROPEAN FRAMEWORK AGREEMENTS

Within European economic integration, Marginson and Sisson (2004) claim to have discerned the creation of a systematic European model of industrial relations to regulate employment across borders. Accordingly, European framework agreements (EFAs) are considered crucial for the management of employment relations within multinationals in Europe. They offer unions the scope to deal with problems of industrial organisation, governance and labour mobility that inevitably result from internationalisation. EFAs cover a great variety of issues, including restructuring, social dialogue, health and safety, human resource management and data protection.

Since the adoption of the 1994/45/EC Directive, EWCs have contributed greatly to the spread of cross-border negotiation activity at the multinational company level in Europe. As most studies report, the majority of EFAs have been negotiated within multinationals with headquarters in Europe and signed by the relevant EWC. However, recent studies illustrate that negotiations for these agreements are increasingly being led by EIFs. In the metal industry sector, for example, the EMF has played an important role in negotiating agreements. In so doing, the EMF has followed the activities of the EWCs and placed an EMF coordinator (generally a union official from the majority union at the headquarters of the multinational) within each EWC. Between 1996 and mid-2007, Telljohann et al. (2009) counted a total of 73 EFAs that had been signed. Of these, 52 were signed by EWCs, in the majority of cases in cooperation with a European trade union at the industry level. In some situations, these agreements were also co-signed by national unions. The first EFA was signed in 1996, the year in which the 1994 EWC Directive became effective. Since 1998, the number of EFAs has expanded rapidly, with an initial peak in 2001 and a steady growth since then.

There is a need in comparative European studies to comprehend the impact EFAs can have on the creation of a European regional dimension for employment regulation. However, to assess correctly the influence of EFAs on the process of Europeanisation, it is crucial to define first what we mean by Europeanisation. In a recent contribution, Hyman (2010) warns about the often 'ambiguous and disputed concept' of Europe and its closely interlinked meanings. Hyman's argument underlies the need for a clear definition of employment and its regulation in Europe, which should automatically imply social relations, not simply contractual issues based on pure market principles. This is because the rules governing employment relations are not directly determined by the market alone, but are mitigated and/or mediated by the strategies of social actors at different levels, influenced in turn by industrial relations institutions (da Costa 2001). However, if Europe constitutes a complementary level interacting with national, sector and company levels, one of the main key issues is not only the levels at which diverse actors act but also, and more importantly, the degree of articulation between structures and processes at the different levels. Accordingly, Hoffmann (2001) claims that the Europeanisation of industrial relations should be defined and understood through the development of a complementary layer of actors, structures and processes at the European (regional) governmental and non-governmental levels that interact with national and local institutions. The main question remains, therefore, that of the interaction between different levels of regulation (company, sector, national, and regional), which are populated by diverse social actors, with probably different strategies, and various and in some cases contrasting interests.

EIFs have developed some structures for the cross-national coordination of union strategies that permit dealing with the previously mentioned difficulties. Accordingly, a common feature of all the EIFs' coordinating activities is the central role played by European experts, model agreements and the guidelines jointly developed and adopted by national unions. This is extended to the negotiation procedures and standards regarding the content of framework agreements, together with the role of EWCs, national trade unions and EWC coordinators. As the following sections will illustrate, the European industry federation in the metal sector (the EMF) is the most developed and first established with regard to dealing with the challenges posed by the rise of transnational company-level social dialogue and (though not exclusively) in situations of multinational change.

CROSS-NATIONAL NEGOTIATION AT THE COMPANY LEVEL: EVIDENCE FROM THE METAL SECTOR IN EUROPE

At the beginning of the new millennium, the EMF started to develop a European-level trade union coordination strategy to be applied in the context of cross-border restructuring within multinational companies. Aiming for joint strategies at the European level, the EMF established several common rules concerning how the metalworkers' unions should handle restructuring in Europe. In so doing, the EMF created binding procedures intended to define the conditions under which an EIF can negotiate at the transnational company level. This allowed closing the gap between structures for employee representation at the local and EU levels (i.e., works councils and EWCs) and trade unions by facilitating the national implementation of framework agreements within multinationals in Europe (Pulignano 2010). Among the ten principles that accordingly should be applied in the context of cross-border restructuring, we particularly note: full compliance with information and consultation rights, including the demand for extraordinary EWC meetings and the setting up of a European trade union coordination group that should be involved in drawing up a platform of common demands, promoting European-level negotiations and organising cross-border action. Moreover, it was decided that '*no negotiation at national level or within one company will be concluded before having informed and consulted with the colleagues concerned at the European level*' (EMF 2005: 4). Furthermore, any strategy agreed upon and any decision taken at the European level should be made binding for all the actors concerned and implemented at the national level.

Negotiating EFAs was planned as a union strategy to widen the scope for the transnational coordination of collective bargaining in the metal sector in the absence of an overall legal framework for transnational collective bargaining in Europe. Therefore, in June 2006, the EMF adopted a set of rules to be followed in the case of transnational negotiations within multinationals.[1] These rules were adopted in response to the increased negotiation activities of EWCs and gave the EMF a mandate from the different national trade unions to engage in negotiation with the corporate signatory of the relevant agreement. There was a need for the EMF to define the conditions and establish the rules under which to receive a mandate from the different national unions to negotiate at the transnational company level. In accordance, in the case of negotiation, it was specifically stated that preliminary information and consultation should involve the national trade unions, the EMF and the relevant EWC. In addition, a mandate to negotiate at the European company level should be decided on a case-by-case basis and given unanimously by the national trade unions, which should also approve the resulting agreement and specify its implementation in the diverse national settings in cooperation with the EWC. The mandate to sign the agreement is given to the EMF. The EMF Secretariat is, in turn, responsible for passing on to the Executive Committee and the relevant policy committees, information about the negotiation process and the signed agreements. At the time of writing, we count 21 framework agreements negotiated (via both EWCs and the EMF) within the metal industry sector. Managing restructuring is the main topic of EFAs in the automotive industry sector. Other topics are the anticipation of change, occupational developments, health and safety, equal opportunities and social dialogue.

CASE STUDIES

The Pioneering Agreements in the Automobile Sector: Ford and GM

In January 2000, the EWC at Ford signed the first European-level agreement in the automotive industry. The agreement was intended to protect those ex-Ford workers affected by the externalisation of its Visteon division. Their new employment contracts gave them the benefits of the same conditions as workers remaining at Ford, including seniority and pension rights. The Visteon agreement was the first substantial agreement negotiated with a multinational corporation at the European level. It was also the first agreement where an EWC in Europe asked to be involved in negotiations and was accepted by the management of a multinational as a partner for bargaining and the signing of an agreement on such substantive issues. Other similar agreements have subsequently been signed at the European level between Ford and its EWC: the Getrag Ford Transmissions agreement of 2000, the International Operations Synergies agreement in 2004 and the 2006 agreement on engineering. All Ford Europe agreements deal with concrete and substantive issues, such as job security and working conditions, and have been signed with management without resorting to industrial conflict. A 'Memorandum of Understanding' jointly agreed to between trade unions and management in 2000 provided the internal rules and indicated the conditions for bargaining at both the European and the national levels. In so doing, it helped to frame general expectations between management and local unions while reinforcing a climate of dialogue within the company. However, in a major restructuring in 2009, the three Visteon UK facilities were closed down without specific guarantees as to redundancy or pension rights. After several weeks of sit-ins and a campaign led by the union UNITE, a settlement was reached at the national level, including notice pay and a lump sum. However, the legally complex pension issue for the ex-Ford Visteon workers who were laid off presently remains unresolved.

The first European agreement between the management of General Motors Europe (GME) and its EWC was signed in May 2000. It had been negotiated in cooperation with IG Metall on behalf of the EMF and after coordination with Fiat's EWC. The agreement protected GM employees transferred to joint ventures between GM and Fiat. Subsequent agreements, signed at GME in 2001, 2004, 2008, and 2010 (dealing with the GM/Fiat joint venture, corporate social restructuring and various restructuring agreements including the closure of the Antwerp plant) are the most significant restructuring agreements signed by an EWC and the EMF with a multinational at the European level, since they theoretically protected all the company's employees in Europe. Only in the case of the restructuring of the Luton plant in 2001, followed by the 'Olympia Plan' the same year, did the EWC alone sign the agreement for multinational restructuring between employee representatives and the management at GM. The GME agreements are the result of a coordinated union strategy at the transnational level. Specifically, after years of GM restructuring negotiated at the local level with plants being pitted against each other, the GM EWC progressively adopted a European-level strategy for transnational solidarity—sometimes referred to as 'sharing the pain'—based on three principles: no plant closures, no forced redundancies and a systematic search for negotiated and socially responsible alternatives. In so doing, the EWC responded to a managerial tendering process for investment by developing a norm for not agreeing to local negotiations and concessions with local management, but instead holding out for a European-level agreement that would allow all plants to survive. The EWC achieved this through formal meetings, official communications and informal socialising between the different EWC members. Local union and employee representatives were actively involved in international work by discussing the importance of being involved in international issues. This strategy included Europe-wide mobilisation followed by transnational negotiation. Notably in 2001, 2004 and 2006, throughout its European sites, up to 50,000 GM workers took part in common strikes or 'action days' against plant closures.

In 2004, the EMF established a European trade union coordination group that comprised members of the EMF secretariat, representatives of the national unions and members of the GM EWC in order to coordinate employee responses at the European level. This experience became the basis for the EMF's European strategy for socially responsible restructuring and transnational solidarity. Accordingly, with the creation of the Joint Delta Working Group, through which the EWC sought to have an input in the choice of production sites for the next-generation of the Astra/Zafira (Delta platform) model, a fair distribution of production volumes was negotiated, allowing for the survival of all the GME plants. In particular, the EWC, the national unions and the local representatives of the Delta Group plants signed a 'European Solidarity Pledge' demanding a European agreement, which was signed in April 2008. In addition, GME signed another EFA in 2008 guaranteeing information and consultation on outsourcing and transfers of employees to suppliers on a voluntary basis. After the car sales crisis in the autumn of 2008, another EFA was signed in January 2009, reducing working time to avoid economic redundancies. However, the management of GME denounced this last EFA in May 2009, after the GM crisis in the USA. The EWC chairman and the CEO of GME tried to work out a plan at the European level to make the European operations independent from GM headquarters and devise a restructuring plan avoiding plant closures and forced redundancies. In November 2009, however, GM (now owned by the US Department of the Treasury) announced its intention not to sell its European subsidiary, Opel/Vauxhall. In January 2010, the management of Opel/Vauxhall presented a new restructuring plan, including 8,300 job cuts in Europe and the closing down of its Antwerp plant (2,600 workers). In April 2010, the Belgian trade unions and the local management of Opel Antwerp agreed on a 'social plan', based on anticipated retirements and voluntary redundancies. A tripartite restructuring group set up by the Flemish government to find investors was given until December 2010, failing which, the plant would shut down. On 21 May 2010, the director of Opel and the president of the EWC finalised another EFA on restructuring called the 'Opel Plan for the Future'. This EFA confirmed job and wage reductions but excluded collective redundancies until 2014.

The 'Missed Opportunities': The Electrolux and Siemens Cases

In response to global competition, in 2004, the Swedish-based multinational Electrolux announced a restructuring aimed at cutting costs in production and purchasing. Under this plan, half of Electrolux's 44 white-goods factories were to be relocated to low-cost countries. In 2005, the management decided to close plants in Fuenmayor, Spain (refrigerators), Parabiago, Italy (lawnmowers) and Nuremberg, Germany (washing machines, dishwashers and tumble dryers). In the case of the refrigerator plant in Fuenmayor, 450 employees were affected and production was moved to Hungary. The closure of the Nuremberg plant affected 1,750 employees and production was gradually moved to Poland. In the face of the restructuring plan, the EMF set up a European trade union coordination group consisting of the trade unions involved in the company, the EWC, the EMF EWC coordinator and the EMF secretary. As in other cases in the metal industry sector (such as GME), this body was intended to develop a European-level coordinated response to restructuring, aimed at ensuring a sustainable future for the European production sites. The European trade union coordination group initially organised a Europe-wide action day in October 2005 to protest against the management's decision. In order to avoid plant closures, the EMF strategy aimed at improving the competitiveness of the existing sites while attempting to safeguard socially responsible restructuring. The EMF urged management to engage in discussions at the European level about alternatives to plant closures. Central management rejected the request of the European unions, and at the end of 2005, it announced the closure of the Fuenmayor and AEG Nuremberg plants. The local union strategy aimed at entering into European-level negotiations encountered not only opposition from the management, but also a lack of conviction on the part of the Swedish EWC members and the Swedish metalworkers' union (IF Metall), which agreed with the strategy of central management that negotiation should be kept at the local level. The opposing position of the Swedish metalworkers' union contributed to weakening the role of the EWC in framing common norms and goals for the effective implementation of a cross-border strategy. Thus, the process of developing a shared, coordinated European-level trade union strategy capable of counterbalancing management restructuring plans entered into crisis. This lack of coordination adversely affected the extent to which a link with the European-level trade union strategy of the EMF could be created. As a result, a EFA was difficult to achieve.

Similarly, in the case of restructuring at the German-based engineering group Siemens, the strong control of the German representatives over the Siemens EWC (known as the Siemens Employee Committee or SEC) constrained the development of transnational mutual trust and employee cohesion in the face of the challenge of cross-border restructuring. On 8 July 2008, Siemens officially announced a plan to cut 16,750 jobs, which corresponded at that time to approximately 4 per cent of its global workforce. The job reductions affected all segments of the group and production sites in various European countries. As a result, the eight divisions that previously made up Siemens were reduced to three: energy, healthcare and industry. In addition to the 16,750 job losses, a further 4,150 jobs were affected by restructuring. The restructuring plan for Germany envisaged some 5,250 job cuts. In other European countries, 5,150 jobs were cut, and outside of Europe, the job reductions amounted to 6,350 employees. In this context, members of the Siemens EWC and trade union representatives met for two coordination meetings organised by the EMF in order to develop a trade union response. The first meeting was held on 17 July 2008, where 30 trade union representatives and members of the EWC were present. Union and SEC members expressed their dissatisfaction with the central management's information policy, as the SEC had not been informed and consulted about the details of the restructuring plan, in particular the closure of the Siemens SKV plant in Prague. The participants in the trade union coordination meeting affirmed their objection to forced redundancies. The meeting concluded with the announcement of Europe-wide support for a demonstration protesting against any plant closures, to be organised in Erlangen (Germany) on 23 July 2008. Contrary to the lack of information provided by management to the workers' representatives in other European countries, the German economic committee of the local works council received detailed information about the German sites that were to be affected by change and some generalised data about other EU Siemens plants. Surprisingly, on 22 July 2008 (one day before the planned European action day), IG Metall signed a preliminary agreement with the central management of the Siemens group on restructuring in Germany without informing the EMF beforehand. In the agreement, Siemens guaranteed not to close or relocate any German-based plants in the period up to 30 September 2010 and stated that the Mobility sector was to remain a strategic element of the German Siemens AG. Thus, there would not have been any closures of facilities in Germany. This initiative, taken by IG Metall and the German central works council, to sign a national-level agreement implied the undermining of the joint European-level strategy and entailed the closure of the Siemens plant in Prague. In order to support the Czech employees, a second European-wide coordination meeting was organised by the EMF in Prague on 19 August 2008. The trade unions and EWC members from 11 countries reaffirmed their objection to plant closures and expressed full solidarity with the employees at the Prague plant by organising strike action on 20 August 2008. After having signed an agreement that excluded plant closures in Germany, IG Metall was able and ready to support OS KOVO (the Czech Metalworkers' Federation) in its endeavors to negotiate acceptable conditions for the closure of the railway plant in Prague. IG Metall officially condemned the intended closure of the Siemens facility in Prague, announced its support for OS KOVO's activities and asked Siemens to negotiate fairly and openly with OS KOVO to achieve the aim of preserving the facility, if necessary by means of a sale. As a result of the support actions on 25 August 2008, a local agreement was reached for employees at the Siemens plant in Prague. This included efforts to preserve the facility by means of sale. In this case, Siemens would have paid every employee a transfer bonus equal to three months' wages. However, in the end, the plant was closed and Siemens offered a severance pay equal to 16 months' wages. SKV also ensured measures for improving workers' qualifications, which were financially supported for up to three months.

The Social Experiences of Agreements in Areva and Schneider

In November 2006, the EMF and the French energy supplier group Areva signed a EFA framework agreement on equal opportunities. Negotiation was requested by management and followed the company's policy strategy to promote greater diversity in employee profiles and career paths. The aim was to mobilise more skills and potential in the development of Areva's market in order to better cope with the process of demographic transformation and the need for skills development. The coexistence of different profiles is considered by the management of Areva to be crucial in providing complementary skills and a major asset in terms of innovation and change. With regard to career development and pay, Areva's management also agreed that there should be social equality between men and women with regard to pay and access to career paths. Accordingly, the recruitment process throughout the structure of the Areva group in Europe also operates according to the same conditions for both sexes: namely, using selection criteria based on the skills, professional experience and qualifications obtained by the person. The agreement identifies relevant indicators to assess the progress achieved and lays the groundwork for the establishment of a follow-up committee in which the EWC is expected to play a central role. In particular the EWC, represented by the select committee, is involved in implementing the agreement in cooperation with national and local representatives in the countries concerned. In an interview, the EMF Deputy General Secretary Bart Samyn[2] clearly points out that the Areva framework agreement on equal opportunities represents an important example of effective social dialogue at the EU company level that fully recognises the importance of European trade union organisations and attributes to them the responsibility for monitoring the transposition and implementation of the agreement in all relevant European countries. Implementation of the agreement follows three stages. Firstly, an information day is held for members of the EWC, as well as for the HR managers in the various European countries, aimed at creating the conditions necessary for implementation. Secondly, the appropriate legal representative within each country signs the agreement for transposition in accordance with national regulations. Thirdly, a local action plan is drawn up within all the entities concerned. A monitoring committee composed of representatives of HR management, the EWC and the EMF carries out an annual review of the action plans and evaluates the practical application of the agreement. Similarly, in July 2007, the EMF signed a European-level framework agreement on anticipating change with the French-based Schneider group. The aim is to promote life-long learning as a Schneider policy initiative designed to overcome skill discrepancies and increase the long-term employability of its workers, particularly older employees. Negotiation on the agreement was requested by management and viewed positively by the European trade unions, which saw the initiative as widening the scope for labour-management consultation at the European level. In anticipating which skill sets will be required to remain competitive, the agreement highlights three priorities: identifying skill requirements at both the job and workplace level; carrying out individual career path reviews with employees; and developing an active training policy. A key aspect of the Schneider 2007 agreement is the fact the company recognises the social dialogue aspect of it. Specifically, this means that through Schneider's EWC, the company commits to offering employee representatives the chance to voice their opinions and potentially influence company strategy. In line with the Areva case, consultation with the EWC and the EMF is considered by Schneider management as crucial in order to establish effective consultation at the European company level. It offers the negotiating union (the EMF) a key role in monitoring the program of anticipating change. Likewise, it attributes to Schneider's EWC the task, together with the management team, of influencing the characteristics of the company's transnational action plans. By not dealing with substantial aspects of the collective labour contract, such as pay and working conditions, both the Areva and Schneider agreements of 2006 and 2007, respectively, are usually referred to as covering what are termed the 'soft' employment issues. Conversely, in July 2010, following the acquisition of Areva T&D (a division of Areva) by Alstom and Schneider Electric, an agreement was signed on no collective redundancies for a period of three years and the retention of the working conditions for all the former Areva T&D workers who were transferred to Alstom-Schneider Electric. In particular, the agreement, which was signed by the EMF and the CEOs of Alstom, Areva and Schneider Electric, outlines rules and procedures to guide the social integration of employees of Areva T&D. It establishes no-discrimination rules by applying to the Areva T&D employees the same working conditions of employees in Alstom and Schneider Electric. In addition, the agreement states that all employees included in the headcount of Areva T&D at the date of its acquisition by the Alstom-Schneider Electric consortium will be entitled to an equivalent job in the same location. Any new job will reflect the employees' level of qualification, remuneration and seniority in the same way that their previous post did. The content of the agreement is in line with the general company policy, which is to strengthen the social dialogue aspect of the agreement while managing employment under company restructuring. The secretary of the Areva EWC played an important role in the negotiations, and the EWC obtained the guarantees on remuneration and employment for those employees affected by the transfer. After consultation with Areva's EWC, these guarantees were given by the CEOs of Schneider and Alstom in a plenary meeting in December 2009 and were included in the minutes. They were later confirmed in a letter from the French Ministry of Economy to the Secretary of the Areva EWC. In order to make them binding for Alstom and Schneider, the EWCs of Areva, Alstom and Schneider, together with the French unions in these companies (in particular, the CFDT), asked the EMF to negotiate with Alstom and Schneider to transform these guarantees into a European agreement. The secretary of the Areva EWC, together with the secretaries of Alstom and Schneider's EWCs, were part of the EMF negotiation team. All three are members of the CFDT. The agreement was signed by the two acquiring companies and the EMF.

ARTICULATING AT THE LOCAL LEVEL: TRADE UNION AND MANAGEMENT STRATEGIES FOR CROSS-NATIONAL BARGAINING IN EUROPE

An approach focused on the functioning and evolution of the institutions characterising the process of the Europeanisation of industrial relations more generally deserves to be analysed in light of the experiences and practices developed at the local level by the actors operating within such institutions. The 'rule-taker' versus 'rule-maker' model is particularly relevant in this regard. In other words, the fact that, in principle, any rule-following (even if intended to be fully conforming) must call upon what Joas (2005) called the 'creativity of action', implies that no social order can ever be perfectly reproduced in its enactment. Thus, the rule-taker and the rule-maker tend to set in motion interactive processes between them, which make the institutions and their meaning evolve over time. Thus, if we want to understand the functioning and evolution of particular institutions, it is crucial to begin at the micro-level of social action from where it gradually proceeds to institutional structures at the macro-level. With regard to the focus of this chapter, this entails specifically examining the strategies different local actors participating in the transnational company-level bargaining process develop, how these strategies evolve and the extent to which they are the result of cross-border and multi-level (i.e., European, national and company) coordination. In so doing, we aim to comprehend the effective nature of the changes and evolutions occurring in the process of European company-level bargaining. Our hypothesis is that the institutional structures (without reference to the strategies of the actors and what they do within these structures) do not offer a sufficient basis for understanding and assessing the development of bargaining activity at the European transnational level. When we say that actors have strategies, the meaning is that they have characteristic ways of interacting with their environments. Actors are located within a network of other people and the strategies they form are affected by a range of critical factors expressed through the behavior of the others and the wider economic and socio-political influences (Hyman 1994).

According to this interpretation, it is therefore relevant to identify the conditions under which collectively organised actors are enabled to act as 'institutional entrepreneurs' (Crouch et al., 2007). Only actors who somehow break with the rules and practices associated with the dominant institutional logic(s), and thereby develop alternative rules and practices, can be regarded as institutional entrepreneurs (Battilana 2006). Therefore, examining the conditions that offer scope to alter the rules or the distribution of resources requires identifying the factors that contribute towards affecting an actor's strategic course of action. Empirical findings presented in this chapter suggest differentiating between four basic kinds of conditions that enable social actors to be regarded as institutional entrepreneurs: cross-border workers' coordination, supported and facilitated by a solid articulation between the EU level and the national union level; an EWC structure and practice not predominated by headquarters with a strong 'home country' structure for worker representation; local union power; and a centralised HR corporate culture with a high degree of centralised autonomy and the control of local management over labour relations. By reflecting different local experiences, these conditions facilitate diverse political tendencies and strategies by the local actors. In so doing, they also concur to shed light on the different resources and capabilities organised actors mobilise to pursue their strategies. For example, in both cases in the automotive industry, the EWCs, although working under different conditions of labour relations (more conflictual in GM than in Ford), played crucial roles in shaping the hearts and minds of the workers and local unions across (and within) diverse geographical contexts. The EMF supported the EWC activity. In particular, the European trade unions provided the organisational background ('organisational field') where particular conditions could be conducive to action, by structuring principles and attributing social positions within which action could take place.

By recalling Bourdieu's conceptualisation of fields, we propose that the social position of actors in a given field is a key variable in understanding how they are enabled to act as institutional entrepreneurs, despite institutional pressures from pre-existing structures. GM's EWC demonstrated to local union representatives that the international strategy of the EMF was not merely a matter of international union strategies and meetings, but something that greatly affected them and their own local interests. Greer and Hauptmeier (2010: 24) state that the EWC *'promoted closer relationships between its own members'* by developing a lot of commonalities in their interpretation of the situation of company change. These commonalities soon became principles or norms. The solidarity norm of 'sharing the pain' and the 'solidarity pledge of 2005', which were at first introduced as policy principles by the EMF, were subsequently implemented and diffused by the GM EWC. These are just some examples of the ways in which the European trade unions and employee representatives in GME refrained from local concession bargaining until a common framework had first been agreed upon, so as to distribute production fairly and prevent all plant closures. The ability to provide principles or norms indicates the capacity of the local unions to create a frame of reference for their actions, while offering a scope for institutional transformation. As new institutionalism in organisation studies emphasises, *'new institutions arise when organized actors with sufficient resources see in them an opportunity to realize the interests that they value highly'* (Di Maggio 1988: 14). Moreover, while the willingness to act is dependent on actors' interests, their ability to act is also partly determined by the resources that they hold or to which they have access. Lévesque and Murray (2010) identify 'framing' as being important to a union's ability to define a proactive and autonomous agenda that can be used strategically to mobilise coalitions across borders and generate coordination and collective action, even in the situation of the absence of a general right to strike, as is the position in Europe. The GM case suggests that the institution of the EWC provided the resource that was used by local unions to frame new ideas. This was crucial in building up cross-border coordination of workers and articulating with the union at the European level. The EWC at GME became the platform for treating international competition as a grievance. In so doing, the EMF's strategic principle that national union strategies cannot solve the international problems created by international capital was enforced by the EWC. Specifically, as a result, the EWC made a general statement that it used in the specific case of GME to point out the need for local trade unions and workers to cooperate across borders. Accordingly, the EWC implemented the strategy developed by the EMF by creating a shared perception and understanding of problems, interests and strategies among the local workers and union representatives across European borders. This was sustained by transnational strike action in the face of a material conflict of interests, which confirmed the strong union power able to counter the management's whipsawing. Likewise, the Ford case illustrates that although operating under a situation of comparatively less conflictual labour relations, but with strong union power and a stable organizational field, the institution of the EWC became an important resource that the European trade unions used for initiating negotiation with management at the transnational level.

What is innovative in the Ford case is the fact that the EWC worked within a climate of consensus and cooperation with management to achieve its goal. The Ford EWC alone signed with management all the agreements that were concluded between 2000 and 2004, covering the management of restructuring (i.e., spin-offs, joint ventures, corporate social responsibility and fundamental rights). The 'Memorandum of Understanding' provided the context of common norms facilitating negotiation with management. These norms were set up to create a shared understanding of the specific problems and needs that were to be dealt with at the transnational European level, with an internal mandate to negotiate given to the EWC, thus setting up an internal procedure facilitating the emergence of European-level negotiations. One might consider that, because the headquarters of Ford Europe is in Germany, the strong unionisation and important characteristics of German industrial relations might have played a role, but in other cases, such as Siemens, it did not.

In fact, in the Siemens case, the presence of a strong German group works council with strong institutions, representation interests and co-determination rights in the home country converged to undermine the dynamic functioning of the EWC, while challenging its capacity to initiate negotiations with the company at the transnational level. In particular, the case of Siemens illustrates the failed attempt of a joint European-level strategy for transnational labour coordination, by revealing the contradictions between a strategy of company-level corporatism on the one hand, and an approach characterised by transnational solidarity, on the other. The agreement signed in Germany represents the outcome of a competitive company alliance aimed at prioritising local interests. The result of the competitive company pact at the national level consisted of reducing the impact of restructuring processes in Germany and increasing the burden in other countries. In order to reach a relatively favourable solution at the local level, management, on the one hand, and trade union and employee representatives on the other, did not comply with the relevant obligations concerning information. While the management did not respect the right of information and consultation of the SEC, neither did IG Metall inform the EMF about the ongoing negotiation processes and the foreseeable conclusion of an agreement in Germany. Likewise, in Electrolux, the presence of a strong Swedish works council and the union tradition typical of Nordic countries (in accordance with which bargaining has to be kept at the local level as the basis for the unions' power) contributed to reduce the possibility of the EMF obtaining a mandate and respect for its policy on restructuring from the local unions. As a result, the scope of the European trade unions to coordinate responses cross-nationally while requesting negotiations with company management was jeopardized. In this regard, the Electrolux case shows that it was particularly difficult for the European trade union to become effectively involved with central management in the handling of the actual restructuring processes. In particular, two obstacles are evident: the refusal of company management to voluntarily involve trade unions at the European level in the management of restructuring and weak internal cohesion on the part of employees. Hence, the Siemens and Electrolux cases, as with the GM and Ford ones, illustrate that the existence of European institutions such as the EWC do not determine *ex-ante* what local unions do. Conversely, cross-company comparisons show that EWC legislation has mixed effects, since it can both provide resources (in the example of the GM and Ford cases) and create constraints (in the example of the Siemens and Electrolux cases) for worker-side, cross-border cooperation. The extent to which institutions for employee representation at the European level can become good (or bad) working instruments for transnational labor solidarity and negotiation depends on the strategic capability of the local unions and employee representatives to fight by working to rule, and therefore use, these institutions as a means of envisaging feasible prospects for change.

The Areva and Schneider cases confirm the complexity characterising the process of transnational company-level negotiation and the mixed nature of the conditions sustaining or inhibiting it, as well as the strategies followed by local actors when faced with uncertainty. Both the 2006 Areva and 2007 Schneider agreements followed management's interest in negotiating at the European level to create efficiency in the bargaining processes, which involved negotiating at one table rather than undertaking multi-table negotiations at the different local plants. This seems to be typical of multinationals with a centralised HR corporate culture with a high level of centralised autonomy and the control of local management over labour relations. This scenario is characteristic of French-based multinationals. In the cases in point, management considered the European level as a supplementary level for industrial relations and therefore used agreements at the European level to strategically promote the companies' policies with regard to employment. Thus, the principles of equal opportunities, skills development, training and career promotion in the workplace have been endorsed. This can explain why in both the equal opportunities agreement in Areva and the anticipation of change agreement in Schneider, management was one of the willing parties in the negotiations. However, it can be also argued that the nature of the subject of the negotiations (soft employment issues) also created conditions that stopped local unions in France from obstructing the conclusion of agreements. As a result, the trade unions provided a mandate to the EMF to conclude agreements in both cases. In the case of the 2010 agreement on employment guarantees at Alstom and Schneider Electric, the European agreement gave the scope for both acquiring companies to pursue shared views on employment management, training and social dialogue by encompassing the Areva T&D activities. Even though the EMF was recognised as the negotiating party at the European level, the French unions and EWC employee representatives used all their power and influence at the national level to strengthen the negotiations to get the best possible agreement for the restructured workers (no collective redundancies for three years as the result of the acquisition by Alstom-Schneider Electric).

CONCLUSION

Social actors can and do respond strategically when faced with immediate crises and external shocks. Notably, strategic action requires considerations of spatial (scaling) and temporal (framing) horizons, as well as feedback loops for organisational learning and the transfer of knowledge (Lévesque and Murray, 2010). It is these strategic capabilities that contribute to clearly distinguishing between exogenous institutional and structural forces, and endogenous influences, and then striking a fine balance between those structural elements of path dependency on the one hand, and an autonomous capacity for strategic action by local actors, on the other.

The empirical evidence provided in this chapter contributes to illustrating that the issue of institutional entrepreneurship is quite critical in understanding the variance of the interest of social actors in requesting the negotiation of framework agreements at the European company level in the face of specific circumstances. While it is fairly difficult to predict precisely what options actors (management, unions and their representatives) may choose when faced with a critical situation that can potentially entail diverging interests, such as transnational restructuring, one might be able to arrive at a probable solution. Existing literature on institutional change identifies some trajectories of strategic institution shaping by actors. Among these trajectories, institutional 'layering' and *'bricolage'* (Streeck and Thelen, 2005) see the actors creatively using various elements from existing institutions or recombining them to reform and revitalise them. By using strategies of 'exit and voice', they help reinforce institutional change in multi-tiered, multi-level European governance of industrial relations. As the GM and Ford company cases illustrate, vertically and horizontally (cross-national) integrated policy networks have been created by local unions and their representatives in order to influence the regulation of employment relations in Europe. The institution of the EWC has been re-shaped for a different use than its original one, namely to create and enforce a normative social order across workers and unions, and between them and management. This has provided resourceful labor unions at both the national and local levels with strategic opportunities to influence the governance of employment relations at the company level by framing collective interests for transnational negotiation. This depends on the social position of both employee representatives and local unions within the organisational field of policy principles introduced by the EMF. In this respect, the EMF provided to employee representatives and local unions in GME the legitimacy to act as institutional entrepreneurs. When this strategic opportunity was jeopardised by the existence of home-country effects (i.e., the Electrolux and Siemens cases) it was very difficult for the local actors (in particular the unions) to avail themselves of these strategic opportunities. Likewise, by paying specific attention to the enactment of the institutions, in the Areva and Schneider cases, we observe that management took a strategic position in relation to the structure for European bargaining at the company level and used it (by reshaping) as a tool to widely spread company policy to local subsidiaries.

Drawing from the empirical findings, two major conclusions can be pointed out. Firstly, going beyond a pure institutionalist approach to actors' strategies in the study of the trends in multinational-level bargaining in Europe has enabled us to reconcile external factors with internal considerations. It has also enabled us to shed light on the purely artificial character provided by differentiating between local, national and transnational level, while assessing what unions do in a multi-level and multi-actor environment. In so doing, and this is the second conclusion, we overcome the simplistic description of successful and unsuccessful experiences in the context of transnational bargaining in Europe by providing a deep understanding of the underlying processes as social actors adapt to external change. This highlights the importance of learning more about the actors and their interplay with institutions as a crucial basis to form a better understanding of the functioning of the process of transnational bargaining in Europe.

NOTES

1. EMF (2007), 'Internal EMF Procedure for Negotiations at Multinational Company Level', Internal Policy Document.
2. Interview 25 November 2010.

REFERENCES

Battilana, J. (2006), 'Agency and Institutions: The Enabling Role of Individuals' Social Position', *Organization*, 13(5), 653–676.
Crouch, C., Streeck, W., Whitley, R., and Campbell, J. (2007), 'Institutional Change and Globalization', *Socio-Economic Review*, 5, 527–567.
da Costa, I. (2001), 'Globalizacion y relaciones laborales: comparacion entre Francia y España', *Cuadernos Relaciones Laborales*, 19, 95–122.
da Costa, I., and Rehfeldt, U. (2008), 'Transnational Collective Bargaining at Company Level: Historical Developments' in K. Papadakis (ed.), *Cross-Border Social Dialogue and Agreements: an Emerging Global Industrial Relations Framework?*, Geneva: International Institute for Labour Studies / International Labour Office.
Di Maggio, P. (1988), 'Interest and Agency in Institutional Theory', in L. Zucker (ed.), *Institutional Patterns and Organizations*, Cambridge, MA: Ballinger.
EMF (2005), *EMF Policy Approach towards Socially Responsible Company Restructuring—Approved by the 100th EMF Executive Committee*, Luxembourg, June 7–8.
Erne, R. (2008), *European Unions. Labor's Quest for a Transnational Democracy*, Ithaca: Cornell University Press.
Fetzer, T. (2008), 'European Works Councils as Trade Union Risk Communities: The Case of General Motors', *European Industrial Relations*, 14(Summer), 289–308.
Greer, I., and Hauptmeier, M. (2010), 'Identity Work: Sustaining Transnational Worker Cooperation at GM Europe', unpublished paper.
Hoffmann, J. (2001), 'Ambivalence in the Globalisation Process—The Risks and Opportunities of Globalisation', in D. Foden, J. Hoffmann and R. Scott (eds.), *Globalisation and the Social Contract*, Brussels: ETUI.
Hyman, R. (2010), 'Trade Unions, Global Competition and Options for Solidarity', in A. Bieler and I. Lindberg (eds.), *Global Restructuring, Labour and the Challenges for Transnational Solidarity*, London: Routledge.
Hyman, R. (1994), 'Changing Trade Union Identities and Strategies', in R. Hyman and A. Ferner (eds.), *New Frontiers in European Industrial Relations*, Oxford: Blackwell.
Joas, H. (2005), *The Creativity of Action*, Cambridge: Polity Press.
Lévesque, C., and Murray, G. (2010), 'Understanding Union Power: Resources and Capabilities for Renewing Union Capacity', *Transfer*, 16(3), 333–350.
Levinson, C. (1972), *International Trade Unionism*, London: Allen & Unwin.
Marginson, P., and Sisson, K. (2004), *European Integration and Industrial Relations*, London: Palgrave-MacMillan.
Pulignano, V. (2010), 'European Integration and Transnational Employment Regulations: the Company-Level Experience of EFAs in the Metal Sector in Europe', *European Labour Law Journal*, 1, 81–88.
Rehfeldt, U. (1993), 'Les syndicats européens face à la transnationalisation des entreprises', *Le Mouvement social*, 162(January–March), 69–93.

Streeck, W. (2011), 'Taking Capitalism Seriously: Towards an Institutionalist Approach to Contemporary Political Economy', *Socio-Economic Review*, 9: 137–167.

Streeck, W., and Thelen, K. (2005), *Beyond Continuity: Institutional Change in Advanced Political Economies*, Oxford: Oxford University Press.

Telljohann, V., da Costa, I., Muller, T., Rehfeldt, U., and Zimmer, R. (2009), *European and International Framework Agreements—Practical Experiences and Strategic Approaches*, Luxembourg: Office for Official Publications of the European Communities, available at http://www.eurofound.europa.eu/pubdocs/2008/102/en/2/EF08102EN.pdf.

9 European Trade Unions and the Long March through the Institutions
From Integration to Contention?

Richard Hyman

EUROCENTRIC INTERNATIONALISM

For most of its history, trade union internationalism has been primarily European in composition and focus: all formal organisations of global unionism have been located in Europe, headed by Europeans and largely funded by European affiliates. Following Stevis (1998), we may speak of five main historical phases. The process began with the 'First International' in the 1860s and 1870s; its initial congresses were exclusively European affairs, though in its closing years the headquarters (a misleadingly grand term) was moved to New York. From the end of the 1880s came the creation of International Trade Secretariats (ITSs)—much more recently renamed Global Union Federations (GUFs)—and at the turn of the century, the first transnational organisation of national union confederations. Not only were the ITSs European in membership, the majority were based in a single country, Germany (Hyman 2005). Confederal organisation was also purely European until the American Federation of Labor (AFL) participated in 1909. In the third phase, the reconstitution of the International Federation of Trade Unions (IFTU) after the First World War, fundamental differences between the AFL and the socialist-oriented Europeans led the Americans to withdraw in 1921, not to return until 1938. In the interim, the AFL concentrated on building a regional structure in the Americas, a process with longer-term significance, while 'the IFTU had no alternative but to focus its attention on its European base' (Van Goethem 2000: 82–8).

The creation of the World Federation of Trade Unions (WFTU) in 1945 marked a fourth phase of trade union internationalism, one when—according to an enthusiastic commentary at the time—'world labour [came] of age' (Wallace 1945). Efforts to achieve a truly global representation were reinforced by the break-up of WFTU in 1949 and the formation of the International Confederation of Free Trade Unions (ICFTU). After the split, WFTU was resourced and dominated from Moscow, while the key ICFTU affiliates were the leading members of NATO (perhaps not altogether coincidentally, both organisations had their headquarters in Brussels). In the cold war confrontation between international trade union movements, which in many respects were adjuncts of inter-governmental politics, both rivals strove to win allegiance in the non-aligned countries of the world. So did the Christian International, which had not joined WFTU and in 1968 was reconstructed as the World Confederation of Labour (WCL). In effect, trade union internationalism involved a form of clientelism: resources (and control?) remained primarily European (Gumbrell-McCormick 2000a), and establishing 'internationality' (Rütters 1989: 264) was an objective never fully realised. The relationship between the numerically and financially dominant European affiliates, and the European-based headquarters, on the one hand, and unions in the rest of the world on the other, was to be a constant source of tension.

The final phase (to date) commenced with the collapse of the Soviet Union and the end of the cold war, removing the key source of international trade union division. At the same time, the advance of economic globalisation and the weakening of socio-political constraints on unbridled capitalism made genuine unity increasingly essential. The creation of the International Trade Union Confederation (ITUC) in 2006 was the logical culmination. For almost the first time in any global trade union organisation, the ITUC is now headed by a non-European (the Australian Sharan Burrow), and western Europe accounts for only a quarter of total affiliated membership. Nevertheless, it still provides, by far, the largest single block of *paying* membership, and since fee levels are banded according to GNP, the west European unions contribute over 60 per cent of total ITUC income.

EUROPEAN UNIONS TURNING INWARDS?

If one source of tensions in international trade unionism has been a belief that the movement was dominated by 'a powerful European club' (Gumbrell-McCormick 2000b: 336), a reverse concern has existed ever since the creation of the (then) European Economic Community (EEC) in 1957. What was initially a common market between six western European countries has now become the European Union (EU) of 27 member states, encompassing virtually the whole of western Europe and the majority of countries in central-eastern Europe. Unlike other free trade areas, for example the North American Free Trade Area, it possesses an elaborate regulatory architecture, including the capacity to legislate on a wide range of employment issues. Increasingly, European economic integration has set the parameters of trade union action, encouraging 'an extension to the European level of the role unions had sought for themselves in national planning' (Cox 1971: 562). Hence for unions in Europe, 'international' is often understood primarily to mean 'European'. This Eurocentrism was accentuated, as in the interwar period, when in 1969, the AFL-CIO withdrew from the ICFTU, not returning until 1982 (Gumbrell-McCormick 2000b: 333).

The formation of the European Trade Union Confederation (ETUC) in 1973, as a body autonomous of existing global union structures, was widely viewed as a signal of a shift of interests and resources. The ICFTU had established a European Regional Organisation (ERO) in 1950, but affiliates in the new EEC formed a European Trade Union Secretariat in 1958, reconstituted as the European Confederation of Free Trade Unions in the European Community (ECFTU) in 1969. Unions in the European Free Trade Association (EFTA), formed in 1960 by seven countries outside the EEC, created a committee, which in turn became ICFTU-EFTA in 1968 (Buschak 2003: 3), and with the consolidation of these two bodies the ERO was wound up in 1969. The first enlargement of the EEC, in 1973, necessitated a realignment, but there were two main contentious issues among European affiliates of the ICFTU. First, should there be a single organisation encompassing both EEC member states and those outside; second, should the new body be open to non-members of the ICFTU. After intense debate, it was agreed to create a pan-European structure, followed by a decision to open membership to all bona fide unions except affiliates of WFTU. In 1974, the ETUC opened its ranks to all main European affiliates of the WCL. Later the same year, the largest Italian union, the CGIL—which ended its full membership of WFTU—was also admitted, to be followed significantly later by all major (ex-) communist unions in western Europe (Moreno 2001). With the fall of the iron curtain in 1989, membership was extended eastwards, though again with considerable debate about whether the former 'official' unions should be admitted.

The ETUC was founded with 17 affiliates in 15 countries. Today it has 83 member organisations in 36 countries. Creating a coherent common programme with a growing diversity of interests, experiences and traditions is a daunting task. At the same time, the challenges facing trade unions have magnified radically, yet in a period of straitened union finances, income from affiliates has not kept pace in real terms with membership, particularly since the unions from central-eastern Europe pay pro rata only a quarter of the fees of those in the west. For much of its work, the ETUC depends on subsidies from the European Commission. Most notably, its research arm, the European Trade Union Institute (ETUI), is largely funded by the Commission—more than €10 million was paid for its 2009–10 work programme, substantially above the annual affiliation fees—while considerable sums are also received for other projects. In addition, considerable support for workshops and conferences—meeting facilities, interpreters, travel costs—is derived from the same source. The European Trade Union Federations (ETUFs, previously known as European Industry Federations), the (more or less autonomous) regional organisations of the GUFs, likewise receive significant Commission support.

Gläser (2009) has suggested that the ETUC faces two dilemmas that are a source of inescapable weakness. The first is between representativeness and capacity to act—a tension between the logics of membership and of influence, as Dølvik (1997) puts it, or between broad representativity and homogeneity (Braud 2000). The second is between political independence and financial dependence on the European institutions or in the words of Martin and Ross (2001), 'the dilemma of borrowed resources'. The resulting contradictions are central to my discussion below.

THE EUROPEAN UNION: A COMPLEX AND CONTESTED POLITICAL SPACE

The EU is something of an enigma for social scientists. As noted above, it is not just a regional trading bloc; it possesses a significant administrative infrastructure with authority of a political nature. But nor is it, as sometimes asserted, a 'super-state': the competence of the EU institutions is limited to the agenda specified in the governing Treaties, and the principle of 'subsidiarity' insists that the European level should regulate only when this cannot be accomplished effectively at national level (though it is less clear who is to judge whether this is the case). It is also a complex political system with many veto points.

There are four key institutions. The *Commission* consists of nominees from each member state and has the power to initiate policy but not to decide on policy. The *Council of Ministers* consists of the heads of member state governments and is in effect the legislative and decision-making forum. For a long period, there was a unanimity rule, which has been increasingly replaced by qualified majority voting (QMV) on specific issues: in this case, the larger countries have more votes and a roughly two-thirds majority is required for a decision. The *European Parliament* has far fewer powers than most national parliaments, but now possesses some veto powers. The *European Court of Justice* (ECJ) has developed an important quasi-legislative role on some issues, not least as affects equal opportunities in employment. Lately it has adopted a more neo-liberal interpretation of the Treaties than many member states had envisaged, as discussed below.

Much early academic discussion assumed that the political authority and competence of the European level would inevitably expand because powers to regulate in one policy field would 'spill over' into others. But scholars soon proposed a contrasting interpretation: there would never be a truly federal Europe, because national governments were effective protectors of their own autonomy. Europe was not a super-state in the making, but an arena governed by the diplomatic manoeuvres of the member states—hence the emphasis on subsidiarity. More recently, attempts have been made to bridge these conflicting positions. Today, a fashionable notion is 'multi-level governance' (Marks et al. 1996). This implies that both national and European (and also sub-national) levels have an important influence and that it is the interaction between levels that is crucial. Moreover, the primary locus of power may shift over time and may also vary according to policy issue.

Another key question is the character of European integration. For many commentators it once seemed self-evident that if the importance of the European level increased, this would entail a growing body of European rules, including those regulating employment and the labour market. But, subsequently, a more sceptical position was developed, based on the concept of 'negative integration' (Scharpf 1999). The argument here was that integration has occurred primarily through weakening or eliminating national rules that constrain cross-national economic integration, without necessarily establishing supranational rules in their place. For example, central to the single European market are the 'four freedoms' of movement (for goods, services, capital and labour). Freedom of movement meant eliminating national barriers; but for neoliberals and advocates of flexibility, it was neither necessary nor desirable to create positive regulation at the European level.

This question overlaps with the relationship between economic and social integration. The 1957 Treaty of Rome established a European Economic Community (or Common Market), and market integration was, in the eyes of many observers (both supporters and opponents), the be-all and end-all. However, there were some fears that countries with inferior employment conditions would gain an unfair advantage in the common market (what would later be described as 'social dumping'). For this reason, the original Treaty of Rome included a clause enabling the Commission to propose measures aimed at the harmonisation of working conditions and another prescribing equal pay for women.

In the 1970s (when centre-left governments were in power in many member states) there were more ambitious efforts to adopt directives that would ensure upwards harmonisation of employment regulations. But this was halted with a shift to the right in European politics (notably Thatcher's election in Britain in 1979) and the more general enthusiasm for labour market deregulation. A new phase began when Jacques Delors became Commission President in 1985. He helped drive the 'single market' project, but also insisted that greater integration must possess a 'social dimension'. This developed into the initiative for a European 'social charter', which had no binding status, but gave a green light for further Commission initiatives. This was followed by the 'social chapter' agreed at Maastricht in December 1991, which enlarged the EU competence in the employment field and extended the range of issues on which directives could be adopted by QMV.

A key element in the Delors initiative was the 'social dialogue' between unions and employers at the European level, conventionally known as the 'social partners'. Didry and Mias (2005) describe the launch of the social dialogue at Val Duchesse in 1985 as a 'cunning plan' (*grande ruse*) to establish a 'subtle dialectic' between market, state and civil society at the pan-European level. The aim was to counteract the Thatcherite agenda of market liberalism, but also to breathe new life into this dormant process of social regulation. The precondition of the process was to embed the ETUC and their employer counterpart UNICE (now BusinessEurope), together with the public sector employers' body CEEP, in the next stage of European construction, and in the process, to transform the character and function of the European 'social partners' themselves. By cultivating authoritative interlocutors from the two sides of industry, the Commission might strengthen its own supranational authority and acquire greater room for manœuvre within the complex politics of EU decision-making. The Maastricht Treaty gave 'social partners' at the European level the right to negotiate European-level agreements that could be implemented as directives (the main form of EU legislation) by a 'Council decision'. After Maastricht, there was a considerable acceleration in employment legislation, but from the late 1990s, the pace slowed again. Right-wing governments now dominated western Europe, while many argue that enlargement to central-eastern Europe has now created a large bloc without the traditions of 'social Europe' and with a competitive interest in preventing new employment regulation.

Is the 'social dimension' of European integration simply a fig-leaf to make a neoliberal economic project more acceptable, or is it a thing of substance? How far has the relationship between economic and social changed over time? If the whole idea of a social dimension is little more than rhetoric, the possibility of significant European-level employment regulation is minimal; if it has real meaning, then the Europeanisation of industrial relations seems more feasible. In terms of the EU 'constitution', the Single European Act of 1986 prescribed a large agenda of economic integration, with disagreements in many instances resoluble by QMV. The Treaty imposed far fewer obligations concerning social regulation, and most decisions still required unanimity (though the Maastricht and Amsterdam Treaties of 1991 and 1997 increased the scope for QMV on employment issues).

TRADE UNIONS AND THE 'EUROPEAN SOCIAL MODEL'

European economic integration provoked conflicting reactions among trade unions. To some extent, these reflected the familiar political divisions within labour movements. Unions affiliated to, or sympathetic with, the WFTU denounced the original EEC as the institutional expression of the interests of large-scale capital. Conversely, affiliates of the ICFTU and the WCL tended to adopt a more positive view: European integration had an inherently progressive character, not least as heralding the end of military conflicts among (West) European nations. But national circumstances have also proved important. Marks and Wilson (2000), in a study of party-political attitudes to European integration, suggest that social-democratic parties with limited strength and effectiveness at the national level have tended to regard European integration positively; while those with a greater power to shape national policy have resisted the idea of subordinating national decision-making capacity to an (almost certainly more conservative) European regime. A similar distinction applies to trade unions: where Labour or social-democratic governments have been relatively common (as in Britain and the Nordic countries), unions have been more sceptical of European integration. Confronted with the tension between a process of European integration that seems in principle desirable, and the potential threats from economic integration to national industrial relations practices, four broad categories of response might be identified. The most negative could be termed 'no, because': for example, the French CGT long opposed existing Europeanisation as a conspiracy driven by multinational capital to undermine workers' protections. A more nuanced position could be termed 'no, unless': the position of opposition groups within many trade union movements, particularly in the Nordic countries. This shades into what might be termed the 'yes, if' stance: for example, the Austrian ÖGB in 1988 endorsed accession to the EU on nine specified conditions. More positively, many trade unions have embraced a 'yes, and' posture: their support for integration is virtually unconditional, but they articulate a 'wish list' of desired accompaniments to Europeanisation. As discussed further below, this has been the position of the ETUC.

Dølvik (1997: 29) has proposed that 'the incentives for trade unions to engage in Europeanisation . . . are influenced by interplay between the particular structure of opportunities related to the social dimension and the structural bias of the broader trajectory of European integration'. As this interplay has developed, both ideological and nation-specific sources of resistance have weakened over time: it is possible to discern a 'conversion experience' (Martin and Ross, 1999: 355) through which even sceptical organisations have changed position. This conversion owed much to the exhaustion of the old ideologies (communist, christian, or social-democratic) which once provided a vision and utopia for trade union movements: 'Europe' seemed to represent a new moral inspiration.

Crucial for this view of the normative value of the EEC/EU was the idea of 'social Europe', which as indicated above has been part of the rhetoric of European integration for the past half century. The discourse of the 'European social model' presents both an idealised account of reality and a programme. As the literature on 'varieties of capitalism' (Albert 1993; Hall and Soskice 2001) emphasises, capitalist societies are marked by substantial differences in regulatory frameworks and institutional arrangements, including their systems of industrial relations. In much of continental western Europe these frameworks and arrangements differ substantially from those in much of the rest of the world. There are substantial limits to the ways in which labour (power) can be bought and sold, often imposed through elaborate employment protection legislation and reinforced by extensive public welfare systems. Partly as a corollary, collective agreements usually have priority over individual employment contracts, further limiting the freedom of individual labour market actors; moreover, centralised bargaining and, in some countries, legal extension mechanisms result in high levels of coverage (even when union density is low). There is broad social and political acceptance that labour possesses distinctive collective interests that need independent representation; from this follows the idea of labour as a 'social partner', often with a key role in shaping social policy and administering public welfare. Fourth, almost universally, there is a standardised system of workplace representation at least partially independent of management (underwritten by law or peak-level agreement, or both). The autonomy of employers is thus constrained to a degree unknown elsewhere in the world.

'Social Europe' can be seen, first as a celebration of these features of employment regimes in which workers are assigned both individual and collective rights and status. Second, the term symbolises the goal of generalising and extending these rights and protections through the harmonisation and upward standardisation of outcomes across the community. From the late 1960s this aspiration was symbolised by demands for the generalisation of the rights of worker representation and co-determination most strongly established in Germany, as I discuss further below.

In the uphill struggle for a meaningful social Europe, trade unions confront not only the gravitational pull of the existing constitutional framework, but also the force of weighty opponents. There is the familiar imbalance within the institutions of the EU itself: the Parliament, the most 'popular' (directly elected) element in the decision-making architecture, and the most reliable supporter of an effective social dimension to European integration, is also the most limited in its powers. The Commission, while dependent for its own status on the extent of EU regulatory capacity, is at best an ambiguous ally. While the Directorate-General for Employment and Social Affairs (DG EMPL) may be sympathetic to many trade union aspirations for social regulation, its own influence is subordinate to that of the many others with a primarily market-making mission. Note that in recent years, the DG EMPL has always been assigned a Commissioner from a 'peripheral' country, after the more influential briefs have been carved up amongst the heavyweights. Within the Prodi Commission, Commissioner Bolkestein—responsible for the internal market—pursued a fervently neoliberal agenda, including pressing the notorious directive on the liberalisation of services, and the current Barroso Commission is even more dominated by free market fanatics.

To these biases is, of course, added the imbalance of influence between labour and capital. This is not simply a matter of organisational resources. In many respects, the ETUC is organisationally more robust than BusinessEurope, though we should not forget the ranks of lobbyists and representatives retained in Brussels by individual companies and national associations, vastly outnumbering the European officials of national trade unions. Far more than veto power is exercised by the European Round Table of Industrialists:

the single market project of the 1980s, and the more general commitment to liberalisation of European societies, was largely the outcome of its strategic initiative (Balanyá et al., 2003; van Apeldoorn, 2000). But the issue is also structural: employers and industrialists work with the grain of entrenched EU policy, while trade unions (if they are serious about 'social Europe') seek a major change of course. In such a context, veto power is typically more effective, as well as more discreet. Recall the argument of Offe and Wiesenthal (1985: 191–3) concerning the 'structural asymmetry' of capital and labour in their relationship with the state: since governments are dependent on the investment decisions of a multiplicity of individual firms, capital exerts political pressure without the need to mobilise collectively. The normal economic rationality of company decision-makers has a political significance that may not even be intended. Against this background, the relative organisational weakness of BusinessEurope may constitute a strength for capital: even if its professional representatives were inclined to compromise on principles that some employers consider sacrosanct, it lacks the capacity to commit those it supposedly represents.

At the national level, employment regulation typically takes the form either of collective agreements between unions and employers (in many countries, with binding status) or of legislation, the two commonly operating in conjunction. In the EU, the analogue to national collective bargaining is the social dialogue, only exceptionally resulting in anything more than 'joint opinions', with the number of agreements reached under the Maastricht social partners' route still minimal; while, the analogue to national legislation is the directive, an instrument that is always slow (that on European Works Councils was first proposed in 1980 and finally adopted in 1994), and rarely does more than codify existing practice in the great majority of member states. Over and above this, there has been a marked shift in recent years away from regulation by directive to 'softer' methods.

Indeed economic integration, and in particular the single market project, has pointed in a diametrically opposite direction to an extended social dimension. In one sense, Europe can be seen as a particularly strong example at the continental level of 'globalisation', involving transnational product market integration, corporate restructuring and financial liberalisation—threatening the traditional basis for autonomously created national socioeconomic regimes. As Scharpf (1999) has argued, the preferred mode of Europeanisation has been 'negative integration', the elimination of national regulations that constitute obstacles to free movement. Negative integration reflects the priority of economic over social and political integration: a common market can be understood primarily in terms of freedom *from* regulations that inhibit cross-national exchange, whereas the creation of a social community depends on *rights* that are entrenched in new regulatory institutions. The Treaty of Rome established community competence primarily in market terms; the Single European Act was most mandatory and specific in the field of market-making (with the formalisation of qualified majority voting primarily directed to this end); the Maastricht Treaty, though celebrated by the trade union movement for its social chapter, was most binding in outcome in respect to the notorious deflationary convergence criteria for economic and monetary union (EMU); the Stability and Growth Pact of 1999 reinforced the commitment to budgetary restraint; and the Lisbon Treaty of 2007 reaffirmed neoliberal economic imperatives in unambiguous terms while giving far more diffuse approval to social goals. This conception of 'anti-social Europe' has been brutally asserted by the ECJ in a series of landmark decisions. In the Viking and Laval cases in 2007, it adopted the principle that, irrespective of national law, industrial action that interfered with freedom of movement was legitimate only if it satisfied a 'proportionality' test. These were followed in 2008 by the Rüffert and Luxembourg cases, which set very strict limits on the extent to which public authorities could prescribe minimum employment standards if these interfered with the freedom to provide services. Are Anglo-Saxon principles of 'shareholder value', and associated practices of labour market flexibility, necessary concomitants of the single market?

Accordingly, a more defensive conception of 'social Europe' focuses on damage limitation. This perspective, increasingly embraced by the ETUC in the past decade, addresses the EU as a potential mechanism of 'collective defence' of the existing architecture of social regulation in the Member States, in the face of external pressures to dismantle workers' rights at the national level (Grahl and Teague, 1997). Yet the defence of 'civilised' capitalism against threats from unfettered, casino capitalism still contradicts the dominant logic of actually existing European integration, and indeed the dominant mode of 're-forming' national capitalisms, as Streeck (2009) has demonstrated in the German case.

Reconciling workers' rights with the imperatives of capital accumulation ('competitiveness') encourages a double-edged strategy: attempting to demonstrate 'the economic dimension of the social dimension' (Streeck 1992: 315). This view is consistent with the varieties of capitalism approach: protecting workers against dismissal, providing an institutionalised 'voice' within the workplace and establishing a developed infrastructure of social welfare all contribute to investment in skills, long-term planning and a high-quality production paradigm. A strong 'social dimension' is thus necessary as a 'productive factor' (Andersson 2005; Streeck 2001). This argument is very evident in much of the discourse of the ETUC in recent years. Yet it carries two dangers. First, what if capitalists and policy-makers are unconvinced, or no longer convinced? Second, to propose that worker rights and welfare provision are to be justified primarily in terms of their contribution to competitiveness is to abandon the long-established arguments of labour movements in terms of equality and democracy, and to disregard the extent to which social and employment policy is an arena of contest within a class society.

BETWEEN ELITE EMBRACE AND CONTESTATION

Some years ago, Ramsay (1997: 528) wrote that 'ETUC efforts are focused almost entirely in the EU lobby circuit'. This is not wholly true: the ETUC has always played an important information and coordination role, has attempted to transform the diverse and at times conflicting aims of its affiliates into a coherent policy agenda and has even organised the occasional mass demonstration in support of these objectives, as I discuss below. Nevertheless, it remains the case that its limited resources are substantially concentrated on engagement with the Brussels institutions. What are the implications?

As noted above, Dølvik (1997), in his detailed insider study of the ETUC, distinguishes between a 'logic of membership' and a 'logic of influence'. The former requires unions to maintain their representative credentials by articulating the wishes and interests of their constituents. The latter requires them to adapt their aims and methods to the actual decision-making processes on which they wish to exert an impact. Balancing the two logics is a difficult art: neglect the logic of influence, and one's demands may be ineffectual; neglect the logic of membership, and one loses representative legitimacy. The Brussels embrace can all too easily achieve the second outcome. 'The seductive appeal of the social partnership rhetoric has been instrumental in bolstering legitimacy and support around union claims for recognition and influence in the EU polity,' but with the risk 'that the ETUC representatives might become co-opted by the EU institutions' (Dølvik and Visser 2001: 32).

The decision-making process within the EU is often termed 'comitology': initiatives are formulated, analysed, revised, debated, further amended and reformulated, within an elaborate network of interacting committees, until an outcome emerges (or fails to emerge). This process has a strong technocratic bias: the focus of argument is diverted from principle to detail. One could say that this takes the politics out of policy: as Goetschy comments (2003: 32), 'a relative "depoliticisation" of decision-making and the reliance . . . on expert networks and procedural routine does not facilitate public political debate'. Likewise, de la Porte and Pochet note (2003: 34) that the involvement of the 'social partners' in the policy process is intended to counteract the EU's democratic deficit but fails to do so because those involved 'operate through unknown mechanisms behind closed doors', resulting in an essentially technocratic dynamic of integration (Erne 2008; Storey 2008).

The outcome of comitology is reminiscent of what, at the British TUC, is known as the composite resolution. Different member unions submit conflicting proposals on a contentious policy issue, but are then pressed to agree through backroom negotiation to a form of words that somehow embraces the opposing viewpoints. In this way, potentially embarrassing disputation is removed from the public arena. The outcome of Brussels comitology seems similar. For example, in the European Employment Strategy (EES), strongly supported by the ETUC, the underlying message seems to have been that the prescriptions of Keynesianism and monetarism, of social regulation and of deregulation, can somehow be harmonised through a technocratic fix that transcends hard political choices. The Lisbon European Council in March 2000 famously declared that 'the Union has today set itself a new strategic goal for the next decade: to become the most competitive and dynamic knowledge-based economy in the world, capable of sustainable economic growth with more and better jobs and greater social cohesion'. But can all these desirable goals be achieved simultaneously; and if not, who decides the priorities? In the evolution of policy since Lisbon, the goal of 'better jobs' has been transformed into the slogan of quality, which has in turn been redefined primarily in terms of productivity. Competitiveness links directly to the 'adaptability' pillar of the EES, with its synonym flexibility. The joint statement on *Key Challenges Facing European Labour Markets*, signed by the ETUC with the employers' organisations in October 2007 at a time of intense controversy over Commission proposals to 'modernise' employment protection legislation, is a clear but depressing example of this technocratic approach.

The ETUC is sucked into this process in part because of its dependence on 'borrowed resources'. 'Because national union movements in Europe were reluctant to allocate resources and to grant it significant opportunities to acquire capacities on its own, the ETUC had to seek its building materials elsewhere, from friendly, but self-interested, European institutional elites' (Martin and Ross 2001: 54). Gobin (1997) and Wagner (2005) have charted in detail how this material dependence has constrained the ETUC's agenda and made comitology the line of least resistance.

More insidious, perhaps, is the subtle interaction between discourse, ideology and practice. All who are familiar with the Brussels process, whether as participants or as observers, have come to talk a strange language. They speak easily of horizontal objectives and open methods, of the social partners' route and co-decision, of macroeconomic dialogue and transposition. They can master a whole lexicon of acronyms. When they refer to Barcelona, Stockholm or Nice they do not—unlike most normal people—think of them as tourist destinations. This is the world of Eurospeak! European integration has generated an organising discourse that—presumably unintentionally—most effectively distances professional Europeans from the citizenry of European states. There is 'a multitude of common understandings, inter-institutional agreements and informal modes of behaviour which are reproduced every day in the political and administrative practice of the EU'; and 'a lobbying community has produced an entire political class that shares the language' (Christiansen et al. 1999: 539, 541). To the extent that Eurospeak has become the working language of the ETUC (and national union representatives active within its structures), their logic of membership is undermined by the fact that they speak a different language from those they seek to represent. Not only different, but actually opposed: 'analysis of the official statements of the ETUC clearly shows a gradual integration of the employers' vocabulary and, increasingly, a vocabulary produced by the administrative apparatus of the Commission, at the expense of a vocabulary expressing traditional trade union demands' (Gobin 1997: 116).

The consequence of the elite embrace is a suppression of both political alternatives and mobilisation capacity. Political alternatives are suppressed because, in effect, European unions have lacked the nerve to say no, which in turn dilutes the logic of influence. Take two of the biggest issues of economic integration. The 'social dimension' was invented by Delors to provide a 'human face' to the completion of the single market, and to turn the trade union movements of Europe from potential opponents into reliable allies. This offered the opportunity for significant influence, if and only if the unions had been prepared to campaign against the Single European Act unless it gave labour social rights that matched the economic benefits for capital. Likewise with the EMU: 'despite judging the design of EMU as fundamentally flawed, the ETUC continued to back it, arguing that it was needed politically to keep integration going' (Martin and Ross 1999: 349; 2001: 72). Yet if the Maastricht convergence criteria were the price for the single currency, it was a Faustian bargain. The same has been true with ETUC support for the—at best ambiguous—revisions to the Treaties that were blocked by the referendum rejections in France and the Netherlands in 2005 but ultimately adopted in 2009 (Hyman 2010).

Having assented to the underlying architecture of actually existing Europeanisation, is unions' capacity to mobilise around an alternative vision of social Europe thereby neutralised? Not entirely. Visser and Ebbinghaus (1992: 232) note that the ETUC organised a number of demonstrations against unemployment between 1978 and 1983, while Groux et al. (1993: 60–1) discuss these in more detail, identifying an oscillation between a trade unionism of 'mobilisation' and of 'pure institutionalisation'. They conclude, however, that the potential for trade unionism of mobilisation faded. However, there has been some revival of the mobilising mode from the late 1990s, with regular mass demonstrations in conjunction with EU summits (Gajewska 2008: 110–3). 'There is . . . evidence that the ETUC is beginning to combine its role as an institutionalized "social partner" with the more campaigning approach associated with "social movement unionism"' (Taylor and Mathers 2004: 268; see also http://www.etuc.org/r/1258). Perhaps most notably, in 2006 the ETUC organised a mass demonstration in Strasbourg while the European Parliament debated the Bolkestein draft directive for the liberalisation of services.

The significance of such actions should not be exaggerated, however. Mass mobilisation under the auspices of the ETUC is invariably symbolic, controlled and subordinated to its 'real' work within the Brussels institutions. (In its 2003–07 Report on Activities, the ETUC devoted four pages to the social dialogue and half a page to campaigns and mobilisations.) In general there has been an overriding concern to maintain a distance from more radical forms of protest and from social movements perceived as hostile to the existing dynamic of European integration (Bieler 2006; Bieler and Morton 2004; Mathers 2007; Tarrow 1995). Relations with *altermondialiste* groups opposed to neoliberal Europeanisation have been typically hostile (Lefébure 2002; Lefébure and Lagneau 2002). There is no indication of a strategic integration of a bargaining and a contestatory approach to the EU institutions.

CONCLUSION: THE LONG MARCH, WITHIN OR AGAINST THE INSTITUTIONS?

Martin and Ross (2001: 54, 74) argue that while the ETUC has had to seek resources 'from friendly, but self-interested, European institutional elites', its orientation to a technocratic insider role has been freely chosen because of its 'commitment to a general vision of European integration close to the one held by the Commission and other key institutional players'. Its core identity has become that of a social partner and a participant in social dialogue.

What has been the outcome? The 'social partners' route' to legislation embodied in the Maastricht Treaty has absorbed substantial energy and resources but with limited results. On major issues, such as European Works Councils, agreement has proved impossible. The three pieces of negotiated legislation between 1995 and 1999—on parental leave, part-time work and fixed-term contracts—involved far less contentious issues. Moreover, these agreements were reached 'in the shadow of the law': if legislation seemed imminent, the employers saw legislation, the terms of which it could negotiate as a preferable alternative to an externally imposed directive. With the shift to the right in EU governments and eastern enlargement, this 'shadow' has been almost completely lifted.

Nevertheless, in the past decade, the ETUC has become even more intensively involved in social dialogue, but now largely on the employers' terms. With the one exception of a joint statement on revision of the European Works Council directive—when legislation seemed inevitable with or without agreement—the employers have been willing to reach a common position only if the outcome is not applied as European legislation. Since 2001, the ETUC has been willing to approve a series of 'autonomous' joint work programmes with the employers' organisations, resulting in framework agreements on telework, work-related stress, harassment and violence at work and a revised framework for parental leave—which unlike the original agreement was not given legislative backing (causing significant disagreement among ETUC affiliates).

Is the ETUC committed to the process of dialogue as much as the outcome? Emilio Gabaglio, general secretary from 1991 to 2003, wrote (2003: 51–2) that 'the process itself, that is negotiating agreements in order to negotiate agreements, is more important than their content. To establish yourself and be recognised as a key actor, you have to produce agreements, if necessary whatever they may be.' More recently Maria-Helena André, then deputy general secretary, defended the principle of non-binding agreements in similar terms (2007: 6–7): 'the biggest net benefit of the agreement is having it,' adding that 'we have to face facts—the days of social directives may not be over, but are increasingly numbered'.

In his discussion of the limited transnational protest mobilisation by European trade unions, Imig (2002: 923) suggests that 'groups who are already organised, such as workers, are not likely to abandon their well-worn opportunity structures to organise at the European level'. But what happens when the 'well-worn opportunity structures' provide diminishing opportunities? Since 2008, the financial, economic and fiscal crises have exposed how little influence the ETUC exerts in the corridors of power in Brussels. Its calls for an expansionary macroeconomic response to minimise job losses were disregarded, as EU governments insisted on austerity measures to reduce public debt as the overriding priority. By early 2011, key governments were proposing to link austerity to a 'competitiveness pact' that would impose wage reductions. 'Europe is heading on a collision course with its social model,' declared the retiring ETUC general secretary John Monks (press release, 4 February 2011). Yet a month later, the austerity plans were intensified through the adoption of the 'Euro-Plus pact' by all 17 eurozone countries and the majority of the other member states.

As the cuts bite, protests are already mounting at the national level. Will the ETUC, which in 2009–10 already raised the tempo of its mass demonstrations, decide on a strategic shift to a genuinely contestatory role—giving reality to the slogan 'On the Offensive' that decorated its 2007 Congress platform? At the Athens Congress in May 2011, the new general secretary, Bernadette Ségol, insisted that 'fundamental social rights must get a priority over economic freedoms' and that 'we will have to oppose uncompromisingly the anti-social practices that attack the heart of trade unionism' (*nous devrons nous opposer, sans compromis, aux pratiques antisociales qui attaquent au coeur du syndicalisme*). What this means in practice remains unclear.

What is to be done? To maintain the relevance of trade unionism at the EU level, there are three central priorities. First, trade unions need to negotiate their own policy agenda, not just in the Brussels committee rooms but through involvement with their memberships. In most countries, EU policy has traditionally been treated as a matter for 'European experts', who have typically been absorbed into the perspectives and discourse of the EU elite. Lack of an organic connection to the rank and file has translated, inevitably, into the absence of effective bargaining power. What is needed is an 'internal social dialogue' in which serious debate on European issues is fostered with the mechanisms of trade union democracy.

Second, as part of this process, they must define, and campaign for, a concrete vision of a real European social model to meet the needs of workers and citizens in the 21st century. 'Social Europe' must be recognised as a terrain of struggle: unions have to launch a battle of ideas to present an alternative vision to neoliberalism. The Athens Congress adopted the slogan 'Mobilising for Social Europe'; what this means in practice is far less clear, though it is evident that the goals and priorities of different national affiliates are on many issues in conflict. Typically, the response is to seek a form of words that papers over the differences, rather than openly negotiating the competing visions of the future.

Third, 'on the offensive' has to mean a willingness to say no, shifting from social dialogue to the mobilisation of opposition to actually existing European integration. Though its leadership has changed, the ETUC still seems determined to maintain the priority assigned to social dialogue—on an agenda defined by its opponents—with the mobilisation for an alternative restricted to token demonstrative action. This is to leave unambiguous opposition to actually existing Europeanisation to the political fringes and, in particular, the xenophobic far right. Europe's workers deserve better.

REFERENCES

Albert, M. (1993), *Capitalism against Capitalism*, London: Whurr.

Andersson, J. (2005), 'Investment or Cost? The Role of the Metaphor of Productive Social Policies in Welfare State Formation in Europe and the US 1850–2000', paper presented to the World Congress in Historical Sciences, Sydney, July.

André, M.-H. (2007), 'European Framework Agreements: "The Best Option as the Politics Stand"', *HESA Newsletter*, 33, 6–7.

Balanyá, B., Doherty, A., Hoedeman, O., Ma'anit, A., and Wesselius, E. (2003), *Europe Inc*, 2nd ed., London: Pluto.

Bieler, A. (2006), *The Struggle for a Social Europe: Trade Unions and EMU in Times of Global Restructuring*, Manchester: Manchester University Press.

Bieler, A., and Morton, A. D. (2004), 'Another Europe Is Possible? Labour and Social Movements at the European Social Forum', *Globalizations*, 1(2), 305–27.

Braud, M. (2000), 'Représentation et représentativité syndicales au niveau européen', *Chronique Internationale de l'IRES*, 66, 105–12.

Buschak, W. (2003), 'The European Trade Union Confederation and the European Industry Federations', in U. Optenhögel, M. Schneider, and R. Zimmermann (eds.), *European Trade Union Organisations: Inventory of the Archive of Social Democracy and the Library of the Friedrich-Ebert-Stiftung*, Bonn: Friedrich-Ebert-Stiftung.

Christiansen T., Jorgensen K. E., and Wiener A. (1999), 'The Social Construction of Europe', *Journal of European Public Policy*, 6(4), 528–44.

Cox, R. W. (1971), 'Labor and Transnational Relations', *International Organization*, 25(3), 554–84.
de la Porte, C., and Pochet, P. (2003), 'A Twofold Assessment of Employment Policy Coordination', in D. Foden and L. Magnusson (eds.), *Five Years' Experience of the Luxembourg Employment Strategy*, Brussels: ETUI.
Didry, C. and Mias, A. (2005), *Le moment Delors: Les syndicats au cœur de l'Europe sociale*. Brussels: P.I.E.-Peter Lang.
Dølvik, J.-E. (1997), *Redrawing Boundaries of Solidarity? ETUC, Social Dialogue and the Europeanisation of Trade Unions in the 1990s*, Oslo: Arena/FAFO.
Dølvik, J.-E., and Visser, J. (2001), 'ETUC and European Social Partnership', in H. Compston and J. Greenwood (eds.), *Social Partnership in the European Union*, London: Palgrave.
Erne, R. (2008), *European Unions: Labor's Quest for a Transnational Democracy*. Ithaca: Cornell University Press.
Gabaglio, E. (2003), *Qu'est-ce que la confédération européenne des syndicats?* Paris: l'Archipel.
Gajewska, K. (2008), 'The Emergence of a European Labour Protest Movement?', *European Journal of Industrial Relations*, 14(1), 104–21.
Gläser, C. (2009), 'Europäische Einheitsgewerkschaft zwischen lähmender Überdehnung und umfassender Repräsentativität: EGB-Strukturen und die Herausforderung der Erweiterung', *Mitteilungsblatt des Instituts für soziale Bewegungen*, 42, 215–34.
Gobin, C. (1997), *L'europe syndicale: entre désir et réalité*, Brussels: Labor.
Goetschy, J. (2003), *The Open Method of Coordination and EU Integration*, Berlin: Fachhochschul- Fernstudienverbund der Länder.
Grahl, J., and Teague, P. (1997), 'Is the European Social Model Fragmenting?', *New Political Economy*, 2(3), 405–26.
Groux, G., Mouriaux, R., and Pernot, J.M. (1993), 'L'européanisation du mouvement syndical: la Confédération européene des syndicats', *Le Mouvement Social*, 162, 41–66.
Gumbrell-McCormick, R (2000a), 'Facing New Challenges: The International Confederation of Free Trade Unions (1972–1990s)', in A. Carew, M. Dreyfus, G. Van Goethem, R. Gumbrell-McCormick, and M. van der Linden, *The International Confederation of Free Trade Unions*, Bern: Peter Lang.
Gumbrell-McCormick, R. (2000b), 'Globalisme et régionalisme', in A. Fouquet, U. Rehfeldt, and S. Le Roux (eds.) *Le syndicalisme dans la mondialisation*, Paris: Editions de l'Atelier.
Hall, P. A., and Soskice, D. (eds.) (2001), *Varieties of Capitalism: The Institutional Foundations of Comparative Advantage*, Oxford: Oxford University Press.
Hyman, R. (2005), 'Trade Unions and the Politics of European Integration', *Economic and Industrial Democracy*, 26(1), 9–40.
Hyman, R. (2010), 'Trade Unions and "Europe": Are the Members out of Step?', *Relations industrielles/Industrial Relations*, 65(1), 3–29.
Imig, D. (2002), 'Contestation in the Streets: European Protest and the Emerging Euro-Polity', *Comparative Political Studies,* 35(8), 914–33.
Lecher, W. (ed.) (1994), *Trade Unions in the European Union: A Handbook*, London: Lawrence and Wishart.
Lefébure, E. (2002), 'Euro-manifs, contre-sommets et marches européennes', in B. Cautrès and D. Reynié (eds.), *L'opinion européenne*, Paris: Presses de Sciences Po.
Lefébure, E., and Lagneau, E. (2002), 'La difficile promotion de l'Europe sociale', in D. Georgakakis (ed.), *Les métiers de l'Europe politique*, Strasbourg: Presses Universitaires de Strasbourg.

Marks, G., Hooghe, L., and Blank, K. (1996), 'European Integration from the 1980s: State-Centric vs. Multi-Level Governance', *Journal of Common Market Studies,* 34(3), 341–78.

Marks, G., and Wilson, C.J. (2000), 'The Past in the Present: A Cleavage Theory of Party Response to European Integration', *British Journal of Political Science,* 30, 433–59.

Martin, A., and Ross, G. (1999), 'In the Line of Fire: The Europeanization of Labor Representation' in A. Martin and G. Ross (eds.), *The Brave New World of European Labor,* New York, Berghahn, 312–67.

Martin, A., and Ross, G. (2001), 'Trade Union Organizing at the European Level: The Dilemma of Borrowed Resources', in D. Imig and S. Tarrow (eds.), *Contentious Europeans,* Lanham: Rowman & Littlefield.

Mathers, A. (2007), *Struggling for a Social Europe: Neoliberal Globalization and the Birth of a European Social Movement,* Aldershot: Ashgate.

Moreno, J. (2001), *Trade Unions without Frontiers: The Communist-oriented trade unions and the ETUC,* Brussels: ETUI.

Offe, C., and Wiesenthal, H. (1985), 'Two Logics of Collective Action', in C. Offe (ed.), *Disorganized Capitalism,* Cambridge: Polity.

Ramsay, H. (1997), 'Solidarity at Last?', *Economic and Industrial Democracy,* 18, 503–37.

Rütters, P. (1989), *Chancen internationaler Gewerkschaftspolitik,* Frankfurt: Otto Brenner Stiftung.

Scharpf, F. (1999), *Governing in Europe: Effective and Democratic?,* Oxford: Oxford University Press.

Seideneck, P. (1993), 'Vertiefung oder Erweiterung? Zu aktuellen Problemen der europäischen Gewerkschaftspolitik', *Gewerkschaftliche Monatshefte,* 9/93, 543–52.

Stevis, D. (1998), 'International Labor Organizations, 1864–1997: the Weight of History and the Challenges of the Present', *Journal of World-Systems Research,* 4, 52–75.

Storey, A. (2008), 'The Ambiguity of Resistance: Opposition to Neoliberalism in Europe', *Capital & Class,* 96, 55–85.

Streeck, W. (1992), 'National Diversity, Regime Competition and Institutional Deadlock: Problems in Forming a European Industrial Relations System', *Journal of Public Policy,* 12(4), 301–30.

Streeck, W. (2001), 'International Competition, Supranational Integration, National Solidarity: The Emerging Constitution of "Social Europe"' in M. Kohli and M. Novak (eds.), *Will Europe Work?,* London: Routledge.

Streeck, W. (2009), *Re-Forming Capitalism: Institutional Change in the German Political Economy,* Oxford: Oxford University Press.

Tarrow, S. (1995), 'The Europeanisation of Conflict: Reflections from a Social Movement Perspective', *West European Politics,* 18(2), 223–51.

Taylor, G., and Mathers, A. (2004), 'The European Trade Union Confederation at the Crossroads of Change? Traversing the Variable Geometry of European Trade Unionism', *European Journal of Industrial Relations,* 10(3), 267–85.

Van Apeldoorn, B. (2000), 'Transnational Class Agency and European Governance: The Case of the European Round Table of Industrialists', *New Political Economy,* 5(2), 157–81.

Van Goethem, G. (2000), 'Conflicting Interests: The International Federation of Trade Unions (1919-1945)' in A. Carew, M. Dreyfus, G. Van Goethem, R. Gumbrell-McCormick and M. van der Linden (eds.), *The International Confederation of Free Trade Unions.* Bern: Peter Lang.

Visser, J., and Ebbinghaus, B. (1992), 'Making the Most of Diversity? European Integration and Transnational Organization of Labour', in J. Greenwood, J. Grote and K. Ronit (eds.), *Organized Interests and the European Community*, London: Sage.

Wagner, A.-C. (2005), *Vers une Europe syndicale: Une enquête sur la confédération européenne des syndicats*, Broissieux: Éditions du Croquant.

Wallace, B. (1945), *World Labour Comes of Age*, London: Lawrence & Wishart.

Part III

International Trade Unionism: Crafting Institutions for the 21st Century

10 The International Labour Movement
Structures and Dynamics

Rebecca Gumbrell-McCormick

International trade unionism is based on structures that for the most part were formed over a century ago: the first International Trade Secretariats (now called Global Union Federations, or GUFs, based on industrial unions) were founded from the 1880s onwards, and the first international confederal structures (those based on national centres) in the first decade of the 20th century. Yet the trade union movement has continued to grow and develop new forms of organisation and action over the last century, creating tensions and sometimes breaking the articulation between formal structures and trade union action. Major changes to the formal structures took place in 1945, with the creation of the unitary World Federation of Trade Unions (WFTU); in 1949, when the International Confederation of Free Trade Unions (ICFTU) was founded as a breakaway from WFTU; and, most recently, in 2006 with the foundation of the International Trade Union Confederation (ITUC). The ITUC brought together the ICFTU and the Christian-inspired World Confederation of Labour (WCL), along with a number of previously non-aligned national centres. The creation of the ITUC also marked the beginning of a new era in relationships between previously independent bodies, primarily between the ITUC itself and the GUFs, which retained their formal autonomy within a new mechanism for collaboration with each other and with the ITUC through the Council of Global Unions. New regional structures were also set up, bringing a new relationship between the ITUC and the European Trade Union Confederation (ETUC).

Four years later, it is not yet clear to what extent these new structures and formal relationships add anything substantively new to the dynamics of trade union action and organisation, let alone take account of the development of more informal networks and coalitions between unions in different countries. This chapter will first give an overview of the current structure of international trade unionism and its historical origins, followed by more detail on the structure of the ITUC and how it fits into the international trade union and industrial relations structure. I will then discuss the key challenges facing the international trade union movement and attempt to evaluate the performance of the ITUC to date.

THE CONFIGURATION OF THE INTERNATIONAL TRADE UNION MOVEMENT IN HISTORIC CONTEXT UP TO 2006

The structure of contemporary international trade unionism is complex and has developed piecemeal over time, like an old house that still has some of its original foundations intact but has had many subsequent additions and renovations, sometimes tearing down and starting anew and sometimes plastering over what went before (see Figure 10.1). It is almost impossible to explain all the historic detail briefly and coherently. I shall instead attempt to portray it here with the help of a crude division based on three factors: *membership base, geographical coverage* and *ideology*. These factors have operated to a degree independently of each other, creating a complex pattern of authority and relationships that has evolved over time and which the recent restructuring has not entirely succeeded in consolidating.

If we look first at the *membership base,* we can distinguish between organisations based on *industrial sectors* and those based on *national centres*. [There are to our knowledge no significant contemporary international trade union organisations based on direct individual membership, with the possible exception of the Industrial Workers of the World (IWW).] The earliest trade union internationals, founded at the end of the 19th century, were industry-based, covering most but not all of the leading industrial sectors of the time: the first, the International Federation of Tobacco Workers (later part of the International Union of Food and Allied Workers) was founded in 1889 but initially comprised only unions from the Nordic countries. The International Metalworkers Federation, founded in 1893, and the International Transport Workers Federation, founded in 1898, represented larger industries but were also initially restricted to industrial unions in northern Europe. These and other similarly based organisations became known as international trade secretariats (ITSs) (re-named global union federations, or GUFs, in 2002). The first body to bring together national trade union centres was founded in 1901 as the International Secretariat of Trade Unions and reconstituted as the International Federation of Trade Unions (IFTU) in 1913. Both types of organisations were at that

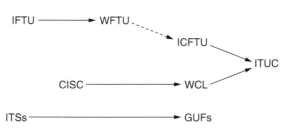

Figure 10.1   The Historical Evolution of International Trade Union Organisations

time entirely Europe-based, with much of their leadership and the strongest affiliates in Northern Europe, in particular Germany and the Nordic countries, although they soon found members in other industrialised countries. The relations between the two types of organisation were not formalised, but in practice they both formed part of the expansion of international organisation under the aegis of the Socialist International (Dreyfus 2000; Van Goethem 2000).

From the late 19th century until the foundation of the ITUC in 2006, an accepted *division of labour* grew up between these two types of organisations: the ITSs/GUFs, which concentrated on practical organising and solidarity work within their sectors, and the IFTU/ICFTU, confederations of national centres that tended to address broader political issues and represented their affiliates in relation to other international bodies, such as the ILO (Reinalda 1997; Van Goethem 2000). This formally autonomous but close relationship between the two types of organisations applied only to international trade unions within the Socialist camp; the Christian and communist trade union internationals, both of which were founded subsequently in the 1920s, were based on a more integrated model. Indeed, the fear of loss of autonomy among the ITSs was one of the main causes of the break-up of WFTU (MacShane 1992). The WFTU had sought to integrate them within its structures as 'industrial departments', but the ITSs were generally much older, stronger and more established than the new internationals, and the national centres that formed the ICFTU were willing to defend their tradition of autonomy (MacShane 1992; Koch-Baumgarten 1999; Reinalda 1997).

This autonomy between the ICFTU and the ITSs meant that there was no formal body regulating or coordinating the relations between them. Instead, their relations were set out at the 1951 ICFTU Congress in Milan (Carew 2000; Gumbrell-McCormick 2001): 'i) the ICFTU recognises the autonomy of the ITSs; the ITSs and the ICFTU will co-operate in all questions of common interest. . . . (ii) the ICFTU and the ITS recognise that they are in fact part of the same international trade union movement. This implies the adoption by the ITSs of the general policy of the ICFTU (Circular no. 5, 12.2.1953)'. While it did not set up a formal coordinating body between the two types of organisations, the Milan agreement did call for the ITSs and ICFTU to attend each other's congresses; a 1990 amendment formalised the representation of the ITSs on ICFTU governing bodies, initially with consultative status. For their part, the ITS set up their own ITS General Conference, which met at least once a year during the International Labour Conference in Geneva with the ICFTU general secretary in attendance (Gumbrell-McCormick 2001).

From the creation of the ICFTU in 1949 until 2006, this general pattern of looser links between the general or social democratic ITSs and the ICFTU on the one hand, and the tighter, more formalised connection between the

Christian and communist industrial federations and their respective internationals, on the other, remained fairly constant. Upon the foundation of the ITUC, a new body was set up, the Council of Global Unions, to coordinate between the new international and the industry-based federations of both the former ICFTU and WCL (but not WFTU). We will explore the relationship between the ICFTU and the GUFs in more detail below, along with the role of the Council of Global Unions.

Geographically, we can distinguish between *regional* and *global* bodies. The first international organisations were almost exclusively European in coverage, and the weight of membership and financial resources has always ensured strong European influence in global unionism. After the Second World War, decolonisation greatly extended the membership of the international bodies and gave a spur to the creation of regional union organisations in the rest of the world. The split in international trade unionism in 1949 reinforced this trend as the three international confederations competed for membership across the globe. The ICFTU set up regional bodies for the Americas (the *Organización Regional Interamericana de Trabajadores*, or ORIT), Asia (the Asia-Pacific Regional Organisation or ARO) and Africa (the African Regional Organisation or AFRO). From the mid-1950s, the process of European integration led to the establishment of regional trade union structures in Europe, which in the case of the socialist-leaning unions became formally independent from the ICFTU in 1973 with the foundation of the European Trade Union Confederation (ETUC). This, in turn, soon opened its membership to affiliates of the WCL and subsequently to former affiliates of the WFTU. Christian trade unions also developed regional organisations in the post-war period, which in the case of Latin America in particular (*Central Latinoamericana de Trabajadores*, or CLAT) enjoyed a high degree of practical, if not formal, autonomy. Regional organisations within the WFTU, for their part, remained subservient within the formal integrated structure of the international (Waterman 2000).

For those regional bodies affiliated to or associated with an international confederation, the relationship between *global* and *regional* bodies is highly complex. This is particularly true at the European level, where the European Trade Union Federations (ETUFs), created to act as interlocutors with European-level employers and EU institutions, have a variety of different relationships with their corresponding GUFs, complicated by the admission of unions from outside the ICFTU from 1974, first those of the WCL and later former affiliates of WFTU. Today, all the global trade unions have their headquarters in Europe, mainly in Brussels and Geneva, where the weight of membership and financial resources has always been concentrated, although most of them also possess regional structures, including committees, offices and staff. The existence of regional structures does not necessarily resolve the differences of interests, resources and perspective between these two groups.

Last but not least, *ideological* divisions have traditionally received the most attention in studies of international trade unionism. The IFTU mainly encompassed unions with a social-democratic orientation, together with more 'business unionist' affiliates in Britain and the USA. After 1920, it faced two smaller rivals, the *Confédération internationale des syndicats chrétiens* (CISC, International Federation of Christian Trade Unions) and the communist Red International of Labour Unions. A new global organisation, the WFTU, was founded as a unitary confederation in 1945, bringing together former affiliates of the IFTU and RILU, but did not win the affiliation of the Christian unions in the CISC, despite the efforts of trade union leaders from both the moderate social-democratic and Christian camps. In 1949, most non-communist affiliates broke away from the WFTU to form the International Confederation of Free Trade Unions (ICFTU) and most of the Christian unions remained in their separate confederation. In 1968, the CISC 'deconfessionalised' and became the World Confederation of Labour (WCL) (Pasture 1994). Meanwhile, the WFTU, consisting mainly of national centres from communist and/or developing countries, especially in Asia, Africa and the Middle East, lost membership rapidly with the rise of 'eurocommunism', followed by the fall of the Berlin Wall in 1989, and today is a skeleton of its former self. However, the WFTU still has some following within unions that are either independent of international affiliation or members of the ITUC. This is particularly the case in unions with a strong communist influence, in Australia and the UK, or in national centres with a formal representation of different ideological tendencies, such as the Austrian *Österreichischer Gewerkschaftsbund* (ÖGB).

Ideological differences remain important despite the foundation at the end of 2006 of the ITUC as a unitary organisation bringing together the ICFTU and most of the affiliates of the WCL alongside a number of independent national centres, some of which had formerly belonged to the WFTU. Within the new ITUC, former ideological identities sometimes overlap with other issues, for example, the question of whether Latin American unions should enjoy regional autonomy (as in the WCL) or be part of a broader pan-American structure in which the US unions exert major influence (as in the ICFTU) or the still open question of the nature of the relationship between the ITUC and the GUFs. The WFTU remains outside, and the ITUC has expressed no intention of seeking its formal merger or absorption by the newly unified body. At the same time, several of the former WCL affiliates have formed a new organisation, World Organisation of Workers (WOW), which groups together some affiliates of the former WCL industry federation for commercial and service sectors and acts as a minor irritant at the national level (mainly in northern Europe) but has no real international influence.

It is important to note here the ways in which, over time, these three dimensions: *membership basis*, *ideology* and *geography* have operated, either in the same or in opposing directions, either facilitating unity of action or, more often, inhibiting it. An example of the former would be the general tendency of progressive unions of the North, whether from the ICFTU or WCL, to support a strong Latin American regional organisation. An example of the latter would be the difficulties faced by the more progressive ITSs in seeking cooperation with communist-led unions (leading to a formal breach between the International Graphical Federation and the ICFTU in the 1960s) or their problems with the ICFTU's model of a single regional organisation for the Americas).

Today, early in the 21st century, we find ourselves in our much renovated old house, built on the foundations of ITSs/GUFs that were set up in the last years of the 19th century, reinforced by international confederations of national centres founded in 1913 (IFTU), 1920 (IFCTU, deconfessionalised in 1968 as WCL), 1945 (WFTU) and 1949 (ICFTU), two of which have now been partially dismantled and then welded together to form a new structure (ITUC). On top of this we have regional organisations of various sorts founded mainly after 1945 and a few small specialised bodies, the most important being the Trade Union Advisory Committee to the OECD (TUAC), which represents the trade unions (mainly former ICFTU and WCL affiliates) of countries affiliated to the OECD. While some of these components are connected to each other either formally or informally, others remain entirely unrelated, so that they are not all linked together and do not all communicate with each other, but do form a series of clusters, as in Europe (with closer links between ETUC, ETUFs and ITUC) (Cotton and Gumbrell-McCormick 2012). All this renovation work leaves behind the detritus of older, now defunct organisations and working relationships that have not been entirely cleared away.

The foundation of the ITUC in 2006 was the culmination of a long process, where the three dimensions of *membership base, geographical coverage* and *ideology* all played a significant role. The main aspects of this process were the rapprochement between the ICFTU and WCL, the rising power of affiliates in the South and a re-thinking of the relationships between the different components of the global labour movement (Gumbrell-McCormick 2000; Pasture 1994). A combination of forces, some internal (strong support for unification from the general secretaries of both the ICFTU and WCL, the example of unity at the European level) and some external (the need to step up joint action in response to neoliberalism and globalisation, the loss of trade union membership and influence world-wide) finally led to the unification of the two former rivals, ICFTU and WCL, inside a new international organisation of national centres that was also open to affiliation from unions that had previously been independent or had left the WFTU and that sought a new relationship with the internationals based on industry and a new approach to representation of regions.

On 31 October 2006, the WCL and ICFTU held their final congresses in Vienna (for the ICFTU it was the 19th, for the WCL the 27th). Each took only half a day and had the main business of voting to dissolve the existing confederations and endorse the new one. The previous ICFTU general secretary became general secretary of the ITUC; the president also came from the ICFTU, while one vice president and one deputy general secretary came from WCL unions. The new body claimed a total membership of around 180 million, including 150 million from the former ICFTU and 26 million from the former WCL.

Clearly, many tensions remained and problems were unresolved at the time of the foundation of the ITUC. Some former WCL affiliates chose to remain outside the new confederation, concerned about the potential loss of identity and autonomy as a minority within a secular 'hegemony'. A number of important previously non-affiliated national centres also remained outside, including the Portuguese CGTP, several important Latin American national centres and the US 'Change to Win' coalition, which broke away from the AFL-CIO in 2005 (Rehfeldt 2007). Other organisations remained affiliated to the WFTU, including some significant unions in India and the Middle East and, of course, the official Chinese unions remained outside, with no immediate plan on the part of either party to seek closer cooperation or affiliation.

Linked to the ideological tensions were the difficulties in building new organisations at the regional level uniting the separate—and often bitterly opposed—old ones. This was particularly a problem in Latin America, given the long-standing conflict between CLAT and ORIT (which included North America). Related to this was the general question of the role and representation of affiliates from the developing and developed countries. The ITUC made some changes in the representation of the global South, but in many other ways affiliates from the industrialised countries continued to play a dominant role. Out of the top elected officials elected at both congresses, only one each was from a developing country. And while women were well represented in the top leadership, a new woman general secretary and deputy president, the same could not be said of the proportion of women delegates and participants at congress.

Another area of disquiet was the relationship between the new unified ITUC and the GUFs. The first ITUC congress did not carry out the integration of the GUFs into the new body that was favoured by some leading figures within the WCL (WCL 2005) and some others involved in the unification process, but instead established a new body, the Council of Global Unions, to coordinate the work of the ITUC and the GUFs. This did not in itself resolve the question of the division of tasks and responsibilities between the two types of organisation. A similar point could be made about the relationship between the ETUC and the new European regional organisation, which was partially resolved by making the general secretary of the ETUC the president of the Pan-European Regional Council (PERC). Both the ETUC and the GUFs remained officially autonomous organisations, and it remained to be seen how effective these efforts to build greater coordination would be in the long term. TUAC also remained an officially autonomous body, and joined the Council of Global Unions.

THE STRUCTURE AND FUNCTIONS OF THE INTERNATIONAL MOVEMENT POST-2006

Looking now beyond the foundation of the ITUC and the restructuring of the international labour movement around it, how does the situation post-2006 differ from the past, how do the policies and programmes of the ITUC differ from its predecessors, and what, if any, additional means of action does it have? And how does it connect to the other parts of the international labour movement, the GUFs and the European and other regional bodies? As an organisation, the ITUC is indubitably in the tradition of 'internationalism from above' described by Hyman (2005), fitting into 'a distinctive model of international trade union bureaucratisation' (ibid: 146) running from the pre-war IFTU through to the WFTU, ICFTU and WCL. The new structure resembles most closely that of the ICFTU, particularly in the recognised autonomy of the GUFs, and follows both ICFTU and WCL practices in the relative autonomy of the regional organisations, the constitutional safeguards for gender equality, and provisions for youth representation. There are some important changes to previous practices. The ITUC has raised the status of regional secretaries to that of deputy general secretary, and that of the presidents of the regional organisations to that of global vice presidents. As was already the case in the former ICFTU and WCL, a disproportionate number of members of the General Council and the Executive Board—in terms of their dues-paying membership, not in terms of their total population—come from the developing countries. In the new body, representatives of the former WCL and the formerly non-affiliated unions are also slightly over-represented, in an attempt to avoid charges of ideological 'hegemony'. The chair and vice chair of the women's committee and the chair of the youth committee sit on the Executive Board (which has a total of 26 members). The chair of the smaller finance committee is a representative of a former ICFTU affiliate and the chair of the Solidarity Fund Management Committee from the former WCL, both from influential industrialised countries. However, the membership of these committees now includes the general secretaries of the regional organisations alongside representatives of the main 'donor' affiliates (ITUC Report on Activities 2010: 36). This follows the ICFTU practice, where European affiliates were dominant in smaller committees dealing with finance (Gumbrell-McCormick 2000).

The autonomy of the GUFs/ITS is reaffirmed—in line with the previous relationship between ITS and ICFTU but unlike the practice of the WCL—with continued representation on the ITUC's governing bodies: up to six delegates per recognised GUF may take part in Congress, with the right to speak but not the right to vote (Article XI f). At the same time, a new 'structured partnership' (Article XI b) has been established through the creation of the Council of Global Unions (CGU), which is to meet annually with up to three delegates from each member organisation (CGU 2007). However, at the time of the creation of the body, it was not yet clear how many existing GUFs would take part, and in the first years of its existence, several key GUFs chose not to do so. Participation in the Council is also largely by general secretaries and other top officials and does not expressly include a regional dimension, although the ITUC and GUFs may continue to cooperate regionally on an ad hoc basis (CGU 2010: 7).

The supreme authority of the ITUC, as with the ICFTU and WCL, is congress, held at least once every four years. The main decision-making body between congresses is the General Council, which meets not less than once a year (Article XXII a), and between those sessions the Executive Bureau, which meets not less than twice a year (Article XXV d). All this is consistent with the most recent practice of both the ICFTU and WCL, but it is worth mentioning that, up to 1992, the ICFTU held two meetings of the Executive Board per year and, up to 1975, held its congress every three years, as did the WCL (Gumbrell-McCormick 2001, ch. 2, 13). The decision to continue with a smaller number of meetings can be seen as unfortunate in terms of internal democracy. Further, the second ITUC congress continued a practice, begun in the last years of the ICFTU, of holding meetings of its Resolutions Committee at the same time as plenary sessions, thus removing much of the substantive debate and disagreements from the main floor of congress.

The top officials and members of the governing bodies of the new organisation naturally have an effect on the policies and programmes it adopts and on its strategic direction. The general political orientation has continued much along the lines set by the ICFTU and WCL, which had grown closer together ideologically over the previous two decades. This could loosely be described as moderate social democracy, with a pragmatic and practical orientation—'a broad church'. This is not to say that there are no differences of position among (and within affiliates): the first ITUC congresses have been notable for open differences of opinion between what could be loosely called a 'right' and a 'left' within the confederation, on such obvious issues as the Israel/Palestine conflict, but also over the orientation towards the international financial institutions—whether to act as 'outsiders' or 'insiders'—an argument already present in the former organisations. These political differences have not, on the whole, been between former affiliates of the ICFTU and WCL, although former ICFTU affiliates such as COSATU and some of the previously non-affiliated unions, such as the French CGT, have emerged as spokesmen for the 'left'. There were, however, significant albeit subtle differences of orientation between the ICFTU and WCL, and some observers have pointed to the greater emphasis on the informal economy, attention to the plight of the world's poorest and unemployed and greater openness to non-governmental organisations (NGOs) as abiding legacies of the former WCL. For example, the WCL 2004 congress resolution on unity stressed the importance of organising women and the informal sector (WCL 2005: 54—55).

Turning now to the means of action, the financial means of the ITUC are limited, again in line with both the ICFTU and WCL. The affiliation fee set for the year 2007, per thousand members of part thereof, was only Euro 182.20, considerably lower than the dues for individual members of most industrialised country national unions. Further, as was the previous practice in the ICFTU and even more in the WCL, there are provisions for organisations in financial difficulties to pay less than the full amount. It has often been observed that the international trade union bodies dispose of considerably more limited means than their national affiliates (MacShane 1992, cited in Devin 1990), and that the ICFTU and WCL both rely on more limited resources than the ETUC, which receives substantial funding from the European Commission (Rehfeldt 2007). Another key point is that voluntary donations above the basic affiliation fee are still accepted to a special Solidarity Fund, which has a separate board. The ITUC founding congress sought to address the general problem of bilateral financial assistance by making 'a statutory commitment to come up with a coherent global strategy of development cooperation' to address this problem, termed a 'Herculean task' by Traub-Merz and Eckl (2007: 6). This is yet another issue that was not fully resolved by the time of the second congress (see ITUC Report on Activities, 85 ff.)

As of 2010, the ITUC claimed a membership of 175 million members in 311 affiliates in 155 countries (ITUC Report on Activities 2010: 9). Leaving aside for a moment the extent to which these figures are accurate, this level of membership is clearly one of the largest if not the largest of any voluntary membership organisation in the world. However, it can be argued that the sheer distance from ordinary members of the ITUC and other international trade union bodies, which are after all 'organisations of organisations', and their reliance on the 'proxy power' of their national or industrial affiliates (Neuhaus 1981, cited in Hyman 2005: 149) to take any action, means that their real strength of numbers is much more limited than the official figures would suggest, although the achievement of unity surely adds some weight to their collective strength. The need to find a way to engage the 'capacity to act' of members and affiliates, to move forward from a past model of 'bureaucratic, top down' internationalism, is one of the key challenges that I will address in the next section.

MAJOR CHALLENGES: INTERNAL AND EXTERNAL

The ITUC has focused much of its energies over its first four years of operation into healing the rifts of the past, creating new structures, developing better coordination and forging a new identity. Its very creation and consolidation are enough to make it a success, but clearly it must do much more than this to become truly effective. In order to achieve its objectives, the new international must respond to a number of challenges, both internal and external. I shall focus here mainly on the internal challenges.

Internal Challenges

First, what seems at first a major advantage for the ITUC, its success in bringing together two separate confederations and a number of non-affiliated national centres in a unified body may be in fact a double-edged sword: unity provides an opportunity for action, but also creates obstacles to it. The extreme breadth of membership of the new body, encompassing former communist as well as former Christian and other independent unions, poses a problem for internal union democracy and debate. As with the supposed 'end of the cold war' more generally, the decline of the WFTU and the affiliation of many of its former affiliates to the new unitary international risks removing a particular ideological strand from international debate, the radical critique of the capitalist system and of the collaboration of many trade unions with it. So far, this does not appear to have transpired. In the coming years, the slight over-representation of the formerly non-affiliated national centres and the former WCL affiliates may counteract any move toward ideological hegemony of the 'centre left', yet it is evident that this remains a possibility over the longer term. The unification may also mean a dilution of the image or 'brand' of the international, which may make it even more difficult than before to interest members and the public at large in international trade unionism and convince them that it has any importance to them. If this happens, the newly won 'unity' might well have the effect of what Hyman calls 'marrying efficiency to impotence' (Hyman 2005: 145).

Related to the challenge of ideological diversity is the potential problem that decision-making might become more unwieldy and consensus more difficult to achieve with a broader range of interests, forms of organisation, means of action and traditions. This is especially the case, as the General Council and Executive Board are large heterogeneous bodies and meet infrequently. Of course, there were different interests—different industrial sectors, regions, genders, etc.—within the former internationals, but the greater ideological breadth adds an extra layer of difficulty to the process of articulating common interests and developing a common programme of action. Added to this is the increased weight of the developing countries, within the new international's governing bodies, the commitment to develop closer cooperation at the European level between the new organisation for the region and the existing ETUC, and to devise a new more collaborative relationship with the GUFs. Each of these will prove challenging in itself; together, they will be fiendishly difficult.

A second series of internal challenges is associated with the attempt to develop new regional organisations and a new relationship between them and the head office. The creation of a single regional body for the Americas was indeed one of the major stumbling blocks in the creation of the ITUC and remained unresolved until well after the first congress. The tensions between ORIT and CLAT went back to the time of the Latin American dictatorships of the 1970s. CLAT and its affiliates had strong links with liberation theology and were involved in opposing the dictatorship regimes, regarding both ORIT and the ICFTU itself as 'nordiste' and dominated by the 'imperialist' countries. ORIT was at that time the recipient of US government funds, channelled through the AFL-CIO, for strongly anti-communist unions with dubious trade union credentials (Thomson and Larson 1978). ORIT was subsequently 'cleaned up' in the 1980s (Gumbrell-McCormick 2000) but remained tainted by its past conduct and continued links with the AFL-CIO. Indeed, while CLAT represented affiliates in Latin America only, ORIT was an 'inter-American' organisation including affiliates in North America, the US AFL-CIO and the Canadian Labour Congress (CLC), which often acted as an intermediary between the two. The difference was significant both for political and for structural reasons. A single organisation for the Americas was founded only in March 2008, a move made possible by an agreement to create sub-regional structures for North and South America.

At the European level, the creation of a single body for West and East Europe, the PERC, was somewhat easier; but the ETUC remains an entirely autonomous organisation. The link between the two is that the general secretary of the ETUC also serves as general secretary of PERC. In practice, PERC deals almost entirely with countries outside the ETUC, that is, the former federations of the USSR (excepting the Baltic states). The trend since the formation of the ETUC towards a greater concentration on European affairs among European national centres continues despite the attempt to create closer coordination of the work of the ETUC with that of the global body, although some authors have argued that it has also opened the perspective of European unions towards new forms of action on the world stage (Collombat 2009).

The third and perhaps most important major internal challenge concerns the relationship between the ITUC and the GUFs (which now describe themselves simply as 'global unions') and the integration of the former ICFTU-linked sectoral bodies with those of the former WCL. In 2006, the WCL had nine 'international trade federations', and there were 12 GUFs in the ICFTU 'trade union family'. The constitution of the ITUC stipulates that only one industrial body per industry will be recognised (CGU 2007, ITUC Article VI b), meaning that the WCL industrial federations have had to merge with or be integrated into the equivalent GUFs. Indeed, some had already done so on their own initiative before the foundation of the ITUC, including the World Federation of Agricultural and Food Workers and the World Federation of Industry Workers. By the time of the second congress, most former WCL industry federations had joined forces with their respective GUFs, with the important exception of the World Federation of Clerical Workers, which opted to remain outside the ITUC and founded the World Organisation of Workers (WOW). It is also important to bear in mind that there is a European aspect to this question, as the ETUFs linked to the ETUC are in some cases separate from their respective GUFs, and the form of relationship they will enjoy under the new arrangements is not yet certain.

Underlying the question of integration of the former industrial federations of the ICFTU and WCL is the more fundamental challenge of finding a way to respect the autonomy of these organisations but at the same time build cooperation amongst themselves and coordination with the confederal body. The creation of a formal body to achieve this, the CGU, in a 'structured partnership' represents a significant change in direction, at least for the GUFs, from the former, much looser and intermittent links through the ITS General Conference and attendance at each other's congresses. The Council (CGU) has the task of coordinating the joint action of the GUFs and the ITUC. Membership is voluntary and representation is mainly by general secretaries and presidents. The Council has led some significant joint campaigns, in such areas as the defence of trade union rights, communications, the response to the crisis and strategies around individual companies that operate in more than one sector (CGU Three-year Review, 2010). While several participants in the second congress pointed out that the representation of GUFs was more limited and at a lower level than they expected, this does not necessarily mean that the GUFs are less involved in the ITUC, rather that they are channelling their participation through bilateral projects, but it is still a warning sign. Indeed, some GUFs, in particular the International Metalworkers Federation (IMF) and to a lesser degree the International Union of Food, Agricultural, Hotel, Restaurant, Catering, Tobacco and Allied Workers' Associations (IUF) have remained aloof from both the Council and the ITUC itself; neither of their general secretaries was present at the second ITUC congress. Both have stressed that the GUFs do not need to work within the structures of the Council or the ITUC to achieve industrial results, and this view is shared off the record by representatives of other GUFs. In its three-year review, the Council and several member organisations pointed to the lack of participation of some GUFs as a major limitation in its work to date. It remains to be seen what impact the anticipated upcoming mergers within the GUFs will have on the work of the Council: the new mega-GUF comprising IMF, ITGLWF and ICEM may feel powerful enough to dispense with the Council, but smaller GUFs such as the IUF may need its operations even more. The challenge for the ITUC is to convince these and other GUFs that their work does indeed need to be more closely coordinated, and for the Council to convince the GUFs that it does 'add value' to their individual campaigns (CGU 2010).

This question of the relationship of the sectoral bodies to the confederal body also has ideological and regional dimensions: the CGU did not envisage a regional dimension, but notes in its three-year review that some discussions of regional issues had taken place and de facto regional cooperation had developed, notably in Asia [among the Association of Southeast Asian Nations (ASEAN) countries] and in the Middle East (CGU 2010). Two of the three GUFs who commented on the report stated they were in favour of developing a regional CGU structure and that there were already some developments on the ground. Ideologically, while the rift between the ICFTU and WCL has been largely healed, the WFTU unions still remain outside the ITUC and its linked organisations. While this is mainly an external challenge (to be covered below), it is important to note here that because these unions include some of the strongest industrial unions in a number of industries, notably in building and woodworking and among seafarers and dockers, their absence from the GUFs and the CGU creates a potentially serious barrier to common action at the sectoral level.

External Challenges

The ITUC and the GUFs obviously face a number of significant external challenges. A first series concerns relations with external organisations, starting with trade unions outside the ITUC. The ITUC leadership has made it very clear so far that it is not interested in dialogue with the WFTU, which has become increasingly marginalised since the break-up of the former Soviet Union and the democratisation (more real in some countries than in others) of the former Soviet bloc. Many important national confederations, in particular the Italian CGIL and French CGT, left the WFTU and are now in the ITUC. Others, such as the Portuguese CGTP, are no longer in the WFTU but remain highly suspicious of the ITUC. But those still within the WFTU are concentrated in particular industries, as mentioned above, and in particular regions, such as the Middle East, where the ITUC and its predecessors have had the most difficulty in organising and where the recent wave of democratisation has created fresh opportunities to bring their democratic unions into the main trade union fold. Further, while the WFTU continues to exist as a separate organisation, it remains an attractive alternative to unionists around the world who take seriously the trade unions' anti-capitalist and radical mission. This is notably the case of COSATU, whose international secretary referred to the option of affiliating to the WFTU instead of the ITUC in a blistering critique of the ITUC second congress (Masuku 2010). Other external organisations include the IWW, which remains active, particularly in North America, and the WCL split-off, the WOW. These are minor irritants to the ITUC, but both organisations may be taking highly motivated activists away at a time that the international movement needs all the activists it can get.

Looking at the challenge of the role of the ITUC within the international trade union movement more generally, writers such as Munck (2002) and Waterman (1998, 2006) have long been critical of the ITUC and its predecessors (especially the ICFTU—few of these critics have paid much attention to the WCL, although Waterman has also written critically about the WFTU) for their timidity in both ideology and action and their increasing irrelevance on the world stage. Waterman (1998) argues that trade union internationals have become 'institutionalised' and have been captured by the official institutions whose policies they seek to influence. This view is shared by some within the international trade union movement, such as Dan Gallin, former general secretary of the IUF and now chair of the Global Labour Institute (2008). In the view of these and other critics (for example, Howard 2007), organisational demarcations and administrative procedures have to be transcended in order to create a 'new' labour internationalism based on a 'bottom-up' internationalism that engages individual workers and union activists at the local or regional level and promotes joint action across boundaries without going through the complex authority structures of the official international movement. Indeed there have been a number of 'bottom-up' actions, the best known being the campaigns of the Liverpool dockers [where the International Transport Workers Federation (ITF) was unable to play a leading role as a result of the UK affiliate's refusal to pursue the case] and of the Australian dockers (which did have significant official trade union support as well as a grass-roots international network). It is important to bear in mind that transport workers, in particular seafarers and dockers, have long been the most successful at organising international solidarity, going back to the early years of the 20th century (Reinalda 1997; Koch-Baumgarten 1999). These and other examples of 'unofficial' international action are covered elsewhere in this book, but it is important to point out here that such actions may be widespread but that no one has yet put forward an alternative to the official structures centred around the ITUC. It is perhaps more important to consider to what extent the ITUC and its associated bodies are capable of encouraging and harnessing the energy of 'bottom-up' actions and networks rather than, as so often in the past, acting as an impediment (Bieler et al. 2010; Hyman 2005). Unfortunately, there is little evidence about these unofficial networks and actions. It is still too early to judge, but there does seem to be a new spirit of openness within the ITUC, which some have claimed relates partly to the greater role played by the former WCL unions as well as some of those that were previously unaffiliated, particularly those in Latin America.

A closely related argument, also brought forward by Waterman (1998), is the need for the labour movement to engage in a broader social movement, as an equal partner with NGOs and civil society (Douglas et al 2004; Stirling 2010). This view also has some support within the international labour movement, and indeed could be seen in the second ITUC congress's panels with speakers from major NGOs. The traditional trade union response, held by most ICFTU affiliates, was that NGOs and social movements, whether operating nationally or internationally, were often small and unrepresentative and lacked the stability, accountability and transparency of trade unions or political parties. Yet many NGOs today do possess clear representative structures and greater accountability. A good example is Amnesty, which has played a significant role in highlighting abuses of human and social rights, both within nations and at the international level. It has often cooperated with UN bodies and had close relations with the ICFTU that it continues to enjoy with the ITUC (Gumbrell-McCormick 2000: 454–8). More generally, it is clear that 'social-movement'-oriented campaigns have been important in shifting the international trade union agenda towards more serious attention to issues such as gender equality, home-working and the 'informal sector'. Significantly, the Self Employed Women's Association, an Indian organisation with a bridging role as trade union and campaigning NGO, was given a platform slot at the ITUC founding congress. We now see greater cooperation between international trade unionism and international NGOs as actors in a 'global civil society' (Waterman and Timms 2005; Douglas 2004; Ghigliani 2010). This can be seen, for example, in the experience of the annual World Social Forum, first convened, mainly by third world NGOs, in Porto Alegre, Brazil in 2001 as a movement for 'globalisation from below' (Sen et al. 2004). Initially the official trade union organisations largely held themselves aloof, but they have become increasingly active participants; the same is true of the European Social Forum, first held in Florence in 2002 (della Porta 2005).

Another immense external challenge is that of how best to organise and represent the overwhelming number of unorganised workers, primarily in the global South but also increasingly in the de-industrialising North. That the world's organised workers are greatly out-numbered by the unorganised is an observation increasingly raised by employers, governments, and other critics of the international trade union movement, potentially calling into question its representativity and legitimacy. It is at the regional level and within affiliates, especially those in the developing countries, that the ITUC is most actively engaged in responding to this challenge. In many countries, its affiliates organise only small, sometimes privileged groups of workers within the formal economy, most typically in public administration, transport and some services such as banking. The vast majority of workers, whether in agriculture or in the informal economy, remain outside the trade unions. Indeed, one of the difficulties faced by the Indian affiliate SEWA in organising women in the informal economy was resistance from the already existing unions in that country. It is not clear to what extent the attitudes of 'official' union confederations in most of the developing countries have changed, but the ITUC regional organisations, especially in Latin America, are pushing for greater attention to the need to organise these workers.

Finally, there is the external challenge of the place of the international labour movement as a whole within what may be called the global international industrial relations (IR) system and the degree to which the movement can achieve concrete results through that system. The international IR system is basically a relationship between trade unions, employers and state institutions at the international level, linked together by custom and regulation along the lines of Dunlop's model of IR systems (Dunlop 1958). The ITUC and the GUFs are the key actors at the international level on the trade union side. They rarely carry out collective bargaining or strikes (the international shipping industry is an exception), but they pursue much the same ends through other means: international campaigns, coordination of national or sectoral demands and coordinated approaches to corporate head offices. The international equivalents for the other actors in the international IR system are less straightforward: International employers' associations are weak, although individual multinational employers do operate on an international scale, with more resources and a higher degree of coordination than most trade unions. The most problematic element, however, is the state: the ILO and other inter-governmental organisations do not have anything close to the power resources of nation states; they depend heavily, if not entirely, on the willingness of member states to implement international labour and other standards in national legislation (Douglas et al. 2004). This international system has been simplified by the creation of the ITUC, which may encourage further streamlining and greater coordination and efficiency, at least on the part of the trade union actors. Whether this will then lead to a stronger international system as a whole remains to be seen. The form and extent of engagement with an international system that remains far less developed than most national systems is one of the main arguments within the global unions, in particular between the ITUC and the GUFs. While the GUFs concentrate on actions aimed at international employers, the ITUC works primarily with international state actors, mainly the ILO but increasingly the international financial institutions. Both parts of the labour movement agree on the need to step up international action and international coordination, but it is not up to them alone to endow the existing international IR institutions with power or influence.

The ITUC and the other global unions now face an uphill struggle to continue to represent the interests of working people on the world stage in a time of economic and social crisis. The unification of the two major confederal bodies removes one level of impediments to action but does not in itself resolve the many other challenges, both external and internal, facing the international labour movement. The pursuit of greater unity of purpose and action is even more necessary today than in the past.

REFERENCES

Bieler, A., Ciccaglione, B., and Hilary, J. (2010), 'Transnational Solidarity, Labour Movements and the Problem of International Free Trade', unpublished manuscript presented at ISA World Congress of Sociology, Göteborg, July 11–17.

Collombat, T. (2009), 'Le débat sur l'eurocentrisme des organisations syndicales internationales : une perspective des Amériques', *Politique européenne*', 27, 177–200.

Cotton, E., and Gumbrell-McCormick, R. (2012) 'Global Unions as Imperfect Multilateral Organizations: An International Relations Perspective', *Economic and Industrial Democracy,* forthcoming.

Council of Global Unions (2007), 'Agreement between the Global Union Federations, the International Trade Union Confederation, and the Trade Union Advisory Committee re: Council of Global Unions', http://www.ituc-csi.org/IMG/pdf/No_03_Annexe_-_Council_of_Global_Unions-2.pdf

Council of Global Unions (2010), 'Council of Global Unions—Three Year Review', Geneva, 25–26.1.1-, index CGU04–05.

della Porta, D. (2005),'The Social Bases of the Global Justice Movement: Some Theoretical Reflections and Empirical Evidence from the First European Social Forum', UNRISD Programme Paper 21, Geneva: UNRISD.

Devin, G. (1990), 'La Confédération internationale des syndicats libres: exploration d'un réseau", in G. Devin (ed.), *Syndicalisme: dimensions internationales*, La Garenne-Colombes: Editions Européennes ERASME.

Douglas, W., Ferguson, J-P., and Klett, E. (2004), 'An Effective Confluence of Forces in Support of Workers' Rights: ILO Standards, US Trade Laws, Unions and NGOs', *Human Rights Quarterly*, 26(2), 273–299.

Dreyfus, M. (2000), 'The Emergence of an International Trade Union Organization (1902–1919)', in A. Carew, M. Dreyfus, G. van Goethem, R. Gumbrell-McCormick and M. van der Linden (eds.), *The International Confederation of Free Trade Unions: A History of the Organization and its Precursors*, Bern: Peter Lang.

Dunlop, J.T. (1958), *Industrial Relations Systems*, New York: Holt.

Gallin, D. (2008), 'Die Gegenmacht der internationalen Gewerkschaftsbewegung', Zürich: Global Labour Institute-German.

Ghigliani, P. (2005), 'International Trade Unionism in a Globalizing World: A Case Study of New Labour Internationalism', *Economic and Industrial Democracy*, 26(3), 359–382.

Gumbrell-McCormick, R. (2000), 'Facing New Challenges: The International Confederation of Free Trade Unions 1972–1990s' in M. van der Linden (eds.), *The International Confederation of Free Trade Unions*, Berne: Peter Lang.

Gumbrell-McCormick, R. (2001), 'The International Confederation of Free Trade Unions: Structure, Ideology and Capacity to Act', PhD Dissertation, Coventry: University of Warwick.

Howard, A. (2007), 'The Future of Global Unions: Is Solidarity Still Forever?', *Dissent*, 11(4), 62–70.

Hyman, R. (2005), 'Shifting Dynamics in International Trade Unionism: Agitation, Organisation, Diplomacy, Bureaucracy', *Labor History*, 46(2), 137–54.

International Trade Union Confederation (2010), 'Report on Activities', report to 2nd ITUC World Congress, Vancouver, June 21–25.

Koch-Baumgarten, S. (1999), *Gewerkschaftsinternationalismus und die Herausforderung der Globalisierung Das Beispiel der Internationalen Transportarbeiterfederation*, Frankfurt: Campus.

Koch-Baumgarten, S., and Rütters, P. (eds.) (1991), *Zwischen Integration und Autonomie*, Cologne: Bund.

Langille, B. (2005), 'Core Labour Rights: The True Story', *European Journal of International Law*, 16(3), 1–29.

MacShane, D. (1992), *International Labour and the Origins of the Cold War*, Oxford: Clarendon Press.

Masuku, B. (2010), 'ITUC World Congress and ILO Conference Outcomes: Spaces for Real Change or Illusions of a Dream Permanently Deferred', *The Shopsteward*, 19(4).

Munck, R. (2002), *Globalization and Labour: Towards the Next 'Great Transformation'*, London: Zed Books.

Neuhaus, R. (1981), *International Trade Secretariats: Objectives, Organisation, Activities*, Bonn: FES.

Pasture, P. (1994), *Christian Trade Unionism in Europe since 1968: Tensions between Identity and Practice*, Aldershot: Avebury.

Rehfeldt, U. (2007), 'Création d'une nouvelle confédération syndicale internationale', *Chronique internationale de l'IRES*, 104, 3–10.

Reinalda, B. (ed.) (1997), *The International Transportworkers Federation 1914–1945*, Amsterdam: Stichting Beheer IISG.

Sen, J., Anand, A., Escobar, A., and Waterman, P. (eds.) (2004), *World Social Forum: Challenging Empires*, New Delhi: Viveka Foundation.

Stirling, J. (2010), 'Global unions: Chasing the Dream or Building the Reality?', *Capital & Class*, 34(1), 107–114.

Thomson, D., and. Larson, R. (1978), *Where Were You, Brother?* London: War on Want.

Traub-Merz, R. and Eckl, J. (2007), 'International Trade Union Movement: Mergers and Contradictions', Briefing Paper 1/2007, Bonn and Berlin: Friedrich-Ebert-Stiftung, International Trade Union Cooperation.

Van Goethem, G. (2000), 'Conflicting Interests: the International Federation of Trade Unions (1919–1945)', in A. Carew, M. Dreyfus, G. Van Goethem and R. Gumbrell-McCormick (eds.), *The International Confederation of Free Trade Unions*, Berne: Peter Lang.

Waterman P. (1998), *Globalization, Social Movements and the New Internationalisms*, London: Mansell.

Waterman P. (2000), 'A Spectre is Haunting Labour Internationalism: The Spectre of Communism', http://www.hartford-hwp.com/archives/26/035.html.

Waterman, P. (2006), 'The International Union Merger of November 2006: Top-Down, Eurocentric and . . . Invisible?' http://www.labornet.org/news/0000/waterman.htm.

Waterman, P., and Timms, J. (2004), 'Trade Union Internationalism and the Challenge of Globalisation: the Beginning of the End or the End of the Beginning?', in M. Kaldor, H. Anheier and M. Glasius (eds.), *Global Civil Society 2004/5*, London: Sage.

World Confederation of Labour (2005), 'La CMT et la nouvelle organisation syndicale mondiale: Cheminement et décisions', *Labor*, édition spéciale, 26th WCL World Congress, Houffalize, November 21–23.

11 Transnational Solidarity around Global Production Networks? Reflections on the Strategy of International Framework Agreements

Michael Fichter, Markus Helfen and Katharina Schiederig

The organisation of transnational solidarity has long been the Achilles heel of (international) trade unionism. In today's world, this predicament is particularly evident in regard to the unprecedented growth and power of transnationally operating corporations (TNC). While TNCs can use diverse employment conditions in different countries and localities to arbitrage labour costs, local trade union resistance is often undermined by the threat—real or perceived—of relocation or substitution. Moreover, a lowering of standards in one place generates downward pressure on the level of standards in general, contributing in the context of widespread deregulation to undercutting, whipsawing and an international 'race to the bottom'.

From a trade union point of view, this vicious circle can only be broken by transnational solidarity, i.e., when workers in different political and socio-economic settings and different locations in global production networks (GPNs) engage in cross-border activities to maintain and increase standards. Over the past two decades, international framework agreements (IFAs)[1] have developed as overarching instruments of global reach towards this end. IFAs are strategically directed at raising standards in TNCs and throughout their GPNs. They are being used to address the challenge of transnational solidarity by aggregating the interests of diverse groups of workers, firstly, around a border-crossing organisation—the Transnational Corporation—and ultimately, throughout a global production network. As such, IFAs are possibly more far-reaching policy instruments than any previous attempts at TNC-specific policies and platforms of transnational unionism.

Is the IFA strategy a step towards organising transnational solidarity around GPNs? To explore this question, we begin by addressing the general power relationship between TNCs and organised labour to explain the broader context in which the corporate-oriented strategy of IFAs has become recognised across major economic sectors as a key instrument of transnational trade union activity. From there, we take a closer look at GPN governance in general and its varying sectoral configuration. This leads directly to the third segment, which focuses on the IFA strategies of the global union federations (GUFs) that have signed over 90 per cent of all agreements: the

International Union of Food, Agricultural, Hotel, Restaurant, Catering, Tobacco and Allied Workers' Associations (IUF), the International Metalworkers Federation (IMF), UNI Global Union Network (UNI), the International
Federation of Chemical, Energy, Mine and General Workers Union (ICEM)
and the Building and Woodworkers International (BWI). While sharing a
common understanding of IFAs as building blocks of transnational solidarity, the corporate-oriented strategy of each GUF develops in a particular
economic field with its own institutional, organisational and political settings. In our conclusions, we will discuss the opportunities and constraints
of IFAs as a corporate-oriented strategy in regard to the extent to which they
provide a focal point for meeting the challenges of global corporate power
and building transnational solidarity around GPNs. And we will argue on
behalf of the need for more in-depth analysis of the organisational dimensions that such a strategy entails.

REDRESSING THE GLOBAL IMBALANCE: A CORPORATE STRATEGY APPROACH

Transnational corporations are the 'prime "movers and shapers"' (Dicken
2011: 109) of economic globalisation. Over the past decades, we have wit-
nessed a massive expansion of global economic activity through the deregulation of the international trade regime and the growth of TNC-driven
investment, production and services. In expanding their reach across borders, TNCs build extensive GPNs that span a wide range of political, economic and labour relations systems. Their power lies in the concentration
and discretionary deployment of material, financial and human resources
that they control. As leading corporations, TNCs have a predominant
influence on shaping product markets from the extraction of raw materials to the individual consumer. Decisions they make on investment and
relocation—singly and collectively—have an enormous impact on the well-
being and economic growth of the localities or regions where they operate.

  With their extensive GPNs, these corporations directly and indirectly
wield power over a relatively small, but strategically significant portion
of the global workforce.[2] Both at individual workplaces and across different national systems of labour relations, management strives to optimise
flexibilisation in work processes. Significantly, GPNs organise production
processes on a new transnational plane, often reconfiguring and building
new relationships and centres of value extraction, fragmenting here and re-
integrating there. The paths and dynamics of GPN development may vary
markedly across time and across sectors, and may be subject to different
levels of 'drivenness' and control (Riisgaard and Hammer 2011). As corporate 'webs of power' (Amoore 2002: 128), they are potentially of crucial
importance for organising the collective voice of labour and implementing
labour standards globally.

GUFs have begun to fashion a strategy for counteracting indiscriminate TNC power over labour around IFAs. With this instrument, their goal is to systematically and globally rectify the power asymmetry between management and employees, which tends to increase in moving from the core of production to the periphery. As reflected in the literature on the governance of GPNs (cf. Gereffi et al. 2005), the collective voice of labour—in particularly beyond the core—is only marginally present and sporadically heard.

Firstly, and as a minimum, IFAs are based on the core labour standards of the International Labour Organization (ILO), although many of the agreements include standards for additional issues as well. Secondly, to varying degrees, IFAs stipulate procedures for monitoring the agreement, for case handling of violations and for resolving other disputes. Thirdly, in the negotiation of an IFA, the boundaries of its application are defined. All entities of the signatory TNC are included and, increasingly, IFAs contain language that extends the coverage to suppliers and sub-contractors. Finally, the effectiveness of an IFA may be significantly influenced by two actor-related factors. For one, the actor constellation during negotiations, especially on the labour side, has a noticeable impact on the outcome (Fichter et al. 2011). Secondly, the recognition and involvement of unions at the workplace is crucial to enabling implementation.

As union strategy for IFAs has developed, it has been especially this last factor that has become the centrefold for the GUFs. Using IFAs as a means of restraining TNC power to unilaterally control the employment relationship hinges on building associational power (Wright 2000) through collaboration, cooperation and coordination among unions operating within distinct national systems of labour relations. As a strategic framework for creating a multi-level and cross-border arena of engagement with corporate management, IFAs may redefine actor constellations within the contested fields of GPNs and open new space for building local union representation.

Based on current research,[3] we conceptualise the intended institutional configuration of current IFA strategies as illustrated in Figure 11.1. In basic terms, the IFA process establishes a new space of labour-management negotiation at the headquarters level with a potential to impact national and local arenas (Müller-Jentsch 2004) of labour relations. On this basis, the IFA process is potentially the foundation for erecting a multi-level arena of labour relations and redefining power relationships in the 'fields of contestation' (Levy 2008) within cross-border production networks. Our figure is of course simplified in that it represents only the primary actors of negotiation and excludes the role of existing national and international institutions. Moreover, it references only that part of GPNs that is built on local subsidiaries linked to a central organisational level and leaves the labour relations at suppliers and distributors out of the picture:

Taking a closer look at the headquarters level, we would emphasise that the introduction of additional actors representing labour increases the complexity of power relationships, both between labour and management and

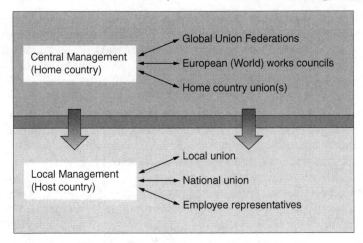

Figure 11.1   The IFA Process. Transnationalising Labour Relations

within the labour camp. Establishing a negotiating process that results in a signed agreement indicates that management must share its decision-making in the policy field of global employment and labour relations with representatives of organised labour. The extent to which the IFA redefines the power relationship in union-management-relations is however only partly revealed in the language of the document. More lasting impacts come from the implementation and monitoring of the IFA as well as from the relationships which develop among the collective representatives of labour in the IFA process.

As for the labour camp, the negotiation of an IFA brings the GUF into a new relationship with existing employee representation in the form of home country union(s) or internal employee representative bodies, such as works councils at the headquarters level. For the GUF, home country unions and employee representatives may be important resources for facilitating negotiations, but they might also turn out to be stumbling blocks in developing a global IFA policy.

As the arrows in the figure show, IFAs are 'top-down' processes, i.e., IFAs are negotiated at corporate headquarters to be implemented in the local arenas of labour relations. The top-down character of the IFA process is never questioned by TNC central management and, indeed, in most cases is incorporated into the standardised policy of the TNC on corporate social responsibility. But on the labour side, it does raise the question of the relationship between labour's actors at the headquarters level and the representatives of labour in host countries and at suppliers and sub-contractors. Although these representatives have seldom participated directly in IFA negotiations, the IFA process assigns them a major role in ensuring implementation. In this, the sense of ownership that the negotiating representatives of labour have developed has to be diffused to the independent local unions. This is not only of paramount importance for policy reasons, it is also relevant since, to varying degrees, the affiliates are also the source of resources for the GUFs. As a consequence, within a company-oriented IFA strategy, unions must address a wide range of issues concerning the modalities of interest aggregation and articulation as, for example, how to channel potential conflicts of interest into a working transnational coordination of actors.

In sum, both horizontally among unions and employee representative bodies at the same level of representation, and vertically between the various levels, the IFA creates a new multi-level arena that may redefine the power relationships among the collective voices of labour. For the GUFs to assert their leading role in the IFA process, they must develop adequate policies along both of these dimensions for successfully negotiating and implementing an IFA. To be sure, an IFA may bolster the recognition of the GUF and enhance its role as a negotiating partner. But beyond this immediate role enhancement, the GUFs also need to raise awareness of the IFA among affiliates, enable them to develop a sense of ownership and concomitantly extend the boundaries of IFA implementation beyond the TNC into its GPN.

TRANSNATIONAL CORPORATIONS, GLOBAL PRODUCTION NETWORKS AND UNIONS

Given the significance of GPNs for TNC operations (Coe et al. 2008), their governance structures have a bearing on the capacity of unions to lever their influence on corporate decisions affecting labour conditions. In particular, we would emphasise three aspects of GPN governance as being especially relevant for developing labour's response. Especially daunting for labour strategies has been the impact of 'financialisation', which has become a key driver of TNC global expansion in recent years. In the name of advancing 'shareholder value', all operations have been increasingly evaluated and organised in terms of the interest of shareholders and financial investors in short-term stock market performance. For labour, this has been evidenced in increased pressure on wages, a casualisation of employment relations and a lowering of labour standards. While this downward pressure is particularly pervasive in the subsidiary units at the lower end of supply chains, it should also be recognised that financialisation as a corporate strategy may affect employment practices within GPNs unequally. As such, the simultaneity of hybrid forms of employment and labour relations with diverging qualities of working and employment conditions is to be found at all stages (Grimshaw et al. 2005). Moreover, wherever 'shareholder value' has become the mantra of corporate governance, formalised processes of worker participation and social dialogue with trade unions are being undermined through restructuring and even targeted as a dangerous throttle on management's investment decisions and employment policies. While unions need to protect their institutional standing, the long-range challenge for unions lies in understanding the varieties of organisational relationships by which production processes are globally distributed and how these are fundamentally shaping employment relations and labour conditions overall.

Secondly, 'global players' are prone to spreading their business activities by disaggregating their production chains towards more network-like organisations, resulting in an erosion of labour standards and practices as they were developed in an organisationally more integrated context (Sydow and Wirth 1999). In this process, the organisational reach of negotiated standards shrinks with every outsourcing step. In many cases, the corporation itself has a "no growth" employment record; rather, its expansion is based on network co-ordination, making the extension of labour standards to workers on the periphery more difficult. As such, the segmentation of workforces into core employees with relatively good benefits and favourable employment conditions and those employed in outsourced units and as temporary and contract workers or day labourers increases noticeably towards the periphery (Atkinson 1985). In short, the more peripheral to the TNC core an organisational unit is, the more likely a violation of core labour standards becomes (Palpacuer 2008).

Thirdly, in addition to the core-periphery dichotomy, the configuration and governance of production varies from one sector to another. Evidence of such variations can be seen in the following examples. Take for instance the long chains of sub-contractors in construction or the vast number of suppliers in the apparel industry, and contrast these to the comparatively stable, centralised and hierarchical structures of production networks in the automotive or chemical industry.[4] In the cases of the global automotive or chemical industries, the configuration of GPNs is characterised by just-in-time supply chains, a stronger centralisation of the overall network under a focal enterprise and the high capital intensity of some production processes (e.g., machinery in final assembly, refineries). In contrast, the apparel industry is marked by fluid and wide-ranging production networks in which design, production facilities and outlets may be easily recombined within short time periods due to low capital intensity and the flexibility provided by information processing technologies. Moreover, the GPNs of individual TNCs in each of these sectors may also vary somewhat from the dominant standard. For this reason, the development of GUF strategies for implementing IFAs may share common elements, but beyond these, they will need to reflect the particular configuration and governance structures of the GPN for which they are being devised.

IFAs AS A UNION POLICY STRATEGY

Given the massive expansion and—for labour—fragmenting impact of GPNs over the past thirty years, the need for developing a new transnational policy strategy to contest the power of TNCs became imperative. The common bond of GUF policy in this sense is to strengthen labour's collective representation and limit the negative consequences of flexibilisation, informalisation and labour market deregulation by bringing globally operating corporations to recognise and uphold basic labour standards. As the primary means in pursuit of this goal, the GUFs have used IFAs to secure their recognition with the goal of bringing the voice of organised labour into the decision-making processes on employment and labour deployment throughout the individual TNCs and their GPNs. Because IFAs are globally scoped around a TNC, giving 'far-flung workers common targets' (Evans 2010: 352), they potentially construct an operational environment for the transnational development of the countervailing power of unions. Especially at the global level, institutional foundations for constructive labour relations are highly tenuous and union efforts to strengthen them by providing international institutions, such as the ILO or the World Trade Organization (WTO), with sanctioning mechanisms, have failed. And, we would argue, that while there may be instances of structural power resulting from tight labour markets or from the strategic location of workers in the production process (Wright 2000) on which a transnational union strategy could build, it is the associational power resulting from collective organisation and networking that is crucial to developing the resources and capabilities (Lévesque and Murray 2010) necessary to counteract TNC power. IFAs construct a multi-level arena as a focal point for strategising cross-border cooperation, which itself is heavily influenced by the vastly different organisational strengths of the participants. While the loss of union power at the national level may induce a shift in the balance of union efforts to the international level (Logue 1980; Fairbrother and Hammer 2005: 422), the ability of the GUFs to pursue the IFA strategy is still inextricably tied to the supporting role of their affiliates. How IFAs have emerged as a policy tool of key GUFs and how this plays out in the context of the sectoral construction of GPNs will be reviewed now in more detail.

EMERGENCE OF IFAs AS POLICY TOOL

IFAs developed out of a history of previous attempts at international coordination spanning several decades (Gallin 2008), in part derived from the corporation committees established by some of the international trade secretariats, the predecessors of the GUFs, in the 1970s (Levinson 1972). The immediate need for a concerted new approach grew out of the unsuccessful attempt to incorporate ILO labour standards into the WTO sanction mechanisms (Gumbrell-McCormick 2004). But it was also connected to the intention of getting workers' rights on the agenda of the global governance debate and reframing this debate to counteract corporate strategies and challenge the legitimacy of voluntary and unilateral codes of conduct. The first

IFA (entitled 'Common Viewpoint') was signed in 1988 by the International Union of Food, Agricultural, Hotel, Restaurant, Catering, Tobacco and Allied Workers' Associations (IUF) and BSN, which is known as Danone today (Gallin 2008: 26). Over the next decade, very few further agreements were reached. But with the defeat at the WTO and the continuing high-profile proliferation of unilateral corporate 'codes of conduct', the international unions mounted renewed efforts to challenge the dominance of TNCs. One sign of this activity was the adoption of a 'Basic Code of Labour Practice' (International Confederation of Free Trade Unions (ICFTU) 1997). After 2000, the number of agreements began to increase slowly, but considerably, supported above all by the formation of the global union federations.

The original ICFTU Basic Code of Labour Practice emphasises two key elements for using IFAs as strategic tools. For one, the existence of an IFA is a commitment to a continuing dialogue between management and labour. Secondly, the substance of having an IFA is to ensure the recognition of ILO labour standards, in particular the core labour standards. References containing these two elements can still be found in the basic IFA templates of several GUFs, including the IMF, UNI and the BWI. However, current bargaining points of the GUFs go beyond these basics since IFAs are increasingly perceived as a policy instrument by which the GUFs might carve out a bargaining role for themselves, counter-balance the power of TNCs over workers in their GPN, strengthen their organisational foundations and promote cross-border union cooperation.

At the end of 2010, over twenty years after the signature of the archetype of IFAs by the IUF and BSN in 1988, there are seventy-six functional IFAs. This tabulation is based on a strict definition including global (not only regional) reach, involvement of GUFs as signatories and reference to ILO core labour standards as a basic minimum. As can be seen in Table 11.1, nine GUFs have signed one or more IFAs, but five of the GUFs (IUF, IMF, ICEM, BWI and UNI) are responsible for over 90 per cent of all IFAs. In our review, we concentrate on the development of these GUFs during the decade 2000–2010 and on their basic differences resulting from the structural, associational and institutional settings in which they operate.

Starting with the IUF, which with its agreement in 1988 with BSN was the 'pioneer' GUF on IFAs, we can see how such factors as the structure of the corporation's cross-border operations and the organisational density of the unions affected the conclusion and further development of this agreement. The signing of the agreement was preceded by regular meetings of an IUF delegation with the directors of BSN over a time span of several years. At first, only the French affiliates accompanied the IUF staff, but soon both sides called in representatives from BSN subsidiaries throughout Europe. With the signing of a 'Common Viewpoint' it was agreed that unions at BSN in other parts of the world would be represented by IUF regional staff (Gallin 2008: 27f).

By 2000, however, the IUF had become dissatisfied with the impact of the agreement. Moreover, the generally positive and extensive engagement with

Table 11.1 Major Global Union Federations with international framework agreements (IFAs)

Global Union Federation	Core industries	No. of organised employees (in million)	No. of affiliates (countries)	No. of IFAs
International Union of Food, Agricultural, Hotel, Restaurant, Catering, Tobacco and Allied Workers' Association (IUF) www.iuf.org	Agriculture, food processing, hotels & catering	12.0 M	336 (120)	5
International Metalworkers' Federation (IMF) www.imfmetal.org	Steel, metal and metalworking industry, electronics	25.0 M	200 (100)	18
International Federation of Chemical, Energy, Mine and General Workers' Unions (ICEM) www.icem.org	Energy, mining and chemicals, pulp and paper	20.0 M	467 (132)	13
Building and Woodworkers' International (BWI) www.bwint.org	Building, building materials, wood-working industry	12.0 M	318 (130)	14
Union Network International (UNI) www.uniglobalunion.org	Commerce, banking, telecommunication	15.0 M	900 (140)	21

The number of IFAs represents the status of December 2010. For a current list of all IFAs, see http://www.global-unions.org/framework-agreements.html. Four IFAs in the list are the result of a joint effort: ICEM/BWI (Lafarge), IMF/ICEM (Umicore), ICEM/PSI (EDF) and BWI/ICEM/PSI (GDF Suez).

BSN/Danone management had not proved to be trend-setting for constructive labour relations with other global players in the food-processing sector, for example, Coca-Cola or Unilever. While the IUF did sign a few other agreements, more importantly, it initiated a policy review to determine how IFAs could be more effectively used to recruit new members and increase union density. The resulting position paper for the IUF World Congress in 2007 set out three conditions for its future IFA policy. IFAs were to be signed only if the TNC adhered to ILO and Organisation for Economic Co-operation and Development (OECD) labour standards, recognised the IUF as a global union and developed a convincing process of implementing the IFA (Platzer and Müller 2009: 349). The 2007 agreement that the IUF negotiated with Danone on diversity policy presents a good example of such a process. It requires the company to pay for an IUF official at headquarters to supervise implementation.

The IUF approach reflects a cautiousness toward signing new IFAs that results not only from its experiences with the marginal effectiveness of the Danone IFA, but also because it strives to have the full backing of its affiliates for the agreement.[5] Organisationally, the IUF and its affiliates cover the full extent of the industrialised global food chain, representing food and farm workers, as well as hotel and restaurant workers. But the unions have a generally low membership level, and many affiliates have only minimal (or no) financial resources for transnational activities (Platzer and Müller 2009: 330). Equally limited is the structural power of the IUF in the highly dispersed production of mass consumption articles, where usually low-paid, replaceable workers are employed in the production networks of globally operating food-processing corporations or in small and family-owned businesses, e.g., restaurants and small farms. As such, the IUF recognised that it could benefit from IFAs only if these went beyond the recognition of the ILO core labour standards and if the IUF would be able to use the agreement to recruit new members. At the same time, the IUF could not expect to have its corporate adversaries voluntarily offer recognition and bargaining. It needed to embed its approach to IFAs within a broader strategy to bring reluctant TNCs to the bargaining table. The IUF began intermittently cooperating with NGOs to anchor union activities in local communities and concentrating more resources on global campaigns (i.e., Unilever[6] und Nestlé) and on organising corporation-based networks such as at Nestlé (Rüb 2004) or Coca Cola. Thematically, IUF campaigns emphasise two basic issues: one is the recognition of the basic human right to form a collective organisation, the other is the recognition of the IUF on the part of employers as the legitimate bargaining agent of the workers.

INTERNATIONAL METALWORKERS' FEDERATION (IMF)

The IFA policy of the IMF has its antecedents in the World Corporation Committees (WCC) in the automobile industry, which never fully developed their potential (Platzer and Müller 2009: 115, 120). As a policy answer to the proliferation of unilateral and voluntary codes of conduct, the IMF has been able to develop a countervailing power approach by relying on traditionally well-organised core sectors such as auto and aerospace. These sectors are dominated by a small number of global players with tightly controlled and integrated production processes primarily located in the industrialised world. The bulk of this production relies on highly-skilled labour forces, whose role and position impart them with structural power. Through unionisation, these workers have also developed a collective capacity to exercise associational power at the workplace (Silver 2003). US unions, such as the automotive workers and the machinists, have, at least until the 1990's, exercised such power, and European metalworking unions, through high levels of membership, political recognition and well-placed employee representatives, have turned their associational and structural power into a strong institutional foundation for their representation of workers' interests.

Regarding IFAs, the German IG Metall has been especially active in using its position of membership strength at key production sites and in cooperation with works councils as institutionalised forms of employee representation to secure over one-half of all agreements signed by the IMF (Rüb 2009). Because of the relatively strong position of its affiliates and the widespread existence of legally mandated employee representative bodies in corporations headquartered in Europe, the IMF has not yet had to resort to disrupting production, public campaigns or to enlisting the support of consumer or community activists to reach an agreement. While core labour standards are included in all of its 18 IFAs, the strength of the IMF is reflected in the fact that in many cases it has been able to incorporate further workplace issues and ensure the extension of implementation beyond the organisational boundaries of the TNC to include suppliers and sub-contractors.

While still operating from a position of relative strength, IMF affiliates have suffered extensive membership losses and have repeatedly come under pressure for concession bargaining. Most distinctively, in the IMF's core industries, GPNs are being reconfigured through the sub-contracting of industrial services and temporary work, thus undercutting the standards of the core firms. Moreover, expanding industries in the IMF domain, such as electronics, information technology and renewable energy have remained largely unorganised. As part of its action program 2009–2013, the IMF has sought ways to both ensure the implementation of existing IFAs and develop the organisational strength necessary to bring more corporations to negotiate and sign an IFA. One approach is to build trade union networks in TNCs. In its guidelines from December 2010, the IMF points to the need to address problems resulting from an increasing 'shift from secure to insecure forms of employment, fragmentation of collective bargaining, corporate restructuring, and abuse of human and workers' rights' in the metal sector. The IMF seeks to encourage its affiliates from the home countries of TNCs to utilise their core sphere of strength at the workplace in key TNCs to build cross-border solidarity. This solidarity should, 'wherever possible extend into supply chains, particularly into outsourced or subcontracted parts of the original company.' An important objective of the strategy, according to the guidelines, is 'to negotiate with management for recognition which may include financing of networks', without sacrificing independence. And regarding the relationship of networks to IFAs, the IMF regards both as viable strategic approaches to ensuring trade union recognition, collective bargaining and decent labour standards, without either approach being solely a function of the other (International Metalworkers' Federation—IMF 2010).

INTERNATIONAL FEDERATION OF CHEMICAL, ENERGY, MINE AND GENERAL WORKERS' UNIONS (ICEM)

In contrast to the IUF and the IMF, the ICEM takes a more pronounced social partnership approach to what it labels "Global Framework Agreements". ICEM affiliates represent workers in eight different manufacturing and resource extracting sectors, which include such global players as BP, Shell, BASF, Bridgestone, Rio Tinto or EDF. Workers, especially highly skilled ones, in certain segments of production possess a significant measure of structural power, but corporations have been able to introduce technological advancements to curtail that power. Moreover, in some sectors, such as chemicals and pharmaceuticals, the sectoral growth of production has shifted from comparatively well-organised industrial countries to areas of the world where unions are weak or under political constraints (International Federation of Chemical Energy Mine and General Workers' Unions— ICEM 2010). At the same time, environmental issues are centrefold in many of the industries represented by the ICEM. Increasing public scrutiny and repeated environmental scandals (for example, the BP oil spill in 2010) have heightened the interest of most leading corporations to present themselves as promoting sustainability and being socially responsible.

Although ICEM has a number of strong unions in the industrialised countries, a large number of its affiliates are in threshold and developing countries whose membership basis is weak and whose financial resources are low. Moreover, the ICEM has experienced a significant amount of organisational fluctuation, partly due to political differences but more generally as a result of conflicts over membership dues (Platzer and Müller 2009: 151). While affiliates from western Europe, in particular the IG BCE from Germany, have considerable influence on policy as a result of their proximity to important European-based corporations and their considerable financial contributions, the integration, participation and representation of the vast majority of the membership in the rest of the world on an equal basis is an ongoing challenge. Attempts to develop the ICEM as a countervailing power to the TNCs in its sectors were reversed after 2000 in favour of strengthening dialogue and bargaining approaches along the lines of a 'participative pragmatic internationalism' (Müller et al. 2003: 671).

In conjunction with its interest in establishing a social dialogue with corporate headquarters, the ICEM has for many years backed the development of regional corporate networks, for example, in Brazil and in Asia (Cumbers et al. 2008). While such networks are important elements of ICEM's policy, its overall approach to framework agreements strongly resembles that of the IMF. The ICEM argues that such agreements 'should be a central aspect of the objectives of the trade union in the country in which the multinational company has its headquarters, as an expression of international solidarity and of the understanding of the interest of the workers in the parent company in improving conditions of work at all points in their company's chain of production' (International Federation of Chemical Energy Mine and General Workers' Unions—ICEM 2010: 58). Thus, while the ICEM is much more explicit in its goal of dialogue and partnership in its relationships with the TNCs in its sectors, its headquarters orientation closely resembles that of the IMF. Seen together, both aspects are a good indication of where associational and institutional power is located in the ICEM.

BUILDING AND WOODWORKING INTERNATIONAL (BWI)

In the two sectors building and woodworking, which fall under the responsibility of the BWI, we find both similarities to and differences with the ICEM social partnership approach. The construction industry is predominantly marked by many small and medium-size companies. The global players are highly flexible organisations, operating project-based networks with a myriad of sub-contractors, the selection of which is first of all determined by the location of the construction site. While workers at large prestigious projects, such as those for international sports events, may wield some structural power, most construction sites do not fall into this category. Moreover, bringing that power to bear is made difficult by the complex chain of contractors and sub-contractors with usually less than 10 employees and the widespread use of migrant labour (see Chapter 13 by Nikolas Hammer in this volume). In woodworking, there are also large numbers of sub-contractors and small to medium-size suppliers, often located in rural areas in close proximity to sources of wood and other raw materials. BWI deals with both the pulp and paper industry and the leading manufacturers of office materials in this sector.

While the Nordic unions have traditionally been a financial mainstay for international activities and had a strong political influence in the BWI and its predecessor organisations, increases in membership (but not finances) since 1990 have come exclusively from the countries of the former Soviet bloc as well as from Africa, Asia and Latin America. With its membership growth outstripping its financial means, requiring significant external project funding, the associational power of the BWI is underdeveloped. For this reason, BWI has initiated a three-prong approach to strengthening its position: organising, campaigning and negotiating (Platzer and Müller 2009: 218f). In its dealing with TNCs, BWI prefers negotiating, opting for social dialogue in a manner similar to that of the ICEM (Hellmann 2007). Recently, however, BWI has invested more resources in building organisational capacities in selected regions (i.e., Africa). Almost one-third of its budget has been earmarked for union development programs, whereas TNC-related activities receive very little financing (3 per cent) (Platzer and Müller 2009: 216). This seems to reflect BWI's recognition of the importance of building union capacities before negotiating with TNCs over new agreements that its affiliates could not service.

UNI GLOBAL UNION (UNI)

UNI covers the diverse employment landscape of the private service sector. Its most important segments are retail and wholesale commerce, banking and telecommunications. As with all private services, there is very little in the way of social partnership tradition on which UNI can build. Even where such an understanding existed at one time, for example, in former state-owned telecommunication or postal services, privatisation has put a definitive end to that chapter of labour relations.[7] In addition, deregulation, flexibilisation through outsourcing and temporary employment and internationalisation have weakened union footholds considerably.

To meet this challenge, UNI is currently revamping its overall approach to transnational unionism, concentrating its resources more heavily on organising. The property services division, while numerically small, has been the progenitor of policy development. This division represents employees in facility management, cleaning and maintenance, as well as security. On the one hand, UNI has taken a lead from the social movement unionism of its US affiliate SEIU (Woodruff 2007) and its organising experiences, targeting specific TNCs as global players for international campaigns and mobilising workers and community support in the process. Working closely with key affiliates at major corporate sites to develop strategies for local activities, UNI's intention is to build solidarity networks and ensure that the affiliates are part of the global agreement (IFA) process from the beginning. This emphasis on involvement and 'ownership' is intended to provide the impetus for successful implementation and trade union recognition. The signing of a global agreement with the British G4S corporation in late 2008, after an acrimonious international battle, is a prime example of this strategy (Fichter and Helfen 2011). Parallel to that targeted approach, UNI has announced its goal of signing as many global agreements as possible in the interest of moving from individual corporate standards to general sectoral standards.

However, this goal of quantity has been a mixed bag as far as quality is concerned. Especially in regard to the applicability to suppliers and sub-contractors and in regard to implementation procedures, many of the recent agreements are not very specific. Exceptions to this may be found in the important cases of G4S and ISS,[8] particularly in regard to trade union recognition and collective bargaining rights. Whether the two strategies of targeting specific global players, on the one hand, and signing as many agreements as possible, on the other hand, are compatible and manageable at the same time is an open question.

CONCLUSIONS

What insights can be drawn from this analysis? In light of the pervasiveness of non-regulation and the violation of elementary labour rights, the need for the union movement to find ways to tackle such problems is evident. Using IFAs as a strategy to set comprehensive and minimum standards for labour in TNCs and throughout their GPNs is a promising means to that end to which other instruments and policies, such as the OECD Guidelines, alliances with NGOs and consumer campaigns, could contribute. Through IFAs, the GUFs have not only given new impetus to enforcing the recognition and implementation of minimum standards, but have also transnationalised the struggle by developing a new level of labour relations and linking their cross-border efforts to national labour relations arenas.

While the importance of developing strategies around TNCs and their GPNs as a means of stemming the erosion of national labour standards worldwide is widely recognised in labour circles, realistically, we should also be aware of the limited impact of the IFA strategy up to now. Firstly, the number of IFAs is still very small, even if UNI continues on its ambitious path to reach 100 agreements within the next few years. The overall number of 80 IFAs[9] finalised to date is less than 10 per cent of the number of European works councils,[10] and not even 1 per cent of the overall number of TNCs. It will require more than an intensification of present efforts to increase the numbers significantly. Secondly, the IFA strategy has been almost totally ineffective toward TNCs headquartered in the industrial centers outside of Europe. Thirdly, companies find ways to hollow-out IFAs, by not implementing them at certain operations, such as special economic zones, joint ventures or in specific national legal contexts. Finally, the GUFs could find IFAs to actually have a restrictive impact on their policy options in building transnational solidarity. Although often projected as extending coverage to suppliers and sub-contractors, the low level of implementation is indicative of the fact that IFAs are still primarily dimensioned along the boundaries of focal TNCs. The danger of a strategy that is incapable of extending its radius beyond the focal TNC is that it may become increasingly corporate-bound, circumscribing union policy choices and turning into a cross-border reproduction of national structural and power-related asymmetries, both among unions and between labour and the TNCs.

Unions have never regarded the task of building transnational solidarity as a cakewalk, despite some claims that it would inevitably follow from globalisation and the expansion of TNCs. And IFAs are not a newly found panacea. But as they have evolved over the past two decades, they can be invoked as a means of stemming the worst kinds of exploitation, e.g., by giving trade unions leverage to push headquarters management to intervene against violations in the GPN. Possibly even more importantly, IFAs can truly open the space needed for local organising and for addressing the labour movement's organisational deficits at the transnational level. This may be seen as a step in 'labor's turn to globalise' (Evans 2010). Yet, as consequential as this argument may seem, the question of just how unions could organise effectively around GPNs using, for example, IFAs to rein in the pervasive power of TNCs and their control over GPNs, is still very much open to debate and investigation. Despite calls for global unions (Lerner 2007) or for hooking the 'trees' of international unionism to the 'rhizomes' of social movements together (Evans, 2010), we know little about how these players, from the local to the international level, can interact and what role the GUFs with their IFA strategy can play in forging an organisational backbone of associational power by developing collaboration, cooperation and coordination.

Much research on this organisational aspect of transnational solidarity is still needed, not only in conjunction with IFAs, but here it becomes particularly obvious. To start with, as a top-down approach, the IFA strategy has generally not generated sufficient momentum to bring national and local unions to recognise their ownership and responsibility for IFA implementation. And yet, remarkably, at the same time, IFAs have set processes in motion that are proving to be at odds with many institutionalised procedures and traditional organisational understandings of international trade unionism with its canon of bylaws, committees and conferences.

Next, using an IFA effectively requires a different concentration of resources and more focused communication at all levels, from the local at the workplace to the GUF. Beyond its signature on an IFA, a GUF rarely has the mandated power to ensure that the provisions of the IFA are met at the workplace. GUFs are not hierarchical and integrated organisations; rather they are facilitators for collaboration and information exchange centers. Power lies in the large, dues paying affiliates.

Finally, as we have pointed out above, organisational strategies must respond to the governance structures of GPNs in order to effectively exercise union power. Organisational approaches in fragmented GPNs, in which the structural power of workers is negligible, will be required to be significantly different from those in more integrated and hierarchical GPNs. In the latter, unions may still be able to rely solely on their own associational power.

Union intervention can build on institutionally based and collectively negotiated standards at core firms, characterised by cooperative labour relations that enhance the performance and motivation of employees, facilitate higher investments in human resources and provide a means of achieving internal flexibility during periods of low demand. In the case of highly fragmented GPN with predominantly low-skilled employees, adjustments are attained through contract terminations unencumbered by protective labour regulation and union contracts. In this case, unions may need to resort to more aggressive and non-conventional strategies built around a broader coalition of union and non-union organisations to achieve that same level of associational power.

It would be short-sighted to couch this challenge exclusively in organisational terms as it is indeed highly political. As Haworth and Ramsay (1986) pointed out many years ago, there are any number of factors that work against building transnational solidarity, not the least of which can be the national embeddedness of unions. And as the experiences with European works councils show, it is often difficult to overcome local and national divisions. We would nevertheless argue that the creation of organisational resources around the IFA strategy will enable the international union movement to move forward on enhancing trade union power in the struggle over the global governance of labour relations.

One means of bringing the necessary resources to bear is to build transnational union networks (TUN): along the nodes of production at a TNC and its suppliers, across local workplaces or throughout a region. To develop and survive, such networks need activists, an agenda and sustainable structures. As a tangible expression of an IFA strategy, such networks can enable unions to develop a strong organisational foundation for transnational solidarity. The involvement and interaction of trade unions across the GPN of a TNC appears to be both a precondition and a goal of a successful IFA strategy.

In this sense we would argue for a strategy that moves beyond the single TNC to encompass the scope of GPNs. This is a necessary step toward overcoming the pitfalls of a singularly corporate-oriented approach. Looking beyond the issue of IFAs and the regulation of labour in TNCs, programs for improving labour laws and their implementation at the national level as well as for strengthening regulatory functions of international institutions can be initiated. Campaigns could be developed that target the (lack of) regulation of international labour relations or the discrepancies between corporate proclamations and the reality on the ground.[11] Alliances among the GUFs to organise new groups of workers could contribute to strengthening international programs. Dynamic shifts in the development of the international division of labour make the importance of strong and independent unions in such countries as India, Brazil, China and Russia evident. In the flexible world of today's global capitalism, the inclusion of such strategically important groups like migrant workers, temporary employees and highly skilled workers is an important challenge. Beyond their own organisational territory, unions must consider whether they can increase their recognition and potential through strategic alliances with non-union activist movements (Bonner and Spooner 2011). In this way, there is a chance for the unions to extend the progress they have made so far via the IFA strategy to organise an even more encompassing level of transnational solidarity to overcome the vulnerability of that Achilles heel.

NOTES

1. Generic term. Other global union federations call them global framework agreements (ICEM) or global agreements (UNI).
2. According to the UNI website, the ILO calculates that TNCs employ over ninety million people, or approximately 5 per cent of the global workforce. http://www.uniglobalunion.org/Apps/iportal.nsf/pages/20090226_ml9xEn.
3. The research on IFAs is co-directed by Michael Fichter and Jörg Sydow with funding from the German Hans-Boeckler-Foundation. See http://www.pol soz.fu-berlin.de/polwiss/ifa_projekt.
4. Although in these industries, increasing flexibilisation through contract and temporary labour undermines trade union organisation capacity as well.
5. See the IFA negotiations with Sodexo. http://cleanupsodexo.org/2011/02/iuf-statement-on-negotiations-with-sodex.php.
6. The IUF was successful in Pakistan in late 2009: http://www.iuf.org/cgi-bin/dbman/db.cgi?db=default&uid=default&ID=6281&view_records=1&ww=1&en=1.
7. The current union campaign directed at T-Mobile, the US subsidiary of Deutsche Telekom, is evidence of this. See http://www.loweringthebarforus.org/.
8. The UNI IFAs are available at: http://www.uniglobalunion.org/Apps/iportal.nsf/pages/20090202_vlnuEn.
9. This number includes IFAs with TNCs that have merged or folded, as well as those agreements that are no longer active.
10. According to the European Trade Union Institute, there were 903 EWCs in transnational corporations in September 2010. See http://www.ewcdb.eu/statistics_graphs.php.
11. See a recent report by Human Rights Watch on European corporations in the US for such an example. http://www.hrw.org/en/reports/2010/09/02/strange-case-0.

REFERENCES

Amoore, L. (2002), *Globalisation Contested. An International Political Economy of Work*, Manchester: Manchester University Press.
Atkinson, J. (1985), *Flexibility, Uncertainty and Manpower Management*, Brighton: IES.
Bonner, C., and Spooner, D. (2011), 'Organizing in the Informal Economy: A Challenge for Trade Unions', *Internationale Politik und Gesellschaft*, 2, 87–105.
Coe, N. M., Dicken, P., and Hess, M. (2008), 'Global Production Networks: Realizing the Potential', *Journal of Economic Geography*, 8(3), 271–295.
Cumbers, A., Nativel, C., and Routledge, P. (2008), 'Labour Agency and Union Positionalities in Global Production Networks', *Journal of Economic Geography*, 8(3), 369–387.

Dicken, P. (2011), *Global Shift. Mapping the Changing Contours of the World Economy*, Los Angeles: Sage.

Evans, P. (2010), 'Is it Labor's Turn to Globalize? Twenty-First Century Opportunities and Strategic Responses', *Global Labour Journal*, 1(3), 352–379.

Fairbrother, P., and Hammer, N. (2005), 'Global Unions: Past Efforts and Future Prospects', *Relations Industrielles/Industrial Relations*, 60(3), 405–431.

Fichter, M., and Helfen, M. (2011), 'Going Local with Global Policies: Implementing International Framework Agreements in Brazil and the United States', in K. Papadakis (ed.), *Practices and Outcomes of an Emerging Global Industrial Relations Framework*, New York: Palgrave Macmillan.

Fichter, M., Helfen, M., and Sydow, J. (2011), 'Employment Relations in Global Production Networks—Initiating Transfer of Practices via Union Involvement', *Human Relations*, 64(4), 599–624.

Gallin, D. (2008), 'International Framework Agreements: A Reassessment', in K. Papadakis (ed.) *Cross-Border Social Dialogue and Agreements: An Emerging Global Industrial Relations Framework?*, Geneva: International Institute for Labour Studies.

Gereffi, G., Humphrey, J., and Sturgeon, T. (2005), 'The Governance of Global Value Chains', *Review of International Political Economy* 12(1), 78–104.

Grimshaw, D., Willmott, H., and Rubery, J. (2005) 'Inter-Organizational Networks: Trust, Power, and the Employment Relationship', in M. Marchington, D. Grimshaw, J. Rubery and H. Willmott (eds.), *Fragmenting Work. Blurring Organizational Boundaries and Disordering Hierarchies*, Oxford: Oxford University Press.

Gumbrell-McCormick, R. (2004), 'The ICFTU and the World Economy: A Historical Perspective', in R. Munck (ed.), *Labour and Globalisation. Results and Prospects*, Liverpool: Liverpool University Press.

Haworth, N., and Ramsay, H. (1986), 'Matching the Multinationals: Obstacles to International Trade Unionism', *International Journal of Sociology and Social Policy*, 6(2), 55–82.

Hellmann, M. F. (2007), 'Social Partnership at the Global Level: Building and Wood Workers' International Experiences with International Framework Agreements', in V. Schmidt (ed.), *Trade Union Responses to Globalization. A Review by the Global Union Research,* Geneva: International Labour Office.

International Confederation of Free Trade Unions (ICFTU) (1997), The ICFTU/ITS Basic Code of Labour Practice, http://www.icftu.org/displaydocument.asp?Index =991209513&Language=EN, (accessed 02.09.2010).

International Federation of Chemical Energy Mine and General Workers' Unions (ICEM) (2010), *ICEM World Conference for the Chemical Industries*. Geneva: ICEM.

International Metalworkers' Federation (IMF) (2010), IMF Guidelines on Trade Union Networks in TNCs, http://www.imfmetal.org/files/10100610594479/ IMF_TNC_Networks_Guidelines.pdf, (accessed January 13, 2011).

Lerner, S. (2007), Global Unions. A Solution to Labor's Worldwide Decline, in *New Labor Forum*, 16(1), 23–37.

Lévesque, C., and Murray, G. (2010), 'Understanding Union Power: Resources and Capabilities for Renewing Union Capacity', *Transfer: European Review of Labour and Research*, 16(3), 333–350.

Levinson, C. (1972), *International Trade Unionism*, London: Allen & Unwin.

Levy, D. (2008), 'Political Contestation in Global Production Networks', *Academy of Management Review*, 33(4), 943–963.

Logue, J. (1980), *Toward a Theory of Trade Union Internationalism*, Gothenburg: University of Gothenburg Press.

Müller, T., Platzer, H.-W., and Rüb, S. (2003), 'Globalisierung und gewerkschaftliche Internationalisierung—Zur Politik der Global Union Federations', in *WSI-Mitteilungen*, 56(11), 666–672.

Müller-Jentsch, W. (2004), 'Theoretical Approaches to Industrial Relations', in B. E. Kaufman (ed.), *Theoretical Perspectives on Work and the Employment Relationship*, Champaign: Industrial Relations Research Association.

Palpacuer, F. (2008), 'Bringing the Social Context Back in: Governance and Wealth Distribution in Global Commodity Chains', *Economy and Society*, 37(3), 393–419.

Platzer, H.-W., and Müller, T. (2009), *Die globalen und europäischen Gewerkschaftsverbände—Handbuch und Analysen zur transnationalen Gewerkschaftspolitik*, Berlin: Edition Sigma.

Riisgaard, L., and Hammer, N. (2011), 'Prospects for Labour in Global Value Chains: Labour Standards in the Cut Flower and Banana Industries', *British Journal of Industrial Relations*, 49(1), 168–190.

Rüb, S. (2004), *Die Entwicklung des globalen Gewerkschaftsnetzwerks im Nestlé-Konzern. Gewerkschaftliche Gegenmacht in transnationalen Konzernen?*, Bonn: Friedrich-Ebert-Stiftung.

Rüb, S. (2009), *Die Transnationalisierung der Gewerkschaften. Eine empirische Untersuchung am Beispiel der IG Metall*, Berlin: Edition Sigma.

Silver, B. J. (2003), *Forces of Labor. Workers' Movements and Globalization since 1870*, Cambridge: Cambridge University Press.

Sydow, J., and Wirth, C. (1999), 'Von der Unternehmung zum Unternehmungsnetzwerk—Interessenvertretungsfreie Zonen statt Mitbestimmung', in W. Müller-Jentsch (ed.), *Konfliktpartnerschaft. Akteure und Institutionen der industriellen Beziehungen*, München and Mering: Rainer Hampp Verlag.

Woodruff, T. (2007) 'Wie die SEIU zur Gewerkschaft mit den höchsten Mitgliederzuwächsen in den USA wurde', in P. Bremme, U. Fürniß and U. Meinecke (ed.), *Never work alone: organizing—ein Zukunftsmodell für Gewerkschaften*, Hamburg: VSA-Verl. pp. 92–116.

Wright, E. O. (2000), 'Working-Class Power, Capitalist-Class Interests, and Class Compromise', *The American Journal of Sociology*, 105(4), 957–1002.

12 Opening the Black Box of Cross-Border Union Alliances
A Case Study

Marc-Antonin Hennebert and Reynald Bourque

The past two decades have seen the emergence of new forms of international employee representation within multinational corporations. In EU member states, management in multinationals finds itself having to deal with statutory European works councils (EWCs), while at a more global level some studies show a rise in the number of solidarity networks and cross-border union alliances. These cross-border union alliances can be defined as groups of union organisations from different countries that represent workers from the same multinational for the purpose of enforcing fundamental worker rights. Under the leadership of some global union federations that have recently made their establishment a strategic priority, cross-border union alliances are of growing interest to organisations seeking to counter the negative effects of globalisation and the increasing power of multinationals. While the establishment of such alliances is not a new phenomenon, recent studies suggest that the current context of globalisation is contributing to their resurgence (Barton and Fairbrother 2009; Croucher and Cotton 2009; Greer and Hauptmeier 2008; Bronfenbrenner 2007; Stevis and Boswell 2007; Harrod and O'Brien 2002). They also have the merit of going beyond the deterministic, even defeatist, views of the various obstacles standing in the way of international cooperation between unions by providing a more nuanced understanding of the conditions in which the new union alliances can be effective.

That being said, there are several grey zones when it comes to the relationship dynamics and structure of power relations within cross-border union alliances. In fact, it is as though the alliances were genuine 'black boxes'. While the participating unions (the inputs) can usually be identified, and although several studies have documented what certain union alliances have achieved in the way of contributions to the social regulation of transnational firms (the outputs), little is as yet known about the social dynamics that move them or the processes of mobilisation and collective action they generate. Little more is known about their internal modus operandi or the logic underpinning each union's position within the alliance.

We base our exploration of these issues on social network theory, which is original in that it conceives of organisations and social entities as networks of actors. To understand collective action within a given group, this approach focuses on the relations between the actors with a view to describing and mapping the structure thereof, identifying the dominant actors and analysing their respective influence on the establishment of a common agenda (Scott 2001; Wasserman and Faust 1994). In so doing, it employs various concepts, such as centrality, autonomy and social capital, in order to correctly understand the position occupied by each member within a social group and to highlight the 'associational' power that may come from being socially connected to the other members (Wright 2000). This approach has already been applied to myriad research subjects, including those relating to corporate structures (Carroll 2004) and social movements (Diani and Mc-Adam 2003), and it appears particularly relevant for shedding light on the internal functioning of international union alliances. The objective of this chapter is therefore more clearly to understand cross-border union alliances, as venues for collective action, using an approach that comprehends spaces of cooperation and mobilisation as networks of relationships between social actors.

In terms of method, the chapter draws on a single case study conducted over the past few years in a Canadian multinational in the commercial printing industry, namely Quebecor World Inc. In recent years, union officials dealing with Quebecor World have sought to coordinate the firm's various unions internationally. Under the leadership of Union Network International (UNI), an international alliance called 'UNI Network@Quebecor World' was established, and a worldwide campaign for union rights initiated. Ambitious in scope, the campaign entailed the coordination of various solidarity actions at the international level involving unions from more than a dozen countries. It culminated in 2007 in the signing of an international framework agreement between UNI and Quebecor World management representatives.

The analysis presented in this chapter is based on empirical data gathered from multiple sources. The core material consists of a series of 40 semi-structured interviews with direct participants in the alliance. The participants were selected according to their position within the national trade union concerned and their involvement in the network. The interviews started by exploring the events that took place and ended with a more detailed analysis of the process by which an international framework agreement had been negotiated. This core material is supplemented by observations collected during union meetings and by documentary material, including the official UNI website, which provides access to information published by different national and local union organisations representing Quebecor World workers.

The chapter is divided into two parts. The first part presents the cross-border union alliance established within Quebecor World. It includes a description of the processes leading to its creation and the centers of strategic action established by its members as part of a transnational corporate campaign called Justice@Quebecor. The second part uses social network theory to analyse the alliance's internal functioning and the relations between the trade union organisations that marked its development.

CROSS-BORDER UNION ALLIANCES: THE CASE OF UNI NETWORK@QUEBECOR WORLD

Quebecor World Inc. is one of the world's largest commercial printing companies. In early 2008, it employed approximately 28,000 workers in a ramified network of more than 115 printing and related facilities in 17 countries on 3 continents (North America, South America and Europe). Since its establishment, the history of this Canadian multinational had been marked by steady growth thanks to the simultaneous deployment of an aggressive acquisition strategy, on the one hand, and expansion in various international markets, on the other. This growth, however, had clearly started to slow down by the early 2000s. The economic downturn caused by the disruption of the publishing market since the events of September 11, 2001 and the greater than expected challenges posed by the integration of World Color Press, a large American commercial printing company with which Quebecor World merged in 1999, gradually undermined the company's economic situation and competitive positioning.

In order to find ways to restore profits, the company adopted a recession-busting programme involving: (1) cost reduction and the disposal of facilities that were not part of its core business; (2) the establishment of a vast retooling programme comprising the purchase of new presses and new high-performance equipment; and (3) the closure of less productive plants (UNI 2006). These measures resulted primarily in numerous job cuts affecting most of the company's installations, especially in North America. Since the early 2000s, more than 15,000 jobs have been lost within the company, equivalent to a third of its total workforce.

Table 12.1 illustrates the diverse nature of the trade unions represented at the Canadian multinational.

It was within this context of restructuring that the first international contacts between Quebecor World employee representatives took place. From the outset, the global union federation representing workers in the commercial printing sector, i.e., UNI, was at the heart of this process. UNI recognised the problems of access to unionisation in some Quebecor World facilities and was anxious to meet the concerns of its affiliates, particularly its sectoral division, UNI Graphical; in 2000, it held the first international meetings aimed at promoting the development of contacts between trade union organisations representing Quebecor World workers around the world. Those meetings provided an opportunity to formalise the existence of a working group called 'UNI Network@Quebecor World'[1] and to set goals, including that of increasing union representation within the company by making the organisation of unionisation campaigns a strategic priority.

Table 12.1 Trade union presence in Quebecor World establishments

Region	Country	Number of factories	Trade union presence	Determination of working conditions	Main trade union organisations
North America	Canada	18	Approximately one-third of company employees are unionised (the proportion of unionised factories is higher in Canada).	At unionised factories, working conditions are governed by locally negotiated collective agreements.	Communications, Energy and Paperworkers Union of Canada (CEP)
	United States	62			Graphic Communications Conference of the International Brotherhood of Teamsters (GCC-IBT), which is affiliated with the Quebec Federation of Labour (QFL)
Europe	England	1	Trade unions are present at all the company's plants.	Working conditions are governed by sector-level agreements that set minimum employment conditions and can be supplemented by local agreements.	AMICUS
	Austria	1			Gewerkschaft, Druck, Journalismus, Papier (GPA-DJP)
	Belgium	1			1. CSC Bâtiment et industrie (CSC)
					2. Syndicat des Employés, Techniciens et Cadres (SETCA-FGTB)
	Finland	1			Viestintäalan Ammattiliitto ry (SAK)
	France	9			Fédération des travailleurs des industries du livre, du papier et de la communication (FILPAC-CGT)
	Sweden	2			Grafiska Facföbundet Mediafacket (Grafiska-LO)
	Spain	5			1. Federación sectorial estatal—Unión General de Trabajadores (FES-UGT)
					2. Federación de Comunicación y Transporte (CCOO)

	Country			
Latin America	Argentina	1	A trade union is present in 6 of 8 company factories.	Non-unionised establishment
	Brazil	2	Working conditions can be governed by both locally negotiated collective agreements and/or sector-wide agreements.	1. Sindicato dos Trabalhadores nas industrias Graficas do Estado de Saõ Paulo (SINDGRAF) 2. Sindicato dos Trabalhadores nas Industrias Graficas do Estado de Pernambuco (SINDGRAF)
	Chile	1		Sindicato no. 1 de trabajadores Quebecor World Chile—Confederación Nacional Gráfica (CONAGRA)
	Colombia	1		Non-unionised establishment
	Mexico	2		1. Sindicato Industrial de Trabajadores de Artes Gráficas (SITAG) 2. Sindicato Unico de Trabajadores de Gráficos Monte Albán (SUTGMA)
	Peru	1		Federación Gráfica del Perú (FGP)

The identification of this strategic priority was relayed to the national and local levels through various union initiatives. In North America, the Graphic Communications International Union (GCIU) launched a recruitment drive by increasing the number of unionisation campaigns and bringing them to fruition more quickly. The campaign met with a number of setbacks, including the particularly disappointing failure to unionise a 650-worker Quebecor World plant in Corinth, Mississippi, in 2001, following a virulent, employer-led local anti-union campaign (Tate 2006). Allegations of anti-union behaviour by local Quebecor World managers in several countries in South America were also filed.[2]

The problems relating to recognition of union legitimacy, coupled with the concern of some union representatives about worker health and safety at different company plants, strengthened union representatives' desire to consult with each other more regularly. Moreover, the new meetings organised for this purpose sparked a process that eventually led to the formalisation and consolidation of a global union alliance within Quebecor World. Several concrete and specific measures came out of these meetings, including, in particular, a clarification of the trade union alliance's goals. At the regional level, i.e., in the Americas, a decision was made by the main national trade union confederations from the US, Canada and Chile, notably, to conduct unionisation campaigns at specific Quebecor plants in the southern US and in Latin America. At the global level, the main goal was the negotiation of an international framework agreement with Quebecor World management along the lines of the agreement co-signed by UNI and the management of the Spanish telecommunications firm *Telefónica* in 2002. Thus what had begun as a transnational forum for consultation and information exchange between Quebecor World trade union representatives had now taken on a more vocal role, with UNI Network ambitiously positioning itself as a legitimate international interlocutor for the multinational's management.

LAUNCHING THE JUSTICE@QUEBECOR WORLD CAMPAIGN

The year 2003 was pivotal in the global alliance's development at Quebecor World. It ended with the Global Quebecor Solidarity Conference, which was held from December 5 to 10, 2003, in Memphis, Tennessee. The conference brought together more than 120 union representatives and workers from 14 different countries to discuss the problems they were experiencing in their respective workplaces. Its high point was the delegates' decision to diversify their strategies for increasing pressure on the company at the regional and global levels. In more concrete terms, this decision led to the official launch of the Justice@Quebecor World campaign, which involved various strategies for action.

The first strategy was to ensure that the relationship between UNI Network members was maintained by organising regular international meetings and developing various solidarity activities. One such activity was the series of 'global solidarity days' held after the Memphis conference, during which workers at Quebecor plants in various countries wore Justice@Quebecor World stickers and T-shirts, signed petitions and distributed tracts demanding employer recognition of their right to unionise. In some cases, they staged rallies at their own plants, demanding that Quebecor World management sign an international agreement recognising the basic labour rights of workers.

The second strategy was to bring the union's demands into the public and political spheres in order to diversify support for the global alliance. To this end, a public awareness campaign was organised and various media events were held. As part of the campaign, in August 2004, members of the Kentucky Workers' Rights Board and of the workers' rights organisation Jobs with Justice organised a gathering in front of company headquarters in Montreal to defend the right of Quebecor workers to organise. In November, a group of more than 20 prominent Canadian and American authors publicly lent their support to the campaign. United under the banner 'Writers Call for Justice at Quebecor World', this group contacted the management of Quebecor World to state their concerns regarding respect for workers' rights at the plants where their books were printed.

In addition to this public awareness-raising strategy, more politically oriented action was also taken. In April 2004, workers, union leaders, students and sympathisers held a vigil in front of the Canadian Embassy in Washington, DC, to protest against what they considered the anti-union practices adopted by the management of Quebecor World in the US. During the 2004 US presidential campaign, North American unions, led by the AFL-CIO and the GCIU, managed to obtain the support of Democratic senator and presidential candidate John Kerry, who stated, in an official letter addressed to the Chairman and Chief Executive Officer of Quebecor World, that he was concerned by the accounts he had heard from some of the company's workers. One UNI leader, during a personal interview, had this to say about Kerry's support:

> So when the presidential campaign was on in the United States, Kerry made several statements and he supported us and to get in the press in Canada (. . .) He played the game a lot. He was good. He needed votes in the South, he needed people (. . .) but even so, I think he actually believed in it.

After targeting public opinion and seeking political support, the Justice@ Quebecor World campaign focused on raising shareholder awareness of the problems surrounding access to unionisation. To this end, several international delegations of workers and union representatives came to Montreal to attend annual shareholder meetings. Their action forced the Chairman of the Board, former Canadian Prime Minister Brian Mulroney, to spend much of those meetings dealing with worker rights and trade union concerns. An AFL-CIO representative summed up this action in a positive light:

> I felt like the shareholders meeting in Montreal, I felt like that was very powerful because I thought it was extremely important that we took the campaign to Montreal, to the home of the company. (. . .) And to be able to take these workers there and have them confront the former Prime Minister of Canada was, I think, for the organizers, for the staff that were there, for those workers, and then they may take their story back to their committees in Mississippi and Tennessee and tell their story about this experience. I think it was really powerful that way and also we got tons of coverage in the Canadian press.

Again with the aim of increasing pressure on the company, Quebecor World unions developed a fourth strategy, which involved putting pressure on some of the company's major customers, raising awareness among them of UNI Network's demands. The GCIU contacted the company's main customers in the US, including Disney, Avon, Kohl's Department Stores, the lingerie retailer Victoria's Secret and the telephone company Southwestern Bell. Demonstrations were held in front of cinemas in the US owned by Time/Warner Bros, which had awarded Quebecor World the contracts to print *Time* and *Sports Illustrated* and was therefore a major customer of the Canadian printing giant. A member of the AFL-CIO Center for Strategic Research explained the strategy as follows:

> The key was that we wanted a public accountability campaign with this company. In Canada, Quebecor is a long-known name and they're not at all in the US. Most people don't have any reason to come across a commercial printer (. . .). But the magazines and the catalogues that they print were with companies that were household names. And so we wanted to make sure that the retailers and the magazine companies that used them for printing were aware of the workplace practices that this company perpetuated and the denial of workers' rights in these facilities. And we thought that if they were informed of these things, they would want to take action. And ensure that, you know, ILO conventions were respected and workers' rights were respected.

Quebecor unions in Europe also played a key role in the development of this strategy by targeting companies in their respective countries that were Quebecor World customers and had signed an international framework agreement, with the aim of making the most of these agreements. Indeed, while international framework agreements primarily cover the trade union organisations and multinationals that have signed them, some contain clauses extending their normative content, in a more or less binding manner, to subcontractors and suppliers. Spanish trade unions used this means to put pressure on *Telefónica*, while Swedish trade union organisations contacted the management of furniture giant IKEA, in both cases to push the companies, in accordance with the international framework agreements they had ratified, to encourage Quebecor World management to sort out its relationship with its workers' representatives. The president of the Swedish trade union *Grafiska* described the strategy this way:

> I called IKEA and I told them that we were preparing an article for one of the biggest newspapers in Sweden and that we knew that IKEA had a good reputation, that they had a code of conduct and some policies regarding sub-contractors. They had an international framework agreement with wood workers. So I told IKEA that they were not applying these mechanisms correctly because of Quebecor. In response, they asked me, "Can you hold this for a week or so?" The management at IKEA spoke with the management at Quebecor. Quebecor and their headquarters in Canada were really upset about it, really upset. You know, the contract with IKEA is worth millions and millions of dollars.

Lastly, North American trade union representatives involved in the campaign developed a fifth strategy, which consisted in taking legal action and gradually filing various complaints to the competent authorities in the US. No legal stone was left unturned in denouncing the anti-union and discriminatory practices said to be used by management at Quebecor World. The labour courts, organisations responsible for the enforcement of health and safety regulations and committees responsible for employment equity were all mobilised.

ASSESSING THE SUCCESS OF UNI NETWORK@QUEBECOR WORLD

The Justice@Quebecor World campaign was created by a worldwide alliance of unions that took shape as a space for interunion cooperation and managed to coordinate various solidarity operations over the years. Of course, some of those operations were merely symbolic, but this attempt to develop a countervailing union power led to some instances of mobilisation that produced results in line with the alliance's goals.

In the US, the activities of UNI Network enabled Quebecor World union representatives to conclude a 'neutrality' agreement[3] on May 5, 2005. The agreement was co-signed by the management of Quebecor World and the Teamsters Graphic Communications Conference (GCC/IBT)[4] and provided for a new unionisation procedure that was more favourable to the unions than that set out in the US regulatory framework. It did not take long, moreover, for the effects of this agreement to be felt. A few months after it was signed, workers at Quebecor plants in Fernley, Nevada, and Versailles,

Kentucky voted in favour of joining the GCC/IBT, thus bringing to fruition unionisation efforts that had been initiated several years earlier (Brecher et al. 2006). In South America, international solidarity actions implemented as part of UNI Network activities also played a crucial role in the unionisation of some Quebecor plants, such as in Recife, Brazil, Santiago, Chile and, more recently, in Lima, Peru (UNI 2006). An AFL-CIO representative praised the concrete results of these global alliance activities as follows:

> To me, one of the exciting things about this campaign was that it produced real results in the US. There are workers today in Kentucky who have a union that didn't before because of this campaign. And there are workers today in Chile, and Brazil, and Peru who didn't before. So it wasn't just, you know, can workers over here help Americans? It was really: how do we come together to help everyone? And there were real results in several countries as a result of this.

At the international level, UNI Network's most significant achievement, at least symbolically, is to have managed to conclude an international framework agreement. Indeed, after several months of campaigning and negotiations, talks between Quebecor World management and the global alliance eventually led to an agreement laid out in the Joint Statement on the Respect and Promotion of International Labour Standards. This international agreement, ratified on May 4, 2007 in Barcelona at a meeting of the Quebecor EWC, is evidence of the company's commitment to respect basic labour rights as enshrined in International Labour Organization (ILO) conventions. Its conclusion was no small feat given that, at the time, it was only the second international framework agreement to be signed by a company with its headquarters in North America.

Lastly, aside from these bipartite agreements of principle, the global alliance's main contribution, according to the representatives interviewed, is to have created a concrete and operational space for transnational union solidarity. Aware that such forms of international solidarity often amount to little more than hollow words, devoid of any concrete outcomes for workers, the president of the global alliance emphasised the success of Quebecor unions in creating real practical international solidarity:

> The fact that when in Lima they decided to organize, that we were able to get people on airplanes within like 48 hours. And show up in Lima and stand in solidarity with them. And basically deliver the message: 'If the company intimidates you, the rest of the Quebecor unions around the world will stand behind you' (. . .) This is something a global union can do. Not just represent us at the WTO, not just do research and documentation, not just issue press releases (. . .) But, do what I call . . . our concept is 'practical global solidarity' (. . .) Five years ago, a local official would not have even thought of that perspective, or of that tool of leverage. But now they know. . .

QUEBECOR WORLD: THE FINAL ACT

The relatively numerous success stories racked up by this global alliance in recent years were soon overshadowed by the company's worsening economic problems. Indeed, despite the countless restructuring measures it undertook and the hundreds of millions invested in modernising its equipment, Quebecor World would never be able to reverse the downward trend first experienced several years earlier. Starting in 2007, its financial problems appeared to be increasingly insurmountable. Its debt peaked at an accumulated amount of over US$ 2.2 billion, and its share value fell by over 97 per cent in recent years.

Its back to the wall, Quebecor World finally decided, on 21 January 2008, to file for protection under Canada's Companies' Creditors Arrangement Act. It would also file for protection under a similar provision in the US, namely Chapter 11 of the US Bankruptcy Code. Quebecor World's European activities, for their part, were sold in June of the same year for US$ 325.8 million to Dutch investment group Hombergh/De Pundert (HHBV).

These events marked the divorce of Quebecor World and its parent company, Quebecor World Inc., which furthermore demanded that its former subsidiary stop using the company name Quebecor. In response, in 2009 Quebecor World changed its name to World Color Press, the name of the American company with which it had merged in 1999. A scant few months later, the shareholders of Quebecor's former industrial subsidiary accepted the acquisition offer of the American firm Quad/Graphics and the Montreal headquarters was shut down for good.

CROSS-BORDER UNION ALLIANCES AS AN ARENA FOR SOCIAL INTERACTION

After having documented the experience of Quebecor World unions in establishing a cross-border union alliance, we now turn to consideration of how such an alliance functions internally. Drawing on social network theory, we shall first identify the various positions occupied by the actors within the alliance before analysing and explaining their degree of involvement and their respective spheres of influence.

The Actors' Positions within UNI Network@Quebecor World

Studies of cross-border union alliances show that they are rarely the product of spontaneous cooperation between peers, i.e., actors with similar resources and occupying the same social positions. In fact, cross-border union alliances differ in nature because they are made up of varying configurations of actors who occupy various positions. UNI Network is no exception, and each of its constituent parts has a different impact on the directions it takes.

By deploying the concepts of structural autonomy and centrality, analysis of social networks helps us to obtain a clearer picture of the positions occupied by the actors. Structural autonomy is defined as the capacity of an individual or collective actor to establish relations with other members of the network without having to go through one or several intermediaries. The concept of centrality, for its part, serves to identify the network's most important actors, i.e. those that, because they occupy the strategic centre, are in a position to influence the distribution of resources and steer the network in a specific direction. Using these two theoretical concepts as a basis, three kinds of structural position occupied by trade union representatives in the UNI Network can be identified. We describe them as peripheral, intermediate and central, respectively.

CENTRAL ACTORS

The central position is occupied by the Canadian, American and French representatives and by UNI officials. These actors have a solid reputation among the alliance's other members, which have no difficulty in identifying them and describing the responsibilities they shoulder. The trade union organisations they represent are not only part of the inter-union alliance and its steering committee, they are also at the core of its structure and development. They have the strongest ties between them, generally have direct links to almost all the members and enjoy great structural autonomy in that they do not have to rely on intermediaries to get in touch with the organisation's members. Their leadership is recognised by all the members, who do not hesitate to point to them as the alliance's most dynamic element.

The autonomy and centrality characterising their position make these members vital actors in the alliance, all the more so in that they occupy key positions in the power and decision-making structure. They do not have absolute control of these strategic spaces, but they are in a position to oversee the participation of other members and to plan the alliance's agenda. They are very committed, as evidenced by their active presence at official meetings. Furthermore, their role as intermediaries in more informal relations ensures the alliance's social cohesion.

Among these central actors, the task of coordinating the alliance internationally falls on two trade unions in particular. The first is the Communications, Energy and Paperworkers Union of Canada (CEP). The director of its Graphical Division is the UNI Network president. He is at the heart of all the alliance's initiatives, sits on all its bodies and takes on a fair share of its public relations. He is also responsible for its internal cohesion and has several times demonstrated his capacity to channel union initiatives. For example, it was he who linked the unionisation campaign conducted by the American trade unions to the demands of other unions wishing to negotiate an international framework agreement with Quebecor World management, while at the same time preserving the coherence of the alliance's activities:

> I was in charge of both objectives. I therefore had the two groups work together. In a way I served as a point of juncture between the unionization campaign in the United States and the other trade union demands being made internationally.

The second most important trade union organisation is no doubt UNI Network. It has the most links to the other members of the alliance and the strongest direct ties to almost all of them. Besides occupying a key central position, it also acts as a necessary intermediary through its regional division in Europe and South America, and it was UNI Network that organised the first meetings at which the members got to know each other. It also sits on the alliance's steering committee, which it even appears to direct.

INTERMEDIATE ACTORS

The union representatives and trade unions from Chile, England, Spain and Sweden play a relatively important role within the alliance and occupy what can be termed an intermediate position. They have relations with several members of the alliance and are relatively close to the centres of power in that they are in contact with the actors most heavily involved. Thus the position they occupy enables them to influence the alliance's decisions and strategic orientations. This applies particularly to the British and Swedish union representatives, who are also members of the alliance's steering committee but do not play a dominant role. The fact that they have direct contact with several members of the alliance facilitates their integration, and they are never dependent on another member. In that sense, their structural autonomy is relatively high, because they can obtain information on their own and voice their opinions to the alliance's leaders and other members. As one British trade unionist recounts:

> As a rule, if I have something to say about our alliance's strategic orientations, I have no problem doing so. The meetings give me the opportunity to speak. [. . .] I know practically everyone in the alliance, and that makes communication easy. Sometimes, if I don't know who to contact, I get in touch directly with the UNI representatives.

These actors sometimes act as intermediaries and facilitate the integration of other members of the organisation, although this does not happen frequently. Such is the case with the Chilean union which, because of its age and the relations it has with important stakeholders, plays a certain leadership role among the Latin American trade union representatives, although that role is not defined in any formal structure and does not pertain to a given task. In short, while the participation of these actors is above all a means to an end, and although they sometimes benefit from the action taken, they also express a desire for more sustained involvement and to play a greater part in the organisation's life than the peripheral actors.

PERIPHERAL ACTORS

The representatives of trade unions from Austria, Brazil, Finland and Mexico occupy a peripheral position. They are members of the alliance but are not major actors and are not identified as such by the alliance's other members. They often appear isolated in terms of collective action, without being totally cut off, and do not belong to tightly bound subgroups within the coalition. While some of them participate regularly in the alliance's official meetings, others are much less diligent and several make no particular effort to interact with the alliance's other members. They take part via an individual or limited group of participants they know better than the others and who serve as intermediaries, as required, for forging links with the alliance's dominant organisations. Their structural autonomy is therefore limited in that they have to resort to 'middlemen' to obtain information and convey their point of view. These peripheral members almost never play the part of intermediary and do not facilitate close ties between other members of the alliance. When asked about his relations with the other trade union representatives who are members of the alliance, a Brazilian trade unionist described the situation as follows:

> I don't have much contact with the members of the alliance. Of course, I know several of the union representatives taking part, but I can't claim to talk or engage in regular exchanges with all of them. Language is a barrier for me. I also have a lot of work to do locally. The working conditions in the factory I represent are very bad. But, when we have an official meeting of the alliance, I always try to be there.

In short, the alliance's peripheral members are there above all as a means to an end, and their involvement is reduced to its simplest expression. However, they are not totally isolated in that they interact directly with at least one of the other members, ensuring they are part of the group and allowing them to voice their expectations, albeit only occasionally.

THE ACTORS' POWER RESOURCES AND POSITIONING

Analysis of the actors' positions serves to reconstitute the social configuration of UNI Network and to highlight the diverse positions occupied by its members. The next analytical step is, therefore, to explain the actors' specific positioning within this relational structure. To that end, in the context of inter-union cooperation at the international level, four power resources, among other variables of course, seem to determine the relative weight of the various trade unions and influence their capacity to guide collective action (Hennebert 2010). The first resource relates to the number of workers represented by a trade union in comparison to the alliance's other member organisations. The second and third resources concern the human, financial and material investment that a trade union organisation deploys within the alliance. That investment capacity depends on the union's resources in its home territory, as well as on the same union's willingness to use some of those resources internationally. The fourth and final resource is associated with the exercise of power and is based on leadership and an actor's capacity to articulate unifying strategies and to frame the alliance's agenda and collective goals (Tarrow 2005). Applied to the workings of the trade union coalition being studied here, this classification of resources provides a partial explanation of the actors' respective positions and the functions they assume within the alliance.

Indeed, the actors in a 'central' position in the alliance are those representing the most workers in the multinational. They are also those providing the alliance with most of its human, financial and material resources. Not only do the representatives of these trade union organisations regularly attend the alliance's meetings, they also assume the alliance's management and mobilisation functions. It is also these organisations that demonstrate the greatest strategic capacity. Since they are at the heart of the alliance, their representatives show the leadership and energy needed to draw up action and mobilisation plans. Nevertheless, their roles and spheres of influence vary.

In the US, the extensive involvement of trade union representatives in the UNI Network can be put down, of course, to the substantial organisational and financial resources invested, but also, at a strategic level, to their need for support for the unionisation campaigns targeting certain Quebecor establishments in a number of southern states. The AFL-CIO, followed by the Teamsters, has mounted ambitious unionisation campaigns among the company's American wage-earners. In this regard, in a region in which labour legislation provides little protection for unionisation rights, active engagement in a cross-border union alliance seems to be both a strategic organisational decision, aimed at bolstering national unionisation campaigns, and a gesture of inter-union solidarity at international level.

In Europe, the *Fédération des travailleurs des industries du livre, du papier et de la communication* (FILPAC), which is affiliated to the *Conférence générale des travailleurs* (CGT) in France, has also played an especially important role. In strategic terms, the FILPAC-CGT, which represents the largest number of Quebecor World European workers, has been prompted to occupy a strategic position on the EWC, for the establishment of which it was a driving force. The FILPAC-CGT has therefore gradually become a key actor among the other European trade union organisations occupying an intermediate position in the alliance. In this sense, both in the US and in France, the national trade unions that found themselves at the core of the alliance have in a way become bridgeheads for sub-regional alliances.

That said, two actors stand out by virtue of their involvement and authority within the alliance, namely the CEP and UNI Network representatives who headed the negotiations leading to the signing of the international framework agreement and who ensured that the various affiliates' action strategies were integrated into a global action plan. They occupy similar positions, but have what appear to be somewhat different sources of power. The power of UNI stems from its cross-border nature, which is the source of its mission to ensure international representation for unionised workers of multinationals. UNI Network appears to have large amounts of social capital, thanks to its many contacts with trade unions from various national sectors; this gives it an organisational capacity and a legitimacy that its national affiliates do not have when it comes to laying the groundwork for a cross-border union alliance. The central role of the CEP, for its part, is explained in part by the fact that its representatives are closer and have more direct access to the company's senior management. Thus even though the CEP has fewer unionised workers at Quebecor World than its American counterpart, it is in a better position to influence Quebecor World management because it can take its campaigns against the anti-trade union practices of this flagship national industry to the Canadian population and authorities. In short, UNI and the CEP are the alliance's key actors by virtue of the special place they occupy in the constellation of trade union members of the alliance.

The Chilean, British, Spanish and Swedish trade unions occupy an intermediate position because most of them invest more financial and human resources than peripheral actors. Although they do not represent a greater number of workers than the trade unions in peripheral positions, the human involvement of trade unions in intermediate positions is more sustained, and they take part more regularly in official meetings and in those concerned more specifically with the activities of the UNI Graphical division.

These trade unions also contribute more to the alliance's activities in terms of material, organisational and financial support. The union that stands out most in this respect is probably Sweden's *Grafiska*, which was in charge of organising the first international meetings leading to the creation of a working group of representatives from the various national trade unions set up within the Canadian multinational. Swedish trade unions tend to have substantial resources, but *Grafiska's* involvement in this case may nevertheless appear surprising, given that the multinational does not have a major presence in Sweden. As the Secretary General of *Grafiska* explains:

> Things change. If, as a trade union, you don't develop a capacity for action at international level, you'll end up falling short in your own

country. As long as we can and as long as our members agree with this strategy, we will be involved internationally. [. . .] This is a tough proposition for the unions, but we have to find a means of countering the growing power of the multinationals. We have no choice. The big multinationals do what they want, and it is our mission to unite our strengths nationally and internationally to be able to deal with them effectively. But, we have to be sure the members understand what we're trying to do.

These trade unions also helped draw up the major strategic orientations framing the international campaigns of solidarity conducted by the alliance. This is particularly true for the British and Swedish trade unions, which take part in the activities of the steering committee and which regularly act when decisions are made. The British and Spanish trade unions are also active at the regional level, both in the activities of the EWCs and in UNI Network's European structures. The history of the alliance's activities also points to the sustained involvement of these trade unions, as in the case of the mobilisation campaign aimed at making the company's main customers aware of the workers' demands.

Among the organisations occupying an intermediate position, the Chilean trade union constitutes a special case. Its scant financial resources have not stopped it from waging major battles for the unionisation of Quebecor's Chilean wage-earners and improvement of their working conditions. It benefits from the solidarity of other alliance members, and its work within the alliance is as much a form of recognition of the other members as an expression of its militant stance as a trade union organisation at the national level. This union plays a particularly important role as a relay between the central core and the trade union organisations of South America, most of which are on the alliance's periphery.

Lastly, the national trade unions occupying a peripheral position are those at the greatest disadvantage in terms of these four resources. They represent relatively few of the multinational's workers and are active in countries in which the multinational has no or few major industrial facilities. They invest very few human and financial resources in the alliance. It is worth noting that this is not so much because they do not have such resources, but more because they have no desire to invest excessively in the alliance. This is borne out by the fact that several trade union organisations from industrialised countries, reputed to be relatively well-off in terms of such resources, nevertheless occupy a peripheral position. However, just because these actors may have a low capacity for action within the UNI Network and tend to trail in the wake of other trade union organisations, this does not mean they are completely uninterested in the alliance's activities or that they are indifferent to the difficulties encountered by the other members. These trade unions, it must be remembered, are full members of the alliance, even if they contribute more modestly to its development than other participants.

CONCLUSION

The growing importance and influence of multinationals in the world economy calls for major adjustments on the part of the social actors, who are today seeking to challenge these organisations in new ways. The cross-border union alliances that are currently emerging are part of that trend; their internal functioning and the factors determining their effectiveness have raised fresh empirical questions and, on a theoretical level, revived long-standing questions of how collective action is constructed that must be reconsidered in an internationalised context. In this respect, the analysis conducted in this chapter serves to open the "black box" such alliances represent and to shed at least some light on how they function and the social relations on which they are based.

More specifically, the study of how UNI Network members are positioned lays open to question several preconceived ideas about the social structuring of cross-border union alliances. First, the analysis clearly shows that union alliances cannot avoid the establishment of some form of hierarchy among their members. The standard image of a network is of loosely structured social relations deployed horizontally, but the case examined here shows that cross-border union alliances also include, albeit less formally, certain elements of a stratified and hierarchical organisation. In this respect, although much attention has been focused on the power struggles between such trade union associations and multinational employers, the analysis reminds us that strategic games and power relations are not an inherent element of the employer-trade union relationship alone, but are also prevalent in relations between actors of the same kind.

Furthermore, the positions occupied by the principal members of UNI Network show the importance of being able to count on key actors or leaders able to bring together and mobilise the various participants and create a common project. In the case of this cross-border union alliance, internal communications and the preparation of shared objectives and common strategies were greatly facilitated by the role of the central actors and the "social entrepreneurship" demonstrated by UNI and CEP representatives. On the other hand, our analysis of the positions of UNI Network members shows that some of them tend to remain on the periphery of the alliance, raising serious questions about the reason for their lack of involvement or, at the very least, limited participation.

Next, the analysis contained in this chapter also shows that the position and sphere of influence of UNI Network members depend, but only to a certain degree, on the resources invested by members and on their ability to take advantage of the relationships they enter into. Here, too, the analysis lays open to question certain commonly held notions about cross-border union alliances. For example, the idea that trade unions from countries of the South are always on the margins of this type of international structure has to be tempered. Trade unions from both the North and the South remain on the alliance's periphery, suggesting there are more complex reasons for the positioning and power of alliance members. In this respect, the analysis of the actors' resources shows that there is no reason to assume that certain members will play a given role and that power can be built within these global union alliances in a number of different ways.

Lastly, the recent developments at Quebecor World described above serve both to highlight one of the major strengths of cross-border union alliances and to reveal their great vulnerability. Indeed, cross-border union alliances are, by definition, organised along the same lines as the multinationals. This serves as a concrete foundation for the development of new forms of trade union solidarity at the supranational level. However, the links that have sometimes taken several years to forge can be easily strained or even completely severed by the constantly changing structure of multinationals entering into mergers, acquiring other companies or neglecting or selling certain production units. This highlights one of the main challenges facing cross-border union alliances today, namely how to guarantee their existence over time in the face of the shifting structures of multinationals.

ACKNOWLEDGEMENTS

This research is part of a larger project funded by the Social Sciences and Humanities Research Council of Canada (SSHRC) and the *Fonds de recherche sur la société et la culture du Québec* (FQRSC).

NOTES

1. Hereafter referred to as UNI Network.
2. According to media reports, for example, workers at the Quebecor World plant in Bogota, Colombia, were forced, under a so-called 'collective agreement', to sign individual employment contracts that *inter alia* restricted potential access to unionisation. During the same period, job transfers between the two Quebecor World plants in Chile came under repeated criticism from the trade union organisations involved, which saw this process as a disguised and pernicious strategy to reduce labour costs and avoid unionisation at the plants (UNI, 2006).
3. This 24-page protocol stipulates, in particular, that Quebecor employees can vote in favour of or against union representation by means of a supervised secret-ballot vote. It thus provides for an accelerated secret-ballot election when requested by a union representing at least 30% of employees in the prospective bargaining unit in any non-unionised facility. The election must take place within 21 days of the request and be organised by a neutral arbitrator designated by the parties rather than by the US Labor Relations Board in order to avoid excessive delays.
4. The Graphic Communications International Union (GCIU) represented all workers at Quebecor World plants in Canada and the United States until 2005 (UNI, 2006). That year, for strategic reasons, the GCIU merged with the International Brotherhood of Teamsters in the United States, thus forming the Teamsters Graphic Communications Conference (GCC/IBT). In Canada,

242 Marc-Antonin Hennebert and Reynald Bourque

however, the majority of local unions in the GCIU rejected the merger with the Teamsters, voting instead in favour of a merger with the Communications, Energy and Paperworkers Union of Canada (CEP).

REFERENCES

Barton, R., and Fairbrother, P. (2009), 'The Local is Now Global. Building a Union Coalition in the International Transport and Logistics Sector', *Relations industrielles/Industrial Relations*, 64(4), 685–703.

Brecher, J., Cosello, T., and Smith, B. (2006), 'International Labor Solidarity: The New Frontier', *New Labor Forum*, 15(1), 9–18.

Bronfenbrenner, K. (2007), *Global Union: Challenging Transnational Capital through Cross-Border Campaigns*, Ithaca: Cornell University Press.

Carroll, W. K. (2004), *Corporate Power in a Globalizing World. A Study in Elite Social Organization*, Oxford: Oxford University Press.

Croucher, R., and Cotton, E. (2009), *Global Unions, Global Business: Global Union Federations and International Business*, London: Middlesex University Press.

Diani, M., and McAdam, D. (2003), *Social Movements and Networks: Relational Approaches to Collective Action*, Oxford: Oxford University Press.

Greer, I., and Hauptmeier, M. (2008), 'Political Entrepreneurs and Co-Managers: Labour Transnationalism at Four Multinational Auto Companies', *British Journal of Industrial Relations*, 46(1), 76–97.

Harrod, J., and O'Brien, R. (2003), *Global Unions? Theory and Strategies of Organized Labour in the Global Political Economy*, New York: Routledge.

Hennebert, M.-A. (2010), *Les alliances syndicales internationales, des contre-pouvoirs aux entreprises multinationales?* Paris : L'Harmattan, Collection Logiques sociales.

Scott, J. (2001), *Social Network Analysis: A Handbook*, London: Sage Publications.

Stevis, D., and Boswell, T. (2007), 'International Framework Agreements: Opportunities and Challenges for Global Unionism', in Kate Bronfenbrenner (ed.), *Global Union: Challenging Transnational Capital through Cross-Border Campaigns*, Ithaca: Cornell University Press.

Tarrow, S. (2005), *The New Transnational Activism*, Cambridge: Cambridge University Press.

Tate, A. (2006), 'The Justice@Quebecor campaign: Lessons for Canadian Unions', *Just Labour*, 8, 40–49.

UNI (2006), *Le réseau UNI Network@Quebecor World et la campagne Justice@Quebecor: Construire une force stratégique*. Nyon: Union Network International, Graphical sector.

Wasserman, S., and Faust, K. (1994), *Social Network Analysis: Methods and Applications*, New York: Cambridge University Press.

Wright, E. O. (2000), 'Working-Class Power, Capitalist-Class Interests, and Class Compromise', *American Journal of Sociology*, 105(4), 957–1002.

13 Labour Standards in Segmented Markets

The Construction Industry in Delhi and Moscow

Nikolaus Hammer

The reconfiguration of global value chains (GVCs) has fractured the links between industrial and managerial power, on the one hand, and work and employment, on the other, along a number of dimensions (Riisgaard and Hammer 2011). Spatial fragmentation, for example, lies at the heart of economic globalisation: multinational corporations' (MNCs') ability to re-locate production to low wage and weakly regulated economies has challenged workers' bargaining power in the Global North. Such restructuring of global production has come with sharp increases in (mostly) export-oriented production as well as commodified employment in the Global South. This was compounded by organisational fragmentation in the form of outsourcing and subcontracting which, together with state regulation favouring foreign direct investment, has further cemented the asymmetry between global product markets and local labour markets.

In attempts to rebalance this asymmetry, various campaigns, international labour networks, and regulatory tools have tried to re-establish a link between the site of industrial and political power, that is the lead firm, and the local workplace and to establish core labour standards (CLSs)—based on the International Labour Organisation's 1998 Declaration on Fundamental Principles and Rights at Work—that take fundamental human rights out of competition. An important route in this project led through MNCs, by implementing and monitoring core labour standards in their production facilities as well as their subcontractor and supplier networks. The 1990s have seen the rise of such campaigns for labour 'standards', either as bilateral standards between MNCs and trade unions (e.g., in international framework agreements, IFAs), or multilateral standards between a range of so-called 'stakeholders'. The Building and Wood Workers' International (BWI) has developed standards in its remit that include provisions crucial to the construction industry: mandatory compliance of subcontractors with fundamental labour rights, the establishment of employment contracts, suitable accommodation, a living wage and a number of health and safety provisions. In a recent revision of its model IFA the BWI has also included a paragraph on the specific rights of migrant workers (BWI 2010a). However, while CLSs and (in many cases) subcontractor compliance form part of

IFAs, while both have been included in the public procurement regulations of the World Bank's lending arm (Hammer et al. 2009), evidence from local case studies points to difficulties of these provisions to reach across complex ownership and inter-firm structures as well as industrial relations systems (Davies et al. 2011). More often than not, CLS awareness at the local level, by both management and labour, is limited.

Trying to grasp the dynamics of CLSs, it is suggested to move beyond a concern with formal implementation mechanisms within MNCs and to look at the way standards formulated at the global level are filtered through MNC, subcontractor and supplier networks, on the one hand, as well as societal and local dynamics in the product and labour markets, on the other. For example, the international construction industry spans long contracting chains across an equally wide range of societal/local markets where international contractors compete for large infrastructure contracts, while the bulk of the work is carried out by local subcontractors competing at the national or even local level (e.g., Bosch and Philips 2003; Strassmann and Wells 1988). The labour markets in the construction industry, particularly in emerging economies, are characterised by migrant and mostly informal labour that constitute important elements in state-backed market despotic production regimes. Here, the spatial and organisational fragmentation that underlie the segmentation of product and labour markets combine into barriers against any unproblematic notions of global-local standards implementation, be it in a managerial or social partnership version.

This chapter explores the challenges for labour standards in the construction industry, particularly those arising out of the increase in outsourcing and subcontracting. It is argued—through a study of the construction labour markets in Delhi and Moscow—that complex subcontracting arrangements have come with an increase in labour market segmentation and forms of labour control that effectively break the chain of monitoring and implementation. The first section discusses the role of value chain governance and market dynamics for labour standards, particularly as it applies in the construction industry. The main section explores the local labour control regimes in detail, for example, how different forms of control based on the employment contract, living arrangements, as well as the regulation of labour mobility, influence interests and capabilities at the workplace. The chapter concludes with a discussion of the role of segmentation for workplace-based labour standards enforcement.

STRATEGIC AND INSTITUTIONAL FACTORS IN SEGMENTED MARKETS

Research on CLSs in IFAs has pointed to certain successes where local and global unions could raise complaints or escalate campaigns to HQ resulting in a resolution of contentious issues (e.g. Papadakis 2011; IFBWW 2004).

However, there are also two more problematic aspects that have been highlighted: on the one hand, an investigation of the impact of an IFA in local construction markets in Brazil, Malaysia and Ukraine has—despite a very established and productive social dialogue at HQ—shown very patchy awareness of the agreement, no local implementation and no direct impact (Davies et al. 2011)—a finding that is compounded in further research on a different set of MNCs in Delhi and Moscow (see below). On the other hand, authors have underscored the unintended consequences of standard-related improvements in work and employment (e.g., Barrientos 2008; Raworth and Kidder 2009; Riisgaard and Hammer 2011). Following improvements in working conditions resulting from standards implementation, these positive changes were subverted as, for example, contractors established a two-tier workforce or as intermediaries decided to source from elsewhere.

How can such a mixed impact assessment of standard-related labour strategies in MNCs and value chains be explained, seeing that HQ management, unions, and international organisations have invested in such strategies? Two approaches, in particular, have formulated theoretical arguments with regard to standards within and across firms in the global economy. In the strategic/organisational view of global value chain (GVC) analysis (see Bair 2009), on the one hand, competitive advantage results from firm strategy, the way firms develop their capabilities and position themselves within the division of labour in the value chain (Palpacuer 2000). In this respect standards are an important element in coordinating and controlling inter-firm networks and play a dual role of differentiation: increasing differences when functioning as entry barriers as well as levelling differences when aiming to establish a level playing field. In the context of the societal/institutionalist take of the national business systems (NBS) approach (see Whitley 1999), on the other hand, standards are a function of societal arrangements as well as the power dynamics between home- and host-country practices. GVC and societal/NBS analysis do, however, have a different focus—lead firms in GVCs as opposed to MNCs and their subsidiaries (see also Lane and Probert 2009), a difference that informs the way standards are conceived of: the outcome of an organisational strategy and a tool to shape the division of labour between firms as opposed to an outcome of the micropolitics between societal arrangements within a MNC.

However, neither a lack of organisational capabilities on the part of lead firms, nor the dominance of host-country societal institutions can sufficiently explain the limited impact of standard-related labour strategies through MNCs and their value chains. While GVC theory differentiates between firms at different positions in the value chain, it does not sufficiently tie these differences back to specific societal frameworks (Lane and Probert 2009). Societal theory, on the other hand, has for a long time neglected how firm capabilities are influenced by scale-and sector-specific dynamics as well as how the integration into global production networks impacts on product market segmentation and competition (Ferner et al. 2006). Neither approach has focused on uneven worker capabilities and the resulting dynamics of worker-to-worker competition in segmented labour markets. By contrast, it is argued here that actors and markets are not unified and that it matters how organisational capabilities are filtered through societal frameworks, at the same time as societal effects are not evenly distributed. In this vein, Grimshaw and Rubery (2005) argue that an analysis of the employment relationship needs to take account of inter-capital relations as well as capital-labour relations.

> It is important to embed the analysis of the employment relationship within an economic and productive system where inter-capital relations structure both distributional and production relations. Divisions within labour both fuel the process of inter-capital competition and can be considered an outcome of the process. From this perspective, the labour market does not operate as a unified entity or value chain with variations in price reflective only of variations in labour productivity or human capital. The failure to embed the analysis of the employment relationship and of labour market divisions within the dynamics of inter-capitalist and capital-state relations provides an inadequate, and in practice often too deterministic, analysis of the position of labour within the economic system. (Grimshaw and Rubery 2005: 1029)

While both strategic/organisational as well as societal factors play a crucial part in the global-local dynamics of work and employment, it is argued that the analysis of the latter is helped through an integration of segmentation—of product as well as labour markets (Grimshaw and Rubery 2005; Rubery 2007). A segmentation perspective, first, underlines the uneven distribution of capacities between and within capital and labour. It thereby re-emphasises one of the concerns of GVC theory, that firm capacities are not distributed evenly and that there are different forms of competition and cooperation, power and interdependency, between firms in a horizontal and vertical dimension. Similarly, the interaction of MNC strategies with societal institutions accounts for different processes of labour market competition and labour allocation and results in differential labour capacities across social groups, sectors, value chain functions and localities. Second, a segmentation perspective establishes different groups in the labour market as active agents in the politics of organisational strategies and societal arrangements and thereby supports non-functionalist explanations of labour market dynamics. Such a perspective allows an explanation as to how a particular societal/institutional context is unevenly structured across firms and workers and how their struggles, in return, shape forms of economic organisation and control.

The contradictory relation between control and cooperation in the employment relationship can only be outsourced or subcontracted superficially. While such forms of externalisation push risks of value extraction to subcontractors and labour, CLSs as discussed here impose the costs of compliance on the upstream end of the value chain—where competition is fiercest and where CLSs shift the frontier of control at work. Non-compliance with CLSs or their unintended consequences, therefore, are not in the first instance caused by a lack of lead firm capability or insurmountable societal barriers but result from the different interests in product and labour market segments. Here, standard-induced shifts in the power relations at the workplace run up against competitive product and/or labour markets, again underscoring the link between inter-organisational relations (of production as well as competition) and employment relations.

PRODUCT AND LABOUR MARKET SEGMENTATION

The increase in subcontracting practices has come with a rise in market despotic and coercive labour regimes in urban growth poles that opened and integrated into the global economy. This required a large construction labour supply, which was drawn from migrant and informal labour and challenged established national as well as inter-national models of collective organisation. Since the 1990s, the BWI has concluded nine IFAs with leading construction MNCs and one in the building materials sector in a strategy to extend CLSs along MNC value chains. The BWI is the global peak organisation for building and wood workers' unions and represents around 12 million workers organised in more than 300 trade unions and 130 countries. Next to attempts to organise the large number of casual and migrant workers through projects on decent labour standards, the BWI has also developed a strong campaigning role for CLSs with regard to MNCs (for example in IFAs), international organisations such as the World Bank and the International Monetary Fund or a number of social and environmental reporting programmes.

Reflecting the specific challenges encountered in the sector, IFAs have successively included a larger number of provisions beyond the CLSs, for example, on the employment contract, working time, living wages, housing conditions, health and safety, as well as HIV/AIDS awareness and prevention. Recently, the BWI included additional provisions into its model IFA, which specifically affirms the rights of migrant workers to equal pay and working conditions, as well as rights concerning identification, travel documents and associated costs (BWI 2010a). Equally important, and a reflection on the complex subcontracting practices in the sector, a large number of these agreements extend validity to 'subsidiaries, contractors, subcontractors, suppliers and joint ventures' (BWI 2010a); such strong provisions can, for example, be found in the agreements with Hochtief, Skanska, Impregilo, VolkerWessels and Pfleiderer. Still, recognising the barriers and long-haul character of this strategy, the BWI considers 'framework agreements as a tool for organising' (IFBWW 2003, 3) rather than a developed tiered social dialogue. This chimes with the difficulties found in segmented construction markets, which are often characterised by social dialogue at home-country level; political strategising of host-country subsidiaries and joint ventures in relation to HQ; and local subcontractors and the informal workforce in market despotic and (at times) coercive labour regime that is disconnected from the CLSs formulated in the home country (Davies et al. 2011). The reminder of this section draws on preliminary research on IFAs in the local construction markets of Delhi and Moscow and emphasises the lines of segmentation that effectively break the channels of CLS implementation.

The internationalisation of the construction industry, while by no means homogenous, has proceeded in the 1990s on the back of the growth and liberalisation in emerging economies (Reina et al. 2005; Strassmann and Wells 1998). Subsectors, such as large civil engineering projects, home building and materials, have benefited from sustained economic growth and offered entry routes for foreign MNCs. Raftery et al. (1998: 729) observed '(1) larger private sector participation in infrastructure projects, (2) increasing vertical integration in the packaging of construction projects, and (3) increased foreign participation in domestic construction'. Advantages of foreign firms stem from technical capabilities as well as access to cross-functional links between finance, design and operation, which are crucial for large projects and finance-led arrangements such as build-operate-transfer (BOT). At the same time, though, MNCs need to integrate these capabilities with regulations that support local firms through mandatory subcontracting requirements or tendering preferences.

This opening up of product and labour market competition was behind a substantive increase in subcontracting, of production functions as well as labour supply. Practices of subcontracting are based on modularity on the one hand (e.g., 40 per cent of the contracting business in Larsen and Toubro, the largest Indian MNC in the sector, are turnkey work in the hydrocarbon, industrial and power sectors, Reina 2005) and Taylorised production on the other. Large, one-off, civil engineering projects, for example, highlight the link between inter-capital competition with forms of production relations: cooperation between MNCs and large national players in securing the high-end value chain functions pushes cost competition and risk down the value chain where relations between subcontractors are competitive and non-cooperative. There are marked differences in the forms of control in contracting arrangements, however. As in most countries, the state also plays an important role in India and Russia: while in the former, government investment in transport and electricity generation infrastructure, for example, as well as the growth of the IT sector, are behind expansion (Reina et al. 2005), the recent recession has underlined the role of the government in Russia as it designated a key role for public-private partnerships (PPPs) in developing large infrastructure projects. Equally, foreign investment is crucial in both markets. India has a number of strong players that are active internationally, but has recently opened its construction sector to 100 per cent foreign direct investment. The Russian market is still characterised by relatively large, vertically integrated contractors that have origins in Soviet industrial structures. Still, foreign MNCs have had access since the 1990s through local agencies, the export of projects or establishing their own subsidiaries, resulting in very complex consortia with considerable foreign participation (Reina 2008).

The implications for work and employment can be seen at both ends of the value chain (see Table 13.1): on the one hand, high-skill design functions normally performed in permanent employment were relocated and/or subcontracted to low-wage economies, such as India, South-East Asia or Eastern Europe. For firms in these countries, the logic here is to develop their capabilities and to move from less complex, lower-value added processes to higher-end ones such as conceptual engineering (Rubin et al 2004). On the other hand, there is a large bulk of unskilled, casual and informal labour that is project-based and recruited from various streams of internal and/or international migrants. Wells (2007) underscores how deregulation and more restrictive employment regulation in many developing countries have led to a decline of permanent work in favour of informal casual work in formal enterprises, as well as a considerable increase in workers sourced through intermediaries that supply labour only at various stages of the construction process. Labour-only subcontracting shifts risks from the buyer to the supplier but also establishes an important function of labour control for these intermediaries/gang masters. In fact, a particular form of labour regime can be made out here in which labour control is exercised through the employment contract (see e.g., Nichols and Cam 2005), the living arrangements (e.g., Pun and Smith 2007) and the restriction of mobility. In addition, direct forms of labour process control are reinforced through paternalist and/or regulatory forms of control and bondage, for example, through late and incomplete payment of wages, the provision of inadequate accommodation on- or off-site, regular movement between sites, as well as the use of registration and residency requirements that perpetuate the workers' irregular status.

LABOUR CONTROL IN DELHI

The construction labour force in India is essentially drawn from rural-urban migration and is estimated to consist of 17 million workers (Economic and Political Weekly 2008). Insufficient subsistence agriculture is a major push factor of outward migration but also a factor in circular migration where large numbers of migrants return home for the monsoon season (see also Breman 1996). Wells (2007: 91) quotes studies that show an increase in the casualisation of urban construction workers between 1983–93 from 58 to 64 per cent for men and 89 to 96 per cent for women. 'If self-employed workers are also included then 89 per cent of men and 97 per cent of women

Table 13.1 Market despotic and coercive labour control regimes

	Contracting	Labour supply	Labour process	Reproduction	Collective action
India/Delhi	Foreign/Indian MNCs + national contractors 2nd tier contractors only employ few skilled workers directly Labour-only contractors	Rural-urban inter-regional (circular) migration Intermediaries: Thekedars Recruitment through loans Day labour	89%/97% informal labour Regular movement between sites Direct control by intermediaries Bondage Paternalism Female labour included in husband's	On-site materials to build own huts/tents Charges for living facilities/ subsistence No registration with welfare board	Skilled workers in unions National Campaign Committee for Central Legislation on Construction Labour, and other NGOs working through legal channels
Russia/ Moscow	Complex foreign consortia Foreign-led MNCs + foreign/national contractors Project import through foreign MNCs Integrated national contractors Labour-only contractors	International high value functions Migrants from former Soviet republics Intermediaries: Brigadiers Trafficking Individual recruiters/ employment agencies Project-tied workers Day labour	Direct control by intermediaries Bondage: late/ incomplete payment Forced labour: passport confiscation, registration, residency	Private Project tied: at times in labour camps No registration	Organisation in former state firms Migrant workers' union NGOs, diaspora leaders, labour attachés provide

working in construction in 1993 could be considered as 'informal labour' (see also Pais 2002; Breman 1996). This informal status, together with the regulation of mobility and the provision of sub-standard living arrangements is what delineates the contours of control.

While circular migration ensures migrant workers remain always on the move and therefore at the margins of local labour markets, once employed, workers are moved every couple of months to a different worksite in order to prevent the formation of more durable solidarities. The prime relation of dependence is with intermediaries who recruit, might hand out loans in advance to tie workers in, and directly control the labour process. Furthermore, bondage is established through late and/or partial payment of wages as well as paternalist dependence on the subcontractor for occasional welfare-related payments (instead of the rights that accrue through simple registration with the welfare board). For example, a study in the period leading up to the 2010 Commonwealth Games in Delhi found that workers received about 40 per cent less than the stipulated minimum wages for unskilled, as well as semi- and skilled workers, respectively (thus, unskilled workers received around 2.4–2.8 USD per day, PUDR 2009). Workers do not receive pay slips, have no proof of any outstanding amounts, are not registered with the welfare board and do not receive shoes or equipment (leading to a high number of accidents, including fatal accidents). The value of women's work is dependent on their marital status and takes the function of a bonus: their output is calculated as part of their husband's, except if they are single.

> Though skilled workers secure jobs directly from employers, unskilled workers by and large, are engaged through intermediaries who introduce the workers to contractors on a commission basis. The payment of wages is routed through the intermediaries who usually enrol workers by offering loans. These loans are then recovered by manipulating the wages of the workers, with the result that the worker hardly gets out of the clutches of the intermediaries. (Ministry of Labour 2002: 634)
>
> At a building site for the Commonwealth Games, for example, second tier contractors only hire directly in a few cases, 'mainly skilled workers like welders and crane operators. . .; these subcontractors normally further subcontract the work to smaller contractors, or *thekedars* for different work operations like shuttering, plastering, flooring, plumbing, etc. (PUDR 2009: 8).

Workers' reproduction also constitutes an important lever of control. As migrants they tend to live on site where they are often charged for substandard living arrangements and facilities. As they are rarely registered with the welfare boards, they are not able to access benefits in their own right but turn to the employer and thereby further reproduce their paternalist dependence. Thus, labour subcontracting is a condition for informality that, in turn, leads to a varied system of multiple controls based on the continuity of informal employment, the management of mobility, as well as the paternalistic provision of workers' housing and welfare arrangements.

In this context, collective action takes isolated spontaneous forms, on the one hand, or, supported by citizen organisations, the route through the courts. Unions organise mainly skilled workers and have great difficulties in penetrating networks based on kinship and paternalism as well as in accessing guarded sites. Therefore, campaigning organisations increasingly make use of formal channels such as public interest litigations (PILs): for example, the National Campaign Committee for Central Legislation on Construction Labour has filed a PIL at the Supreme Court to force the implementation of the Building and Other Construction Workers (Regulations of Employment and Conditions of Service) Act, 1996 and the Building and Other Construction Workers' Welfare Cess Act, 1996 (Economic and Political Weekly 2008). Equally, when a worker at a CWGV construction site was killed from a falling defective crane in December 2008, workers staged a two-day strike and protest that resulted in an investigation by a civil rights organisation, the People's Union for Democratic Rights (PUDR), which then filed a PIL with regard to the workers employed in building facilities for the Commonwealth Games held in October 2010 in New Delhi (PUDR 2009; PUDR 2010). A report by a court-appointed committee subsequently corroborated these findings. Statutory regulations are, in fact, relatively wide ranging (including provisions on wages, workers' welfare and contractors' liability), however, a lack of transparency as well as tangible implementation and monitoring mechanisms put a heavy burden on an informal and fragmented workforce in pursuing complaints.

LABOUR CONTROL IN MOSCOW

A large proportion of workers in the Russian construction sector are external migrants from former Soviet republics, such as Tajikistan, Uzbekistan, Ukraine and Moldova; of the 4–9 million migrant workers in Russia, about 40 per cent work in construction. What is distinctive about the construction sector in Russia is that it overlaps with the trafficking of labour as well as forced labour. Labour market segmentation and different forms of labour control are closely tied to workers' mode of recruitment and entry into the country.

Workers who are recruited through individual employment recruiters or registered employment agencies often become victims of unscrupulous agents. In many cases, such agents take advance payments against the prospect of well-paid jobs and the arrangement of visas but abandon the workers on the way to the construction site. Subsequently, workers are also more likely to fall foul of regulations that require them to register for residency status and a work permit. In 2007, estimates held that around 90 per cent of the migrant workers were irregular. Employers often exploit this situation and, through the confiscation of passports, effectively confine workers to the building site (for fear of being detained by the police and expelled from the country) and force workers to endure abusive work and living conditions as well as physical violence (HRW 2009: 36).

As already seen in India, extensive subcontracting in Russia has also led to the form of labour-only, informal intermediaries, called foremen or brigadiers. Here, however, the function of the brigadier designates a technical skill level in the first instance, although brigadiers tend to recruit from their own ethnic networks.

> A brigadier may informally organize a number of men from his home town or village into a construction brigade that then travels to Russia and works together with them on construction sites. Brigadiers may also recruit people already in Russia, also often of the same nationality and from the same region, to work on construction brigades. A brigade may consist of a just few workers or up to several dozen. The brigadier is usually a person with more work experience who ensures that the brigade fulfils its tasks on time and that the work is of the necessary quality. Very often, the brigadier will be the only member of a brigade to have any direct contact with the construction company, individual contractor, or subcontractor hiring the brigade and will be responsible for receiving wages and then distributing them to the members of his brigade. (HRW 2009: 30)

Thus, the brigadier has a function of recruitment, controlling the labour process and managing pay, and it is mostly the incomplete payment of wages that workers suffer in this set-up; as recruitment is based on personal networks and residency status often irregular, the postponement of payments is less central to keep workers from quitting. Often however, brigadiers themselves do not receive the full sums they have agreed with the contractor.

The considerable inroads made by MNCs from developed as well as emerging economies (e.g., Turkey and China) into the Russian construction sector has also brought arrangements where these companies recruit their workforce from the home country. The conditions of project-tied workers vary, however: while İçduygu (2009) found that Turkish workers engaged in projects in Moscow enjoyed better working conditions than at home, a report on the construction of the landmark Federation Tower in Moscow, in which the China State Construction Engineering Corporation plays a major part, was less encouraging:

> China State employs about 500 Chinese workers on the job, all housed in a construction camp. Western project staff who have visited the camp say living standards are worse than in the Middle East. They report at

least one industrial dispute but [the manager] has no recollection of it. (Reina 2008: 115)

Organised trade unions are mostly confined to larger companies that emerged out of the vertical structures of the Soviet system where each Ministry had its own construction division. In this segment, unions largely continue established functions of social dialogue and service provision to core workers in the former state sector (Kubicek 2004). Although a trade union for migrant workers in construction and other sectors was formed in 2007, the activities of the union, of NGOs as well as labour attachés in the embassies of the sender countries are essentially restricted to information, advice and legal assistance. Occasions where collective action is successful, as in a strike in Ekaterinburg that was supported by a local Tajik diaspora leader, are rare exceptions; more often, collective action by informal migrant workers is met by intimidation and physical violence:

> The brigadiers gathered that day and decided to strike. It was August 30, 2006. We. . . came to the foreman . . . He said, 'You'll get your money on December 31. . .' He called the guards. They started to beat one worker from Samarkand [Uzbekistan] in front of us. We all went back to our work places, and gave some medical assistance to the beaten guy ourselves. We could not bring him to the hospital as he did not have a residency registration. (HRW 2009: 67)

Different degrees of casual and informal employment, modes of accommodation for migrant workers and the regulation of mobility between sites, regions and across borders all play important roles in the specific forms of labour control. There are important differences through, for example, the kinship and communal basis of the relation between labour intermediaries and workers in India as opposed to those of ethnic networks of skilled brigadiers from the former Soviet states. Equally, while circular migration in India is the consequence of employers' recruitment policies (of not recruiting local workers) (see Breman 1996), control over mobility in Russia stems from the irregular residency and employment status migrants are led into, encouraged both by strict bureaucratic procedures as well as employer practices (of not registering workers). To some extent, an important similarity can be detected in that informal migrant workers organise their collective interests, where they do so, independent from those in the formal economy, whether that is through civil rights organisations or separate trade unions. While these labour control regimes subcontract the risk associated with the labour process in different ways, this does not necessarily mean that contractors higher up in the contracting system do not exert any direction over production (e.g., with regard to quality or time). The issue for workplace regulation is to what extent CLSs can be implemented when they shift the power relations in the subcontracting chain.

WORKPLACE REGULATION—UNION STRATEGIES AND STANDARDS

The BWI has tried to address the dimensions of labour control regimes at a number of different levels. First, at the company level, it has concluded IFAs to promote CLSs in lead firms and their value chains. Against the background of extensive subcontracting and informal labour, these CLSs—reinforced again through an emphasis on the employment contract, living arrangements and regular residency and work permits for migrants—directly address the foundations of market despotic and coercive labour regimes. Most crucially, though, the agreements establish strong—often mandatory—compliance for subcontractors. The complex structure of subcontracting and transparency about the parties involved, however, remains one of the most serious challenges in establishing management-labour relations even at the level of the signatory MNC (Davies et al. 2011). Trying to overcome these problems, the BWI has continued working on establishing synergies between different strategies in order to support the monitoring and implementation of standards. For example, unions affiliated to the Dutch FNV have linked part of their international work to following Dutch MNCs abroad and to build management-labour dialogue in construction projects they are involved in. Concerted campaigns in the build-up to major sports events, such as the 2010 Football World Cup in South Africa constitute another example. However, a major factor behind non-compliance as well as the unintended consequences of such standards, it is argued, is that their implementation is likely to shift the frontier of control at work.

Second, the BWI have also gone beyond the firm level and campaigned for the inclusion of CLSs into public procurement provisions. After a long campaign by the Global Unions, for example, the World Bank has integrated the respect of core labour standards for projects supported by its private sector lending arm, the International Finance Corporation (IFC). Compliance is now a condition of all its loans and commits clients as well as subcontractors. While this IFC standard differs from IFAs in that it is imposed by a public (international) organisation, the challenges of implementation, monitoring and enforcement with subcontractors at the societal/local level remain:

> The standard applies to sub-contractors, contract labour and non-employee workers, although these categories are narrowly defined; the standard applies in full only to legal employees (see Martin 2008). The client's responsibility for workers in the supply chain, for example, is restricted to cases where 'low labor cost is a factor' in competitiveness. In such cases, clients will 'inquire about and address' child labour and forced labour (IFC 2006: 2; 6). Thus, while monitoring mechanisms are universal, their actual use and effectiveness is contingent on power relations within the MNC as well as between the firms in the subcontracting chain. (Hammer et al. 2009: 3)

Third, with regard to migrants, a number of BWI affiliates and regional union federations have explored ways to provide support and organisation to workers in sending as well as receiving countries. Unions have developed initiatives trying to control labour mobility, or at least the conditions under which migrants take up employment and return to their home country (Asper n.d.). For example, they have involved themselves directly in the provision of education, information and welfare support to out-migrating and returning construction workers such as between the Filipino NUBCW and the Taiwanese NFCCW:

> such that NUBCW will undertake to facilitate sending its presently unemployed member or an employed member intending to work in the construction sites in Taiwan while the NFCCW will facilitate the acceptance of the Filipino workers in their unionised construction projects at the same time that the union in Taiwan will protect them by helping them organise a separate union for migrant construction workers or integrating them into existing union structures. (Asper n.d.: 19–20)

Affiliates of the BWI in Southern India have created an information and resource network for migrant workers to the Gulf region. Similar projects are developed further under a recently launched BWI campaign on migrant workers, BWI Connect (BWI 2010b), aiming to offer a standard employment contract, legal advice and representation abroad and to facilitate communication between workers. The goal is to reduce differences between workers on the basis of migration status and to improve the conditions of work and employment through organising.

In assessing the potential and problems of IFAs, the difference with regard to other (social, technical and quality management) standards has to be emphasised: the monitoring of CLSs is to function through workplace organisation, which also constitutes the ultimate goal of an IFA. Therefore, the establishment of implementation and monitoring mechanisms might well be necessary but is not sufficient to establish workplace capacity. This can be further illustrated through a consideration of approaches to implementation along the opposite poles of compliance vs. commitment (see Locke et al. 2009). Interestingly, both prove equally problematic as they neglect the dynamics of product and labour markets and instead focus on firm-level capacities. On the one hand, a commitment approach to standards implementation supposes inter-firm relations that are compatible with cooperation and gradual upgrading. On the other hand, a compliance approach is equally problematic in the assumption that lead firms are able to implement and monitor provisions, in other words, dispose of the relevant mechanisms and power to regulate certain aspects within their subcontracting chain. Thus, in both cases, lead firm capabilities and inter-firm relations are abstracted from the competitive relations suppliers and subcontractors work under—competition in a vertical dimension with contractors, in a horizontal dimension with firms providing similar products and services and also competition between different social, technical and productivity standards where they produce for a range of different buyers. This raises two issues: the quality of labour as a value producer as well as the importance of the context of production and competition.

First, the notion of labour standards as a codifiable part of the production process that reduces transaction costs underestimates the contested nature of work and employment. By contrast, standards such as IFAs are an attempt by management and unions at the level of the lead firms to shape the frontier of control by establishing workplace-based monitoring and labour relations at the workplace. However, outsourcing has changed the functional division of labour by further segmenting product and labour markets. It thereby has established an industrial and political distance between the workplace and the lead firm and shifted the leverage points for labour (Riisgaard and Hammer 2011).

> The outsourcing of labour is generally associated with deregulation of labour markets as the intermediaries (subcontractors and labour agents) who are the new suppliers of labour find it easier to avoid registering workers, in order to evade the 'on-costs' associated with employment, than the contractors who previously employed them. Indeed, this is often the motivation for outsourcing in the first place. Hence there has been a great expansion in the number of informal employees who may be found working in both formal and informal enterprises. Together with the self-employed and family labour they make up 'the informal sector of the construction labour force' or 'informal labour'. (Wells 2007: 92)

As shown above, industrial pressures leading to outsourcing and labour market segmentation are shaping forms of local labour control along the dimensions of employment contracts, living arrangements and mobility. At the same time, however, the local embeddedness of the labour and production process reflects place-specific social dynamics. The problem that arises for workplace regulation shifting from state to market sanctions (O'Rourke 2003) is that subcontracting redefines the 'markets', e.g., for construction labour. In the process, the different functions in the policy cycle for standards (Nadvi and Wältring 2004)—standard setting, monitoring, assistance on achieving compliance and sanctions for non-compliance—are assigned to actors in different segments and therefore different interests. Thus, it is the lead firm that defines the standard, together with unions and/or NGOs, but does not have sufficient capacity to monitor. Yet those who have, the contractors of labour-only supplies, have no interest in sanctioning non-compliance. Even the developmental option, where lead firms and unions assist in building up compliance capacity, may run up against production and competition relations.

Second, when it comes to the private regulation of work and employment, there is a tendency to look at labour rights standards as a capital-labour issue between a lead firm and its subcontractors. However, following from Grimshaw and Rubery's (2005) argument, private regulation is always subject to inter-capital as well as capital-labour dynamics and filtered through segments of product and labour markets. Standards whose monitoring and enforcement is supposed to occur through workplace organisation differ from public regulation as well as multi-stakeholder standards. The implementation and monitoring of such standards in subcontracting chains cannot rely on formal mechanisms and the micropolitics between the headquarters and subsidiaries. By contrast, what is a capital-labour issue becomes subject to inter-capital and worker-to-worker competition in that it is filtered not only through the organisational capabilities of the lead firm but also through competitive local contractor markets as well as local labour markets characterised by an over-supply of migrant, informal labour that is tied to the contractor through paternalism and debt-bondage.

While IFAs have no doubt established productive management-labour dialogue on CLSs at the global level, evidence from the construction sector is very mixed. At the level of MNCs' subcontracting chains, problems seem to be tackled constructively once they surface to the headquarters level. However, given the elaborate subcontracting chains and the extent of migrant informal labour on construction sites, monitoring through a complaints mechanism 'as and when issues arise' is inadequate. Given the high segmentation of product and labour markets, standards such as IFAs might be most effective in a differentiated (by market segment) and articulated strategy (between workers and other local interest and campaigning groups, and vertical as well as horizontal inter-national networks; see Lévesque and Murray 2010). Appropriate strategies to link the global and the local and to overcome conflicts of interest must take differences across lead firms' capabilities, sectoral specificities or societal contexts into account.

CONCLUSION

The pronounced outsourcing and subcontracting throw up a number of issues concerning the dynamics of power and interests in the construction sector. First, at the level of the value chain, subcontracting changes the boundaries of product and labour markets and thereby creates a new functional division of labour as well as new interest constellations. However, the central role of the employment relationship for production and competition, and vice versa, means that social and labour standards cannot be seen as a management-labour issue only but must be set in the context of how different functions in the value chain are related. Thus, while standards might be created as a regulatory tool for capital-labour relations, their success is also shaped by the way they influence firms' competitive positions.

Second, with regard to the implementation of CLSs it is important to differentiate between different segments of firms and the extent to which CLSs shift the frontier of control at work.

MNCs do possess organisational capabilities that can be targeted and standards such as IFAs or multi-stakeholder standards can be a useful entry point into value chains. However, segmentation means that labour strategies in different tiers of the product market are different, as are firms' positions and interests in the policy cycle for standards. Thus, while MNCs are likely to have capabilities for standard setting and establishing entry barriers, national contractors at the second tier might be better placed to monitor compliance. Equally, assistance on achieving compliance and sanctions for non-compliance do raise crucial public policy issues. Interestingly, both India and Russia do have an exhaustive set of regulatory provisions to protect workers, yet these are undermined by market dynamics as much as by the state's light-touch approach to shaping power dynamics within the value chain.

Third, subcontracting and the parallel rise of informal employment lie at the basis of divisions within labour that sustain the reproduction of this division. There are a number of problems for organised labour to reach out to the unorganised workforce in the informal economy, not least statutory limitations on trade union organisation as well as the unions' own definition of their social base. Thus, strategies that use IFAs as organising tools take on a series of difficult challenges: the competitive relations between firms, the relations of control at work as well as established boundaries of labour solidarities and interests.

Despite the difficulties resulting from the industry structure and the specific labour control regimes, interesting facets can be made out in existing trade union approaches. Within a European Union context, for example, Lillie and Greer (2007) have analysed strategies aiming to 'relocalise' labour relations as an answer to employer exit from regulated industrial relations systems. In the weaker institutional context of emerging economies, standards concluded at the global level, particularly when encouraging the articulation of different levels of labour strategies as emphasised by Lévesque and Murray (2010), can be one element to support the development of more inclusive union strategies and organising approaches (see BWI 2010b). Wills (2009) uses the service sector to argue that subcontracted employment is becoming paradigmatic and highlights successful living wage campaigns developed in these circumstances (Wills et al. 2007). Finally, the argument made here about the link between capital-labour and inter-capital relations suggests a focus on the state. Coercive and market despotic labour regimes are shored up by the state's policies on production and competition as they are by policies on the regulation of capital-labour regulations. Despite the emphasis on firm strategies, it is labour and the state that have to be seen as equally central actors in the power dynamics within value chains.

260   *Nikolaus Hammer*

REFERENCES

Asper, A. (n.d.), 'Trade Unions and Workers' Migration', paper presented to the IFBWW-Asia Migrant Workers' Project, http://www.bwint.org/pdfs/Asiaregion.pdf, accessed April 4, 2008.

Bair, J. (2009), 'Global Commodity Chains: Genealogy and Review', in J. Bair (ed.), *Frontiers of Commodity Chain Research*, Stanford: Stanford University Press.

Barrientos, S. (2008), 'Contract Labour: The "Achilles Heel" of Corporate Codes in Commercial Value Chains', *Development and Change*, 39(6), 977–990.

Bosch, G., and Philips, P. (eds.) (2003), *Building Chaos: An International Comparison of Deregulation in the Construction Industry*, London: Routledge.

Breman, J. (1996), *Footloose Labour. Working in India's Informal Economy*, Cambridge: Cambridge University Press.

BWI (2010a), 'New BWI Model Framework Agreement', http://www.bwint.org/default.asp?Index=47&Language=EN, accessed January 31, 2011.

BWI (2010b), 'BWI Global Migration Strategy: BWI Connects', discussion paper for the migration ad-hoc working group, http://connect.bwint.org/wp-content/uploads/2010/12/BWI-CONNECTS-120910.pdf, accessed January 31, 2011.

Davies, S., Hammer, N., Williams, G., Raman, R., Ruppert, C.S., and Volynets, L. (2011), 'Labour Standards and Capacity in Global Subcontracting Chains: Evidence from a Construction MNC', *Industrial Relations Journal*, 42(2), 124–138.

Economic and Political Weekly (2008), 'State Apathy towards Construction Workers. Where Are the Cess Funds and Welfare Boards for Construction Workers Decreed More than a Decade Ago?' *Economic and Political Weekly*, 43(21).

Ferner, A., Quintanilla, J., and Sánchez-Runde, C. (2006) 'Introduction: Multinationals and the Multilevel Politics of Cross-National Diffusion', 1–23, in A. Ferner, J. Quintanilla and C. Sánchez-Runde (eds.), *Multinationals, Institutions and the Construction of Transnational Practices: Convergence and Diversity in the Global Economy*, Basingstoke: Palgrave.

Grimshaw, D., and Rubery, J. (2005), 'Inter-Capital Relations and the Network Organisation: Redefining the Work and Employment Nexus', *Cambridge Journal of Economics*, 29(6), 1027–1051.

Hammer, N., Davies, S., and Williams, G. (2009), 'International Union Strategies in Construction: Voluntary Agreements vs. Regulation in the Global Value Chain', paper for the 15th IIRA World Congress, Sydney/Australia, August 24–27.

HRW (2009), *'Are You Happy to Cheat Us?' Exploitation of Migrant Construction Workers in Russia*, New York: Human Rights Watch.

İçduygu, A. (2009), *International Migration System between Turkey and Russia: The Case of Project-Tied Migrant Workers in Moscow*, CARIM Research Reports 2009/18, Florence: EUI/Robert Schuman Centre for Advanced Studies.

IFBWW (2004), 'IFBWW Experiences with Global Company Agreements', http://www.ifbww.org/files/global-agreements.pdf, accessed April 4, 2008.

IFBWW (2003), 'IFBWW "Toolbox" on Social Dialogue and Multinational Companies', http://www.ifbww.org/files/strategy-mnc-en.pdf, accessed April 4, 2008.

IFC (2006), *International Finance Corporation's Performance Standards on Social and Environmental Sustainability*, Washington, DC: International Finance Corporation.

Kubicek, P.J. (2004), *Organized Labor in Postcommunist States: From Solidarity to Infirmity*, Pittsburgh: University of Pittsburgh Press.

Lane, C., and Probert, J. (2009), *National Capitalisms, Global Production Networks. Fashioning the Value Chain in the UK, USA, and Germany*, Oxford: Oxford University Press.

Lillie, N., and Greer, I. (2007), 'Industrial Relations, Migration, and Neoliberal Politics: The Case of the European Construction Sector', *Politics and Society*, 35(4), 551–581.

Locke, R., Amengual, M., and Mangla, C. (2009), 'Virtue Out of Necessity? Compliance, Commitment, and the Improvement of Labor Conditions in Global Supply Chains', *Politics and Society*, (37)3, 319–351.

Lévesque, C., and Murray, G. (2010), 'Local Union Strategies in Cross-Border Alliances: From Defensive Isolation to Proactive Solidarity', *Labor Studies Journal*, 35(2), 222–245.

Martin, B. (2008), *Can Transnational Corporations Legally Apply Conditions to Companies that Supply Them with Contract and Agency Labour?*, Brussels: ICEM.

Ministry of Labour (2002), *Report of the Second National Commission on Labour*, Delhi: Government of India.

Nadvi, K., and Wältring, F. (2004), 'Making Sense of Global Standards', in H. Schmitz, (ed.), *Local Enterprises in the Global Economy: Issues of Governance and Upgrading*, Cheltenham: E Elgar.

Nichols, T., and Cam, S. (2005), 'Labour in a Global World—Some Comparisons', in T. Nichols and S. Cam (eds.), *Labour in a Global World: Case Studies from the White Goods Industry in Africa, South America, East Asia, and Europe*, Basingstoke: Palgrave.

O'Rourke, D. (2003), 'Outsourcing Regulation: Analysing Nongovernmental Systems of Labour Standards and Monitoring', *Policy Studies Journal*, 31(1), 1–29.

Pais, J. (2002), 'Casualisation of Urban Labour Force. Analysis of Recent Trends in Manufacturing', *Economic and Political Weekly*, 37(7).

Palpacuer, F. (2000), 'Competence-Based Strategies and Global Production Networks. A Discussion of Current Changes and Their Implications for Employment', *Competition and Change*, 4(4), 353–400.

Papadakis, K. (ed.) (2011), *Practices and Outcomes of an Emerging Global Industrial Relations Framework*, Geneva: ILO/Palgrave Macmillan.

PUDR (2009), *In the Name of National Pride. Blatant Violation of Workers' Rights at the Commonwealth Games Construction Site*, Delhi: People's Union for Democratic Rights.

PUDR (2010), *Games the State Plays. A Follow-Up Report on the Violations of Workers' Rights in Commonwealth Games Related Construction Sites*, Delhi: People's Union for Democratic Rights.

Pun, N., and Smith, C. (2007), 'Putting Transnational Labour Process in Its Place: The Dormitory Labour Regime in Post-Socialist China', *Work, Economy and Society*, 21(1), 27–45.

Raftery, J., Pasadilla, B., Chiang, Y. H., Hui, E. C. M., and Tang, B. (1998), 'Globalization and Construction Industry Development: Implications of Recent Developments in the Construction Sector in Asia', *Construction Management and Economics*, 16(6), 729–737.

Raworth, K., and Kidder, T. (2009), 'Mimicking "Lean" in Global Value Chains; It's the Workers Who Get Leaned On', in J. Bair (ed.), *Frontiers of Commodity Chain Research*, Stanford: Stanford University Press.

Reina, P. (2005), 'India's Largest Contractor Begins Flexing Its Muscles', *Engineering News-Record*, 255(21), 61–62.

Reina, P. (2008), 'Russia's Cutting Edge', *Engineering News-Record*, 261(19), 114–116.

Reina, P., Rubin, D., and Post, N. (2005) 'Fast Growth Propels India to the Top of the World's Hot Markets', *Engineering News-Record*, 255(21), 56–59.

Riisgaard, L., and Hammer, N. (2011), 'Prospects for Labour in Global Value Chains: Labour Standards in the Cut Flower and Banana Industries', *British Journal of Industrial Relations*, 49(1), 168–190.

Rubery, J. (2007), 'Developing Segmentation Theory: A Thirty Year Perspective', *Economies et Sociétés*, 26(6), 941–964.

Rubin, D., Reina, P., Powers, M., and Illia, T. (2004), 'As Cost Pressures Mount, Offshoring Is Making the Work Go Round', *Engineering News-Record*, 253(5), 20–24.

Strassmann, P., and Wells, J. (eds.) (1988), *The Global Construction Industry. Strategies for Entry, Growth and Survival*, London: Unwin Hyman.

Whitley, R. (1999), *Divergent Capitalisms: The Social Structuring and Change of Business Systems*, Oxford: Oxford University Press.

Wells, J. (2007), 'Informality in the Construction Sector in Developing Countries', *Construction Management and Economics*, 25(1), 87–93.

Wills, J. (2009), 'Subcontracted Employment and Its Challenge to Labour', *Labor Studies Journal*, 34(4), 441–460.

Wills, J., Datta, K., McIlwaine, C., Evans, Y., Herbert, J., and May, J. (2007), 'From Coping Strategies to Tactics: London's Low Pay Economy and Migrant Labour', *British Journal of Industrial Relations*, 45(2), 404–432.

Part IV
Conclusion

14 Futures of Transnational Trade Unionism

Christian Lévesque, Marc-Antonin Hennebert and Peter Fairbrother

Recent studies on labour internationalism and cross-border trade union actions have opened up different ways of viewing transnational unionism. The argument presented here is that cross-border relations are shaped by a variety of actors differentiated along functional and territorial lines within and between different places and spaces of regulation (Anner 2007; Gajewska 2009; Munck 2010; Webster et al. 2008). The chapters in this book analyse a range of ways that unions organise in relation to transnational space. These spaces are an integral part of their strategies at local, national and international levels. This final chapter draws on the contributions to this collection to revisit three issues: the contours and shape of transnational unionism, the question of power and the conditions for building and sustaining solidarity.

THE CONTOURS AND SHAPE OF TRANSNATIONAL UNIONISM

Transnational unions often have been viewed as an outcome of a set of hierarchical relations, with international forms of unionism proposed to address the problems of multinational corporations, an argument for countervailing power relations (Levinson 1971). Alternatively, union activity at a local level focuses on the ways that international or transnational support could be secured and promoted to strengthen local claims (Carter et al. 2003; Bronfenbrenner and Juravich 1999). While opening up important themes, transnational trade unionism is more comprehensive and complex than this twofold contrast suggests. Such unionism takes various forms that can be understood through a consideration of four distinctive features. These relate to transnational space, rootedness, multi-level governance and the contested nature of transnational unionism.

First, various transnational spaces are emerging out of structured interactions between trade unions located in more than one national setting. The issue of space is becoming a central concern not only with regard to transnational unionism (Munck 2002; Lillie and Martinez Lucio 2012) but also in relation to employment relations in general (Rainie et al. 2007).

This focus on transnational spaces in relation to trade unionism has three dimensions to it (for a synthesis of the concept of transnational space, see Morgan and Kristensen 2006). The first dimension is concerned with the new space transnational unionism opens up through the development of multiple forms of linkage between trade union actors. Such linkages comprise exchanges, participation in forums and campaigns. These linkages can be relatively loose and de-centred, involving horizontal relations between workplace and national trade unions, as in the coalition of Canadian, Peruvian and Chilean trade unions (Dufour-Poirier and Lévesque, this volume). In some cases, they may be more formalised and involve union actors at the local, national and regional levels as shown by the mobilisation campaign at Renault in Romania (Descolonges, this volume) and the actions of European works councils (EWCs) in the six multinationals studied by Pulignano and colleagues in Europe (this volume). These linkages may be driven by international organisations, such as global union federations (GUFs), illustrated by the Quebecor example (Hennebert and Bourque, this volume) or by local unions in alliance with GUFs, as is the case with the maritime unions (Fairbrother, this volume). In a different setting, non-governmental organisations (NGOs) may constitute a driving force with local workers and their unions, as highlighted by the Russell case (Anner, this volume), where the spaces of production and of consumption were intertwined and thus provided the opportunity for relatively unusual alliances.

The second dimension deals with the creation of transnational regulatory arenas where new solutions, forms of activity or regulations are emerging. Over the last few decades, these dimensions have taken different forms across various spatial landscapes. They include global company councils, EWCs and national-based corporate and employer forums (see Pulignano et al.; Hennebert and Bourque; and Descolonges, this volume). Union involvement ranges from individual unions to national confederations to international trade union bodies, such as the European Trade Union Confederation (ETUC), International Trade Union Confederation (ITUC) and the GUFs (Gumbrell-McCormick; Fichter et al.; Hyman; and Dufour-Poirier and Lévesque, this volume).

This form of union activity is associated with the production and refinement of a variety of types of regulation. They range from the exchange of information through transnational bodies, which involves looser forms of regulation, to the negotiation of rules and standards, such as international framework agreements (Hammer; and Fichter et al., this volume), European framework agreements (Pulignano et al., this volume) or collective agreements (Anner; Descolonges; and Fairbrother, this volume). Increasingly, these forms of regulation cover or have implications for the local, national or transnational levels.

The third dimension concerns the elaboration of narratives to define transnational unionism. As illustrated by many of the contributions, developing and expressing these narratives involves a deliberative process, whereby narratives are formulated, changed and shaped via collective engagement involving union leaders, members and others in the transnational process, such as international agencies and employers (derived from Fearon 1998). The process of rule-making, even when it produces soft regulation, often involves a deliberative process that reinforces or puts into question the orientations and conceptions of transnational unionism. Out of such deliberative processes come new and competing narratives about globalisation and the forms of transnational unionism. The emergence of such narratives is well illustrated by the Gumbrell-McCormick chapter on the dynamic and structure of the ITUC and Hyman's analysis of the evolution of the ETUC (both in this volume). The elaboration of IFAs and EFAs is also about defining new rules as an opportunity to nurture a community of interest and of action between trade unionists (Hennebert and Bourque; Pulignano et al., this volume). Looser coalitions from below are also about creating a sense of identity and solidarity in order to build narratives about globalisation and the prospects of transnational unionism.

The second key feature of transnational unionism is that this form of unionism is anchored locally, not only in labour and product markets but also in the household, the community and in relation to the state. As Burawoy (2010) suggests, local endeavours are paramount to trade unionists, and we need to understand their patterns of action, forms of involvement and objectives according to the local contexts where they own their stories. Two complementary processes are at play here: an internalising and an externalising process (Tarrow 2005; Turnbull 2007). The first process focuses on the way that actors mobilise in relation to international issues, drawing on symbols or resources to frame domestic issues as global ones. This process neatly characterises the struggle of workers in Romania against Renault (Descolonges, this volume) and the action undertaken by the Ghanaian mine workers to access new resources for internal capacity building (Adanhoumne and Lévesque, this collection). The second process focuses on the spatial extension of specific local practices and patterns of influence into transnational space; the local is in the global. Several cases illustrate this process of externalising these domestic claims and practices: the GM coalition (Pulignano et al., this volume), the UNI Quebecor network (Hennebert and Bourque, this volume) and the creation of new transnational forums by trade unionists in the aerospace industry in both France and Canada (Lévesque et al., this volume). These two processes are not mutually exclusive. The struggles of the Russell workers in Honduras (Anner, this volume), of the Mineros in Mexico (Adanhounme and Lévesque, this collection) and the coalition between the Australian maritime transport unions (Fairbrother, this collection) involve both internalising and externalising processes, reinforcing the point that transnational unionism actions are rooted and embedded in local realities but articulated to transnational spaces.

The third defining feature, multi-level governance, is a central organisational principle of transnational unionism. It involves multiple arenas of regulation and linkage between the local, sub-national, national and supra-national levels of organisation. Such unionism is not exclusively a top-down or a bottom-up process, but a combination of both. A number of scholars focus on the latter relation, whereby trade unions move from the local to the global, although this does not adequately represent the way that spatial scales operate (Herod et al. 2007; Webster et al. 2008). These authors marshal evidence to the effect that spatial scales are not nested but are interconnected in fragmented and heterogeneous ways. A defining characteristic of Quebecor UNI Network (Hennebert and Bourque, this volume), the Russell campaign (Anner, this volume) and the coalition between South-American and Canadian workplace trade unions (Dufour-Poirier and Lévesque, this volume) is their multi-centred coordination processes. The story of the struggle of the Australian maritime transport unions (Fairbrother, this volume) shows that transnational unionism operates at multiple scales to capture the variations in and reflect the heterogeneity of the preferences of workplace and national trade unions. Pulignano et al. (this volume) illustrate the complexity of the negotiation processes within MNCs in Europe, where multiple and independent regulatory bodies (EWC, EMF, IMF) fulfil distinct but also complementary tasks.

A defining characteristic of such negotiations is that there are multiple opportunities for trade unions to collaborate and compete in shifting coalitions. Following Voss and Sherman (2000), several chapters show that it may be misleading to place bottom-up and top-down processes in opposition to each other. Equally, the association of innovation with bottom-up processes and bureaucracy with top-down is not supported. Rather a process of interlinkage between the top-down and bottom-up relations may be the key to the development and expansion of transnational unionism, as highlighted by the Quebecor UNI Network (Hennebert and Bourque, this volume) and the Russell Campaign (Anner, this volume). Without such interlinkage and the mutual reinforcement associated with it, then the intention as shown in the coalition between South-American and Canadian industrial and workplace trade unions may be unrealised (Dufour-Poirier and Lévesque, this volume). All chapters emphasise the necessity of understanding the varied forms, whereby claims and concerns are articulated at multiple levels of action.

The fourth feature of transnational unionism is that it remains a contested terrain, subject to political bargaining and negotiation. It is a social construct that brings into play different sets of interests, rationalities and power resources (Gajewska 2009; Lillie and Lucio Martinez 2012; Lucio Martinez 2010; Harrod and O'Brien 2002). It is an open-ended process that encompasses convergent and divergent and competing and complementary developments (Anner 2007; Hyman 2005; Waterman 2011). The chapters in the book highlight three distinct characteristics of the contested nature of transnational unionism.

In the first place, the main characteristic of employment relations— structural antagonism and interdependence—is carried over into the transnational terrain (Edwards and Bélanger 2009). The inherent duality of employment relations shapes the strategies of trade unions and their patterns of interaction with employers, as highlighted by several chapters. This is especially apparent in the struggle undertaken by workers in Honduras (Anner, this volume), Romania (Descolonges, this volume) and Australia (Fairbrother, this volume) as well as in the Quebecor UNI Network (Hennebert and Bourque, this volume). In other cases, the structural antagonism is paramount, such as in the battle of the Mineros in Mexico or the mutual interdependence between workers and employers are more apparent, pushing union leaders towards some form of micro-corporatism (Pulignano et al. and Lévesque et al., this volume). It is perhaps the Hammer chapter that best underlines how transnational actions are embedded in labour control strategies in the construction industries in both New Delhi and Moscow.

In the second place, transnational unionism is characterised by asymmetrical power relations, resources and capabilities. Although participation from the South in international bodies is increasing, trade unionists from developing countries are often excluded as highlighted in the Gumbrell-McCormick chapter. This aspect is particularly evident in the composition of the governance structures that are usually dominated by the richer countries, mainly European and American. Even in Europe, this asymmetry is manifest within the ETUC, where the powerful countries dominate the agenda and are able to mobilise their resources to ensure that this is the case (Hyman, this volume). This asymmetrical distribution of power resources is also noticeable in the relations between international bodies and national and industrial unions from emerging or transitional economies, such as India and Russia (Hammer, this volume) and Ghana (Adanhounme and Lévesque, this volume). It is also quite evident in coalitions involving industrial national unions from the North and the South where the latter is in a position of dependency not only in terms of access to financial resources (Anner, this volume) but also in terms of agenda setting (Dufour-Poirier and Lévesque, this volume).

In the third place, transnational unionism encompasses competing and contrasting logics and meanings. Tensions within and about the forms of transnational unionism are not new, as shown in the Gumbrell-McCormick and Hyman chapters. The historical landscape of transnational unionism has from the beginning been divided by contrasting geographical, ideological and industrial logics, but nowadays they take different configurations. Gumbrell-McCormick, in particular, argues that the ITUC is confronted with the challenge of articulating common interests and means of action through deliberative processes among trade unions that draw on different and even contradictory frames of reference. She also emphasises the tension within the ITUC between various organisational forms, in particular between a social movement approach from below and a more centralised approach. Hyman's chapter highlights the way these tensions are also active within the ETUC. He argues that the ETUC is caught between two contrasting logics: a logic of representativeness and a logic of influence. Competing logics also characterise the GUFs, as shown by Gumbrell-McCormick, Hammer, Fichter et al. and the Hennebert and Bourque chapters. Fichter et al. (this volume) demonstrate the ways that GUFs differ in their approach and logic of actions. They range from a social dialogue focus to networking to enhancing organising drives. In some cases, these three approaches are pursued jointly, while in other cases they are followed independently and one by one. Nonetheless, the tensions between these competing logics are not restricted to transnational bodies; they are also apparent within EWCs (Pulignano et al. and Lévesque et al., both in this volume) and looser forms of coalition from below (Dufour-Poirier and Lévesque, this volume).

These four defining features (emerging transnational space, rootedness, multi-level governance and the contested nature of transnational unionism) underscore the ways that new practices, rules and systems of meanings are transforming the way trade unions act and organise at different levels and across borders. There is no evidence that a coherent and integrated form of transnational unionism is emerging; rather, what is evident is the heterogeneity of practices, mechanisms and processes. Transnational unionism involves both the reproduction of old patterns and practices and the development of new patterns of relations, repertoire of actions and ways of framing international issues that provide opportunities for trade unionists to make new combinations among elements of various paths. This recombining process opens up new avenues for strengthening trade union power (Crouch 2009).

THE QUESTION OF POWER

Over the last two decades, the balance of power between capital and labour has significantly shifted. Through their integrated processes of production and distribution and their subcontracting arrangements, corporations are able to shift production across the global landscape and to extract value-added activity in many locations (Coe et al. 2008; Gereffi et al. 2005). Such corporations are active in shaping globalisation not only through the control of global value chains, but also through their capacity to frame the agenda of economic and social development (Dörrenbächer and Geppert 2011). In this process, governments have embraced a neo-liberal agenda that provides an opportunity for these developments as well as shaping and influencing outcomes (Harvey, 2000).

Several contributions show how MNCs are able to shift production from one location to another and to split and fragment the production process to cut costs and increase their control over the labour process (Hammer, Descolonges and Anner, this volume amongst others). Hyman demonstrates how employers through their organisations and the CEE infrastructure have the capacity to set agendas, often placing the ETUC on the defensive and in a position of dependence. Several chapters also highlight how the promotion of neo-liberal policies through structural adjustment programs (e.g., Ghana) and deregulation policies and anti-trade union legislation (e.g., Australia) have weakened trade union power. Nonetheless, such assaults on trade unions can be more straightforward and less subtle, as in the case of the Mineros in Mexico.

There are however limits to the capacity of employers to realise their interests. Their capacity to shift production from one location to another is not unlimited. In fact, as shown by economic geographers, capitalists may be just as fixed as are workers (Herod 2009; Sassen 2006). Even the most footloose corporations are, to some extent, spatially rooted in particular places. Spatial arrangements in relation to investment, infrastructure and the dynamic of the labour market limit the mobility of capital. Hence, according to their location within the global value chain, both in terms of product and labour markets, workers can limit the margin of manoeuvre by employers. This restriction is particularly obvious in the chapters that reported on high technology producer-driven industries, such as the aerospace and auto industries, or resource-driven industries, such as mining. The influence of structural power on strategies and outcomes is made explicit in the chapter by Fichter et al. They show that the strategies of GUFs are shaped by the way the global value chain is structured and, more precisely, on workers' positions within the GVC.

Workers and their representatives are neither defenceless nor passive. In addition to the resources they can draw from their market location (structural power), workers can use their collective power and their distinctive capabilities to put forward and realise their collective interests. This argument builds on a longstanding tradition in industrial relations where trade union power is paramount to understanding the dynamics of employment relations (Batstone et al. 1977; Hyman 1975; Offe and Wiesenthal 1980; Reynaud 1989; Sainsaulieu 1973; Sayles and Strauss 1953). The main purpose of trade unions is to enhance the control of workers over their conditions of employment by exerting 'power for' them through the establishment of a set of rules and mechanisms that can be mobilised by workers to enable a degree of control over their environment. To accomplish this task, trade unions must exercise 'power over' actors, like employers and state representatives, prompting them to do something that they might not otherwise do (Lukes 2005; see also Dahl 1957). To exercise 'power over' other actors, trade unions need the 'power to', that is, the capacity to act and achieve goals that does not necessarily entail power over others.

'Power to' emphasises the dispositional dimension of power. This refers to the ability of trade unions to use their capabilities and to mobilise their resources, as exemplified in recent contributions about trade union power (Dufour and Hege 2010; Ganz 2004; Lévesque and Murray 2010; Pocock

2000) and social movement theories (Benford and Snow 2000, McAdam et al. 1996; Snow et al. 1986). Recent contributions on labour internationalism and trade union cross-border actions present the range of ways that unions organise to strengthen their power (Anner 2007; Turnbull 2007; Webster et al. 2008). Transnational trade union power relations are indeed organised and exercised in complex ways within unions and between unions and their employer counterparts. Building a comprehensive framework to understand these dynamics is critical. While such an endeavour goes beyond the purpose of this book, the contributions provide the foundation for the development of such a framework.

Several chapters contribute to our understanding of trade union 'power over' employers. The expansion of supranational structures and processes and the capacity to organise across borders provide new spaces to challenge corporations' practices and narratives. Campaign coalitions, such as the one described by Anner (this volume), the negotiation and implementation of IFAs or EFAs (Fichter et al. and Pulignano et al., this volume), the creation of international networks and campaigns targeting corporations like Quebecor (Hennebert and Bourque in this collection), or an entire sector, such as the maritime industry (Fairbrother in this collection), are amongst the forms of transnational action undertaken by unions to contest the power of employers. Transnational unions also provide opportunities to explore ways of reshaping these relationships via the development of varied forms of social dialogue. They may open up new spaces for social dialogue at both the transnational and local levels, with MNCs as organisational entities and with management at the regional and local levels. Pulignano et al. and Fichter et al. show that social dialogue is one of the avenues pursued by transnational unions to influence employers.

Other chapters provide the basis to understand trade union 'power for' workers. Transnational trade unionism is also about the creation and the development of rules and mechanisms that can be mobilised by workers, local and national trade unions. The purpose of these rules and mechanism is to enhance workers and trade unions control over their conditions of employment. IFAs, EFAs, collective agreements, global company networks and the various forms of coalition are mechanisms and forums that enable workers and trade unions potentially to strengthen their capacities and power. However, there is no mechanical association between these rules and mechanisms and an increase in the power of trade unions and workers. Hammer makes this point forcefully in his chapter, with regard to the implementation of IFAs in the construction industry in Moscow and New Delhi. The uneven impact of transnational rules and mechanisms is also quite apparent in relation to the operations of EWCs (Pulignano et al. and Lévesque et al., this volume).

All chapters highlight the question of trade unions 'power to' and the way that power resources and/or capabilities come into play. Several chapters show that distinct sets of resources and capabilities can enhance the capacity of unions to act. Fairbrother, for example, shows how a GUF can play a decisive role in the integration of the rules and mechanisms of transnational regulation into workplace and national trade union repertoires of action. However, Fichter et al. (this volume) remind us that GUFs differ in their strategy and capacity to empower national and local trade unions. A crucial ingredient lies in their capacity to articulate and mediate between both the varied interests of workers and the contrasting repertoires of action used and developed by national trade unions (Hennebert and Bourque and Fairbrother, both in this volume). In the cases described by Pulignano et al., the EMF is, in actual fact, acting as a broker, framing events and actions in particular ways and articulating these meanings at multiple levels, from the local to the transnational. Many chapters show that national unions with a robust set of resources at their disposal are more likely to integrate transnational regulation in their repertoires of action (Pulignano et al. and Hennebert and Bourque, both in this volume). Specifically, Fairbrother (this volume) highlights the importance of national leadership and particularly their capacity to articulate their repertoires of action at different levels of the union and to mediate between contending interests. Similarly, workplace trade unions that have built collective structures and active networks and established strong deliberative processes are more likely to engage in transnational campaigns or regulation (Anner, Pulignano et al. and Lévesque et al., all in this volume). In particular, Lévesque and colleagues (in this collection) show that workplace trade unions strategic capabilities play a pivotal role in the integration of transnational issues into their repertoires of action.

In contrast, various chapters show that a deficit in power resources and capabilities reduces the capacity of trade unions to act. For instance, according to Hyman (this volume), the ETUC clearly needs to develop its internal resources, in particular its deliberative processes and proactive agendas in order to strengthen its capacity to act through the formulation of a proactive agenda. Likewise, Gumbrell-McCormick (this volume) considers the reinforcement of debates and deliberative processes to be one of the main challenges facing the ITUC. The problems facing confederations are paralleled by those confronting the GUFs. Hammer (this volume), for example, demonstrates that BWI does not have sufficient resources to overcome the dynamics of product and labour markets in the construction industry in Moscow and New Delhi. These deficits are also evident at a workplace level. Lévesque et al. (this volume) show that workplace trade unions with weak deliberative processes and fragile leadership arrangements cannot modify their traditional repertoires of action and are unable to integrate transnational issues into their repertoires of action. Further, the involvement of workplace trade unions in transnational action with weak resources can reinforce traditional frames of action prompted by 'localist' and instrumental conceptions of their interests.

Transnational action encompasses complex dynamics that combine trade union resources and capabilities across different levels (workplace, industry, nation-state, transnational). Each sphere has a relative autonomy but they are interconnected in a rather complex way across both scales and spaces. Resources and capabilities mobilised by actors at different levels can be complementary and reinforcing. For example, several chapters show that the capacity of GUFs is related to the power resources and capabilities of national and workplace trade unions. Similarly, the dynamics and logics of action at the workplace and national levels are connected to the resources and capabilities of actors at the supranational level. However, transnational unionism is also a contested arena characterised by tensions between competing actors pursuing different goals and mobilising their power resources to attain them. The exercise and control of power resources, as highlighted by various chapters, then become an issue of contestation. Both of these dynamics characterise and shape transnational trade unionism.

BUILDING AND SUSTAINING SOLIDARITY

Research on transnational unionism shows the ways that threats and derived opportunities provide unions with the incentives to move into the global arena (Burgoon and Jaccoby 2004; Greer and Hauptmeir 2008). Most chapters in the book support such a view. The Russell, Quebecor, Renault, GM and maritime transport cases, amongst others, illustrate the importance of key or critical incidents and events, such as lay-offs, restructuring announcements or lock-outs. While these events do not necessarily lead to transnational forums, campaigns or networks, they nonetheless often provide the occasion for such transnational activity. Even so, the very same events and incidents can provide the circumstance for inward looking responses, where unions focus on 'localist' and limited agendas. Accordingly, threats and crises offer only a partial understanding of the building process of transnational unionism.

Trade unions also require power resources to build transnational unionism. These include robust deliberative processes from the workplace to international bodies, proactive and inclusive agendas and dense and diversified networks. The relevance of these power resources to build transnational unionism is supported by all the chapters in this book and by a growing body of research (Croucher and Cotton 2009; Gajewska 2009; Lillie and Martinez Lucio 2012; Turnbull 2007; Webster et al. 2008). Power resources are a necessary condition to build transnational unionism, although they may not be sufficient to sustain it.

To sustain transnational unionism, new sets of capabilities are required: framing, bridging and transformative capabilities. Each is dealt with here in turn.

First, framing supposes an ability to alter the script and enlarge action frames (Benford and Snow 2000; Snow et al. 1986) to justify new practices and repertoires of action that are cross-border in focus and intent. Framing involves the rearticulation of frames of reference, that is, the range of values, shared understandings and beliefs that aggregate identities and interests, and translate and inform motives. Such aggregations constitute a body of interpretative and collective frames that can be mobilised to explain new situations and new contexts. Several processes are at play (frame bridging, frame extension and so on) and they appear to be an essential ingredient for enlarging repertoires of action at the transnational level. Several chapters (Anner, Hyman, Fairbrother, Lévesque et al. and Pulignano et al.) show how the framing capabilities of trade unions play a pivotal role in the integration of transnational issues into repertoires of action. Various chapters suggest that trade union involvement in cross-border actions can trigger a redefinition of frames of reference. Such frames then act as a mental map providing the basis for trade union strategies. For example, the Russell campaign, the struggle of the Renault workers in Romania and the success of unionisation drives in the Quebecor case became what Voss (1996) labels 'fortifying myths'. Such 'myths' inspired activists and allowed them to give meaning to their actions so that the campaigns could be sustained and pushed forward. Perhaps, most importantly, these new frames became a source of mobilisation in other transnational campaigns.

Second, to be successful, transnational trade unions must bridge the multiple levels at which they exert an influence. This obligation has been noted in several recent studies (Croucher and Cotton 2009; Turnbull 2007). The crucial point is that it is necessary for union leaders to bridge issues at the local, national and international levels. Since transnational unionism involves different types of networks, trade union leaders need to articulate points of tensions that arise in coordinating actions across countries. The ability to span boundaries and to bring together the varied interests pursued by workers is a mark of transnational trade unionism. In this process, the role of transnational bodies, such as GUFs, EWCs and European federations, is crucial. Several chapters, in particular Fairbrother and Pulignano et al., show that these transnational bodies can act as brokers by linking and mediating the relationships between unconnected actors. Bridging capabilities is not restricted to actors within these transnational bodies. Workplace trade unionists and union representatives from national or industrial federations also act as brokers, as shown by Anner, Lévesque et al., Fairbrother and Hennebert and Bourque (all in this volume). These workplace trade unionists not only articulate claims between the local and the global, but also connect trade unionists across place and space.

Third, trade unions need to develop their capabilities to transform both institutions and themselves (Dufour et al. 2009). As highlighted by Hyman (in this collection), trade unions must be autonomous from supra-union institutions, such the ETUC. If they do not achieve such autonomy they are likely to become prisoners of these institutions. Such an observation is not restricted to trade unionists operating within transnational bodies, such as the ITUC or the ETUC. It also concerns workplace and national trade unionists. Pulignano et al. (this volume) show how workplace trade unionists transform a EWC into a bargaining forum. Lévesque et al. (this volume) highlight the way workplace trade unions in the aerospace industry in France and Canada, respectively, transform and craft transnational consultative committees. They are acting as rule-makers instead of rule-takers.

In addition, the capacity of trade unions to transform themselves is related to the ability to modify and focus their repertoires of action and meaning. This form of reflexive capacity is often refined and developed over time, reflecting the changing capacities of unions. Several chapters document how transnational unionism can trigger a transformative process. Fairbrother's analysis (in this collection) highlights how transnational campaigns can bring about changes not only in the repertoires of action developed by trade unions, but also a shift in trade union identity. The Ghanaian Mine workers and Mineros in Mexico studied by Adanhoumne and Lévesque (this volume) clearly went through a transformative process. The two unions followed different paths and developed various capabilities; these unions used transnational action to break from rather traditional and conservative types of trade unionism. However, as highlighted by Gumbrell-McCormick (this volume) in her discussion of the history of the ITUC, this transformative process is complex and can engage actors in contradictory directions

Transnational unionism thus is an open-ended process that encompasses convergent and divergent, competing and complementary developments. It is a social construct built around and in relation to power relations. Our perspective draws attention to the importance of actor-centred analyses in relation to the emergence and development of the current forms of transnational unionism. Further research is needed to understand more fully how capabilities can reshape institutions.

THE CHALLENGE

Trade unions are and will remain a force within the world of work and employment. The strength of trade unions resides in their organisational form as part of the employment relationship. In capitalist society, work and employment is and will remain a core experience of most people most of the time, whether working in large mass production units, as the car factories across the world once were, or employed as casuals in fast food retail outlets, or providing services or contributing to the increasing digitalised world. In this context, trade unionism as a collective form of organisation will remain salient. For most union members, most of the time, this is a form of organisation that begins and ends in the workplace. This feature of the work and employment relation defines the parameters of this form of organisation.

Nonetheless, work and employment, and the ownership and management of the labour process, have become increasingly international in focus and practice. It is now the case that production and consumption is multi-layered and cross-border, with complex governance relations. For unions, these developments create challenges for the way unions organise, for their capacities and capabilities and for their purpose. No longer does it suffice to restrict union concerns to the spatially immediate. Many unions have long histories of connection across the globe, arising out of the past colonial and related relationships of the nineteenth century and transformed during the twentieth century, in contested and uneven ways. Workers and their unions face challenges that derive from the very feature of capital, as international and often relatively mobile.

In this context, the future for unions is uncertain. Debates, often bitter and divisive, have taken place within unions and between unions about the future. Some unions, particularly in the developed capitalist economies have sought to embrace forms of active organisation and representation that had become stultified during the twentieth century, and particularly in the post-war period from the 1940s to the 1980s. With the embrace of a neo-liberal agenda by many governments in the 1980s and 1990s and the predominance of international agencies in trade and related relations, many unions found that the nation-state neither had the capacity nor the inclination to regulate and contain capital, even in the partial ways of the postwar period. At the same time, the former verities of the Soviet Union and an underdeveloped 'third' world underwent profound shifts, reshaping international relations and hence production and consumption relations in decisive ways.

The question for unions is how to address these changes. Transnational trade unionism is one step towards an answer. As presented, this step has been uneven, contested and hesitant, although on occasion workers and their unions have taken up the challenge and initiated novel and imaginative ways of dealing with the internationalisation of the modern world. Central to this agenda is how to deal with capital in these circumstances and the governments that enable and often encourage these developments. At times, this will result in divisions within unions and with leaders and their members at variance with each other as to how to proceed. On other occasions, it will mean tentative arrangements are brokered between unions, within states and across borders. These moves are not straightforward and often contested.

Even so, unions remain embedded in the workplace and this remains the well-spring of transnational trade unionism. The problem for unions is to harness the strengths and capacities of workers in traditional mass-based workplaces as well in the individualised and socially isolated workplaces. Unions are caught in a tension between local needs and concerns and global imperatives. If they focus only on their local needs they become isolated and likely to embrace sectionalist and instrumental concerns. However, if they focus only on the global, they become disconnected and removed from their membership. The challenge to unions therefore is how to enable workers to pursue their interests via transnational unionism; it is a process of articulating local concerns, aspirations and interests in a scalar way that locates the local in the global and the global in the local. However this is done, transnational unionism is likely to develop and become a primary future of unionism in the twenty-first century. In this way workers will continue to challenge the depredations of capital.

REFERENCES

Anner, M. (2007), 'The Paradox of Labour Transnationalism: Trade Union Campaigns for Labour Standards in International Institutions', in C. Phelan (ed.), *The Future of Organised Labour: Global Perspectives*, Oxford: Peter Lang.

Batstone E., Boraston I. and Frenkel S. (1977), *Shop Stewards in Action: The Organisation of Workplace Conflict and Accommodation*, Oxford: Blackwell.

Benford, R. D., and Snow, D. A. (2000), 'Framing Processes and Social Movements: An Overview and Assessment', *Annual Review of Sociology*, 26, 611–639.

Bronfenbrenner, K., and Juravitch, T. (1999), *Ravenswood: The Steelworkers' Victory and the Revival of the American Labor Movement*, Ithaca: ILR Press.

Burgoon, B., and Jacoby, W. (2004), 'Patch-Work Solidarity: Describing and Explaining US and European Labour Internationalism', *Review of International Political Economy*, 11(5), 849–879.

Burawoy, M. (2010), 'From Polanyi to Pollyanna: The False Optimism of Global Labor Studies', *Global Labour Journal*, 1(2), 301–313.

Carter, C., Clegg, S., Hogan, J. and Kornberger, M. (2003), 'The Polyphonic Spree: The Case of the Liverpool Dockers', *Industrial Relations Journal*, 34(4), 290–304.

Coe, N. M., Dicken, P., and Hess M. (2008), 'Global Production Networks: Realizing the Potential', *Journal of Economic Geography*, 8(3), 271–295.

Crouch, C. (2009), 'Collective Bargaining and Transnational Corporations in the Global Economy. Some Theoretical Considerations', *International Journal of Labour Research,* 1(2), 43–60.

Croucher, R., and Cotton, E. (2009), *Global Unions, Global Business. Global Union Federations and International Business*, London: Middlesex University Press.

Dahl, Robert A. (1957), 'The Concept of Power', *Behavioral Science*, 2(3), 201–215.

Dörrenbächer, C., and Geppert, M. (2011), *Politics and Power in the Multinational Corporation. The Role of Institutions, Interests and Identities*, Cambridge: Cambridge University Press.

Dufour, C. and Hege, A. (2010), 'Légitimité des acteurs collectifs et renouveau syndical', *La Revue de l'IRES*, n° 65, 2010/2, 67–85.

Dufour, C., Hege, A., Lévesque, C., and Murray, G. (2009), 'Les syndicalismes référentiels dans la mondialisation: une étude comparée des dynamiques locales au Canada et en France', *Revue de l'IRES*, 61(2), 3–37.

Edwards, P. K., and Bélanger, J. (2009), 'The MNC as a Contested Terrain', in S. Collinson and G. Morgan (eds.), *Images of the Multinational Firm*, Chichester: John Wiley & Sons.

Fearon, J. (1998), 'Deliberation as Discussion', in J. Elster (ed.), *Deliberative Democracy*, Cambridge: Cambridge University Press, 44–68.

Gajewska, K. (2009), *Transnational Labour Solidarity: Mechanisms of Commitment to Cooperation within the European Trade Union Movement*, London and New York: Routledge.

Ganz, M. (2004), 'Why David Sometimes Wins: Strategic Capacity in Social Movements', in J. Goodwin and J.M. Jasper (eds.), *Rethinking Social Movements: Structure, Meaning and Emotion*, Lanham, MA: Rowman & Littlefield Publishers.

Gereffi, G., Humphrey, J., and Sturgeon, T. (2005), 'The Governance of Global Value Chains', *Review of International Political Economy*, 12(1), 78–104.

Greer, I., and Hauptmeier, M. (2008), 'Political Entrepreneurs and Co-Managers: Labour Transnationalism at Four Multinational Auto Companies', *British Journal of Industrial Relations*, 46(1), 76–97.

Harrod, J., and O'Brien, R. (2002), *Global Unions? Theory and Strategies of Organized Labour in the Global Political Economy*, London and New York: Routledge.

Harvey, D. (2000), *Spaces of Hope*, Berkeley: University of California Press.

Herod, A. (2009), *Geographies of Globalization*, Malden: Wiley-Blackwell.

Herod, A., Rainnie, A., and McGrath-Champ, S. (2007), 'Working Space: Why Incorporating the Geographical is Central to Theorizing Work and Employment Practices', *Work, Employment and Society*, 2(2), 247–264.

Hyman, R. (2005), 'Shifting Dynamics in International Trade Unionism: Agitation, Organisation, Bureaucracy, Diplomacy', *Labor History*, 46(2), 137–154.

Hyman, R. (1975), *Industrial Relations: A Marxist Introduction*. London: Macmillan Press.

Lévesque, C., and Murray, G. (2010), 'Trade-Union Cross-Border Alliances within MNCs: Disentangling Union Dynamics at the Local, National and International Levels', *Industrial Relations Journal*, 41(4), 312–332.

Levinson, C. (1971), *Capital, Inflation and the Multinationals*, London: Allen & Unwin.

Lillie, N., and Martinez Lucio, M. (2012), 'Rollerball and the Spirit of Capitalism. Competitive Dynamics within the Global Context, the Challenge to Labour Transnationalism, and the Emergence of Ironic Outcomes', *Critical Perspectives on International Business*, 8(1), 74–92.

Lucio Martinez, M. (2010), 'Dimensions of Internationalism and the Politics of the Labour Movement. Understanding the Political and Organisational Aspects of Labour Networking and Co-ordination', *Employee Relations*, 32(6), 538–556.

Lukes, S. (2005), *Power: A Radical View*, New York: Palgrave Macmillan.

McAdam, D., McCarthy, J., and Zald, M. (1996), *Comparative Perspectives on Social Movements*, Cambridge: Cambridge University Press.

Morgan, G., and Kristensen, P. H. (2006), 'The Contested Social Space of Multinationals: Varieties of Institutionalism, Varieties of Capitalism', *Human Relations*, 59, 1467–1490.

Munck, R. (2010), 'Globalization and the Labour Movement: Challenges and Responses', *Global Labor Journal*, 1(2), 218–232.

Munck, R. (2002), *Globalisation and Labour: The New 'Great Transformation'*, London and New York: Zed Books.

Offe, C., and Wiesenthal, H. (1980), 'Two Logics of Collective Action: Theoretical Notes on Social Class and Organizational Form', *Political Power and Social Theory*, 1, 67–115.

Pocock, B. (2000), 'Union Renewal: A Theoretical and Empirical Analysis of Union Power', Research Paper Series, No. 12, Center for Labour Research.

Rainnie, A., Herod, A., and McGrath-Champ, S. (2007), 'Spatialising Industrial Relations', *Industrial Relations Journal*, 38(2), 02–118.

Reynaud, J.-D. (1989), *Les règles du jeu. L'action collective et la régulation sociale*, Paris: Armand Colin.

Sainsaulieu, R. (1973), *Les relations de travail à l'usine*, Paris: Editions des Organisations.

Sassen, S. (2006), *Territory, Authority, Rights. From Medieval to Global Assemblages*, Princeton: Princeton University Press.

Sayles, L.R., and Strauss, G. (1953), *The Local Union*, New York: Harper.

Snow, D. A., Rochford, E. B., Worden, S. K., and Benford, R. D. (1986), 'Frame Alignment Processes, Micromobilization and Movement Participation', *American Sociological Review*, 51, 464–81.

Tarrow, S. (2005), *The New Transnational Activism*, Cambridge: Cambridge University Press.

Turnbull, P. (2007), 'Dockers versus the Directives: Battling Port Policy on the European Front', in K. Bronfenbrenner (ed.), *Global Unions: Challenging Transnational Capital Through Cross-Border Campaigns*, Ithaca: ILR Press.

Voos, K. (1996), 'The Collapse of a Social Movement: The Interplay of Mobilising Structure, Framing and Political Opportunities in the Knights of Labor', in D. McAdam, J.D. McCarthy and M.N. Zald (eds.), *Comparative Perspectives on Social Movements*, Cambridge: Cambridge University Press.

Voos, K. and Sherman, R. (2000), 'Breaking the Iron Law of Oligarchy: Union Revitalization in the American Labor Movement', *American Journal of Sociology*, 106 (2): 303–349.

Waterman, P. (2011), 'Beyond Polanyi and Pollyanna—Oscar Wilde?', *Global Labour Journal*, 2(1), 78–83.

Webster, E., and Lambert, R. (2008), *Grounding Globalization: Labour in the Age of Insecurity*, Oxford: Blackwell Publishing.

Contributors

Armel Brice Adanhounme is a Banting postdoctoral fellow at the Labour Law and Development Research Laboratory (LLDRL) based at McGill University and associate researcher at the Interuniversity Research Centre on Globalization and Work (CRIMT). Prior to his postdoctoral research on the juridical origins of exclusion at work, he completed his PhD in Business Administration at HEC Montreal on an institutional and comparative analysis of citizenship at work in a multinational firm. He investigates questions of development and globalisation concerning the treatment of workers in both the North liberal economy context (Canada) and the South postcolonial context (Ghana).

Mark Anner is an assistant professor of labor studies and political science at Pennsylvania State University. He holds a PhD in Government from Cornell University and a Master's Degree in Latin American Studies from Stanford University. His research examines local and transnational labor strategies in global manufacturing industries, international workers' rights and corporate social responsibility in the apparel industry. He is the author of over twenty-five academic publications, including the book, *Solidarity Transformed: Labor Responses to Globalization and Crisis in Latin America*. Prior to his academic career, he lived in Central America for ten years where he worked with labor unions and a labor research centre.

Reynald Bourque is a professor of collective bargaining at the School of Industrial Relations-University of Montreal, and a researcher at the Interuniversity Research Centre on Globalization and Work (CRIMT). His recent research focuses on the impact of globalisation on trade unions, collective bargaining and industrial relations in multinational corporations. He has published extensively on comparative and international collective bargaining, trade union renewal, comparative industrial relations and transnational trade union action. He has co-edited seven books and published several articles and book chapters.

Isabel da Costa (CNRS-IDHE, France) is a senior researcher at the Institutions et Dynamiques Historiques de l'Economie (IDHE) research unit of the Centre National de la Recherche Scientifique (CNRS), located at the Ecole Normale Supérieure de Cachan near Paris. She teaches industrial relations at the University of Paris-X Nanterre. Her research and publication themes include industrial relations theories, comparative industrial relations and industrial relations developments at the national, European and global levels.

Michèle Descolonges is a sociologist. She is a researcher at the Centre de Recherches Sociologiques et Politiques de Paris (CRESPPA). Her recent research focus deals with the testing of standards, rules and values of the union actors in the process of globalisation. She has published on corporate social responsibility (CSR) and the renewal of social negotiation on an international scale. Her latest book focuses on collective action for the protection of workers of subcontractors in various cultural areas.

Christian Dufour, sociologist, associate researcher at the University of Avignon and the Interuniversity Research Centre on Globalization and Work (CRIMT). His research focuses on comparative industrial relations and workplace representation in Europe and North America. He has done extensive fieldwork, especially in Europe. He has published on employee representation, collective bargaining and trade union renewal in a context of globalisation. From 1990 to 2010, he was deputy director of the Institut de Recherches économiques et sociales (IRES) in France and the editor of the *Revue de l'IRES*.

Mélanie Dufour-Poirier is an assistant professor in Labour Relations at the School of Industrial Relations of the University of Montreal (Canada). She is also a core researcher at the Interuniversity Research Centre on Globalization and Work (CRIMT). She holds a PhD in administration from HEC Montreal (Canada). Her research focuses on impacts of globalisation on trade unions, their identities and strategies and trade union renewal, as well as emerging actors and news forms of international labour regulation. She has done extensive field work in various countries in the Americas. She has published on trade union renewal and transnational union action taking place in under-institutionalised contexts.

Peter Fairbrother is a professor of International Employment Relations and Director of the Centre for Sustainable Organisations and Work at RMIT University. He is also a core researcher at the Interuniversity Research Centre on Globalization and Work (CRIMT). He has researched and published widely on trade union renewal, industrial restructuring and re-generation and the privatisation and reorganisation of public services and utilities. His recent work focuses on the mobilisation of labour in relation to the social and political transition towards low carbon economies. He has published nine books and numerous articles and book chapters.

Michael Fichter recently retired from his long-term position as senior lecturer and researcher in labour relations in the Institute of Political Science at Freie Universität Berlin. He continues to be active on the teaching staff of the Global Labour University. He has published widely both on German trade unions and labour relations as well as on labour issues in the process of European Union integration and expansion. His current research and publications focus on the regulation of labour in global production networks. From 2008 to 2011, he co-directed a multinational and interdisciplinary research project on international framework agreements.

Rebecca Gumbrell-McCormick is a lecturer in the Department of Management at Birkbeck, University of London and is a former international trade union official and official of the ILO. She specialises in European and international industrial relations, trade unions and equality. She is currently working on a book with Richard Hyman on their recently-completed research project on trade unions in ten western European countries for Oxford University Press.

Nikolaus Hammer is a lecturer in employment studies at the Centre for Labour Market Studies at the University of Leicester, United Kingdom. He has published articles on industrial relations with regard to cross-border trade unionism and international framework agreements. Current research focuses on work and employment in global value chains.

Adelheid Hege, sociologist, is a senior researcher at the Institut de Recherches économiques et sociales (IRES) in France and an associate researcher of the Interuniversity Research Centre on Globalization and Work (CRIMT). Her research focuses on comparative industrial relations and workplace representation in Europe and North America. She has done extensive fieldwork, especially in Europe. She has published on employee representation, collective bargaining and trade union renewal in a context of globalisation. She is a former editor of the *Chronique internationale de l'IRES*.

Markus Helfen is a senior research fellow at the Institute of Management, Chair for Inter-firm Cooperation at Freie Universität Berlin. He holds a doctorate in business administration from Aachen University. His current research focuses on institutional analysis of international industrial relations, human resource management and the relevance of collective action for organisation theory.

Marc-Antonin Hennebert is an assistant professor in HR and Labour Relations at HEC Montréal and a core researcher at the Interuniversity Research Centre on Globalization and Work (CRIMT). He holds a PhD from Université de Montréal and recently completed a postdoctoral fellowship in the Department of Management at King's College London. His recent research looks at the emergence of new forms of international labour regulation, such as corporate codes of conduct, global framework agreements and international collective bargaining and its impact on actors and their strategies. He has recently published various articles and a book on international union alliances.

Richard Hyman is an emeritus professor of Industrial Relations at the LSE and is founding editor of the *European Journal of Industrial Relations*. He has written extensively on the themes of industrial relations, collective bargaining, trade unionism, industrial conflict and labour market policy, and is author of a dozen books (including *Strikes* and *Industrial Relations: A Marxist Introduction*) as well as numerous journal articles and book chapters. His comparative study *Understanding European Trade Unionism: Between Market, Class and Society* (Sage, 2001) is widely cited by scholars working in this field. He is currently working on a book for Oxford University Press comparing trade union strategies in ten European countries.

Christian Lévesque is a professor of Employment Relations at HEC Montréal and Co-director of the Interuniversity Research Centre on Globalization and Work (CRIMT). His research focus concerns the impact of globalisation on trade unions, employment practices in multinational corporations and union-management relations. He has done extensive fieldwork in various parts of the world, including México, various countries in Europe, Ghana and China. He has published on trade union renewal, comparative employment practices in multinational corporations and transnational union action. He has co-edited a book and four special journal issues and published several articles and book chapters.

Gregor Murray is Canada Research Chair on Globalization and Work and a professor in the School of Industrial Relations at Université de Montréal. He is also Director of the Interuniversity Research Centre on Globalization and Work (CRIMT). He holds a PhD from Warwick University. His recent research looks at the evolution of workplace partnerships, employment relations practices in multinational firms, how unions contend with globalisation and forms of regulation in global firms.

Valeria Pulignano is a professor in Labour Sociology and Industrial Relations at the Center voor Sociologische Onderzoek (CESO) at the Katholieke Universiteit Leuven (Belgium). She is an associate fellow at the

IRRU at Warwick University (United Kingdom) and core researcher at the Interuniversity Research Centre on Globalization and Work (CRIMT; Canada). She has widely published in comparative industrial relations nationally and internationally. Her research interests include employment relations and restructuring in multinational companies, system of employee representations at both the European and national levels, trade unions and the labour market. In 2008, she co-edited a book entitled *Flexibility at Work: Critical Developments in the International Automobile Industry*, which was published by Palgrave Macmillan.

Udo Rehfeldt (IRES, France) is a senior researcher at the IRES (Institut de Recherches Economiques et Sociales) in Noisy-le-Grand near Paris. He also teaches comparative industrial relations at the University of Paris-X-Nanterre. His research and publication themes include European works councils, trade unions, employee representation and collective bargaining at the national, European and global levels.

Katharina Schiederig is a lecturer and a research fellow at the Chair for Gender and Diversity in the Institute of Political Science at Free University Berlin. In her PhD thesis, she deals with diversity politics in transnational corporations, with a special focus on global framework agreements. Katharina holds a Master's degree in Political Science from Free University Berlin and in Development Studies from Sciences Po Paris. Her research interests centre on labour, gender and diversity and development issues.

Volker Telljohann (IRES EmiliaRomagna, Italy) is a senior researcher at the Institute for Economic and Social Research (IRES) Emilia-Romagna in Bologna. His research activities centre on working conditions and employee representation as well as on national and transnational industrial relations. In particular, his research and publication themes include employee participation, the functioning of EWCs, European and international framework agreements as well as experiences of transnational social regulation in the context of restructuring processes.

Index

A

A. & L. Group Inc. (ALGI) 32
aerospace industry *see* Canada and France cross-border actions
AFL *see* American Federation of Labor
AFL-CIO *see* American Federation of Labour and Congress of Industrial Organisations
ALGI *see* A. & L. Group Inc.
alliances *see* cross-border alliances
Alstom-Schneider Electric 152, 157
Alta Gracia factory 37
American Center for International Labour Solidarity 32
American Federation of Labor (AFL) 161
American Federation of Labour and Congress of Industrial Organisations (AFL-CIO) 11, 32, 189, 232; in Justice@ Quebecor World campaign 230; Kerry support for North American unions 229; NAFTA opposition and 131; ORIT and 194; unionisation campaigns of Teamsters and 237; withdrawal from ICFTU 162
Amnesty International 198
Amsterdam Treaty 166
André, Maria-Helena 175
ANS *see* Australian National Stevedores
anti-sweatshop activism: in apparel global value chains 27–9; centralisation as advantage to 25; Knights Apparel 13, 36–8; naked marches 31, 39; Nike Just Pay It campaign 36–8; normative power used in 26, 38; outcomes 23; political power and 27, 29, 38; Russell case 23, 30–6; young activists in 25
anti-union campaigns 228, 241, 271
apparel industry: GVCs 28–9, 38; horizontal outsourcing in 24; MNC common strategy 30; power sources for workers 23–7; quota system for Central American 27, 29; worker power sources 23–7
Areva and Schneider cases: Alstom-Schneider acquisition of Areva 152; Areva social equality issues 150–1, 157; EFAs completed by 142, 150–2; EWC effectiveness in 151–2, 157; Schneider initiative on skill discrepancies and working conditions 151–2; social experiences of 150–2
Argès County teachers 92–3
Asian Financial Crisis 83
associational power 7, 38, 117; cross-border actions context for 61, 71–2; institutional arrangements with structural and 74–6; labour internationalism and 122–3; resource mobilisation and 25; TNC power counteracted through 209
ATUF *see* Australian Transport Union Federation
Australian National Stevedores (ANS) 106
Australian transport maritime unions 101–19; *see also* Maritime Union of Australia
Australian Transport Union Federation (ATUF) 110; ITF and 113–14; local and global mediations with 114–16

Austrian ÖGB 167, 187
automotive industry case study 142;
    EWCs impact on workers
    154–6; pioneering agreements
    by Ford and GME 146–8; *see
    also* Canada and France cross-
    border actions
autonomy 51–2, 275; of GUFs and
    ETUC 189–90; GUFs/ITS 191;
    ICFTU and WCL 195; structural
    234; workplace union 51, 54
auto parts industry, case study firms
    62–3

B

Barcelona 232
bargaining *see* collective bargaining;
    EU-level bargaining
BJ&B factory 37
BNS *see* National Trade Unions Block
Bolkenstein Directive 82
bottom-up/top-down processes and
    relations 51, 197–8, 268
Bozich, Joseph 37
Brasov tractor factory 91
Brazil 232
brigadiers 253, 254
British trade unions, in UNI Network
    238
Brussels 186; embrace 171, 172
Building and Woodworking
    International (BWI) 211,
    215–16, 243; IFAs of 247–8;
    labour control regimes
    addressed by 255–6
bureaucracy, trade union 25
BWI *see* Building and Woodworking
    International

C

CAFTA-DR *see* Central American-
    Dominican Republic Free Trade
    Agreement
Canada: Canmin1 workplace unions
    in 42; creation of North-South
    alliances 44–8; cross-border
    alliances with South America 42;
    see also Canada-South America
    alliances
Canada and France cross-border
    actions 58–78; aerospace
    MNCs overview 63, 64;
associational power in 61,
    71–2; auto parts MNCs
    overview 62, 63, 64;
    conclusions 76–8; cross-
    border interaction dynamics
    64–9; dimensions and patterns
    overview 66; domain of
    contention 65; global economy
    context for 58–61; institutional
    and power analyses 74–6; local
    union involvement 65; modes
    of interaction analysis 65, 66,
    67, 68; patterns of involvement
    69–73; power dynamics in
    60–1; proactive pattern 67, 75,
    76; research methods and case
    description 61–4; risk reduction
    pattern in 65, 67, 75; spatial
    dimension 65, 66, 67; structural
    power impact on 71; subsidiary
    pairs in 62–4; transport
    equipment MNCs overview 62,
    63; unionisation level 72
Canada-South America alliances 9,
    13; breakup and withdrawal
    2007–2008 48–50; Canmin1
    growth and inclusion phase
    for 44–6; conclusions 53–5;
    description 43–4; expansion and
    consolidation 2005–2006 46–8;
    growth and inclusion 1990–2004
    44–6; issues and challenges
    50–3; meetings in Canada
    47, 48; organisation issue 54;
    research methods 44; resource
    allocation 54
Canadian industrial trade union:
    collective bargaining by 53;
    Euromin unions 2007 meeting
    with 49–50; mobilisation of
    47; as official coordinator of
    alliances 48; role of 51, 54
Canadian Labour Congress (CLC) 194
Canmin1: acquisition of 46–7; North-
    South alliances created 44–6;
    workplace unions 42, 44
Canmin 2 47–9, 53
capacity-building: overview of GMWU
    135; variation among GUFs 273
capital, hyper-mobility of 28; *see also*
    labour-capital relations
Caribbean Basin Trade Partnership Act
    (CBTPA) 28

Cartel ALFA *see* National Trade Union Confederation
case studies *see specific cases*
casualisation of labour 249–52; GPNs 207
CBTPA *see* Caribbean Basin Trade Partnership Act
Central America apparel production, 1990s 27–8
Central American-Dominican Republic Free Trade Agreement (CAFTA-DR) 28–9
centralisation: GPN 208; local actors impacted by 51; MNC culture of 156–7; production 24, 25; *see also* decentralisation
Central Latinoamericana de Trabajadores (CLAT) 194
CEP *see* Energy and Paperworkers Union of Canada
CES *see* Confédération Européenne des Syndicats
CFDT *see* French Democratic Confederation of Labour
CGC *see Confédération genérale des cadres*
CGT *see Confédération générale du travail*
CGU *see* Council of Global Unions
child labour 28
Chile: Euromin mining sites in 43; North-South alliances with Canada and Peru 44–8; in UNI Network 232, 235–6, 238, 239
China State Construction Engineering Corporation 253–4
Chinese unions 189
Christian trade unions: in historic context 186, 187; ITUC challenges with 193
circular migration 251
CISC *see Confédération internationale des syndicats chrétens*
class relations 2
CLAT *see Central Latinoamericana de Trabajadores*
CLC *see* Canadian Labour Congress
clientelism 162
CLSs *see* core labour standards
coalitions 5, 133; MUA 108–9; *see also* cross-border alliances
codes of conduct 69; TNC unilateral 209–10

Cold War 9, 161–2
collaboration, competition and 54–5, 124
collective bargaining 53, 58; in metal industry 145–6; in Romania 85; in Russell case 31; social dialogue and 169
colonialism 9–10
Commons, John 24
competition: collaboration and 54–5, 125; inter-capital 248; inter-site 74
Confederación de los Trabajadores de Mexico (CTM) 130, 131
Confédération Européenne des Syndicats (CES) 88
Confédération genérale des cadres (CGC) 87
Confédération générale du travail (CGT) 14, 30, 32, 35, 73, 237–8; Dacia and 96–7; Europeanisation opposed by 167; Renault and 89, 94; Renault-Dacia interviews with 82–3
Confédération internationale des syndicats chrétens (CISC) 184, 187
confederations, as transnational trade unionism form 7–8
Congreso del Trabajo (CT) 131
construction industry: in India 249–52; internationalisation of 248; outsourcing impact on 257; in Russia 252–4; segmented labour markets of 243–59; study on IFA impact in 245; subcontracting 244, 248–9, 250; *see also* Delhi and Moscow labour standards
contestation, elite embrace and 171–4
contract terminations 33, 34; Nike 36–7
cooperation: East-West inter-union 96; precondition for 3; study of EU-NAFTA 13
core labour standards (CLSs): cost of compliance and 247; IFAs and 243–4, 255–6, 258; ILO 205, 210; in MNC value chains 247; monitoring 256; subcontracting and 254, 255
core-periphery dichotomy 207–8

Council of Global Unions (CGU) 191, 196
Council of Ministers 164
cross-border actions: dynamics of 64–9; by GUFs 217; GVC fragmentation creating space for 59; motives for 122–3; NAFTA as intensifying 57; supranational institutional arrangements and 57–8; sustained 77; vulnerability creating conditions for 75; *see also* Canada and France cross-border actions
cross-border alliances 5, 101; anti-sweatshop campaign 25; coalitions and 5, 108–9, 133; definition of 223; factors and resources for 43; formal partnerships 5; globalisation and 223; global trade union 11; GUFs role in 42, 52; MUA 109–11; multiple forms of 266; Quebecor World case 223–42; as social interaction arena 233–4; social network theory approach to studying 223–5, 233–41; strengths and weaknesses 241; success of 16; *see also* Canada-South America alliances; North-South alliances
cross-national negotiating, company level: Areva and Schneider social experiences 150–2; EMF evidencing 145–6; Ford and GME 142, 146–8, 154–5; IG Metall 146–7, 150; missed opportunities for 148–50; union and management bargaining strategies in Europe 152–7
CSDR *see* Democratic Trade Union Confederation of Romania
CT *see Congreso del Trabajo*
CTM *see Confederación de los Trabajadores de Mexico*
Czech Metalworkers' Federation (OS KOVO) 150

D
Dacia: annual sales increase of 2007 84; CGT and 96–7; platform 84; Renault acquisition of 83–4; wage negotiations by management 90, 91

Dacia automobile union (SAD) 87, 96, 97
damage limitation 170
decentralisation 24
Delhi and Moscow labour standards: despotic and coercive regimes 250; labour control in Delhi 249–52; labour control in Moscow 252–4
Delor, Jacques 165
democracy 117
Democratic Trade Union Confederation of Romania (CSDR) 87
deregulation 110–11, 165, 249, 271; outsourcing linked with 257
Designated Suppliers Program 37
de-unionisation 107, 111
developing countries 199, 214, 269
Directorate-General for Employment and Social Affairs (DG EMPL) 168
dispositional dimension 7
diversity management issue 52–3
Dominican Republic *see* Knights Apparel
DP World (DPW) 105

E
Easter celebration, Romania's 92
Eastern Europe, Western and 13–14, 96
East-West inter-union cooperation 96
ECFTU *see* European Confederation of Free Trade Unions
ECJ *see European Court of Justice*
economic and monetary union (EMU) 170
Economic Community of West African State (ECOWAS) 126, 134–5, 137
economy *see* global economy; *specific countries*
ECOWAS *see* Economic Community of West African State
EEC *see* European Economic Community
EFAs *see* European framework agreements
EIF *see* European Industry Federation
Electrolux and Siemens cases 142–3; EMF weakened in Electrolux case 156; EWC undermined in Siemens case 155–6; institutional arrangements and 156; missed opportunities 148–50

elite embrace, contestation and 171–4
EMF Secretariat 146
employment contracts 230–1, 249
employment regulation:
Europeanisation and 143–4,
169; European-level 166; factors
determining 144
employment relations: power and
domination as embedded in
6; power imbalances 58, 59,
206–7; structural antagonism
and interdependence in 269; *see
also* labour-capital relations
EMU *see* economic and monetary union
Energy and Paperworkers Union of
Canada (CEP) 234–5, 238
England, UNI Network in 235
ERO *see* European Regional
Organisation
ETUC *see* European Trade Union
Confederation
ETUFs *see* European Trade Union
Federations
EU *see* European Union
EU-level bargaining 141–58; conditions
influencing 141; metal industry
and 145–6; MNCs selected for
case study 142–3; *see also* Areva
and Schneider cases; Electrolux
and Siemens cases; Ford and
General Motors Europe
Eurocentric internationalism 15, 161–2
Euromin 43, 48–50, 53
Europe: bargaining at EU-level in
141–58; Eastern-Western
collective action 13–14, 96;
local level strategies for cross-
national bargaining in 152–7;
Quebecor unions in 226, 230;
transnational unionism in 15
European Confederation of Free Trade
Unions (ECFTU) 163
European Court of Justice (ECJ) 164
European Economic and Social
Committee 85
European Economic Community (EEC),
EU and trade union concerns
162–4
European framework agreements
(EFAs): Areva and Schneider
completion of 142, 150–2; case
study overview 142–3; common
feature of all 144; EWCs

facilitating signatures 143–4;
Ford and GME completion of
142, 146–8; issues covered by
143
European Industry Federation (EIF)
143–4
Europeanisation (European integration)
165, 166–70; employment
regulation and 143–4; of
industrial relations 152–75
European Metalworkers' Federation
(EMF) 144, 145–6, 148–9;
Alstom-Schneider negotiation
team 152, 157
European Parliament 164
European Regional Organisation (ERO)
163
European Round Table of Industrialists
168–9
European Solidarity Pledge 147
European Trade Union Confederation
(ETUC) 82, 86, 97; autonomy
of GUFs and 189–90; dilemmas
facing 163–4; founding and
subsidizing 163; logic of
membership and influence 171;
strikes organised by 173–4; *see
also* European Union
European Trade Union Federations
(ETUFs) 186
European trade unions, Renault-Dacia
strike solidarity 93
European trade unions and
institutional arrangements
161–76; elite embrace and
contestation 171–4; Eurocentric
internationalism 161–2;
European social model 166–70;
institutional approach issue
174–6; inward direction
162–4
European Union (EU) 13; comitology
171–2; contested political
space of 164–6; EEC and
162–4; employment regulation
and 166; EWCs and 57; key
institutions 164, 168; legislative
authority of 162; negative
integration concern 165;
relocalising labour relations
in 259; Romania's entry into
81, 85–8, 94; social dialogue
practices in 11, 151, 169, 174;

see also European Trade Union
Confederation
European Works Council (EWC) 42,
57, 67, 85, 151–2, 157; auto
workers impacted by 154–6;
EIFs as facilitated by 143–4;
local-level influence and mixed
results 156; number of TNCs
having 220; reshaping of 158;
sharing the pain strategy of 147,
154; *see also specific cases*
Eurospeak 172–3
EWCs *see* European Works Council
exit and voice strategies 158
export processing zones 27–8

F
Facebook 33, 36
Fair Labour Association (FLA) 27, 32,
34
FDI *see* foreign direct investments
*Fédération des travailleurs des
industries du livre, du papier et
de la communication* (FILPAC)
237
Federation Tower, Moscow 253
FEM *see* Fonds européen d'ajustement
à la mondialisation
Fiat 147
FILPAC *see* Fédération des travailleurs
des industries du livre, du papier
et de la communication
FILPAC-CGT alliance 237–8
financialisation 207
FLA *see* Fair Labour Association
Flag of Convenience campaign 10, 42
flexibilisation 209, 220
Fonds européen d'ajustement à la
mondialisation (FEM) 88, 97
Football World Cup in South Africa
255
Ford and General Motors Europe: EFAs
completed by 142, 146–8; Ford
innovation 155; Ford plants
in Mexico and US 59; GME
framing 154; influence and
resources from EWCs 154–5;
restructuring plan and 148
foreign direct investments (FDI) 122
formal partnerships 5–6
formative period 7–9
fortifying myths 275
four freedoms movement 165

Fox, Vicente 131
fragmented institutional arrangements
7–9
framing 274–5
France 13; French-Romanian trade
unions relations 88–9; Renault
sites in 87; trade between
Romania and 81; trade union
relations between Romania and
88–9
French Democratic Confederation of
Labour (CFDT) 82–3, 87, 89,
93, 94; in Areva-Schneider cases
151–2, 157
French media, during Renault-Dacia
strike 93

G
Gabaglio, Emilio 175
galamsey 126
GCC/IBT *see* Teamsters Graphic
Communications Conference
GCIU *see* Graphic Communications
International Union
General Motors Europe (GME) 148,
154–5; *see also* Ford and
General Motors Europe
General System of Preference petitions
28
German central works council 150
Ghana and Mexico labour
internationalism 14–15,
121–38; comparison 133–7;
conclusions 137–8; context
for 125–7; Ghana trade union
vulnerability of 122; Ghanian
economy and institutional
arrangements 126–7; Mexican
economy and institutional
arrangements 130–1; modes
of interaction 124, 129, 135;
patterns in Ghana 127–31;
patterns in Mexico 131–3;
research method 125–7; spatial
dimension 123–4; trade unionist
interests dimension 124–5
Ghana Mine Workers Union (GMWU)
125; capacity-building focus
of 128, 134, 135; craft
identity focus 134; economic
vulnerability context 134;
ICEM affiliation of 127–8;
modernisation process 127;

transnational solidarity obstacles in 129
Ghana Trade Union Congress (TUC) 126
Gifford, Kathie Lee 28
global economy, transnational unionism building in 58–61
global framework agreements, ICEM's 214–15; *see also* International Framework Agreements
globalisation: cross-border alliances in context of 223; grounding 121; in Mexico 130; spatial fragmentation from 243; TNCs and 204
global production networks (GPNs): casualisation of labour and 207; industry sectors and 208; standards raising in TNCs and 203; TNC dominance and 204; TNCs, trade unions and 207–8
global solidarity days 229
global trade union alliances 11
global union federations (GUFs) 1, 4–5, 57, 104; activities of today's 11; autonomy of ETUC and 189–90; autonomy of ITs and 191; capacity variation among 273; chart of signed IFAs by industry 211; cross-border action conclusions 217; in cross-border alliances 42, 52; founding of 183; history of ITSs and 185–6; in IFA process 206; IR institution coordination of ITUC and 199–200; ITUC relations with 16, 189–90, 194–5; pioneer of 210; predecessors of 161, 209
Global Union Network *see* Union Network International
global value chains (GVCs): apparel industry 27–9, 38; extension of 58; hyper-mobility of capital in 28; reconfiguration and fragmentation of 59, 243; societal theory compared to theory of 245–6; strategic/ organisational view 245; workplace unions at apex of 77
global workforce, TNC employment percentage 220
GME *see* General Motors Europe

GMWU *see* Ghana Mine Workers Union
Goldin, Adrian 32
governance structures: monitoring by transnational 27; multilevel 267–8; neo-liberal policies and 1, 2, 270, 271, 277; TNC core-periphery dichotomy 207–8
GPNs *see* global production networks
Grafiska 238
Graphic Communications International Union (GCIU) 228
Great Divide period 9–10
Greenhouse, Steven 35
Grupo Mexico 132
GUFs *see* global union federations
GVCs *see* global value chains

H

HERE *see* Hotel Employees and Restaurant Employees Union
Hermansoon, Jeff 32
Holland, John 33
Honduras: Goldin's visit to 32; as outsourcing choice 30; political access in 30; political power and 26; post-coup government 35; *see also* Russell case
horizontal outsourcing 24
Hotel Employees and Restaurant Employees Union (HERE) 32
hyper-mobility of capital 28

I

ICEM *see* International Federation of Chemical, Energy, Mines and General Worker Union
ICFTU *see* International Confederation of Free Trade Unions
IFAs *see* International Framework Agreements
IFC *see* International Finance Corporation
IFTU *see* International Federation of Trade Unions
IG Metall 146–7, 150
IKEA 231
ILO *see* International Labour Organisation
IMF *see* International Metalworkers' Federation; International Monetary Fund

India 198, 199; BWI in Southern 256; construction industry in 248–52
industrial relations (IR): Europeanization 152–75; system 199–200
industrial sector organisations, history 184–5
informal labour: organising by informal migrant workers 254; product and labour market segmentation impact on 247–9; workplace regulation in subcontracting and 255–8; *see also* casualisation of labour
information politics 27, 31, 36
Institut de recherches économiques et sociales (IRES) 82
institutional entrepreneurs 153–4, 157, 158
Institutional Revolutionary Party (PRI) 130
institutional specificity 58
institutions and institutional arrangements: capability to transform 275; as constraining and facilitating 60; cross-border actions and power 74–6; definition of 59–60; as dependent on local management 156; exploitation variability by workplace unions 76; fragmented 7–9; Ghanian 126–7; local actor strategies and 153; local power dynamics and 60–1, 74, 76; period of fragmented 7–9; in segmented markets 244–7; *see also* European trade unions and institutional arrangements
inter-capital competition 248
inter-capital dynamics, labour-capital relations and 246, 258
international aid, to Central America 27
International Confederation of Christian Trade Unions 162; renaming of 8
International Confederation of Free Trade Unions (ICFTU) 2, 161–2, 166; autonomy of WCL and 195; new ITUC structure and 195; WCL unification with 188–9
international dimension 15–16
International Federation of Chemical, Energy, Mines and General Worker Union (ICEM) 10, 127–8, 211, 214–15
International Federation of Trade Unions (IFTU) 8; historic context and divisions 184–5; union orientation in 187
International Finance Corporation (IFC) 255
International Framework Agreements (IFAs) 12, 16–17, 203; BWI 247–8; CLSs and 243–4, 255–6, 258; construction industry impact 245; effectiveness factors 205; GUFs in process of 206; ICEM's 214–15; IMF 211, 212–13; listed by industry 211; number of functional 210; other names for 220; as policy tool 208–12; power imbalances addressed by 59, 206–7; Renault 88; resources required for 218–19; signing conditions 212; as strategy for restraining TNC power 205–7, 208–9; UNI 216–17; UNI Network 224, 232; as union policy strategy 208–9
international labour movement 183–200; early and recent structural changes in 183
International Labour Organisation (ILO) 8, 32, 34, 85; core labour standards of 205; labour standards 205, 210
International Metalworkers' Federation (IMF) 88; core industries and approaches 213–14; IFAs 211, 212–13; Mineros joining 131–2
International Monetary Fund (IMF) 2
International Secretariat of National Trade Union Centres (ISTNUC) 8
International Trade Secretariats (ITSs) 8; as GUF predecessors 161, 209; history of GUFs and 185–6; renaming of 161, 184
International Trade Union Confederation (ITUC) 1, 162; autonomy and integration challenge 195; congressional

meetings 191; constitution 195; external challenges of 196–200; financial resources and membership 192–3; GUFs relation with 16, 189–90, 194–5; ideological diversity in 193–4; increasing activity of 5; internal challenges 193–6; IR institution coordination of GUFs and 199–200; new structure and practices 190–3; politics 191–2; Romania and 85; WCL unification with 183

international trade unionism: Achilles heel of 203–4; geographical division of organisation types 186; ICFTU-WCL unification 188–9; ideological division of organisation types 187; industrial and membership division of organisations 184–5; industrial-national division of organisation types 184–6; ITUC-GUFs tensions 189–90; organisational configurations up to 2006 184–90; structure and functions post-2006 190–3; *see also* global union federations; transnational solidarity

International Transport Federation (ITF) 10, 11, 101, 197; ATUF and 113–14; global affiliations 111–12; inspectorate 115–16; local and global mediations with 114–16; MUAV relation with 104–19; national coordinating committees and 113; strategies and capacities 112–13; working group 106–9

International Typographers' Union 8

International Union of Food, Agricultural, Hotel, Restaurant, Catering, Tobacco and Allied Workers' Associations (IUF) 210–11

International Working Men's Association (IWMA) 8

inter-site competition 74

interviews: France-Canada case study 62; Ghana and Mexico case 125; MUAV and ITF 104; Quebecor World case 224; Renault-Dacia 82–3

IR *see* industrial relations

IRES *see* Institut de recherches économiques et sociales

Iron Law of Oligarchy (Michels) 25

ISTNUC *see* International Secretariat of National Trade Union Centres

ITF *see* International Transport Federation

ITGLWF *see* Textile, Garment and Leather Workers' Federation

ITSs *see* International Trade Secretariats

ITUC *see* International Trade Union Confederation

IUF *see* International Union of Food, Agricultural, Hotel, Restaurant, Catering, Tobacco and Allied Workers' Associations

IWMA *see* International Working Men's Association

J

Japanese MNC 64

Joint Delta Working Group 147

joint text 141

Justice@Quebecor World campaign 228–31

K

Kentucky Workers' Rights Board 229

Kerry, John 229

Klein, Naomi 25

Knights Apparel 13, 36–8

L

labour: casualisation 207, 249–52; decentralisation 24; informal 247–9, 254, 255–8; labour-capital relations 102–4; Europeanisation and 168; inter-capital dynamics and 246, 258; transnationalising through IFA process 206; *see also* employment relations

labour control: BWI strategies against regimes of 255–6; in Delhi 249–52; market despotic and coercive regimes 250

labour internationalism: bottom up 197–8; definitions of 3; dimensions of 123–4, 135; Ghana and Mexico context for 125–7; rooted 122–5, 137, 138;

Southern Hemisphere 121–2; *see also* Ghana and Mexico labour internationalism

labour markets *see* labour standards in segmented markets

labour standards: erosion 208, 213, 217; subcontracting and temporary work undercutting 213; TNCs lowering of 203; *see also* core labour standards

labour standards in segmented markets 243–59; construction industry subcontracting and 244, 248–9, 250; despotic and coercive regimes in Delhi and Moscow 250; labour standards in segmented 243–59; product and labour market segmentation 247–9; product and market segmentation 247–9; strategic and institutional factors 244–7

Latin American unions 187, 188, 189, 198

lay-offs, importance of critical events such as 274

legal framework, European Commission for 141

legislation, social partners route to 174

Levinson, C. 10

Lima 232

Lobo, Porfirio 35

local actors 42; adaptation of 158; centralisation impact on 51; company-level cross-national bargaining 145–6; in cross-border actions 65; local-global movement as beyond scope of 138; relocalising labour relations 259; strategies and responses 142, 153; in transnational structures 141–58; *see also* cross-national negotiating, company level; UNI Network@ Quebecor World

local-global bridging 122; double movement 138

local power dynamics: institutional arrangements and 60–1, 74, 76; institutional specificity and 58

logic of appropriateness 26, 34

logic of consequences 34

logic of influence 171

logic of membership 171

Luxembourg *see* Rüffert and Luxembourg cases

M

Maastricht Treaty 166, 173

Mangalia shipyard strike 92

Maritime Union of Australia (MUA) 5, 10; alliances and solidaristic activity 109–11; coalition-building and recruitment drives 108–9; founding and membership of 105; international framework of 108; local and global mediations 114–16; maritime industry transnational unionism 118–19; outside support for 107; RTBU and 110; transnational unionism in 118–19; *see also* Port of Melbourne

Maritime Union of Australia, Victoria Branch (MUAV) 101; assessment of case 116–18; ITF relations 104–19; ITF Working Group of 106–9; organising method 106; Patricks Corporation membership in 106; Patricks de-unionisation and lockout 107, 111; study of 14, 104

Melbourne Port *see* Port of Melbourne

membership base, industrial-national division of organisation types 184–6

Memorandum of Understanding 155

mergers 5

metal industry 88, 131–2, 211, 212–14; collective bargaining 145–6

Mexican Miners' Union *see* Mineros

Mexico 14–15, 59; economy and institutional arrangements 130–1; globalisation in 130; labour internationalism patterns in 131–3; mining industry in 122; trade union vulnerability 122; *see also* Ghana and Mexico labour internationalism

Michels, Robert 25

Middle East 196

migrant workers: BWI support for 256; circular migration 251; IFAs and 243–4; organising by informal 254; product and labour market segmentation impact on 247–9

Milan agreement 185

Mineros (Mexican Miners' Union) 125; coalition-building strategies 133; exile of 132; IMF joined by 131–2; USWA alliance 132–3

mining industry: in Ghana 122, 126; in Mexico 122; Western NGOs and 129

mining industry coalitions 47–8

Mining Law, in Mexico 130

Ministry of Labour 30

Mioveni 84, 93, 95

Mittal 92

MNCs *see* multinational corporations

modes of interaction: in Canada-France cross-border actions 65, 66, 67, 68; Ghana-Mexico trade unions 124, 129, 135

Monks, John 175

Moscow, labour control in 252–4; *see also* Delhi and Moscow labour standards

MUA *see* Maritime Union of Australia

MUAV *see* Maritime Union of Australia

Mulroney, Brian 229–30

multilevel arrangements 10–12

multinational corporations (MNCs) 11; with centralized corporate culture 156–7; emergence of 10; growing importance and influence of 240; negotiation trends in 141–58; power imbalances increased by 58; production location shifting 270–1; relocation threats and coercion 58; segmentation and 259; transnational governance structures and 27; *see also specific cases*; *specific corporations*; *specific industries*

N

NAFTA *see* North American Free Trade Agreement

naked marches 31, 39

National Basketball Association (NBA) 33

national business systems (NBS) approach 245

National Farmer's Federation 107

National Trade Union Confederation (Cartel ALFA) 85, 87, 92, 97

national trade unions 184–5; EFAs as cosigned by 144; EMF coordination with 145–6; leadership in transnational activities 51; legal framework for European 141; local-global bridging by 122; overview of study on 14–15; study overview 14–15, 121–2; workload of 54

National Trade Unions Block (BNS) 87, 92

Nautilus UK-Nautilus Netherlands partnership 5

NBA *see* National Basketball Association

NBS *see* national business systems

neo-liberal policies 1, 2, 270, 271, 277

neutrality agreement, US-UNI Network 231–2, 241

New York Times 35

NGOs *see* nongovernmental organisations

Nike 13; Just Pay It campaign 36–8

Nissan 83–4

nongovernmental organisations (NGOs): equal partnership needed for 198; GMWU relations with 128–9; mining operations and Western 129

Nordic unions 215

normative power: in anti-sweatshop activism 26, 38; against child labour 28; in Russell case 33–4

North American Free Trade Agreement (NAFTA) 13, 57, 131, 136, 137

North American Internationals, colonial relations and 10

North-South alliances 9, 44–50; bottom-up and top-down processes balance needed in 51; focus on 13; Mineros-USWA 132–3; UNI Network example of 240–1; *see also* Canada-South America alliances

North-South divide 9–10, 51

O

ÖGB *see* Österreichischer Gewerkschaftsbund

Organización Regional Interamericana de Trabajadores (ORIT) 186, 194
OS KOVO *see* Czech Metalworkers' Federation
Österreichischer Gewerkschaftsbund (ÖGB) 167, 187
outsourcing 30, 147–8, 208, 216; deregulation linked with 257; horizontal 24; segmentation from 257; subcontracting and 258–9; *see also* Delhi and Moscow labour standards

P

Pan-European Regional Council (PERC) 194
Paris Commune 8
partnerships *see* cross-border alliances
Patricks Corporation 115; deunionisation 107; lockout 107, 111; MUAV members in 105; PGE and permanent staff 105–6
pattern bargaining 44, 47
People's Union for Democratic Rights (PUDR) 252
PERC *see* Pan-European Regional Council
permanent guaranteed wages (PGE) 105–6
Peru 232; Euromin sites in 43; North-South alliances with Canada and Chile 44–8
PGE *see* permanent guaranteed wages
PILs *see* public interest litigations
Pitesti demonstration 91–2, 93, 95
political power 26, 38; in Mexico 131; political access in Honduras 30; in Russell case 29
politics 191–2; EU contested political space 164–6; Honduras political access 30; information 27, 31, 36; ITUC 191–2; Romanian 87
Port of Melbourne 101; stevedoring operators within 105–6; trade and revenue 105
positional power 24
power 270–4; concept of 6–7; definition of 23; IFAs for redefining relational 59, 206–7; imbalances 58, 59, 206–7, 269; local power dynamics 58, 60–1, 74,

76; need for power resources 274; overlooked dimensions of 116–17; 'power to' 271–3; UNI Network resources of 236–9; *see also* associational power; normative power; political power; structural power; worker power
PPPs *see* public-private partnerships
PRI *see* Institutional Revolutionary Party
proactive pattern, cross-border actions 67, 75, 76
product and labour market segmentation 247–9
Professional and Managerial Staffs Association Union 129
public interest litigations (PILs) 252
public-private partnerships (PPPs) 248
PUDR *see* People's Union for Democratic Rights

Q

qualified majority voting (QMV) 166
Quebecor World Inc. case study: anti-union campaign 228, 241; closing of headquarters 233; context for 223–4; history and restructuring of 225; Justice@ Quebecor World campaign 228–31; major customers and contracts 230–1; research method 224–5; trade union presence by region and country 226–7; World Color Press and 225; *see also* UNI Network@ Quebecor World
quota system 27, 29

R

Rail, Tram and Bus Union (RTBU) 104, 108; MUA and 110
recruitment, brigadier function of 253, 254
recruitment drives 108–9
Régie nationale des usines Renault (RNUR) 83–4
relocation threats 58, 93–4
Renault-Dacia strike 13–14, 81–97; borrowed features and legacy of 89–93; changing relations between Romanian and French trade unionists 95–7; conduct 96; Easter and 92;

as European strike 90; European trade union solidarity during 93; failed wage negotiations leading to 90; industrial know-how *vs.* relocation 93–4; lawfulness 90–1; media presence 92, 93; national identity *vs.* international action 95; nationalised RNUR transition to MNC 83–4; Pitesti demonstration 91–2, 93, 95; Renault acquisition of Dacia 83–4; Renault IFAs 88; Romanian trade unions' integration into Europe 81–3; social justice *vs.* Europe 94; support for strikers 92–3, 95; trade unions and Romanian EU membership 85–8

Renault Group Committee 88–9, 90

resource mobilisation, associational power and 25

Rio Tinto mining campaigns 42

risk reduction pattern 65, 67, 75

RNUR *see Régie nationale des usines Renault*

Romania: Easter and 92; EU entry by 81, 85–8, 94; strikes and participant numbers in 2007 89–90; trade between France and 81

Romanian trade unions 85–8; changing relations between French and 95–7; political orientation 87; relations between French and 88–9; unionisation rate 87

rooted cosmopolitanism 123

rooted labour internationalism 122–5, 137; double movement basis of 138; *see also* Ghana and Mexico labour internationalism

RTBU *see* Rail, Tram and Bus Union

Rüffert and Luxembourg cases 170

Russell case: ALGI report 32; anti-sweatshop campaign 23, 30–6; collective bargaining process 31; company names 38; contract terminations 33, 34; implementation phase 35; importance of case 12–13; naked marches 31, 39; Nike and Knights Apparel after 36–8; Nike campaign compared to 36–7; normative framing in 33–4; plant closing 31, 32, 39; restructuring process of 29–30; union creation 30; USAS protests 31, 32–3; worker dismissals 31; worker power in Honduras 29–36; WRC report 31

Russia: construction industry in 249, 252–4; government role in 248; subcontracting in 253; *see also* Delhi and Moscow labour standards

S

SAD *see* Dacia automobile union

Samyn, Bart 151

SAP *see* structural adjustment programs

SEC *see* Siemens Employee Committee

segmentation perspective 246–7; MNCs and 259; product and labour market segmentation 247–9; *see also* labour standards in segmented markets

Self Employed Women's Association (SEWA) 198, 199

SEWA *see* Self Employed Women's Association

shareholder value, as TNC mantra 207

sharing the pain strategy 147, 154

Siemens *see* Electrolux and Siemens cases

Siemens Employee Committee (SEC) 149

Single European Act 169–70

single market project 165

skill discrepancies 151–2

skill recognition, strikers' desiring 94

social dialogue practices 12, 272; collective bargaining and 169; in EU 11, 151, 169, 174

social dumping 86, 87–8, 89, 165, 186

social entrepreneurship 240

social equality issues, Areva's focus on 150–1, 157

social Europe 168, 176

social network theory 223–5; UNI Network in light of 233–41

social partners route 174

societal theory, GVC compared to 245–6

soft employment issues 152, 157

solidarity *see* transnational solidarity
South Africa 255
South America: Canmin1 workplace
    trade unions in 42; cross-border
    alliances between Canada and
    42; trade union dependency in
    51
Southern Hemisphere: labour
    internationalism in 121–2; *see
    also* North-South alliances
Southern India BWI 256
Soviet Union collapse 162
Spalding 33
Spanish trade unions: in Quebecor
    World 230–1; in UNI Network
    235, 238
spatial dimension 4, 265–6; of
    cross-border actions 65,
    66, 67; fragmentation
    from globalisation 243;
    Ghana and Mexico labour
    internationalism 123–4; spatial
    scales 4, 24, 26
spatial extension 3, 23, 59
Stability and Growth Pact 170
Strasbourg, ETUC demonstration in
    173
strikes: Constitution of 2003 covering
    Romanian 90; ETUC 173–4;
    European demonstration of
    2010 82; GME plant closure
    147; Mangalia shipyard 92; in
    Mexico 132; naked marches
    31, 39; in Romania prior to
    Renault-Dacia 89–90; *see also*
    Renault-Dacia strike
structural adjustment programs (SAP)
    122, 126
structural autonomy 234
structural power 6, 38, 117, 269;
    apparel workers and 24, 29;
    in cross-border actions 71;
    definition of 60–1; institutional
    arrangements with associational
    and 74–6
subcontracting 213, 220; CLS
    implementation and 254,
    255; construction industry
    244, 248–9, 250; inter-capital
    competition and increased
    248; outsourcing and 258–9;
    in Russia 253; workplace
    regulation in informal labour

and 255–8; *see also* Delhi and
    Moscow labour standards
Summit of the Americas, 2001 45
supranational institutional
    arrangements: cross-border
    actions and 57–8; list by firm
    70
sweatshop practices: proliferation
    context for 27; sweat-free
    factory 37; *see also* anti-
    sweatshop activism
Sweden, UNI Network in 235,
    238–9
Sydney *see* Maritime Union of Australia
symbolic power 26

T
Tarrow, Sidney 31, 32
Teamsters Graphic Communications
    Conference (GCC/IBT) 231,
    237, 241
Telefónica 230–1
temporary work 213
Textile, Garment and Leather Workers'
    Federation (ITGLWF) 32
Thatcher, Margaret 166–7
TNCs *see* transnational corporations
Trade Union Advisory committee to the
    OECD (TUAC) 188
trade unions and unionists: agency
    of 103–4; British-UNI 238;
    bureaucracy in 25; challenges
    facing 10–11, 276–8; class
    relations and 2; cross-border
    actions of 57–78; democracy in
    117; deunionisation 107, 111;
    Eurocentric internationalism
    history 161–2; European
    integration of Romanian 81–3;
    GPNs, TNCs and 207–8; IFA as
    policy tool 208–12; institutional
    opportunities seized by 60;
    interests defined by 124–5;
    investment capacity 237; localist
    conception of 59; main purpose
    of 271; organisational capacity
    building 7; proximity to workers
    74; Quebecor World by region
    and country 226–7; Romanian
    85–8; Romanian-French
    relations 88–9; solidarity of
    European 93; spatial extension
    of 3, 23, 59; strength of 276;

theoretical considerations
102–4; transformative capacity
of 1–2; transnational solidarity
task viewed by 218; uncertain
future of 277; unionisation
levels 72, 87; unionism
conceptions 101; workplace
as wellspring of transnational
unionism 277–8; *see also* cross-
border alliances; European
trade unions and institutional
arrangements; international
labour movement; national trade
unions; transnational unionism;
workplace unions; *specific cases*;
specific topics; *specific unions*
transnational activism 3
transnational corporations (TNCs):
core-periphery dichotomy in
governance by 207–8; global
workforce percentage employed
by 220; GPNs, trade unions
and 207–8; IFAs hollowed
out by 217; IFA strategy for
restraining power of 205–7,
208–9; IMF trade union
networks in 213; threats to
international trade unionism
posed by 203; TUN and 219;
unilateral codes of conduct of
209–10
transnational solidarity 43, 117;
building and sustaining 274–6;
Eastern/Western European trade
union 81; EWC sharing the
pain strategy 147, 154; Ghana
and Mexico case 137–8; global
solidarity days at Quebecor
229; MUAV and 116–18;
obstacles to Ghanian 129; TNC
standards raised through 203;
transport industry example
116–18; UNI Network creating
232; unions' view of task of
building 218
transnational spaces 265–6
transnational unionism: Australian
transport maritime unions and
101–19; from below 43, 53–4;
bottom-up/top-down processes
51, 197–8, 268; competing
logics and meanings in 269–70;
competitive and collaborative

relations in 54–5, 124; as
contested terrain 268–70;
contours and shape 265–70;
diversity management for 52–3;
Eurocentric history of 161–2;
formative period 7–9; forms of
4–8, 64; frame of reference for
52; global economy in building
58–61; ITF strategy and 116;
local issues and 52; local
rootedness of 267; maritime
industry example 118–19;
multilevel arrangements of
current period 10–12; multilevel
governance and 267–8;
narratives defining 266–7;
national union leadership in 51;
overview of Europe's 15; power
concept and 6–7; regulatory
variation in 266; relational
framework 104; scholarship
overview 2–4; social dialogue
period of 11–12; spatial
extension feature of 3, 23, 59;
study overview for European 15;
twentieth-century Great Divide
period of 9–10; twofold view
of 265; workplace as wellspring
of 277–8; *see also* cross-border
actions; cross-border alliances;
International Framework
Agreements; international labour
movement; *specific related topics*
transnational union networks (TUN),
TNCs and 219
transport equipment MNCs *see* Canada
and France cross-border actions
transport industry *see* International
Transport Federation; Victorian
Transport Union Working Group
Transport Workers Union (TWU) 104,
107
treaties: Amsterdam 166; Maastricht
166, 173; Treaty of Rome 165,
169–70
Treaty of Rome 165, 169–70
trust network 32, 36
TUAC *see* Trade Union Advisory
committee to the OECD
TUC *see* Ghana Trade Union Congress
TUN *see* transnational union networks
Twitter bombs 33
TWU *see* Transport Workers Union

U

UAW *see* United Auto Workers
UNI *see* Union Network International
UNI Network@Quebecor World (UNI
    Network): actors' positions in
    233–41; central actors 234–5;
    hierarchy in 240; IFAs 224,
    232; intermediate actors 235–6;
    Justice@Quebecor World
    campaign 228–31; need for key
    actors shown in 240; neutrality
    agreement with US 231–2,
    241; North-South presence in
    240–1; peripheral actors 236;
    power resources and positioning
    236–9; president 234–5; success
    assessment 231–2
Union Network International (UNI) 16,
    211, 216–17; Quebecor World
    working group formed by 225
unions *see* global union federations;
    international labour movement;
    international trade unionism;
    trade unions and unionists;
    transnational unionism
unitary organisations, de facto 5
UNITE 5, 32, 146
United Auto Workers (UAW) 11
United States (US): Ford plants in
    Mexico and 59; Quebecor
    World trade unions in 226;
    quota system for Central
    American apparel production
    27, 29; UNI Network in
    237; UNI Network neutrality
    agreement 231–2, 241; WFTU
    withdrawal 9
United Steelworkers of America
    (USWA) 5–6; Mineros work
    with 132–3
United Students Against Sweatshops
    (USAS) 31, 32–3, 36–7, 38
unorganised workers 198–9
US *see* United States
USAS *see* United Students Against
    Sweatshops
US Change to Win coalition 189
USWA *see* United Steelworkers of
    America

V

Velázquez, Fidel 131
Victorian Transport Union Working
    Group (VTUWG) 106–9; local

and global mediations with
    114–16; significance of 108,
    117; waterfront dispute and
    lockout origins of 107; Work
    Choices attack on unions and
    111
Visteon agreement 146
VTUWG *see* Victorian Transport Union
    Working Group

W

Wassa Association of Communities
    Affected by Mining 128–9
waterfront dispute and lockout,
    Patricks Corporation 107, 111
Waterside Workers' Federation 105
WCL *see* World Confederation of
    Labour
Western Europe, Eastern and 13–14, 96
Western NGOs, mining operations and
    129
WFTU *see* World Federation of Trade
    Unions
Wharf Labourer's Union 105
Work Choices project 110
workers: code of conduct specifying
    rights of 69; international
    influences on 102; 'power to'
    271–3; unorganised 198–9, 259;
    workplace unionist proximity to
    74; *see also* global workforce,
    TNC employment percentage;
    labour; migrant workers; *specific
    industries*
worker power: Russell/Honduras and
    29–36; sources of 23–7, 38;
    see also local power dynamics;
    power
Worker Rights Consortium (WRC) 27,
    31, 36
Workers Uniting 5–6
workplace unions: autonomy of 51,
    54; Canmin1 42, 44; cross-
    border alliances of 42; at GVC
    apex 77; as organisation basis
    276; understanding patterns of
    involvement 69–73; variability
    in institutional opportunity
    exploitation 76
World Bank 255
World Color Press 225
World Confederation of Labour
    (WCL) 8, 162, 163; autonomy
    of ICFTU and 195; ICFTU

unification with 188–9; ITUC
unification with 183
World Federation of Trade Unions
(WFTU) 163; breakup of
185; creation of 183; EEC
denounced by 166; Eurocentric
internationalism and 161;
marginalisation of 196–7;
membership decrease 5; US
breaking away from 9
World Organisation of Workers
(WOW) 187

World Trade Organization (WTO)
29
World Works Councils 5, 9
WOW *see* World Organisation of
Workers
WRC *see* Worker Rights Consortium
Writers Call for Justice at Quebecor
World 229
WTO *see* World Trade Organization

Z
Zelaya, Manuel 30, 34